THE DESIRE FOR CHANGE, 2004–2007

Professor Tom Frame AM has been a naval officer, Anglican Bishop to the Defence Force, a member of the Australian War Memorial Council and various ethics oversight bodies, and a theological college principal. He became Professor of History at UNSW Canberra in July 2014 and was appointed Director of the Public Leadership Research Group in July 2017 with responsibility for establishing the John Howard Prime Ministerial Library. He is the author or editor of more than 50 books, including *HMAS Sydney: Loss and controversy*, *Stromlo: An Australian observatory*, *The Life and Death of Harold Holt*, *Evolution in the Antipodes: Charles Darwin and Australia* and *Gun Control: What Australia got right (and wrong)*.

THE DESIRE FOR CHANGE, 2004–2007

THE HOWARD GOVERNMENT
VOLUME IV

EDITED BY TOM FRAME

UNSW PRESS

A UNSW Press book

Published by
NewSouth Publishing
University of New South Wales Press Ltd
University of New South Wales
Sydney NSW 2052
AUSTRALIA
newsouthpublishing.com

© Tom Frame 2021
First published 2021

10 9 8 7 6 5 4 3 2 1

ISBN: 9781742235837 (paperback)
        9781742244136 (ebook)
        9781742248554 (ePDF)

A catalogue record for this book is available from the National Library of Australia

Design Josephine Pajor-Markus
Cover design Luke Causby
Cover image John Howard holds a media conference at Parliament House, Canberra, 31 July 2007.

CONTENTS

CONTRIBUTORS

PHILLIP BARRESI was a Liberal member of the Australian House of Representatives from March 1996 to November 2007. He represented the Division of Deakin, Victoria. Born in Patti (Sicily), he was educated at the Australian National University and Swinburne University (then the Swinburne Institute of Technology). He was a psychologist, training officer and consultant before entering politics. He was defeated by Labor's Mike Symon at the 2007 election. Barresi again contested Deakin for the Liberals at the 2010 election but was defeated in a rematch with Symon. He is now National Employment Relations Director for the Australian Retailers Association.

ROGER BEALE is an artist, having painted for over 50 years, and was previously one of Australia's most senior public servants. Appointed Secretary of the Department of the Environment, Sport and Territories in 1996, he remained head during its transition to the Department of the Environment and later Department of the Environment and Heritage. In 2004, Roger retired from the Australian Public Service after 37 years. He was made a Member of the Order of Australia for his contribution to national economic reform in 1995, received the Centenary Medal and was made an Officer of the Order of Australia in 2006.

ANDREW BLYTH, a senior member of staff at UNSW Canberra, was previously CEO of the ACT & Region Chamber of Commerce and Industry and a former chief of staff and senior adviser in the Howard Government. He holds an undergraduate degree in government and postgraduate qualifications in business and international relations. In 2012 he was awarded a Fulbright Professional Scholarship in Australia–US Alliance Studies that he used to conduct research at the University of Texas at Austin into off-grid energy solutions. He is a contributing author to *The Long Road: Australia's train, advise and assist missions* (UNSW Press, Sydney, 2017) and the previous volumes in this series. He is currently researching the role and effectiveness of think tanks in the development of public policy through a professional doctorate at UNSW Canberra. He has been admitted as a graduate of the Australian Institute of Company Directors.

KATE CARNELL is the Australian Small Business and Family Enterprise Ombudsman. Kate brings extensive experience and knowledge to the role of ASBFEO, having run her own small businesses for 15 years before becoming Chief Minister of the Australian Capital Territory in 1995 for a five-year period. Prior to her appointment as the ASBFEO, Kate held the position of CEO of the Australian Chamber of Commerce and Industry (ACCI), which represents more than 300,000 businesses across Australia. She has also served two years as CEO of Beyond Blue and four years as CEO of the Australian Food and Grocery Council. Kate is a pharmacist by profession and was the inaugural chair of the ACT Branch of the Pharmacy Guild of Australia and the first woman to become the National Vice-President of the Pharmacy Guild of Australia. Kate was appointed an Officer of the Order of Australia in 2006 for services to the community through contributions to economic development and support for the business sector, knowledge industries, the medical sector and medical technology advances.

SHAUN CARNEY is a visiting fellow at the School of Humanities and Social Sciences at UNSW Canberra who has written extensively about leadership, politics and industrial relations since the Melbourne afternoon newspaper, the *Herald*, first sent him to work in the Canberra Press Gallery in 1979. He is a political columnist with the *Age* and the *Sydney Morning Herald*, and a former associate editor of the *Age* and columnist at the *Herald Sun*. He is the author and editor of several books, including *Australia in Accord – Politics and industrial relations under the Hawke Government* (1988), *Peter Costello – the New Liberal* (2001), *The Change Makers – 25 leaders in their own words* (2019) and a memoir, *Press Escape* (2016).

ANNETTE CARTER is the Exhibitions Coordinator at the Howard Library. She studied a Bachelor of Arts with Honours while working at the Australian National University transcribing 19th-century birth, death and marriage records from Tasmania. She has since had curatorial roles at the Australian War Memorial, the Victoria and Albert Museum in London, and a 17th-century town hall in rural England, and as a volunteer for the National Trust (United Kingdom). She also worked at the Imperial War Museum on a project aiming to protect war memorials from metal theft. In 2012, she completed a Master of Science in Museum Studies and is currently studying for a Graduate Diploma in Information Management.

ALEXANDER DOWNER is Executive Chair of the International School for Government at King's College London. From 2014 to 2018, he was Australian High Commissioner to the UK. Prior to this, he was Australia's longest-serving Minister for Foreign Affairs, a role he held from 1996 to 2007. Alexander Downer also served as Opposition Leader and leader of the Parliamentary Liberal Party from 1994 to 1995 and represented the electoral division of Mayo for more than 20 years. In addition to a range of other political and diplomatic roles, he was Executive Director of the Chamber of Commerce and the United Nations Secretary-General's Special Adviser on Cyprus, in which he worked on peace talks between Turkish Cypriots and Greek Cypriots. He is currently Chairman of the British think tank, Policy Exchange, and a trustee of the International Crisis Group.

NICK ECONOMOU, a PhD graduate from the University of Melbourne, is a Senior Lecturer in the School of Political and Social Inquiry at Monash University. Nick has been teaching Australian politics and governance at Monash since 1992 and previously taught at the then Swinburne Institute and the former Gippsland Institute of Advanced Education (now Monash Gippsland). He was the Sir Robert Menzies lecturer in Australian Studies at the Institute of Commonwealth Studies (London University) in 1995 and 1996. His publications include *The Kennett Revolution* (co-edited with Brian Costar), *Media, Politics and Power in Australia* (co-authored with Stephen Tanner) and *Australian Politics for Dummies* (co-authored with Zareh Ghazarian). There have also been numerous academic journal articles on subjects ranging from Australian state and federal and even local government elections through to analyses of environmental policy-making. He has also published on Australian political parties, with particular emphasis on the ALP and the Greens. His research interests include Australian national and state governance, federal, state and local elections and electoral systems, and the role and behaviour of Australia's political parties.

Contributors

KAY ELSON was elected to the House of Representatives for the south-eastern Queensland seat of Forde on 2 March 1996. She was re-elected three times (1998, 2001 and 2004) before retiring ahead of the 2007 election. Prior to entering parliament, she was a special events co-ordinator for the Handicapped Association (Horizon Foundation), a shop proprietor and financial consultant. One of nine children, she left school at 13 to work in a factory to support her family. As a mother of eight children, she dedicated her parliamentary service to restoring the value of the family, giving parents more responsibility for their children, and fostering community citizenship. She served on several parliamentary committees including family and community affairs, employment, education, training, agriculture, fisheries and forestry, health and ageing. She was appointed Government Whip during the Second Howard Government (1998–2001).

DAVID FOOTE has been the official photographer for Parliament House in Canberra since 1992. During that time, he has covered seven election campaigns and more than 60 overseas visits following prime ministers Howard, Rudd, Gillard, Abbott, Turnbull and Morrison as official photographer. He has also photographed thousands of formal Guests of Government to Australia. David was in Washington DC on 11 September 2001 as part of Prime Minister Howard's delegation.

ZAREH GHAZARIAN is Lecturer in Politics and International Relations in the School of Social Sciences at Monash University. He is a leading commentator on politics and government, and he frequently contributes to political debate by appearing on national and international media. He has published widely in academic journals and his teaching and research interests include political parties, elections and public policy. He was a Fellow in the Prime Ministers Centre at the Museum of Australian Democracy at Old Parliament House, 2015–16. His publications include *The Making of a Party System: Minor parties in the Australian Senate*.

MURRAY GOOT is Emeritus Professor in the Department of Modern History, Politics and International Relations at Macquarie University. His most recent book is *The Conscription Conflict and the Great War* (2016), co-edited with Robin Archer, Joy Damousi and Sean Scalmer. He contributed to the first three volumes of this series on the Howard Government, and is currently exploring the history of political campaigning in Australia and the history of opinion polling in Australia, Britain and the United States.

JOHN HOWARD was the 25th Prime Minister of Australia, leading the nation from March 1996 to December 2007. He was the federal member for Bennelong in the House of Representatives (1974–2007) and filled several ministerial and shadow ministerial posts prior to 1996. He was made a Companion of the Order of Australia (AC) and a member of the Order of Merit in 2012. He is the second-longest serving prime minister of Australia.

ELIZABETH LUCHETTI has over 25 years' experience working in libraries. She spent 12 years at the National Library of Australia before moving to the Department of Defence as Manager, Document Services. In 2011 she joined the Department of Parliamentary Services, Parliamentary Library, as Director, Collection Management. Major initiatives during this period included the introduction of e-books and other electronic resources, implementation of a web scale discovery service and procurement of a new integrated library system. In 2013 Liz was promoted to Assistant Secretary,

Library Collections and Databases Branch. In this role she has significantly increased the range of news and media services available to parliamentarians, enhanced digital delivery of library products and services and completed several large-scale digitisation projects that will ensure the Parliamentary Library's historic resources are preserved for long-term access. Apart from library management, Liz has significant experience in government procurement, project management and staff management. She is passionate about motivating, mentoring and developing staff and using new technologies to improve the delivery of library services. Liz has a Bachelor of Arts in Library and Information Studies and is currently completing her Masters in Information Leadership.

Maria Maley is a Senior Lecturer in the School of Politics and International Relations at the Australian National University where she teaches public administration and public policy. Her research focuses on the work of political advisers; political–administrative relations; comparative advisory institutions; gender and political leadership; and the careers of ministers and political staff. Her Australian Research Council-funded research is about public servants who work as ministerial staff. Her work has appeared in *Public Administration*, the *International Journal of Public Administration*, the *Australian Journal of Political Science* and the *Australian Journal of Politics and History*.

Patrick McClure was CEO of Mission Australia (1997–2006) when it evolved into an international charity with revenue of $300 million and 3000 staff providing employment, training, housing, youth and family services. He was also CEO of the Society of St Vincent de Paul (New South Wales/Australian Capital Territory) and CEO of The Retirement Villages Group. McClure chaired the

Reference Group on Welfare Reform (1999–2001). The final report, 'Participation support for a more equitable society', was supported by all of the major political parties. He was a member of the Prime Minister's Community–Business Partnership (1999–2007) and Commissioner of the Australian Fair Pay Commission (2006–09). He was also Chair of the Reference Group on Welfare Reform (2014–15) and Review of the Australian Charities and Not-for-profits Commission (2017–18). He is an Officer of the Order of Australia and was awarded the Centenary of Federation Medal. He is an AFR True Leader (2005) and received the EQT CEO Award for 'Lifetime Achievement'.

Nicola McGarrity is a Senior Lecturer in Public and Criminal Law in the Faculty of Law, University of New South Wales, and Director of the Terrorism Law Reform Project in the Gilbert + Tobin Centre of Public Law. She has published extensively on Australian and comparative anti-terrorism law and policy, her most recent publications being *Foreign Terrorist Fighters and Anti-Terrorism Law* (2018, co-authored with Jessie Blackbourn and Deniz Kayis) and *Inside Australia's Anti-Terrorism Laws and Trials* (2014, co-authored with Andrew Lynch and George Williams). Her particular area of expertise is in the prosecution of terrorist suspects, drawing on her academic research and her experience as a barrister at the New South Wales and Victorian bars. Most notably, she spent the second half of 2010 appearing as defence counsel before the Victorian Supreme Court on behalf of one of five men accused of planning an attack on Holsworthy Army Barracks. Nicola has worked with a range of community and political organisations on advocacy campaigns relating to the reform of Australia's anti-terrorism laws and is often called upon to give background information and interviews for the print and electronic media.

Contributors

GREG MELLEUISH is a Professor in the School of Humanities and Social Inquiry at the University of Wollongong, where he teaches Australian politics, political theory and ancient history. He is currently a member of the Australian history and non-fiction judging panel for the Prime Minister's Literary Awards. He has written widely on Australian political ideas, and his books include *Cultural Liberalism in Australia*, *A Short History of Australian Liberalism*, *Australian Intellectuals* and *Despotic State or Free Individual*.

GARY NAIRN was elected the Federal Member for Eden-Monaro in 1996, after 25 years in the surveying and mapping profession, including running his own business. His 12-year parliamentary career included Parliamentary Secretary to Prime Minister Howard with responsibility for water reform and Special Minister of State with responsibility for e-government, the Australian Electoral Commission (AEC) and five government business enterprises. After parliament he operated his own spatial sciences consultancy, and was the inaugural Chairman of the Northern Territory Planning Commission, and Chairman of the Tasmanian Spatial Information Council. He is currently Chairman of the Mulloon Institute, Chairman of the Duke of Edinburgh's International Award in Australia, and a Board Member of the New South Wales Biodiversity Conservation Trust.

BRENDAN NELSON was the Director of the Australian War Memorial from 2012 to 2019. He was previously the Australian Ambassador to Belgium, Luxembourg, the European Union and NATO (2010–12). He holds a Bachelor of Medicine and Surgery, and was a medical practitioner in Hobart from 1985 to 1995. From 1993 to 1995, he was the National President of the Australian Medical Association (AMA). In 1996, Brendan was elected to the House of Representatives, representing the electoral division of Bradfield, later serving as Minister for Education, Science and Training, and then Minister for Defence. As leader of the Liberal Party, Brendan was Leader of the Opposition from November 2007 to September 2008. He holds many awards and honorary appointments, and was appointed an Officer of the Order of Australia (AO) in January 2016 for his services to the community, the Parliament of Australia, diplomacy and cultural leadership. He is currently President of Boeing Australia.

SCOTT PRASSER has worked in senior policy and advisory positions in both state and federal governments including as senior adviser to three federal cabinet ministers from 2013 until his retirement in July 2019. He also held academic positions, the last at professorial level. Scott's publications include: *Royal Commissions and Public Inquiries: Practice & potential* (with Helen Tracey, 2014); *Audit Commissions* (with Kate Jones, 2013); and *Restraining Elective Dictatorship: The upper house solution?* (with Nicholas Aroney and JR Nethercote, 2008). Scott is a graduate of Queensland and Griffith universities. He is currently completing a book on recent Commonwealth attempts to reform school funding.

TIM ROWSE is a historian of Australian affairs, with honorary appointments at Western Sydney University and the Australian National University. His publications include *Nugget Coombs: A reforming life, Divided nation? Indigenous affairs and the imagined public* (with Murray Goot), and *Indigenous and non-Indigenous Australians since 1901*. With Laura Rademaker at the ANU he has edited a collection of essays about the history of Indigenous self-determination in Australia. His recent writings include studies of the violence of Australia's 19th-century frontiers and commentary on the ways scholarship on colonial violence troubles Australia's military heritage.

Marija Taflaga is a lecturer in the School of Politics and International Relations at the Australian National University. She researches Australian politics in comparative context. Her research examines political parties' relationships with parliament and the executive. Marija also undertakes research in Australian political history. Recently she has begun researching the career paths of political elites. Marija has undertaken research fellowships at the Australian Parliamentary Library and the Australian Museum of Democracy, Old Parliament House. She has also worked in the Australian Parliamentary Press Gallery as a researcher at the *Sydney Morning Herald* and the *Age*.

Alan Wilson, a retired librarian, has been a volunteer in the Howard Library since 2018. After working in public and college libraries in Britain, he served in senior positions in the National Library of Australia for 12 years, and in the Commonwealth Parliamentary Library for 22 years, where he headed Information Resources with a staff of 50, processing and indexing more than 400 press clippings per day in addition to media releases and media transcripts for inclusion in the ParlInfo database. He was involved in the early days of library automation in both institutions and in the establishment of the parliament's website. He was the inaugural winner of Australian Society of Indexers' Web Indexing Award in 1996.

DISCLAIMER

The views expressed by contributors are their own opinions and do not necessarily represent the position of the Commonwealth of Australia, the University of New South Wales or any other tertiary education institution, the Australian Labor Party, the Liberal Party of Australia, the National Party of Australia or any organisations with which the contributors were or are now associated. The publication of their chapter in this book does not imply any official agreement or formal concurrence with any opinion, criticism, conclusion or recommendation attributed to them.

PREFACE

TOM FRAME

This series casts critical light on the four Howard governments. The first volume covered the 1996 election and the foundational year of Coalition rule, focusing on the campaign and the results, budget repair and the imposition of financial discipline, and the National Firearms Agreement. The second began with the 1997 *Workplace Relations Act*, covered difficulties arising from the ministerial code of conduct, the challenge of introducing 'A New Tax System' and ended with the Aston by-election on 14 July 2001, which produced an unexpected Coalition victory. The third volume looked closely at the tumultuous events of August–October 2001, marked by the collapse of Ansett Airlines, the 11 September terrorist attacks on New York City and Washington DC and the subsequent invasion of Afghanistan, the MV *Tampa* controversy and the 'children over-board' affair.

This volume begins with the October 2004 election campaign, examines a range of portfolio matters such as welfare reform, energy policy and anti-terrorist legislation, considers the influence of leadership tension within the Cabinet, WorkChoices and the ACTU's 'Your Rights at Work' protest on voter attitudes, and ends with the Coalition's heavy defeat to Kevin Rudd and the Labor Party in November 2007.

When introducing the previous volumes I have posed a series of historiographical questions: Who is best placed to examine the Howard years? When is the best time to engage in critical reflection? What kinds of judgments can be made now and which are best left until official records are available? The answers to these questions relate to perspective and objectivity, and ultimately to the reliability of interpretations and the accuracy of conclusions. There is value in standing back from any major analytical project, especially one involving a large number of authors, and assessing whether there may have been bias or distortion in either the identification of contributors or the selection of topics.

The contents of this fourth volume were being agreed as the Liberal Party was marking the 75th anniversary of its foundation in 1944 and the National Party was preparing for its centenary in 2020. These highly significant anniversaries provided an important element of context for this book. What did the Coalition parties now think of the Howard years? Were these views colouring popular perceptions and influencing scholarly opinions? Was the Fourth Howard Government viewed differently from its predecessors, given the unpopularity of its workplace relations reforms, the controversial intervention in Indigenous communities in the Northern Territory, blunders in managing the immigration program, and the rejection of a fifth-term policy platform by the electorate? After all, the Howard Government was resoundingly removed from office by voters.

Notwithstanding its demise, the Howard Government's performance still looms large in the corporate memory of both parties. As the Liberals and the Nationals look back on their histories, they have found comfort in reliving the glory days and insight from discerning how and why the good times began and how they can be revived. The Liberal Party celebrated the 75th anniversary of its founding in October 2019. The party's present leadership saluted those from the past and paid tribute to their achievements. The Menzies and Howard governments were singled out for special mention. They were longstanding governments; 16 years in the case of the former and nearly 12 years for the latter. Both Sir Robert Menzies and John Howard, respectively the longest- and second-longest serving prime ministers of Australia, were recognised as effective leaders of both the Liberal Party and the nation. Very few who marked the occasion personally recalled the Menzies years or were voting when his long reign ended in January 1966. As Howard spoke warmly of his hero's many achievements and attainments, those with more recent parliamentary service lauded the Howard Government's contribution and its leader's convictions. In the minds of the party faithful, the Menzies Government and the Howard Government were accorded equivalent status. Menzies and Howard were considered model leaders worthy of emulation and their administrations the standard by which other Liberal governments will be judged.

It is, in one sense, contentious to make too much of a celebration in which a little pride and hubris are expected and excused. Unlike the Labor Party, which draws much of its identity and purpose from its history and traditions, the Liberal Party has never invested seriously in the study of its history nor required its members to have a detailed understanding of its traditions. It is more pragmatic than philosophical, focusing on emerging opportunities and practical initiatives. And yet, there is ample scope for the present leadership to discern the ways in which its minimalist philosophy has served the needs of its parliamentary representatives and where the party ought to sharpen its thinking in the continuing contest of ideas. Whereas Labor looks to the past to determine where things went wrong, the Liberal Party should look to the past for explanations of why things went right. In the years since its founding, the Liberal

Party has been vastly more successful in electoral terms. Over the past three-quarters of a century, the Coalition has held power for 48 years while the Labor Party's time in office runs to 27 years. The Liberal Party has also been more effective in selling its agenda to the electorate although the Whitlam, Hawke, Keating, Rudd and Gillard Labor governments were never short of reforming zeal.

Armed with enough information to misrepresent the past, there is a tendency among Liberal supporters to turn the Howard Government into something it was not. Part of this misrepresentation is intentional 'over-correction' in the face of a continuing refusal among partisan commentators to give the Coalition any credit for its achievements between 1996 and 2007. There are critiques of the Howard Government contending that it simply exploited the benefits of greatly enhanced commodity prices and the economic and labour market reforms initiated by the Hawke–Keating governments. It squandered budget surpluses on middle-class welfare and tax cuts for the affluent. The Coalition manipulated racist sentiment in its management of immigration to secure electoral advantage, and committed Australia to costly and potentially illegal invasions of Afghanistan and Iraq in its desire to secure American goodwill. In attempting to counter claims that the Howard Government did nothing right, there is a counter-tendency among its supporters to insist it did nothing wrong. Conceiving of history as a pendulum is mistaken. Accuracy is not achieved through manufactured consensus or balancing one set of flawed contentions with another equally flawed set of conclusions. No government is ever without its frailties and failings. Strengths and weaknesses ought to be acknowledged in moving towards a more objective assessment of the Howard Government.

Another reason the Howard Government has been misrepresented is sheer nostalgia. The Howard years preceded a decade of political turmoil within both major parties that many commentators already consider to have been the low point in postwar Australian political life. Neither the Rudd and Gillard Labor governments nor the Abbott and Turnbull Coalition governments will be judged favourably by historians. Although each began with high hopes of ending party in-fighting and providing stable government, what they achieved will be assessed in the context of what they might have done had leadership tensions not distracted both parties. It will be the feuds between Kevin Rudd and Julia Gillard, and Tony Abbott and Malcolm Turnbull, that will occupy as many pages in the history books as the achievements of their governments.

In addition to these misrepresentations, a number of aspects of the Howard Government are often overlooked. The first is its precarious existence. After its substantial election victory in March 1996, the Coalition performed very poorly in 1997 and nearly lost the next election. It secured the most seats but not the most votes. It was expected to lose in November 2001 after trailing consistently in the polls but was effectively 'saved' by a number of external factors not of its own making, principally the 11 September terrorist attacks in the United States. The October 2004 election would have seen it swept from office but for Labor being unable to produce a leader the electorate could trust. With Kevin Rudd's triumph over Kim Beazley in December 2006, the electorate now believed they could trust the alternative prime minister if only because he could be depicted as 'John Howard-lite'. By 2007, the Coalition was destined to lose office. The only question was the margin.

Second, to think the Howard Government consistently enjoyed the goodwill of the people based on policies that the voters endorsed is a serious error. There were protracted periods when the Coalition was consistently unpopular in the polls. The difference was that, unlike the Labor Caucus, which thought changing the leader would improve its polling, the Coalition held its nerve and stuck with John Howard. It needs to be said, moreover, that the Coalition was just as willing to 'buy' votes as Labor in an attempt to improve its standing in the polls. Indeed, it had greater scope to do so because the economy was performing well. Once government debt was repaid, budget surpluses might have been applied to infrastructure development for long-term growth. Instead, they were partly exploited for short-term political gain — a point made openly on several occasions by the Treasurer, Peter Costello.

Third, the Howard Government had practical shortcomings ranging from its handling of bonds paid to aged care facilities and the slowness of its response to the High Court's Wik judgment, to its indifference to the cause of constitutional reform and neglecting the continuing need for the electoral system to be modernised. The Coalition committed Australia to hugely expensive military deployments in Afghanistan and Iraq, neither of which would qualify as a strategic success or a foreign policy triumph, that have imposed an enormous burden on the public purse in addition to committing future Australian governments to a very substantial veteran support bill.

Notably, the Howard Government did not pursue its philosophical convictions to their political conclusions. It did not always deregulate markets or ensure greater competition, such as in the airline industry, while it retained industry protection where and when the electoral consequences of removing it were deemed too great. There are good reasons for analysing success but more compelling is the need to learn from failures. There has been a reluctance to engage in this kind of introspection for fear any admissions will be gleefully seized upon by opposition parties as a confession of guilt or an admission of shortcoming. This is a regrettable mindset and a lost opportunity for the Liberals, whose internal cohesion, or lack of it, remains a work in progress.

There is also much for the National Party, the junior Coalition partner, to learn from the past, particularly the Howard years, as it reflects on its foundation as the Country Party in 1920. The National Party continues to provide the deputy prime minister and around three Cabinet ministers in a Coalition government. Its senior leadership can point to important reforms and significant decisions that specifically addressed the needs of its stakeholders. It can highlight initiatives that would never have been implemented by a Labor government. While not wanting to diminish these things, the National Party is struggling to find its place in a highly urban and suburbanised society increasingly oblivious to the particular needs of primary producers and those who live in regional and remote Australia. As the proportion of the population living in the capital cities continues to rise and the 'bush' becomes a distant place – out of sight and, therefore, out of mind – there is a danger of the National Party descending into a political rump preoccupied with special pleading for marginalised voters. During the Howard years, the National vote declined, the party lost seats and its ministerial representation declined. There was also talk of merging the two Coalition parties. While the Liberals needed the Nationals to hold power after 1998, the Howard Government's time in office was not an untroubled time for the junior Coalition partner.

There are many aspects of the Coalition's time in office that have yet to receive the attention they deserve. The contributors to this volume, which focuses on the Fourth Howard Government, are members, servants or close observers of the Howard Government. They were invited to contribute because of their experience and expertise, and have been aware of the need to transcend contemporary commentary and the prevailing mood when assessing events that happened more than a decade ago. The initial draft of each chapter was presented at a conference held in the National

Press Club in Canberra in November 2019, some 15 years after the Fourth Howard Government was sworn in by the Governor General. Although the conference was hosted by UNSW Canberra's Howard Library, the contributors were at liberty either to commend or condemn John Howard (who attended the entire conference) and his colleagues (of which a number were also present). It was a highly productive gathering, especially for the contributors to this book. There was free and open exchange of ideas and, on occasion, profound disagreement over Coalition decision-making. In this sense, the conference certainly exceeded the university's expectations. UNSW has no brief to defend or denounce the Howard Government; its foremost interests are preserving the past and promoting critical scholarship and analysis. (Sadly, the Labor Opposition perspective presented at the conference did not materialise as a chapter submitted for inclusion in this volume. The view of the Howard Government from the Opposition benches was an important element in the first three volumes.)

This book is not an attempt to redress any perceived imbalance in the body of knowledge or opinion presently associated with the Howard Government. In defending my own objectivity, readers should be aware that I have never been a member of the Liberal Party nor been associated with any of its kindred organisations. Contributors who were involved with the Howard Government as parliamentarians, advisers or consultants were asked to be candid in identifying where and how it could and should have done better. They were strongly encouraged to transcend personal self-justification to reveal their doubts and disappointments with the outcomes of policies and the failure of processes.

PART I
INTO THE UNKNOWN

1
SETTING THE SCENE

TOM FRAME

Nothing lasts forever but the Howard Government survived much longer than anyone could have imagined. When the Coalition won a landslide victory on 2 March 1996, commentators believed it was very likely to govern for two terms, given the extent of its majority and the unpopularity of the Australian Labor Party at the end of the Hawke–Keating years. The same commentators expected the Howard Government to lose in 2001, after it had come perilously close to defeat, its majority slashed at the 1998 election when it went to the people advocating 'A New Tax System'. Indeed, polling in 2000 and early 2001 showed consistently that the Labor Opposition led by Kim Beazley was on track for a comfortable victory. The Coalition's lowest point was 17 March 2001: the by-election held in the previously safe Coalition seat of Ryan in Queensland.

The sitting member, John Moore, decided to leave politics when he resigned the Defence portfolio. Labor's Leonie Short won the subsequent by-election with a 9.69 per cent swing. The newly imposed Goods and Services Tax (GST) and climbing fuel prices were blamed for the Coalition's loss, alongside the electorate's anger at being obliged to vote in a by-election less than a year out from a scheduled election. Howard's political obituary was already being written. There was no coming back from such a result. He and the Coalition were destined for defeat. The government claimed it had listened and was willing to respond to voter concerns. After the May 2001 Budget, the mood in the electorate began to change – imperceptibly, at first. The Budget and the continuation of economic prosperity, border protection and the 11 September terrorist attacks, combined to improve the incumbent government's appeal.

The election held on 10 November 2001 returned the Howard Government to office and it even managed to increase its majority by two seats. This was the result no-one had predicted at the start of the year. It was the election John Howard was never expected to win and Labor did not imagine it could lose. Howard was on track to exceed Malcolm Fraser as the second-longest serving Liberal prime minister, while Kim Beazley was considered the best Labor prime minister the country would never have. Beazley resigned the leadership of his party on election night.

Simon Crean succeeded Kim Beazley as the Leader of the Opposition, but stood down in November 2003 when it was clear Labor could not reduce the government's supremacy in the polls. Although he had reformed the internal processes of the Labor Party and initiated significant policy developments that he felt would appeal to voters at election time, a few trusted colleagues pointed out that he no longer enjoyed majority support in the party room. Crean became the first Labor leader since Billy Hughes was expelled from the party in 1916 to be replaced before he had led the party at an election. By this time, Beazley had reconsidered his position and again thought he could lead Labor to victory. He contested the leadership ballot against the party's Treasury spokesman, Mark Latham, but was narrowly defeated by 47 votes to 45. Opting for Latham was a courageous decision on the part of the Caucus majority. The member for Werriwa, a product of the Right faction of New South Wales Labor, was known for aggression and volatility. Other than serving as Mayor of Liverpool (1991–94), he had not been tested in a senior leadership role. When a supporter told Latham that he would need four years and two elections to become prime minister, Latham wrote in his diary: 'Bullshit, I can beat Howard in one'.[1]

From his ascendance in December 2003, Latham fascinated commentators with a political style that could be traced back to the firebrand Premier of New South Wales (1925–27 and 1930–32), Jack Lang, via the self-declared 'Placido Domingo' of Australian politics, Paul Keating. When asked in 2002 about his political outlook, Latham revealed in an interview with the *Bulletin*:

> I'm a hater. Part of the tribalness of politics is to really dislike
> the other side with intensity. And the more I see of them,
> the more I hate them. I hate their negativity. I hate their
> narrowness. I hate the way, for instance, John Howard tries
> to appeal to suburban values when I know that he hasn't got
> any real answers to the problems and challenges we face. I
> hate the phoniness of that.[2]

Like Lang, Latham was big and bold, intense and impulsive. He was also young and exuberant with boundless energy compensating for limited experience. Those who had been drawn to the Coalition by John Howard's plainspoken suburban outlook were enticed back to Labor by Latham's down-to-earth demeanour. He started 'town hall'–style meetings across the country, campaigned on the primacy of values, talked about the 'ladder of opportunity' and promoted the slogan 'ease the squeeze', to emphasise the struggles families were facing. The electorate initially liked him and, by March 2004, Latham enjoyed a higher personal approval rating than any other opposition leader since Bob Hawke's brief tenure in February 1983. The 'outsider' might yet become the prime minister by the year's end, despite the Coalition managing a strong and growing economy and exerting firm leadership in the global 'war on terror'.

Of Howard's foremost political opponents over the previous decade, Latham was the maverick and the one who appeared most threatening with his utter unpredictability. For instance, on 10 February 2004, he wrong-footed the government on superannuation entitlements for federal politicians, a matter that was mentioned periodically but that the media and the people largely overlooked, by announcing that a Labor government would close the existing scheme. Latham claimed the provisions of the scheme:

> are well outside the community standard in Australia and have become out-of-date. They offer superannuation benefits seven times more generous than the current contribution scheme available to the general public. Parliamentary superannuation has become a major source of public dissatisfaction and cynicism in modern politics. That is why a Labor Government will pass legislation closing the scheme to new entrants.[3]

Two days later, Prime Minister Howard said the government would close the existing scheme and establish less generous superannuation arrangements for new members and senators who entered parliament after the next federal election.[4] Howard justified his hasty decision on the basis of:

> a community perception that this super is too generous. I think the overall package is not too generous but people think the super is generous and rather than this thing drift

on for months as the subject of a partisan political debate,
I've decided to act immediately to get it off the agenda as a
partisan political issue so that we can have a focus on issues
that are really important to the future of this country such as
the Free Trade Agreement with the United States.[5]

This was an impressive political achievement on Latham's
part, strong-arming the Coalition into an action it had not contemplated. Commentators claimed that Latham was setting the
agenda with new perspectives and fresh energy. While health and
education were always Labor's strong points, Latham knew where
he wanted to place the emphasis of policy and the investment of
resources. He championed the introduction of parenting classes
for those who failed to discipline their children adequately; proposed a nationwide ban on junk food advertising during children's television hours; advocated substantial investment in early
childhood literacy and providing free story books; foreshadowed
banning single-use shopping bags throughout Australia; and advocated extending the Commonwealth's vilification laws. The Labor
leader never lacked ideas and initiatives that seemed to resonate
with the practical challenges key metropolitan fringe electorates
like his own of Werriwa were facing. With hindsight, his later drift
to the political right – he became the New South Wales leader of
One Nation in November 2018 and was elected to the Legislative
Council in March 2019 – began with the positions he promoted
while Federal Labor leader.

Latham was personally less committed and politically less convincing when it came to showing leadership in the external portfolios of international trade, foreign affairs and national defence.
He started badly and never really recovered. In March 2004, a year
after the invasion of Iraq had failed to uncover any weapons of mass

destruction, Latham sparked controversy by committing a Labor government to withdrawing Australian troops from the Middle East by Christmas 2004.[6] The prime minister accused Latham of a 'cut and run' approach and remarked: 'It's not the Australian way not to stay the distance'. The polls showed Labor lost support over Latham's stance, support which rebounded after the Abu Ghraib detainee abuse scandal made worldwide headlines. But Latham's confrontational style left little room for diplomacy. In 2003 he claimed George W Bush was 'the most incompetent and dangerous American president in living memory'.[7] When Bush described Latham's pull-out policy as 'disastrous' and implied Labor should not be elected, Latham told Bush and his administration to stay out of Australian domestic politics. It was messy on all sides.

Anti-American sentiment within Labor looked certain to deepen when Latham announced that Peter Garrett, the lead singer of the rock band Midnight Oil and former Senate candidate for the Nuclear Disarmament Party, would be Labor's nominee for the safe Sydney seat of Kingsford Smith at the 2004 election.[8] Garrett had co-written the band's strident anti-American anthems 'Short Memory', 'US Forces' and 'The Power and the Passion'. Garrett had not previously been a member of the Labor Party and seemed a much better fit for the Greens.[9] He was, however, key to Latham's strategy to parade Labor's environmental credentials, particularly in Tasmania, where he seemed indifferent to the fate of timber workers, whose jobs John Howard seemed more committed to preserving.

Having fulfilled many of its domestic policy aspirations by 2004, the Third Howard Government was focused predominantly on international affairs: hosting the Commonwealth Heads of Government Meeting conference in March 2002; the continuing global war on terror with Australian forces deployed to Afghanistan from

November 2001; dealing with grief following the Bali bombings in October 2002; continuing whole-of-government commitments in Bougainville, East Timor and, from July 2003, the Solomon Islands; the hugely controversial invasion of Iraq in March 2003; a massive natural gas agreement with China; and free trade agreements with Singapore and Thailand. The emphasis on affairs abroad was made possible by favourable conditions at home.

The Treasurer, Peter Costello, continued to deliver budget surpluses with net government debt on target to be repaid by 2006–07 (which it was). National productivity increased and this fed strong economic growth. Unemployment continued to fall from 8.1 per cent at the start of Coalition rule and was heading towards 4.1 per cent (which would be achieved in 2007). Average weekly earnings grew substantially in real terms although household debt in relation to disposable income rose considerably; interest rates were at an acceptable level; and inflation was low, but housing affordability was becoming a problem. Australians thought they were doing well although comparable nations such as Canada and New Zealand were doing just as well. Was the Coalition doing a good job or simply exploiting favourable conditions? Were its interventions reaping a substantial dividend for the country or were the Hawke–Keating reforms the actual origin of the sustained prosperity Australia was experiencing?

From his incredibly high approval rating in March 2004, Latham inevitably lost support during the coming months. By August, there were rumours that John Howard would call a slightly early election although, by the middle of that month, three opinion polls showed that Labor was again in front. On 16 August, the children overboard affair was revived after a former senior adviser to then Defence Minister Peter Reith claimed publicly that he told the prime minister three days before the 2001 election that reports of children being thrown overboard from Suspected Illegal Entry Vehicle 4 (SIEV 4) were wrong, only to have Howard repeat 'the lie' the next day in an address to the National Press Club.[10] Labor sought to exploit the lingering controversy by convening a one-day Senate inquiry in the hope of damaging the prime minister's credibility. This was high-stakes politics. Labor thought John Howard's personal standing made the Coalition vulnerable. It told the electorate Howard could not be trusted. He was untruthful and duplicitous.

On 29 August, the prime minister advised the Governor General to issue writs for an election to be held on 9 October for both Houses of Parliament. Howard then told the assembled media:

> This election, ladies and gentlemen, will be about trust … Who do you trust to keep the economy strong, and protect family living standards? Who do you trust to keep interest rates low? Who do you trust to lead the fight on Australia's behalf against international terrorism?[11]

At the campaign launch on 26 September 2004, the Coalition promised tax breaks for small business, extra funds for government and non-government schools, childcare support and stay-at-home parent support and a boost to formal technical training. In what proved a turning point in the campaign, Howard told Tasmanian timber workers gathered in Launceston on 7 October that a re-elected Coalition government would 'preserve an extra 170 000 hectares of Tasmanian old-growth forest, while ensuring no job losses'. The proposed preservation area was condemned by Latham, the Greens and the Democrats, but applauded by the audience of 1500 timber workers, by the local Labor member, Dick Adams, and by the Construction, Forestry, Mining and Electrical Union (CFMEU).

In response, Latham said Labor was offering a plan that would make Australia 'stronger, fairer, safer' whereas, he claimed, John Howard's only plan was retirement during the next term of parliament. Launching the Labor Party's election campaign on 29 September 2004, he spoke of:

> The urgent need for an Australian Labor Government. Unless we change now, it will be too late to save Medicare – too late to increase bulk-billing and improve our public hospital system … Unless we change now, it will be too late for the families under financial pressure – too late to solve the family debt crisis and deliver tax relief for all Australian taxpayers. Unless we change now, it will be too late for the security and safety of our nation – too late to shift policy and resources to our part of the world, getting it right in Asia in the fight against terror. And unless we change now, it will be too late for the basic decency and honesty of government in this country – too late to restore truth in government and end the deceit and buck-passing of the Howard years.[12]

On the morning of the day before the election, Howard and Latham crossed paths at the ABC's Sydney studios. A film crew recorded the encounter, in which the Opposition Leader appeared to drag the prime minister towards him with an aggressive twist of the hand. This was the defining, dramatic image of the entire campaign. Latham saw it differently. He later told Labor staffer Sean Kelly that:

> Every time they saw each other during the campaign, Howard would try to crush Latham's hand, 'shaking with his arm, instead of his wrist, like a flapping motion. It's a

small man's thing, trying to show you can match the big guy at something'. On the last Sunday of the campaign, Latham says, Howard did the same thing to his wife. Latham decided, 'we're not going to have any more of that'. When he ran into Howard again, Latham 'put on the squeeze and got a bit closer to him, so he couldn't do the flapping thing. The weak animal looked startled, so it had the desired effect.'[13]

The incident might have seemed this way to Latham; it looked different to everyone else.

The media said Latham's conduct was 'aggressive', 'bullying' and 'intimidating'.[14] The Liberal Party's campaign director, Brian Loughnane, later told the National Press Club that this one incident generated more feedback than anything else during the previous six weeks, and that it 'brought together all the doubts and hesitations that people had about Mark Latham'.[15] The Labor campaign had, however, started to unravel long before that infamous handshake. Labor had placed Latham at the forefront of its campaign. It thought he was the decisive factor. It tried to paint Howard as ageing and weary and his government as stale and complacent. The Coalition would campaign on Latham's unpredictability, and contend that Labor's policies would weaken national security and imperil economic prosperity. Coalition television ads focused on Latham's time as Mayor of Liverpool, featuring yellow motor vehicle 'L' plates, claiming that Latham could not manage a budget, could not control spending, could not deliver savings and could not limit borrowings. He was out of his depth and had not passed any competence test for public office. He lacked experience and expertise.

One side was offering opportunity; the other reliability. It seemed that voters had come to a clear view on John Howard's question 'Who do you trust?' when they were asked whether they wanted a fourth Howard government on 9 October 2004.

2

MISSING THE WOOD FOR THE TREES: EXPLAINING HOWARD'S 2004 VICTORY

MURRAY GOOT

The Coalition returned to office, in 2004, with an increased share of the vote and an increased share of the seats. Seeking a fourth term, the Liberal and National parties lifted their share of the first-preference vote from 43.0 to 46.7 per cent, and their share of the two-party preferred vote from 50.9 to 52.7 per cent. This was the Coalition's best performance since the Howard Government was first elected in 1996. Increasing the government's vote share and share of the seats on two successive occasions was something no other prime minister had achieved since Federation. Only one other government had achieved it – the Liberal–Country Party government led by Robert Menzies in 1963 and by Harold Holt in 1966.[1] The Coalition also secured a majority in the Senate for the first time since 1977 – a possibility 'which had fallen beneath every expert pundit's radar', former Labor Senator and expert pundit Graham Richardson noted ruefully.[2] Labor recorded its lowest first-preference vote in 70 years, and Latham became the first Leader of the Opposition since the Second World War, leading his party for the first time, to see its vote go backwards.

Early in 2004, after Mark Latham had replaced Simon Crean – the man with the 'worst' public image 'of any Labor leader since

Arthur Calwell'[3] – the Coalition parties' prospects looked very different. Labor's lead in the opinion polls, at times, was of 'landslide' proportions. Latham himself enjoyed 'the highest personal approval ratings for an opposition leader since Hawke'.[4] Even after the May Budget, which forecast a surplus while still allowing tax cuts and increases in spending, Newspoll showed that Labor was 'perilously close to a landslide'.[5] Latham, it was widely agreed, had made Labor competitive again.[6]

When John Howard called the election at the end of August on the last day of the 2004 Athens Olympics, he appeared to be 'facing the fight of his long political life'.[7] According to Newspoll – the poll that politicians and pundits watched most closely – the Coalition trailed Labor, 46–54, two-party preferred; in the ACNielsen poll, also taken two weeks before Howard's announcement, the Coalition was trailing, 47–53; in the Morgan Poll, a week before the announcement, it was even further behind, 44–56. 'Running a poll during the Olympics is insanity', Liberal pollster Mark Textor remarked about polls that showed Labor ahead.[8] Labor 'started the campaign on broadly level terms with the government', not ahead, wrote political scientist Rodney Tiffen.[9] But only in the Galaxy poll – a poll yet to establish a track record – were the two sides on level terms. Latham thought Labor was actually 'behind but still reasonably competitive', a judgment for which there is no publicly available evidence.[10]

The election result, Howard was reported to have said, as the campaign got underway, was 'very much in the balance'.[11] Howard 'had always said that the Coalition needed to be ahead on the primaries by at least three points to be assured of winning', journalist Mungo MacCallum noted.[12] The Coalition was ahead by exactly three percentage points in the most recent polls conducted by Newspoll and ACNielsen, and by four points in the most recent Galaxy poll, before the election was called; in the Newspoll completed on the day the election was announced, it was ahead by five (Table 1). Only in the Morgan poll was it not ahead by three points or more; it was two points behind.

To write that 'the Coalition was consistently ahead of Labor', as the political scientists Ian McAllister and Clive Bean do, is mistaken.[13] Immediately after the election was called, almost all the polls showed the Coalition gaining ground. Newspoll now had the two sides on even terms, two-party preferred. So did ACNielsen. In the Galaxy poll, the Coalition moved ahead of Labor. Only in the Morgan poll was the gap unchanged. Across the 12 Liberal marginals polled by Newspoll – seats the *Sunday Telegraph* said Labor 'need[ed] to win government' – the Liberals were ahead, although this did not mean that the Liberals were ahead in all these seats.[14]

The campaign saw the Coalition make further inroads – most clearly in terms of first preferences – though none as dramatic as its initial gains. In the final days, the LNP was ahead by 12 points in the ACNielsen poll, and by six (Newspoll) or seven (Galaxy, Morgan) in the others; the gap after the votes were counted (9.1 percentage points) split the difference.[15] On the two-party preferred, the Coalition's position had improved by four points (54–46) in the ACNielsen poll, and by five (49–51) in the Morgan poll. But in the Galaxy poll, where the Coalition led 52–48, and in Newspoll, where they were 50–50, the parties finished as they started.[16] In the Liberal marginals, there was no change either, the Coalition slipping notionally from 52 to 51.5 per cent of the two-party preferred.[17]

Not until mid-way through the campaign was the Coalition's ascendancy evident. In the first three weeks, according to three polls – Newspoll, ACNielsen and Galaxy – there was nothing to separate the Liberal–National parties (LNP) from Labor. Other polls had Labor ahead, not the Coalition: the Morgan poll, in the first two

Table 1 Voting intention during the campaign*

Poll	Week	Sample size	Fieldwork	First preferences						Two-party preferred	
				LNP (%)	ALP (%)	LNP lead	Greens (%)	AD (%)	PHON (%)	LNP (%)	LNP lead
2001 (E)			10 Nov	**42.7**	**37.8**	**4.9**	**5.0**	**5.4**	**4.3**	**51**	**+2**
Newspoll	One	1145	27–29/8	43	40	3	6	1	na	48	-4
Newspoll	One	1734	3–5/9	45	40	5	8	1	na	50	0
ACNielsen	One	1415	3–5/9	46	40	6	9	2	1	50	0
Galaxy	One	1000	3–5/9	46	39	7	8	na	na	52	+4
Morgan	One	1866	28–29/8 & 4–5/9	41.5	43	-1.5	10.5	2	1	44	-12
Newspoll	Two	1707	10–12/9	46	40	6	6	1	na	50	0
Morgan	Two	na	11–12/9	42	43.5	-1.5	8	2	1	45.5	-9
ACNielsen	Three	1408	14–16/9	48	40	8	8	1	1	51	+2
Newspoll	Three	1674	17–19/9	43	41	2	7	1	na	47.5	-5
Galaxy	Three	1010	17–19/9	46	41	5	7	2	na	51	+2
Morgan	Three	1046	18–19/9	45	41	4	7.5	1	1	47	-6
ACNielsen	Four	1417	21–23/9	50	36	14	8	1	1	54	+8
Newspoll	Four	1701	24–26/9	43	40	3	7	1	na	48	-4
Morgan	Four	1323	25–26/9	48	40	8	9	1	1	50	0
Newspoll	Five	1680	1–3/10	46	39	7	7	1	na	50.5	+1
ACNielsen	Five	1397	30/9–2/10	48	39	9	8	2	1	52	+4
Galaxy	Five	1000	1–3/10	45	39	6	7	2	na	52	+4
Morgan	Five	1010	2–3/10	45.5	40.5	5	9	1	1	48.5	-3
Galaxy	Six	1200	5–6/10	46	39	7	7	1	na	52	+4
ACNielsen	Six	2029	5–7/10	49	37	12	7	1	1	54	+8
Newspoll	Six	2500	6–7/10	45	39	6	7	1	1	50	0
Morgan	Six	1311	7–8/10	45.5	38.5	7	9.5	1	1	49	-2
2004 (E)			9 Oct	**46.7**	**37.6**	**9.1**	**7.2**	**1.2**	**1.2**	**52.7**	**+5.4**

*Excludes the daily *Bulletin–Nine* (ANU) poll

weeks, had the Coalition facing its biggest defeat since the Second World War, the Coalition trailing throughout the campaign; the Bulletin–Nine (ANU) poll, which also had Labor ahead, predicted a 54–46 split in Labor's favour (Table 1).[18] If Labor needed to win 51.3 per cent of the two-party vote to secure an absolute majority, as the Mackerras pendulum indicated, or 50.8 per cent to form a minority government, then a 50–50 split meant that Labor was in a worse position than the Coalition.[19] But this is quite different from saying that in the polls the Coalition was ahead.

The turning point – taking an average of the Newspoll, ACNielsen and Galaxy results – appears to have come half-way through the campaign. In week four, after Labor released its schools package, the Coalition was back to its winning margin in 2001, 51–49. In week five, following the parties' official campaign launches – 'Crazy John's Closing Down Clearance Sale', as Labor called Howard's '$30 million a minute' spending spree, followed by Labor's promise to introduce Medicare Gold as part of a big health spend – the Coalition was averaging 51.5 to Labor's 48.5 across these polls.[20] And in the middle of the sixth week, after Latham announced Labor's forests policy but before Howard announced his, the Coalition led 52–48 – not far short of the actual result, 52.7–47.3.[21] Note, however, that the steady improvement in the Coalition's position suggested by these figures does not mean that the Coalition had the better of Labor on key announcements to do with education, health or even the environment. Using the Australian Election Study (AES), health economist Stephen Duckett argues that those who decided to vote Labor during the campaign were more likely to prefer Labor to the Coalition on all three policy areas than those who made up their minds before the campaign.[22]

Howard had started the final week 'by announcing that while the contest was still very close, he believed he was ahead and that he would win'. To declare himself the likely winner was a marked and revealing departure from modern ways of managing electoral expectations. Leaders do not usually declare themselves the likely winner, preferring underdog status.[23] On election day, according to a later report, he had expected to win 'probably with the loss of two or three or four seats', leaving the Coalition with a majority as small as six.[24] In fact, he won with a gain of five, a much more comfortable majority of 24.

Of the issues included in the AES, the biggest drivers of the Coalition's success were not education or health. Nor was the contrast between the Coalition's and Labor's environment policies a significant factor. The issues that defeated Labor were: economic management, especially interest rates; terrorism and defence (though not the war in Iraq); and immigration. The economy had long been regarded as central; terrorism and immigration, dating from 2001, were more recent. All were issues on which the Coalition's advantage was evident well before the formal campaign got underway. In June, Newspoll had Labor behind the Coalition as the preferred party on interest rates, inflation, immigration, defence, and national security. In August, ACNielsen had Labor behind on the economy, interest rates, border protection, national security, and international relations (see Table 2).

Leadership was another Labor weakness. Before the election, Newspoll, ACNielsen, and Morgan had Howard ahead of Latham by between eight and 11 percentage points as the prime minister respondents preferred. In their last polls of the campaign, Newspoll and ACNielsen had Howard ahead by between 14 and 17 percentage points (Galaxy did not ask this question). The polls also sought to compare Howard and Latham on other measures; here, too, Howard generally prevailed.

Even if the images of the leaders mattered, it is likely that the

Table 2 Importance of issues and best party to handle them, national surveys, June–December 2004 (percentages)

Issue	Newspoll June 2004		ACNielsen Sept/Aug 2004		AES Post-election		Newspoll Post-election	
	Very important	LNP-ALP	Two most important	LNP-ALP	Extremely important	LNP-ALP	Very important	LNP/ALP respondents [LNP-ALP]
Health & Medicare	82	-6			76	-6	na	64/76 [-12]
Health & hospitals			52	-23				
Interest rates	50	27	14	22*	48	29	na	49/30 [19]
The economy			31	35			na	77/43 [34]
Inflation	40	30						
Taxation	57	7			44	14		
Unemployment	55	0	10	-1	46	10		
Industrial relations	34	-3			31	10		
Education	80	-10	29	-21	69	-9	na	58/71 [-13]
Border protection			na	11				
Refugees & asylum seekers					54	27		
Immigration	44	11			32	17		
National security	66	24	16	14			na	61/40 [21]
Defence	54	24						
Terrorism					51	25		
International relations			9	19				
War in Iraq					36	11		
Leadership	65	na					na	63/49 [14]
Honesty in government			23	na				
The environment	60	-8	13	-28	52	-6	na	38/48 [-10]
Welfare & social issues	59	-18						
Family issues	61	-11						
Women's issues	46	-10						
Aboriginal & native title issues	25	-13						
n	1155		1415	1413	1769		1099	

*'Do you think interest rates are likely to be higher under a John Howard led government or a Mark Latham led government?'

Questions:

'Would you say each of the following is very important, fairly important or not important on [sic] how you personally would vote in a federal election?' 'Which one of the (Labor Party, Liberal and Nationals Coalition or someone else) do you think would best handle each of the following issues?' (Newspoll, 18–20 June)

'I am going to read out a number of issues. For each one please tell me which of the major parties, the Labor Party or the Liberal-National Coalition, you think would best handle that issue.' (ACNielsen, 13–15 August)

'I am now going to read out a list of issues. Which of these issues is most important to you personally in deciding who you will vote for at the election? Which is the next most important to you?' (ACNielsen, 3–5 September)

'Here is a list of important issues that were discussed during the election campaign. When you were deciding about how to vote, how important was each of these issues to you personally: Extremely important, quite important, not very important?' (AES, October–December)

'Would you say each of the following issues was very important, fairly important or not important to you in deciding who you voted for in the federal election held last Saturday?' (Newspoll, 15–17 October)

SOURCE <www.newspoll.com.au/opinion-polls-2/opinion-polls-2/>; ACNielsen Issues Report, 16 August 2004, 6 September 2004; Bean and McAllister, 'Voting behaviour', p. 329, for the AES

images of the parties mattered more. Party research pointed to the importance of the party standing for something – something beyond the quest for office that targeted marginal seats, fuelled by focus groups. In his memoirs, Howard attributes the Liberals' success in 2004 – as in 1996 and 2001 – not only to the 'economic security my Government delivered', but also to its being 'socially conservative' and to its taking 'great pride in the Australian achievement'.[25] Howard, as the rhetor Peter Clark notes, 'was an outstanding stander'.[26] On this, however, the polls – and the AES – had almost nothing to say.

Issues

'This election ... will be about trust', Howard told journalists when he called it:

> Who do you trust to keep the economy strong, and protect family living standards? Who do you trust to keep interest rates low? Who do you trust to lead the fight on Australia's behalf against international terrorism? Who do you trust to keep the budget strong so that we can afford to spend on health and education?[27]

In his policy speech, he repeated these questions.[28] A few days out from the election, he ran through the list again.[29]

Howard framed the election around the issues he thought the voters he sought to persuade regarded as most important, presented them in terms of widely supported values, and hoped to make it a contest over which party was more likely to deliver the agreed ends – low interest rates, protection from terrorism, higher spending on health and education – rather than a contest over which policies voters might prefer as a means of getting there. On some issues, however, such as health and education, the debate was not so much about which party would be more competent but about which party's policies would be better.[30]

The economy, economic security, interest rates

There are, as MacCallum would later note, two quite different theories about the way economic prosperity affects elections: the 'common sense' view, that good times help governments because voters (mis)attribute peace and prosperity to their actions and are happy to see them re-elected; and the alternative view, that good times help oppositions – at least Labor oppositions – because it is only in good times that voters feel sufficiently confident to take a risk.[31] The evidence, according to academic economists Andrew Leigh and Justin Wolfers, supports the 'common sense' view;

specifically, incumbents are more likely to be re-elected if inflation is low and unemployment is low. Based on three different economic models, they would have expected the Coalition to win between 51.3 and 51.7 per cent of the two-party preferred vote.[32]

When the election was called, '[t]he Australian economy was wonderfully buoyant',[33] Australia enjoying 'arguably the best macroeconomic times in a generation'.[34] In Labor's research, '60 per cent of people thought the country was headed in the right direction, mainly due to its economic strength', Latham noted.[35] In the second half of 2004, business investment, commodity prices (iron ore, in particular), and building approvals were rising, as were average earnings, while unemployment was falling; consumer price inflation was within the Reserve Bank's target range; but the growth in real gross domestic product (GDP) was slowing. Although the sharp rise in housing prices since the mid-1990s had stalled, interest rates were rising alongside household debt.[36] Some of these were incorporated into the models devised by Leigh and Wolfers; most were not.

If the state of the economy helped build the Coalition's credentials as an *economic manager*, Labor's lack of credibility may have helped build it as well. In August, ACNielsen reported that Labor lagged behind the Coalition by 35 percentage points as the party better able to handle 'the economy' (Table 2). 'At the time of the policy launch', Crean recalled, 'polling showed that we had passed the Coalition in terms of our ability to manage the economy'.[37] Liberal research showed that Howard's spending spree – not pre-tested on focus groups – had undermined his claim to be a good economic manager.[38] But Labor's research showed that it had raised doubts about its own 'capacity to pay for [its] promises'.[39] Three days out from the election, in its tracking poll across marginal seats, the Liberals led Labor as the party 'best able to manage the economy and finances' by 43 percentage points and as 'able to keep interest rates low' by 34 percentage points.[40] In the Liberal's post-election research, the Coalition led Labor as the party [sic] 'best able to keep the economy strong' by no less than 49 points, according to Brian Loughnane, the party's federal director. This was an extraordinary margin; 63 per cent of respondents are also reported to have said that 'Labor did not have a credible and convincing plan to keep the economy strong'.[41] For those who thought the times were good, Labor could not afford to be riskier; if most thought economic management 'very important' (see Table 2), it could only afford to be riskier for those who thought Labor offered something not far short of what the Coalition offered – and that it was time to 'throw the rascals out'.[42]

The AES did not ask about the parties' competence. Instead it asked a series of questions about changes in the country's economic situation, looking back and projecting forward; and changes in the wellbeing of the respondents' households, looking back. On balance, these judgments also favoured the government. Respondents who thought the *general economic situation in Australia* was 'a lot better' or even a 'little better' after the election than it had been 12 months earlier (41 per cent of the sample) were 21 percentage points more likely to have voted for the Coalition than for Labor; respondents who thought the 'general economic situation' was likely to be better in the next 12 months (29 per cent) were 31 percentage points more likely to have voted for the Coalition than for Labor; but those who thought the 'general economic situation in Australia' was 'worse' than it had been 12 months earlier (16 per cent) were not significantly less likely to have voted for the Coalition than for Labor. And while respondents who thought their *household* situation was better than it had been 12 months earlier (27 per cent) were not significantly more likely to have voted for the Coalition over Labor, respondents who thought their household was worse off (24 per cent) were 13 percentage points less likely to have voted for the Coalition over Labor.[43]

Clearly, this evidence does not support McAllister's conclusion that voters are 'motivated by … evaluations of the national economy, rather than by evaluations of their own economic circumstances', and by 'prospective economic judgements rather than retrospective ones'.[44] Nor do they corroborate Leigh and Wolfers' modelling, since this would require respondents to be focused on retrospective judgments and the national economy. Judgments that one's household's circumstances had improved were not related to how respondents voted, but judgments that one's household's circumstances had worsened were.[45] Judgments (prospective) that the country's economic circumstances would either improve or get worse were related to how respondents voted; but so, too, were judgments (retrospective) that one's household's circumstances were now worse.[46]

While it may be true that 'unless there is a serious recession it is very difficult for any opposition to best a government on economic policy',[47] among respondents who thought their household had gone backwards, the probability of voting Labor rather than LNP increased by 16 percentage points – the absence of 'a serious recession' notwithstanding. We should also note how evenly divided respondents were about the future of the economy (29 per cent expected it to get better, 22 per cent expected it to get worse); and how evenly matched were the propensities to vote for the Coalition among those who thought the future was bright (31 per cent more likely compared to the probability of voting Labor), and to vote for Labor among those who thought the future was bleak (32 per cent more likely compared to the probability of voting LNP).[48]

Being concerned about unemployment, as one might expect, worked against the government. But with Labor having little to say about it – Latham simply promising, in his policy speech, to 'bring more people into the labour market'[49] – the issue worked against the government in only a small way. Among those (44 per cent of the AES sample) who indicated that 'unemployment' was 'extremely important' when they 'were deciding how to vote', the probability of voting for the Coalition rather than Labor declined by just 8 percentage points.[50] On unemployment, respondents may have preferred the Coalition to Labor, as McAllister contends.[51] As a measure of its electoral potency, however, this is misleading.

The Liberals' attempt to leverage 'economic security', especially in television ads, involved: talking up their own performance in 'delivering'; emphasising the risk of putting a 'learner' like Latham – a leader with an 'L-plate' – in charge of taxing, spending, and borrowing, given his record as Mayor of Liverpool; and rehearsing the history of interest rate increases under Labor.[52] '[T]hey killed us with their ads', Latham lamented. The report presented to Labor in July by UMR, the party's market research consultants, which Tim Gartrell, the Labor Party Secretary, then 'rubber-stamped as our campaign strategy', he complained, 'mentioned interest rates only once', and it took Gartrell 'ten days to come up with a rebuttal ad'.[53]

It was the Liberals' advertising man, Ted Horton, who proposed that interest rates should be central.[54] Liberal advertising that 'flooded marginal electorates' included a 'mortgage calculator', reminding voters of how high interest rates were under the Whitlam, Hawke and Keating governments and inviting them to 'calculate what their rates would be like under Latham', the journalist Annabel Crabb noted. With his 'constant repetition of the mantra that interest rates would always be higher under Labor', Howard 'reinforced the claim at every interview he could'.[55]

The idea of having interest rates front and centre came out of the research. When Howard suddenly turned to regional security, in the fourth week of the campaign, Mark Textor, the Liberals' pollster, 'warned that unless the interest rates attack was restored within days', the government 'would be in real trouble'.[56] In week five, Labor's polling showed that 'Howard's interest rate scare campaign was causing voters to leach away from Labor'.[57] Three days before the election, the 'majority of swinging voters agreed that "even though I think it's time for a change, I can't take even the smallest risk of interest rates going up".' The 'growing unease' that 'Labor was a threat to low interest rates' is something Labor heard during the campaign 'from candidates with strong links to their communities, from unionists talking to members in workplaces and from our own research', Gartrell revealed in his overview of the election.[58]

It was 'the interest rate election', observed journalist George Megalogenis.[59] Electoral geography appears to bear this out. 'Seats with the highest proportion of mortgagees were generally those which recorded the biggest swings against the ALP', Gartrell noted.[60] Similar analyses, conducted by journalists, confirmed this.[61] The attempt to demonstrate that the association largely disappeared once one allowed for the presence of people born in non-English speaking countries (NESB) and that it was Labor's NESB orientation, not its economic credentials, that cruelled it, proved misconceived.[62] As the political scientist Simon Jackman demonstrated, after controlling for the presence of NESB voters, the mortgage hypothesis held up.[63]

In their analysis of the AES, Bean and McAllister concluded that this 'was *not* an election about interest rates'.[64] This does not hold up either. On the contrary, of the 12 issues included in the AES, interest rates appeared to matter most. While the proportion (48 per cent) who considered interest rates 'extremely important' was not nearly as great as the proportion who rated some of the other issues 'extremely important' – 'health and Medicare' (76 per cent); 'education' (69 per cent)[65] – interest rates ticked three other boxes that mattered more. First, it most clearly divided LNP from Labor respondents: 61 per cent of LNP respondents compared with 42 per cent of Labor respondents rated it 'extremely important', a gap matched in the post-election Newspoll (Table 2). Second, when respondents were asked which party's position was closest to their own, 46 per cent of LNP respondents, compared with 17 per cent of Labor respondents, said their party's policies on interest rates were closer to their own position, a gap (29 percentage points) unmatched by any other issue;[66] of all the issues, this was the one that the LNP most clearly 'owned'.[67] Third, among those respondents who considered interest rates 'extremely important', the probability of voting for the LNP was 24 percentage points higher than the probability of voting Labor. No other issue was associated with a greater probability of voting for the Coalition.[68] While a cross-sectional survey like the AES cannot establish what *caused* respondents to vote the way they did, it can show what factors were most *closely related* to the way they voted.

Journalist Margaret Simons noted Latham's 'failure to campaign on economic issues'.[69] On the importance of these issues, Latham's form of engagement with the electorate – travelling across 'the vast suburbs and regions of our nation', as he observed in his policy speech, 'listen[ing] to the Australian people' so that he could now 'speak … for them' – had misled him.[70] 'Interest rates and economic management were not concerns raised … at any of the community forums Latham held, either before or during the election campaign', Simons records. 'This may mean that the people who turn up to such forums are unrepresentative of the wider electorate.' It could also mean that those who attended the forums 'did not have the knowledge or confidence' to raise these issues.[71] When asked why they had voted Liberal, 40 per cent of those interviewed in an exit poll conducted for Labor in New South Wales marginal seats said it was because of interest rates and the economy.[72] In the end, as McAllister conceded in another account, 'the prospect of higher interest rates' was a 'concern to many voters' – one that the Coalition used 'to great effect'.[73]

Health and education

If Howard wanted an election fought on health and education, so did Latham. Responding to Howard's election announcement, Latham declared: 'Australia needs a new government that's willing to invest in the education of our children and the healthcare of our families'.[74] Done 'well enough', Latham thought, 'our positive education and health ads will carry the day'.[75] In a bidding war on health funding, Labor promised $3.4 billion to increase the proportion of home visits paid for by Medicare; Howard, having earlier promised '100 per cent Medicare' to increase GP Medicare rebates, now promised 'Round the Clock Medicare' to increase access to GPs; and Latham came back with promises to boost bulk-billing for GP visits, massively increase specialists in out-patient departments, introduce 'Medicare After-Hours', and – for those aged 75 and over – a $5.1 billion 'Medicare Gold' package, and a national dental program.[76]

On education, Labor promised to take $520 million from wealthy private schools and redistribute it to low-income private schools. Howard described the policy as 'old-fashioned class warfare'; he thought Labor's 'hit list' put off 'young families who, while they may not have used the schools in question, wanted the opportunity to do so in the future'.[77] Latham, heavily invested in the politics of 'aspiration', appeared to have imagined aspiration differently rather than to have discounted it entirely.[78] Capital grants to poorer schools were included in the joint Coalition policy speech, but the money was not to come from wealthy schools.[79] For the Liberals, Labor's health and education policies threatened 'social stability': Medicare Gold privileged age over need; its schools funding policy was sectarian. Liberal policies were 'community based', the argument ran, not based on 'the politics of envy'.[80]

Health was not a Coalition strength, nor was education (see Table 2).[81] In Howard's policy speech he insisted that of all the issues that divided the parties, Medicare was not one. Here was acknowledgment that Medicare was an issue on which the Coalition could not afford to be found wanting, nor an issue on which it could hope to prevail.[82] Following the announcement of Medicare Gold, support for Labor among respondents aged 50 and over increased by three percentage points, its two-party preferred by seven points, in the party's research.[83] Medicare Gold had pre-tested 'quite well', though some respondents thought it 'favoured the old unfairly'.[84] In the Liberals' research, too, Medicare Gold sent support for the Liberals backwards.[85] In its final tracking poll, the Liberals trailed Labor as the party that 'believes in a responsive health system' by 24 percentage points – or by 47 points among 'soft voters'.[86] In an exit poll conducted for Labor in New South Wales marginal seats, 37 per cent of respondents said they had voted Labor because of health and Medicare, a higher proportion than for any other issue.[87] Among those (76 per cent) in the AES who indicated that 'health and Medicare' was 'extremely important' in deciding their vote, the probability of voting Labor was 19 percentage points greater than voting LNP.[88] The inference, by political scientists Wayne Errington and Peter van Onselen, that on health the Coalition was 'given the benefit of the doubt', is valid only if, as Latham argued, the election was 'a referendum on the future of Medicare'.[89] But elections are never referendums. Nor is there any warrant for McAllister's conclusion that Labor's health policy was electorally 'disastrous'. His work on 'defectors' – respondents in the AES who said they had voted differently in 2004 to how they had voted in 2001 – shows that this was not true.[90]

Labor's advantage on education survived the Coalition's attempt to frame it as 'class warfare' (see Table 2). Among those (68 per cent) in the AES who indicated that education was 'extremely important', the probability of their voting Labor rather than LNP was 10 percentage points greater – though on education, minor parties also appear to have benefited at the Coalition's expense.[91] Labor's research, according to Latham, showed that its school policy was its best 'vote-switcher'.[92] In its final tracking poll, the Liberals trailed Labor as the party 'committed to improving the education system' by 33 percentage points – or by 52 points among 'soft voters'.[93] McAllister and Bean argue that, among 'defectors', Labor's schools policy damaged the party's standing with voters; Duckett argues otherwise.[94] Even if it did, the damage could hardly warrant McAllister's claim that it was 'disastrous'.[95]

The environment and old-growth forests

In the AES, the environment was another issue that saw the Coalition at a disadvantage (see Table 2). Among those who indicated that this issue was 'extremely important' (50 per cent), the probability of their voting for the LNP rather than Labor dropped by 19 percentage points, half the advantage going to Labor and half to other parties – presumably the Greens.[96] In McAllister's analysis of party 'defectors', 'the environment' was associated with shifts from Labor to the Greens.[97] Would these conclusions have been different had the AES enquired not about 'the environment' but about the forests?

Early in the campaign, Howard had declared that while 'everybody would like to see old-growth logging stopped' – logging in Tasmania was what he had in mind – he would not throw 'regional communities on the scrap heap in order to achieve a particular environmental objective'.[98] Howard was keen 'to win mainland seats in green-tinged marginal city-electorates'.[99] He was also keen to win the preferences of green-tinged voters further afield.[100] His targets: first, 'the "doctors' wives" in the leafy suburbs of the capital cities who were considering deserting the Liberal Party over such issues as asylum seekers and the environment'[101] – 'doctors' wives', 'a put down', Megalogenis wrote, 'meant to signify that they were rich enough to have the luxury of embracing the Keating social agenda'.[102] The second target was 'Howard's battlers', regarded as crucial to his long run in office, who prioritised jobs.

In August, the pollsters UMR, working for Labor, asked a sample of 1500 Tasmanians whether they supported the idea of protecting areas of old-growth forest, 'including the Tarkine, Styx, and Blue Tier forests' – a plan, respondents were told, 'supported by the Australian Conservation Foundation'; 71 per cent said they did. In Labor's most marginal seats the figures were similar: Bass, 74 per cent; Braddon, 66 per cent. While the proportion 'strongly' in favour is not publicly known, those 'strongly opposed' amounted to just 10 per cent. Asked whether old-growth logging was more important than protecting jobs in the forestry industry, opinion was more evenly divided: '43 percent said that stopping logging was more important, 38 per cent said the industry should be preserved at all costs', Crabb reports.[103] Latham understood the research to show 'overwhelming support for a strong conservation initiative that also provided job protection'. A policy that inscribed these outcomes 'would win us support in every Tasmanian electorate'.[104]

How was the issue playing on the mainland? In Sydney, a survey conducted in September on behalf of the Tasmanian forest industry reported that for about a third (32 per cent) of respondents, the logging of Tasmania's old-growth forests was a 'very important' election issue. Having a third of the sample rate an issue as 'very important' is not particularly impressive; every issue raised by the AES was rated 'very important' by at least 30 per cent.[105] And even if these respondents were opposed to logging, it is not clear that they were opposed regardless of the loss of jobs.[106]

At the beginning of the last week of the campaign, Latham visited Tasmania to announce that Labor would protect 'the overwhelming majority' of its old-growth forests and to pledge $800 million to retrain workers whose jobs would be lost.[107] Latham, Crabb noted, had rejected the suggestion that the policy be launched in Victoria.[108] Nevertheless, he had decided to prioritise 'Green preferences over Tasmania's forest industry'.[109] The Tasmanian Labor Premier, Paul Lennon, and the forestry workers' union, looked on in horror.[110] Latham's strategy, like the one that Howard had been mulling over, was designed to win back voters lost to the Greens in 2001 over the arrival and subsequent handling of MV *Tampa*.[111] How sensible this was, when no less than 75 per cent of Green preferences in 2001 flowed to Labor, is another matter; in 2004, the corresponding figure (80 per cent) turned out to be much the same.[112]

Two days after Latham's visit, at an overflow meeting attended by hundreds of forestry workers in Launceston's Albert Hall, in the heart of Bass, Howard announced that the Coalition would allow logging (with limited conservation); but, more importantly, it would protect existing jobs. Liberal polling, apparently, showed the forests 'near the bottom of the list of vote changing issues'.[113] By coming down on the side of the 'battlers', Howard had defied the 'entire [prime minister's] office' which had wanted him 'to go for the green votes'.[114] The extraordinary reception accorded Howard in Tasmania made the evening news and the front pages of the morning papers.[115] Having led Labor to believe he might match Latham's pledge, Howard had delivered a sucker punch.[116]

'The polling was wrong', Latham lamented when he contended: 'we cut Sid Sidebottom's throat in Braddon, and Michelle [O'Byrne], who was already in trouble on interest rates, lost Bass'.[117] But it is unlikely that UMR's polling attempted to anticipate how 'conservation' and 'jobs' would be reconciled, or how the party and industry politics would play out. What 'would have happened if [Dick] Adams [Lyons] and the union officials had kept their head down', Latham would 'always wonder'. Their opposition might have been muted, if only he had come up with a different way of saving old-growth forests.[118] The seats of Braddon – where there were swings of more than 15 per cent in some forestry polling booths[119] – and Bass, represented half the Coalition's net gain of four seats nationwide. The two-party swing in the rural seat of Braddon (7.1 percentage points) was the biggest in Tasmania; in the provincial seat of Bass (4.7 percentage points), it was the second biggest. These swings were all the more impressive for being against second-term incumbents – the average swing against Labor incumbents in their second or subsequent terms across the country being just 1.7 percentage points.[120] The significance of the forestry issue seemed to be underscored by the fact that neither Braddon nor Bass had a particularly high number of electors paying off mortgages.[121]

For Gartrell, it was Latham's policy announcement that 'cost our party at least two seats and crucial momentum in the final days of the campaign'.[122] But, according to Errington and van Onselen, it was Howard who 'killed off any chance of Mark Latham ever becoming prime minister'.[123] For journalist Paddy Manning, it 'was arguably the moment Howard clinched the election'.[124]

How much of the Coalition's success can be attributed to either Latham's announcement or Howard's pledge? Less than these assessments suggest. A poll in the first week of September, conducted by EMRS, already reported the Liberals ahead in Braddon (54–46) and in Bass (54–46). Should Howard be tempted to chase 'the pale Green vote in the trendier marginal electorates in Sydney and Melbourne', the *Examiner* warned, 'he might well lose two seats here that are looking more than a fair bet'.[125] Although the sample sizes were small (200 in each seat), and 17 per cent were 'undecided', the polling identified the eventual winners in all five Tasmanian seats. In Lyons, a rural seat, the swing to the Liberals was 4.5 percentage points, notwithstanding that it had been held since 1993 for Labor by a long-time supporter of the forestry industry. In the inner-metropolitan seat of Denison, the swing was just one percentage point. In Franklin, an outer-metropolitan electorate where the forestry industry had long been contentious, the swing against Labor was even less.[126] The swing to the Coalition in Tasmania (3.5 percentage points) was not very different to the swing in Western Australia (3.8) or Victoria (3.1).[127]

By the middle of the final week, before the last of the polls had been completed, the odds against a Labor win were 'unbackably' long.[128] In an exit poll conducted for Labor in New South Wales marginals, 29 per cent of Labor respondents compared with 17 per cent of Coalition respondents said that they had made up their minds in the past week. Had the forestry issue advantaged the Coalition we might have expected these figures to have been the other way around.[129] The Greens increased their vote from 5 per cent in 2001 to 7.2 per cent in 2004, McAllister and Bean arguing that Labor voters defecting to the Greens were motivated by the forestry issue.[130] But the polls predicted a 7 per cent Green vote throughout the campaign (see Table 1); for the Greens, there was no forest bump.

Political scientist John Wanna's claim that Howard's policy of allowing logging and saving jobs 'was the straw that broke Labor's back'; Nick Cater's insistence that the images out of Tasmania 'tell the story' of how the 'election was won and lost'; and Paul Kelly's declaration that 'the final tight week … turned Howard into a blue-collar workers' hero' – all seem far-fetched.[131] This interpretation has, however, become entrenched in popular memory. More recently, Dennis Shanahan and David Tanner have written that when 'Howard backed forestry in Tasmania to shore up two seats on the island' he 'got a huge boost on the mainland because he was protecting jobs'.[132]

Even before Launceston, Howard boasted that the Coalition had 'been a better friend to the workers of Australia than Labor could ever dream of being'.[133] Labor's stand on the forests, he would later insist, 'alienated traditional Labor blue-collar voters'.[134] In 2004, blue-collar workers appear to have shifted their first preferences from Labor to the Coalition: 48 per cent had voted Labor (35 per cent LNP) in 2001, compared with 44 per cent (41 per cent LNP) in 2004, according to the AES. Whether they swung on the basis of Howard's forestry policy is a different matter. Professionals, about whom Howard remained silent, may have swung to the Coalition (39 per cent, 2001; 42 per cent, 2004) as well – even if they also swung, at the expense of the minor parties, to Labor (33 per cent, 2001; 38 per cent, 2004).[135] The idea that Howard's forests policy appealed to both job-focused blue-collar workers and environmentally sensitive professionals is difficult to credit.

The war in Iraq

Australian forces had been engaged in the 'war against terror' since October 2001 – first in Afghanistan, then in Iraq. Late in March 2004, Latham committed a Labor government to bringing the troops home by Christmas – assuming that there was a new government in Iraq. Far from being 'undoubtedly popular', as Errington and van Onselen claim, it failed to garner majority support.[136] On the other hand, Latham did not 'pay a heavy price', as the political scientist Robert Manne asserts, nor did it contribute 'to the derailing' of Latham's 'push for the Lodge', as historian James Curran believes.[137] Immediately after Latham made the promise, Megalogenis observed, Labor's lead in the polls 'vanished'.[138] It did not. Latham's popularity took a hit, with voters concerned about the wider implications. As preferred prime minister in the fortnightly Newspoll, Howard benefited. But, in Newspoll, March had been an uncommonly good month for Latham and an uncommonly bad month for Howard. Still, Labor led (two-party preferred) from the beginning of March to the end of August, falling behind in just one poll (at the end of May) and finishing on even terms in another (at the end of July), in Newspoll; Labor led every month in the ACNielsen poll, there being little change in support for Latham; in the Morgan poll, which did not measure leaders' support, Labor never fell behind.[139] In July, despite the controversy his promise had engendered, Latham repeated his pledge.[140] The Canberra consensus was clear, however. Latham's commitment had been ill-advised. Delivering the Liberals' policy speech, Howard reiterated his pledge not to 'cut and run before Christmas or any other arbitrary date'.[141] In his policy speech, Latham avoided any reference to Christmas and made no commitment to withdrawing the troops.[142]

While 'Iraq continued to go to hell', journalist Geoffrey Barker complained, 'few in Australia seemed to care about it'.[143] Neither the poll data nor the AES data support Barker's conclusion – unless, like McAllister and Bean, you take as evidence that 'relatively few voters cared' the fact that only 4 per cent in the AES rated it their *most important* issue.[144] From May or June, the polls showed that opinion about Australia continuing to fight in Iraq was evenly divided.[145] While most continued to reject claims that Howard had deliberately (rather than inadvertently) misled the public over claims that Iraq had weapons of mass destruction, those opposed to Australia's engagement marked Howard down heavily when asked to rate him as 'honest', 'trustworthy' or 'inspiring'.[146] While Howard insisted that voters wanted Australia to 'stay and finish' the job – a framing that may have been inspired by Liberal Party research – support for the idea that the war was 'worth it', or that it was 'justified', collapsed.[147]

Although the Coalition was preferred to Labor on this issue (Table 2), the war was a liability. Journalist Greg Sheridan may think it 'fair' to see in the election result 'a validation of Howard's handling of the war in Iraq', but AES respondents were more likely to 'strongly disapprove' (30 per cent) than to 'strongly approve' (18 per cent) Australia's involvement in Iraq.[148] While 61 per cent of LNP respondents thought the war 'worth the cost', only 16 per cent of Labor respondents took this view, the difference of 45 percentage points exceeding the difference on any other issue.[149] And although the proportion who thought the war 'extremely important' (36 per cent) may have been relatively low, the proportion of Labor respondents who thought it 'extremely important' (45 per cent) was higher.[150] Among those who thought the issue 'extremely important' – much higher than the proportion who regarded it as their 'most important' issue – the chances of voting for the Coalition over Labor declined by 26 percentage points.[151] On this evidence, Latham had not 'saved Howard the trouble of finding another *Tampa*', as journalist Laurie Oakes had predicted.[152] Having originally argued that Iraq counted for nothing across the electorate, McAllister and Bean subsequently showed respondents swinging from the Coalition to Labor because of their position on the war itself and because of the damage it did to their view of Howard.[153]

At the end of July, Labor's pollster had suggested that Latham 'stay away from Iraq – this is not a vote-switching issue'. Latham put it differently: 'For some people [Iraq] is seen as Howard's greatest weakness, with his lies and sucking up to Bush. For others [Iraq] raises questions about my foreign policy experience and belief in the American Alliance'.[154] In his post-election review, Gartrell let Iraq pass without mention.[155] Yet if Iraq 'remained a "liability" for the Crean–Latham Labor Opposition', as Manne claims, or if '[n]o serious commentator claimed that the issue had damaged the Coalition', it is far from clear that they were right.[156] 'Howard's choice of election date – one month ahead of the US presidential election', writes McAllister, 'seemed timed to avoid adverse consequences in case George W. Bush was defeated'.[157]

International terrorism

While the war in Iraq appeared to work for Labor, 'terrorism' continued to work for the Coalition; this, notwithstanding that from as early as March, two-thirds of those polled thought Australia's fighting in Iraq had increased the risk of terrorism.[158] After the bombing of the Australian Embassy in Jakarta, during the second week of the campaign, Labor's polling showed that 'concerns about defence and terrorism tripled', and the Coalition established 'its first substantive lead on the key "deserves to win" question'. The 'relative approval ratings of the two leaders changed dramatically in Howard's favour', there was a rise of two percentage points in the Coalition's support, a fall of three points in Labor's support, and expectations of a Coalition victory jumped by 20 points; it blew out the odds against Latham among the bookies.[159] Jakarta, according to one campaign account, would 'snuff out' Latham's 'chance of winning the election': support for Labor's tax and family package, launched a few days earlier, collapsed from 35 per cent to 'single figures' in Labor's research and Latham 'accepted the possibility of becoming prime minister was remote'.[160] The effect of the bombing was short-lived; a few days after the leaders' debate, '[s]upport for Labor and its leader returned to pre-Jakarta levels', according to Labor's research.[161]

As an issue, however, terrorism had not been neutralised. Half (49 per cent) of the AES respondents said 'terrorism' was 'extremely important' to the way they had voted. Among these respondents the chances of voting for the Coalition rather than Labor were 19 percentage points greater. The relationship between terrorism and party choice in 2004 was stronger than in 2001; the probability of voting Labor among respondents who thought the issue 'extremely important' in 2001 declined by 11 percentage points.[162]

'Defence', too, worked for the Coalition, and did so with equal strength (Table 2). For those (51 per cent) who regarded it as 'extremely important', the issue increased the chances of voting for the LNP by 19 percentage points. In 2001, 'defence' had not helped the Coalition, notwithstanding that half the respondents in that survey also regarded the issue as 'extremely important'.[163] On Barker's assessment, 'security and national defence were far less prominent than expected in an atmosphere of high international and regional tension'. But given what he characterised as 'the widening differences between the parties on some key security policy issues', an electoral advantage for one party is something we might have expected.[164] In the Liberals' post-election research, no fewer than 65 per cent of the respondents said that the Coalition – not Labor – was 'best equipped to handle national security'.[165] If, 'surprisingly', foreign policy seemed 'inconsequential', there was not much evidence of this in the AES.[166]

Immigration and border security

Although not as important as it had been in 2001 – in their policy speeches neither Howard nor Latham mentioned 'immigration', 'refugees', 'asylum seekers' or 'border(s)' – 'immigration' again appears to have worked for the Coalition (Table 2). Of those who thought the issue 'extremely important' (30 per cent, in 2004; 48 per cent, in 2001), the probability of voting for the Coalition increased by 11 percentage points; the chances of voting for Labor decreased by six percentage points (12 percentage points in 2001).[167] This may help to explain the success the Coalition enjoyed in attracting most of the Hanson vote it had not won at the 2001 election.

If 'immigration' benefited the Coalition, the issue of 'refugees, asylum seekers' did not; this, despite the fact that almost identical proportions rated the issue 'extremely important' and that on both issues the LNP was preferred to Labor (Table 2).[168] At a time when, according to one observer, the *'Tampa* episode' had 'consolidated public opinion to the advantage of the Howard Government';[169] and when, according to another, 'where you stood in Australian politics was defined by a single symbolically charged political issue – how you reacted to the sudden influx of hundreds of foreign nationals into our immigration zones and detention centres';[170] the failure of 'refugees, asylum seekers' to benefit the Coalition is puzzling.

One possibility is that while the architects of the AES conceived of 'immigration', and 'refugees, asylum seekers', as entirely separate issues, many respondents did not. Respondents may not have been opposed to 'asylum seekers', *per se*, much less to 'genuine' refugees; certainly, the Coalition said it was not. What respondents may have opposed were 'illegal immigrants'. This was the Coalition's position.[171] In so far as this is the case, respondents' views about boat people may have been registered by the item in the AES on 'immigration', not the item on 'refugees, asylum seekers'.

For Latham and Gartrell, among others, Howard had called the election to deny the House of Representatives the opportunity to scrutinise allegations about to be aired in the Senate about the government's dishonourable part in the 'children overboard affair'.[172] On this view, it was not his handling of 'illegal immigrants', or of 'refugees, asylum seekers', that made Howard vulnerable. The issue was his alleged dishonesty.

Leaders

Howard's decision to frame the election as a contest around 'trust' was greeted by some with complete disbelief; it 'floored the cynical gallery journalists'.[173] Doubts about the prime minister's truthfulness were 'a regular part of public commentary in 2004', one political scientist observed.[174] 'Credibility and truth' were the prime minister's Achilles heel, Labor's pollster was said to have told the party. A couple of weeks ahead of Howard's election announcement, Labor followed up by releasing 'Truth Overboard', a pamphlet by a shadow minister, Craig Emerson, purporting to list Howard's 27 best 'lies'.[175] Latham, inspired by the success of a campaign against New York Republican Senator Al D'Amato – 'too many lies for too many years' – thought Howard vulnerable to this line of attack.[176] Perhaps he was. Howard was certainly keen to rebut the attack. But the vulnerability of Achilles' heel, according to legend, left Achilles invulnerable everywhere else.

What did the public think about the relative trustworthiness of Howard and Latham – or about their other qualities? Early in September, ACNielsen had Howard ahead of Latham, 38–27, as 'untrustworthy'.[177] Similarly, in mid-September, in the last of a series of polls on the qualities of the two leaders, Newspoll had Howard trailing Latham, 51–61, as 'trustworthy'. It also had Howard lagging on other measures: 'in touch with the voters', 60–75; someone who 'cares for people', 66–78; 'likeable', 59–70. But it had Howard ahead of Latham as 'decisive and strong', 78–69. More importantly, it had Howard well ahead of Latham on his ability to manage 'national security', 50–31; and, by an extraordinary 34 points, on his ability to manage 'the economy', 59–25.[178] Differences of roughly this magnitude were not new; they dated to March 2004.[179] So, contrary to foreign policy scholar Allan Gyngell's view, Latham's promise to bring the troops home by Christmas did no (further) damage to his standing on 'national security'.[180] If Labor's research, ahead of the campaign, showed that '"the contrast between the two leaders [was] greater in voters' minds" than at any time since 1996' – a Labor 'positive'   what was the research measuring?[181]

In the last polls of the campaign, Howard clearly had the edge on Latham as preferred prime minister: 51–36 (Newspoll), 53–39 (ACNielsen), and 54–37 (Morgan) – an average of 53–37, a lead of 16 points.[182] If the Coalition outpolled Labor at the election, 46.4–37.6, a lead of about nine points, that put support for Howard about seven points ahead of support for the Coalition; support for Latham about the same as support for Labor; and support for Howard over Latham, as preferred prime minister, about seven percentage points ahead of support for the Coalition over Labor. On these figures, Howard may have lifted the Coalition's vote, but it is doubtful that Latham could have depressed the Labor vote by very much. On this evidence, Labor's 'Messiah complex' may have led it astray.[183] Equally, there is not much evidence for Loughnane's view that 'Latham's leadership was a significant contributor to Latham's electoral defeat'.[184] 'The economy', political scientist Judith Brett judges, 'was a bit player in the 2004 election … the real issue was Latham's leadership credentials'.[185] On this evidence, this seems even less likely.

In designing the AES, McAllister and Bean (along with Rachel Gibson and David Gow) decided not to include a question about which leader respondents would have preferred as prime minister. Instead, they chose to present respondents with a number of 'words and phrases people use to describe party leaders' – a variation on the approach Newspoll had used – and to ask 'how well' each of them described the two leaders – 'extremely well, quite well, not too well or not well at all'. Most of the descriptors ('intelligent', 'sensible', 'provides strong leadership', 'knowledgeable', 'inspiring') drew responses that favoured Howard over Latham, generally by large margins; some ('compassionate', 'honest') drew responses that enabled Latham to outshine Howard, however narrowly; some ('trustworthy') drew responses that favoured neither. Absent from this list, as it is from Newspoll's, are descriptors such as 'ready', and 'reliable' – descriptors that may have found Latham wanting.[186] Whether the differences between Newspoll's findings and those reported by the AES – notably on trustworthiness – reflected change over time or something else is impossible to say. After adding the responses together (thereby treating all responses equally) Bean and McAllister concluded that respondents who 'strongly liked' Howard were 25 per cent more likely to have voted for the LNP, while those who 'strongly liked' Latham were 15 per cent more likely to have voted for the ALP – each of the leaders, on their reckoning, better explaining the party vote than any single issue.[187] Unfortunately, findings of this kind do not reveal what proportion of respondents 'strongly liked' either Howard or Latham; if the proportions at the extreme end of the distribution were small, the effect on the vote would have been small.

In earlier work, Bean argued that the key criteria against which leaders-as-vote-winners should be measured were their scores on 'effectiveness', 'caring', 'listens to reason' and 'sticks to principles' – a rejection of the idea that all descriptors were equal.[188] In another study, he argued that judgments about the leaders' 'competence' and 'integrity' were what really mattered. The American neuropsychologist, Alex Todorov, demonstrated that perceived competence, involving both strength and trustworthiness, was a much better predictor of voting behaviour than was likeability.[189] Yet in the AES none of the descriptors Bean once argued for appears; only 'compassionate', a rough equivalent to 'caring', comes close. British research suggests that having respondents say which leader they would prefer as prime minister may better predict their vote than responses to the kinds of qualities on which Bean and McAllister focus. Indeed, the preferred prime minister measure can work to the advantage of the leader not favoured by these more discrete measures.[190]

Instead of asking 'Do I like this person?', British political scientist David Runciman suggests that voters are more likely to wonder 'Would this person like me?'.[191] Journalist Imre Salusinszky's observation that Howard spoke *for* the '"forgotten people" or middle class, voicing their concerns and values in their own language' is one way of coming at this.[192] Tom Clarke notes Howard's 'often overlook[ed]' practice of 'speaking directly to his audience, always engaging with them'.[193] Howard's celebration of what he called 'practical mateship', stressed by Brett in her account of

Howard's remaking of the Australian legend, is another way coming at the question.[194] Howard as comforter-in-chief, after the Bali bombings in October 2002 had 'rocked Australia', illustrated practical mateship in action.[195]

The qualities against which respondents were asked to judge the leaders, in the AES and in the work of Bean and others, were all *positive*. It is striking, therefore, that when illustrating the ways in which he thought Latham damaged Labor, Loughnane refers not to Latham scoring low on positives but to his high scores on negatives; he highlights Latham's 'propensity to blame others', and repeatedly calls him 'erratic'.[196] (Simons spoke with two women after the election who told her 'that they had not wanted to vote for Latham because he was a wife batterer'.[197]) For his part, Gartrell notes the emphasis in Labor's ads on 'Howard's propensity to avoid responsibility and blame others for his many failures'.

Among the weaknesses in Latham's image that Labor research picked up were concerns about what he stood for, and a sense that 'he was inexperienced and needed more time'.[198] Being a 'conviction politician', as Simons and former Labor minister John Button describe Latham, was not enough. Along with some of his colleagues, voters may have struggled to identify 'the core of this conviction'.[199] The question of 'trust', which Howard used to frame the election, was really a 'metaphor', Howard's chief of staff, Arthur Sinodinos, observed, 'for experience versus inexperience'.[200] (Adapting a line out of Ross Perot's campaign against George Bush Senior, when Bush said that Perot lacked government experience, Latham suggested that Labor respond to the Liberals by having him say: 'That's right, I don't have any experience attacking Medicare, making education less affordable or covering up Kids Overboard'.[201])

A re-analysis of the AES data by van Onselen and another political scientist, Peter Senior, offers several other ways of estimating how much the two leaders mattered. The first is based on responses to a question asking respondents to say, on a scale from 0 to 10, how much they 'like[d]' or 'dislike[d]' each of the two. They show that someone who gave Howard the best possible rating was 17 per cent more likely to vote for the Coalition than someone who gave Howard the lowest possible rating. Similarly, the strongest supporters of Latham were 9 per cent less likely to vote for the Coalition than those who liked Latham least.[202] These are much more modest effects than those reported by Bean and McAllister, based on their eight descriptors. But because they are based on an unknown number of respondents at the extremes of the distribution, their findings are equally difficult to interpret.

Another approach involves a counter-factual: imagining the impact of: (i) 'the less popular ['liked'] leader not achieving the higher rating of the more popular leader'; (ii) 'the more popular leader achieving the higher rating rather than the same lower rating as the less popular leader'; (iii) or both leaders achieving a 'neutral rating'. On any of these assumptions the Coalition's vote would have increased by between 1.0 and 1.6 percentage points. On the other hand, had the two leaders been 'as popular as their parties', the effect would have been much smaller: a gain for the Coalition of just 0.3 percentage points.[203] Elections, however, are not contests for 'father of the year', as someone once remarked. Using the preferred prime minister measure, rather than likability measure, a low figure (0.3 per cent) is what we might have expected. In shaping the outcome of the election, it would have barely registered.

Senior and van Onselen also asked respondents: 'Regardless of how you feel about the parties, would you say that any of the individual party leaders in the last election represents your views reasonably well?' If so, 'who was it?' On this measure Howard led Latham by 17 points; this was similar to the gap in the polls between the two as preferred prime minister. The proportion nominating Howard was the same as the proportion identifying with the Liberal Party; the proportion nominating Latham was less than the proportion identifying with the ALP. Respondents who thought Howard represented their views 'reasonably well' were 16 per cent more likely to vote for the Coalition, while those who thought Latham did were 12 per cent less likely to vote for the Coalition – effects that almost cancel each other out. Substituting the answers to this question for the answers to the likeability question made little difference.[204] On none of these measures did the contest between the two leaders matter very much.

This is not the conclusion at which the parties arrived. Loughnane, who saw 'the Prime Minister's record of leadership' as a key plus for the Coalition, noted that voters baulked at 'the risk posed by … an inexperienced leader', and thought 'Latham's leadership … a significant contributor' to Labor's electoral defeat.[205] Gartrell does not portray Howard as a Coalition advantage. On the contrary, he reports that in Labor's final poll 'Howard's lack of credibility' was the second most frequently given reason – behind 'time for a change' – for moving away from the Coalition. But he acknowledges 'the effectiveness of the … personal attacks on Latham' – attacks that Latham thought Labor could have countered early in the campaign by running 'positive ads' about his 'life story'.[206]

Nor is Senior and van Onselen's conclusion one that McAllister and Bean support. After looking not at the individual qualities respondents in the AES ascribed to each leader but at the extent to which the two leaders were 'liked' on a scale of 0 ('strongly disliked') to 10 ('strongly liked'), they argue that both mattered, Howard more than Latham. Howard, they conclude, encouraged defectors from Labor to the LNP, and vice versa. Latham – who pushed Labor voters to the Greens – both repelled and attracted, though less powerfully than Howard.[207]

Labor made much of the idea that Howard was about to be replaced by Peter Costello, the Treasurer and Howard's heir-prescriptive: 'I'm ready to lead. He's ready to leave', was Latham's one-liner.[208] Keen to feed doubts about Howard's future, even before the election was called, Labor distributed 'scratchies' across marginal seats, enjoining voters to stop and think: 'Who are you really voting for?' Each had three images of Howard. When scratched, one revealed another image of Howard, the others revealed images of Costello. The implication: after one more year of Howard voters would get two years of Costello.[209] When ACNielsen asked respondents early in September whether they would be 'more likely or less likely to vote for the Coalition' if 'it was certain that Mr Costello would replace Mr Howard during the next term of Parliament', 21 per cent said they would be 'more likely' to vote for the Coalition while 40 per cent said they would be 'less likely'. 'By the end of the campaign', Gartrell reports, 'the thought of a leadership handover to Costello' made 28 per cent of respondents – 'a staggering' 40 per cent among 'soft voters' – less likely to vote for the Coalition. In Labor's final poll, 'the likelihood of a handover to Costello was the fourth biggest vote-switcher away from the Coalition.[210]

On election day, Labor bunting at polling booths read: 'Peter Costello, Prime Minister, Don't Risk It'. For Latham, this ran contrary to UMR's advice: 'It is important not to make ... Peter Costello [and the question of whether Howard would stay] the sole issue ... disliked though he is by many swingers'. Latham was incredulous: 'Gartrell didn't follow Utting's polling for our most expensive, highest profile advertising in the campaign'.[211] The Liberals, too, thought Labor's manoeuvre a mistake. In their post-election research, 82 per cent of respondents, including 77 per cent of Labor respondents, said 'that the treasurer's economic stewardship was a positive for the Government'.[212] An exit poll conducted for Labor in New South Wales marginal seats found that '17 per cent of voters said they had been less likely to vote Liberal because of the Costello factor' – or, as Latham put it, '[o]nly 17 per cent'.[213]

Conclusion

When Howard called the election, the bookies rated the Coalition a 60 per cent chance to win.[214] If the punters were reading the polls, they certainly were not following them.[215] Once the election was called, however, most of the polls immediately tightened. One could ask: what were the polls measuring before the election was called? But one could also take the shift at face value, and seek to explain it in terms of the advantages of incumbency: 'The most common pattern' in how 'the electoral contest is played out in the media', Tiffen argued, 'is for governments … to gather various scars … to be equal or somewhat behind in the polls … but when the election approaches [and] there is much more scrutiny of the opposition … for governments to claw back support'.[216] Still, whether a shift immediately after the election is called can be explained in terms of this 'scrutiny' is not entirely clear. Tiffen nominated the 'scare campaign' around interest rates, which did not come until later in the campaign.[217] What is clear is that with the shift in the polls, Labor lost its winning position. If 'political professionals' anticipate an 'inevitable tightening of the polls' as each election day draws near – as journalist Aaron Patrick reported – it did not happen this time.[218] In the last three weeks of the campaign, the Coalition slowly consolidated its position.

Of the final polls, Galaxy had the LNP leading, 52–48, a little low; Nielsen finished a little high, 54–46. Newspoll, on 50–50, substantially underestimated the Coalition; its marginal seats poll, 51.5–48.5, underestimated the LNP by almost as much.[219] Morgan, easily the worst, had the Coalition trailing, 49–51. If, at the beginning of the final week, 'the parties were neck and neck in the polls', as Errington and van Onselen declare,[220] this was only because they were 'neck and neck' in the much-vaunted Newspoll.

The fact that most of the polls underestimated the Coalition's winning margin is just what one would expect if there was a late swing. But a late swing is not the most plausible explanation of the polls falling short. The difference between the two-party preferred vote recorded by LNP (52.7 per cent) and the weighted average of the best three polls (51.8 per cent) or all four (51.3 per cent) is not great; sampling variance is the most obvious explanation. The median error was almost the same as the median error in the telephone polls conducted by ACNielsen, Newspoll and Morgan from 1993 to 2010; that is, 1.8 points.[221] On first preferences, there was virtually no difference between the vote for the LNP (46.7 per cent) and the weighted average of Galaxy, ACNielsen and Newspoll (46.6 per cent) – or, if Morgan is included, the weighted average of all four polls (46.6 per cent).

It is true that Labor lost eight seats, three more than it should have lost on a swing of 1.7 percentage points on the pendulum. But it was not all one-way traffic: Labor won four of the Coalition's most marginal seats – four of the seats that Newspoll included in its marginal seat poll.[222] So, whatever might be said about the superiority of the Coalition's campaign in general – and in its own marginal seats it recorded a slightly greater swing than in the electorate as whole (1.7 percentage points) – it yielded one seat less than might have been expected.

Reflecting on the election, Tiffen thought that Howard did not 'campaign well'. What Howard did do well was 'the constant emphasis on interest rates' and 'the tactical ambush on Labor's Tasmanian forests policy in the last week'.[223] The evidence that interest rates mattered is strong. The evidence that the forests policy mattered, even in Tasmania, is less strong. The images of Howard being cheered by timber workers at the rally, 'struck a chord with every campaign in every marginal seat across the country', observed Sam Crosby from the McKell Institute.[224] What 'chord', he does not say. Errington and van Onselen do: 'Howard knew that voters across the country concerned about job security would take notice of the division in the ALP about promoting economic growth'.[225] For Loughnane it was not about Labor's 'division' but about Latham's intervention: it 'fed the impression' that Labor 'had formed an electoral alliance with the Greens' – an 'impression' the Coalition worked hard in marginal seats to cultivate.[226] Even so, in his account of why the Coalition won, Loughnane emphasises the issues of economic management and national security – not forests or the Greens. In the end, Howard takes the same line.[227]

In 'the final week, insiders in both parties could feel the momentum shifting Howard's way', Errington and van Onselen report.[228] At the beginning of that week, wrote Crabb, Labor's internal polling indicated that 15 per cent remained 'undecided'. During the next few days, the undecided moved 'increasingly' to the Coalition. By Thursday, after Howard's announcement on logging, Gartrell believed the election was lost.[229] On the evidence of the published polls, the momentum had shifted well before then. Victory did not require 'undecided voters … to break the Coalition's way', as Errington and van Onselen surmise. Perhaps '[c]ampaigns can be won and lost in the last week'. This just was not one of them.[230]

'The very last visual [sic] image in just about every paper on the morning of the poll … in which Latham seemed too aggressive ("almost violent vigour")', noted Warhurst, 'may well have influenced some last-minute voting choices' – a reference to Latham's handshake as the leaders' paths crossed outside a radio studio on the final Friday.[231] Errington and van Onselen describe Latham 'looking like a bully' as an 'equally important image' to that of Howard being cheered by forestry workers in Launceston.[232] 'It's silly to say it cost us votes – my numbers spiked in the last night of our polling', Latham claimed.[233] On Friday night, according to Latham, nearly half (45 per cent) of those polled said 'Howard deserve[s] re-election', but almost as many (43 per cent) said it was 'time to give Latham a go'. Latham's approval rating was now 49 per cent, 37 per cent disapproving (among those interviewed between Wednesday and Friday) compared to 46–40 (Tuesday to Thursday).[234] The 'last night', of course, may not have been a good guide to reactions the following (election) morning. Mostly, however, the impact of the handshake is vastly over-estimated. For some, the handshake has even become the turning point that gave 'Howard the upper hand', the moment when the Lathams were 'one overly firm handshake away from the Lodge'.[235]

The 'Howard battlers' – central, as he sees it, to his electoral success – were 'socially conservative', Howard insists.[236] The AES is blind to this. Nothing relating to social conservatism figures in the list offered respondents asked to name issues that had been important to them when casting their vote. Writing about 'morality issues' – including the decriminalising of marijuana – raised elsewhere in the survey, McAllister refers to '[t]he unwillingness of political parties to become embroiled in these difficult questions'.[237] Perhaps. But the Liberals picked up drugs as a concern, incorporated it within 'border security', and used it to target the Greens.[238] Howard's 'battlers' also took 'great pride', he asserts, 'in the Australian achievement' – a reference, one imagines, encompassing the revival of Anzac as a defining moment of nationhood, and the rejection of 'the black armband' view of Australian history.[239] The AES does not touch directly on these either. If it had, it might have shown what aspects of social conservatism and nationalism mattered – and whether other things that mattered, mattered less.

Party images – those 'automatic associations' with a party, as British political psychologist Graham Wallas described them, that 'need to be as clear as possible, shared by as large a number as possible', and able to 'call up as many and as strong emotions as possible' – also need to be part of our understanding of electoral behaviour.[240] Loughnane noted that while there are 'a myriad of factors behind an election victory', in 2004 there was one that stood out: after Labor had 'spent more than eight years in Opposition, Australians still did not know what Labor stood for'; a sense of 'doing anything for a vote', did not cut it.[241] Wanna wrote of Labor 'looking shallow and making policy on the run', its 'almost random policy announcements ... ultimately damaging the party's credibility'.[242] Barry Jones, installed as president of the Labor Party, thought that '[g]iven a choice between two conservative parties ... voters chose the one that really believed what it said'.[243] Lindsay Tanner, a shadow minister under Latham, had earlier warned: 'We have got to decide who we are'.[244] By contrast, there was 'a clearly defined message about what the government stood for', said Loughnane[245] – though in May, participants in Liberal focus groups said that Labor was making the Liberals look 'reactive'.[246]

Other 'major reasons for the Coalition's success', said Loughnane, included the 'strength and experience of the Government team', and 'the unity and the discipline of the Coalition'.[247] In its final tracking poll, the Liberals led Labor by 55 percentage points as the party with 'a strong and experienced team', and by 34 points as 'politically competent and able to manage things well'.[248] What a party stands for – as well as the propensity of voters to associate it with (in)experience, (dis)unity and (ill-)discipline – goes a long way towards establishing its image. Issues on their own mattered little, Wallas implied. Images, party colours included, mattered much more.[249]

The AES assumes that while the images of leaders matter, the images of parties do not; it included 16 questions about the qualities of Howard and Latham, none on the qualities of the Liberal or Labor parties.[250] Yet asked 'which was most important to you in deciding how to vote', a plurality of respondents (48 per cent) replied 'the policy issues', followed by 'the parties taken as a whole' (26 per cent); in a three-horse race, 'the party leaders' (18 per cent) came third.[251] The validity of these answers is difficult to determine. For McAllister, issue voting has always been minimal.[252] Instead, he has emphasised the increasing pulling power of party leaders.[253] More recently, however, he has conceded that while leadership preferences may shape party choice they may also be shaped by party choice, and that, with the AES distinguishing between the two, cannot be done. Based on a study of 70 parliamentary elections, across 30 developed countries, from 1996 to 2016, he has now concluded that leaders account for 6 per cent of the vote, on average, a figure he thinks so 'modest' that it 'challenges the prevailing narrative that leaders are decisive in winning elections'.[254]

The images of leaders are not fashioned in a matter of weeks or dismantled in a matter of days. The same is true of parties. 'You can't fatten the pig on market day', John Carrick, Howard's mentor, never tired of repeating.[255] 'I think in 2004, despite optimism about Latham … the election was a done deal … some six months out', former Labor minister and political scientist Neal Blewett observed.[256] Social researcher Hugh Mackay expressed a similar view: 'elections are rarely won or lost during election campaigns'. During the 1993 and 1996 campaigns, Mackay had encouraged

Paul Keating in the belief that campaigns mattered.[257] But 2004 was not one of the 'rare' ones: 'voters do not change their minds … in response to the thrust and parry of an election campaign; they make quiet judgements in the months – or even years – that precede it'. In March, he had said that the Coalition was 'by no means "on the nose"' and 'seem[ed] likely to be returned to office'. The election, he thought, 'was always going to be about the economy and national security', and 'Labor', he said, 'never got on the community's radar on either issue'.[258] Given the state of the economy and the government's apparent success at keeping the country 'secure', perhaps these were issues Labor could not have successfully prosecuted.

On election night, Howard singled out the Galaxy poll for having been 'the most reliable of the campaign'.[259] Galaxy was the only poll that had the Coalition ahead throughout: at the beginning of the campaign, in the middle, and at the end. If the Coalition led all the way, perhaps the campaign made no difference. Even a year before the election, economic modelling pointed to a Coalition victory with an increased majority. But if the modelling underestimated the size of the Coalition's two-party vote this may not mean, as Leigh and Wolfers suggest, that the models 'understate[d] the importance of robust economic conditions'; it may mean that in addition to economic factors, political factors worked in the Coalition's favour.[260] More generally, the predictability of election outcomes ahead of the campaign may not indicate the determinism of the dismal science, but the way voters respond to things they learn about the parties during the campaign.[261]

PART II

INTERACTING WITH A CHANGING WORLD

3

THE 'CONTINUING WORK' OF INDUSTRIAL RELATIONS

SHAUN CARNEY

On Thursday 26 May 2005, after 31 years of hard political slog – and a career in which he had enjoyed great successes interspersed with several disappointments, even a few humiliations – John Howard had reached the highest point of his parliamentary career. He rose in the House of Representatives and declared his intention to devise and implement what stood to be the biggest and most transformative reform during his time as prime minister: a comprehensive recasting of the nation's workplace laws, a legislative package that would come to be known as WorkChoices. Howard had dreamed of this day for a long time, right back to his days as an active Liberal Party member aspiring to enter Parliament in the early 1970s. WorkChoices would dwarf his previous forays into industrial relations policy since leading the Liberal–National coalition into office at the 1996 election, the *Workplace Relations Act 1996* and the waterfront reforms of 1997–98.

Howard told the House of Representatives that his package embodied 'one of the great pieces of unfinished business in the structural transformation of the Australian economy'. He described the nation's longstanding system of industrial awards as 'a product of a bygone era of crippling nationwide disputes and a small, inward-looking economy' that he was now about to see off. The time when 'a select few' could make industrial relations decisions for the many was over, he said.[1]

Work on the legislation had not yet begun but this was no mere statement of intent. The key points he outlined were: scrapping the no-disadvantage test that had guaranteed no worker would be worse off overall if they moved from the regulated system to an individual contract; shunting the Industrial Relations Commission to the margins, removing its powers to approve collective agreements and set wages; a new Fair Pay Commission that would take over wage-setting responsibilities; stripping down awards so that they covered a mere 16 conditions; doubling the probationary period for new employees from three to six months; and exempting a substantial proportion of businesses from unfair dismissal laws. The objective was to turbo-charge a move towards the individually negotiated contracts, known as Australian Workplace Agreements, that had been introduced in the first wave of industrial relations changes in 1996 at the expense of collective agreements and anything that involved unions.

For Howard, this moment had been many years in the making and now, having recently led the Liberal–National Coalition to a fourth consecutive election win in which it had also secured a majority in the Senate, he was savouring the moment. I saw this up close the day after his statement to the House when he visited the Melbourne newspaper the *Age*, where I was working at the time, for a private lunch with a small group of senior editorial staff. It was clear that Howard, assisted by a fellow true believer in this field, the Deputy Leader of the Liberal Party Peter Costello, was seeking to smash the last vestiges of the notion that there should always be a role for the state in setting incomes, a belief that had prevailed in the collective Australian mind to varying degrees ever since the Arbitration Court established centralised wage fixation conceptually through the 'living wage' in its Harvester judgment in 1907. Howard was pursuing policy ambition of the highest order. And yet, at the lunch in the fifth-floor dining room at the *Age* building on Spencer Street, he evinced no nervousness. He was in good humour, relaxed and voluble, so much so that it looked like lunch might go on all afternoon. As the clock struck three, the *Age*'s editor, Michael Gawenda, who had been hosting the get-together, had to call proceedings to a close with words designed not to offend: 'Well, John, we have to go back downstairs and make some money'.

It appeared that for John Howard it was all coming together at last. He had made his landmark policy announcement and he was only a little more than a month away from 1 July, when his Senate majority would come into force. He judged that Australians were ready to accept his prescription to apply across every workplace, transforming the way they lived, worked, and did business. But he would be shown to be wrong. Just two years later his government was defeated at the 2007 election, a defeat so profound that Howard lost his seat of Bennelong – making him only the second prime minister to suffer this fate, alongside Stanley Melbourne Bruce, who lost his seat of Flinders in 1929. Community opposition to WorkChoices played an important role in bringing this about.

As the prime minister was supping at the *Age*'s table, across town the Australian Council for Trade Unions (ACTU), under the leadership of its secretary, Greg Combet, and his lieutenant, George Wright, was well advanced in devising a public campaign aimed at thwarting Howard's WorkChoices dream – one that would prove to be perhaps the best-executed community campaign in modern Australian history. Combet had engaged in battle with the Howard Government before, when it tried to destroy the power of the Maritime Union of Australia (MUA) on the nation's docks during its first term in 1997–98. He had been an assistant secretary of the ACTU then, responsible for maintaining the union movement's resistance to the government's reforms. That dramatic and drawn-out encounter had been fought to an honourable draw, with a diminished MUA being forced to agree to new work practices and the government conceding that it could not wipe out the union. Combet concluded that the government's effectiveness in the waterfront fight owed something to the actions of the Minister for Workplace Relations at the time, Peter Reith. Before taking action against the MUA, Reith spent several months conditioning public opinion about what the government regarded as the economically damaging effects of union work practices on the docks. Combet learned from Reith that it was important to get out early with your message in these types of fights and he would put that lesson to good use in his fight against WorkChoices.

He later reflected that Labor's election loss in October 2004 galvanised him into action with a determination that he had never felt before about a political campaign. 'I resolved that we needed to fight like buggery all the way to the next election ... I was determined to see this government off.'[2]

Given Howard's history as an industrial relations warrior, it was not surprising that at some stage in his time as prime minister he would reach for the stars. After all, as Minister for Business and Consumer Affairs in the Fraser Government's first term, Howard had outlawed secondary boycotts by unions by applying the *Trade Practices Act*, an achievement of which he had always been proud.[3] Then, as shadow treasurer in 1983, he began to focus on overhauling the industrial relations laws, calling for the abolition of centralised wage fixing.[4] After beginning his first stint as Liberal leader in 1985, he helped inspire the formation of the HR Nicholls Society, an influential group of activists and industrial relations players, who sought a fully deregulated industrial relations system. And then, for the 1993 election, as shadow minister for industrial relations, he created the Jobsback! package of deregulationist policies, a precursor to WorkChoices.

And yet, when the Governor General, Major General Michael Jeffery, announced the re-elected government's far-reaching plan to remake industrial relations practices substantially in his speech opening the new parliament on 16 November 2004, it came as a surprise. After all, in late September, during the second-last week of the election campaign, the government had outlined only a handful of mild workplace policies – proposals covering independent contractors and labour hire firms, and greater harmonisation of federal and state laws. Crucially, the plan to dump the no-disadvantage test was nowhere to be seen in that announcement. A hallmark of Howard's prime ministership after his first two terms, which had been dominated by international security concerns, had been his transition from moderate reformism to policy pragmatism with an inbuilt resistance to far-reaching, politically taxing big-ticket reforms.

When the Coalition secured a majority in the Senate from June 2005, a result it did not expect to achieve at the October 2004 election, Howard used the opportunity to exert untrammelled legislative power to fulfil his long-held belief that unions should be tamed. He was not alone. Big business began beating the drum for major industrial relations changes on the Monday after the 2004 election and it found an enthusiastic listener in the prime minister. Costello was keen, as was the Leader of the Government in the Senate, Nick Minchin.[5] Most of the Cabinet and the Coalition party room appeared happy, or at least willing, to go along. Speaking for himself after the 2007 election loss, Howard said that he was not going to 'dingo out', because he believed that further industrial relations reform was critical.[6] On the decision to introduce changes for which it had not sought a specific mandate at the 2004 election, Howard was unequivocal about his own commitment and that of his ministerial colleagues:

> The collective attitude of the Coalition was that history would deem us policy cowards if we did not make further workplace relations changes. And by this, I mean going beyond what was promulgated before the 2004 poll.[7]

Once Combet heard the Governor General's speech, he resolved to get the ACTU into action and started establishing a campaign to fight whatever the government would devise. Although Howard had in recent years shown himself to be pragmatic, sometimes ruthlessly so, Combet was convinced that in this policy area Howard's ideology would dictate his judgment.[8] His punt would pay off. In June 2005, shortly after Howard's statement to the House of Representatives, the ACTU launched an advertising campaign and a week of public demonstrations that ran under the rubric, *Your Rights at Work: Worth Fighting For*. The public rallies were well attended and generated much media interest. The advertisements, notably one in which single mother 'Tracy' is told by her boss that she has to leave her son at home alone and come into work if she wants to keep her job, were devastatingly successful in turning public opinion against WorkChoices. Within two months of the ACTU's advertising campaign beginning, the union body's pollster, Essential Media, found that 77 per cent of voters in marginal seats knew of the government's plans and 64 per cent opposed them. Three months earlier, before the ads started running, the corresponding numbers were both under 40 per cent.[9]

While the ACTU was dictating the public narrative, the

Howard Cabinet was bogged down. It spent from late May until November 2005 refining its suite of WorkChoices policies – and progressively going in harder, with Howard driving the process. A debate on which businesses would be exempted from unfair dismissal laws was instructive. Howard was convinced that all businesses with fewer than 100 employees should be exempt, a big step from the government's previously preferred number of 20 employees. The internal resistance to this came, strikingly, from the Minister for Workplace Relations, Kevin Andrews, who felt the figure of 100 was too high. But Howard prevailed.

Howard's response to assertions that he could not guarantee that real wages would not fall under WorkChoices was to urge Australians to trust him because real wages had grown by 14 per cent under his government. His formulation was simple – 'My guarantee is my record'[10] – but, in truth, he could not really guarantee that real wages and conditions would not decline because the reforms themselves were predicated on getting closer to instituting a market-clearing wage. His record was established under the aegis of the no-disadvantage test. A cameo example produced by the government in material designed to spruik WorkChoices demonstrated this point. 'Billy' was a young man who had been out of work for two years. He got a job but without penalty rates or overtime, something the government believed was clearly better than being on the dole. Almost certainly, 'Billy' would have been paid a rock-bottom wage on a take-it-or-leave it basis. Thus, the market would more strongly and definitively determine the price of labour.[11]

The ACTU felt a sense of relief, and vindication, when the full WorkChoices policy was unveiled in November 2005. Its advertising campaign had not been off the mark. The package was tougher than the one contained in Howard's first announcement six months earlier. Workers in any business could be sacked for 'operational reasons' and it was much harder for employees to be represented by unions. Individual employment contracts were required to comply with just five basic employment standards: minimum wage rates; an ordinary working week of 38 hours; four weeks annual leave; 10 days sick leave; and 12 months unpaid parental leave. Employers now held the whip hand and could negotiate away all other entitlements. Essentially, there was barely any safety net for workers. This conformed to the ACTU's warnings.

By this time, the ACTU appeared to have already won the public argument. While in the lead-up to the 2007 election it spent what Combet has said was 'well over $20 million' on advertising,[12] the government allocated a whopping $110 million of public funds to promote WorkChoices, a lot of it rolled out closer to the election – to little avail. Combet knew from the ACTU's own research that by the time the government's ad went to air, 'a lot of people had made up their minds'.[13] This was borne out by independent research. Polling conducted by Nielsen for the Fairfax newspapers found a permanent shift of between 1 and 2 per cent to Labor, beginning in the second half of 2005 after the ACTU's advertising campaign began.[14]

As public opinion remained locked in against the government and WorkChoices continued to test badly in its polling, Howard concluded after the policy became law that it could do with some better messaging. In mid-2006 he appointed Joe Hockey, who had built up a friendly, relaxed public image through regular appearances on the *Sunrise* breakfast television program, as the Assistant Minister for Workplace Relations. The idea was that Hockey could present as more relatable than the more taciturn Kevin Andrews. Little changed. When Kevin Rudd took over as Labor leader in December 2006, replacing the veteran Kim Beazley, and gave his deputy, Julia Gillard, oversight of the Opposition's fight against

WorkChoices, the public opinion polls became very bad for the government. A month later, Howard pushed Andrews out of the Workplace Relations portfolio and installed Hockey. Hockey took little time to conclude that the policy was unsustainable in its current form. He knew it could not be sold while penalty rates could be wiped out by an employer as a matter of course, without any compensation for an employee. He told an adviser that the government had 'provided the lightning rod for every complaint you've ever had about your boss'.[15]

By April 2007, Cabinet ministers finally had concluded that WorkChoices was hurting them badly and that it was not just the messaging but key parts of the policy itself that were to blame. Having lived under WorkChoices, many voters, primed by the ACTU's campaigning, did not like it and were not backward in conveying this to government parliamentarians. It was the policy around unfair dismissals and penalty rates that was the real bugbear. The removal of the no-disadvantage test had turned out to be toxic.[16] This had to change and Howard, getting back in touch with the pragmatism that had previously served him well, agreed. On 4 May, he announced a 'fairness test', essentially a retooled no-disadvantage test that restored entitlements for employees who earned less than $75000 per year.[17] It did not make a lot of difference; the die was cast. The ACTU had been running on-the-ground *Your Rights at Work* campaigns in 24 marginal seats held by the government, aimed at prising them out of Coalition hands. At the election, of the 25 seats that shifted to Labor, 21 were electorates targeted by the ACTU. The national swing to Labor was 5.7 per cent; in the 24 *Your Rights at Work* target seats, the swing averaged 7 per cent.[18]

More than anything, WorkChoices was a passion project for John Howard. His strong sense of mission on driving a stake into the heart of the detested 'Industrial Relations Club', emboldened by the once-in-a-political-lifetime advantage of a Senate majority, led him to a series of misjudgments. The foundational one was his decision, after the 2004 election, to spring on voters a comprehensive, economy- and society-wide program of change that he had not taken to the voters. Memorably, Howard framed the 2004 election leadership contest against Labor's Mark Latham with a personal slogan that posed the question: 'Who do you trust?' Having asked voters that, there was always an enormous risk in taking the course he chose after the votes were counted.

The failure to establish a mandate might not have been a fatal mistake but for three other misjudgments. Howard underestimated the campaigning smarts of the union movement's leaders and their ability to motivate members to pay for, and participate in, the *Your Rights at Work* campaign over a sustained period. Underpinning this was the residual attachment within the community to the value of collective action in certain circumstances and of the existence of laws and conventions to protect against injustice. Although an increasingly large majority of workers were opting not to belong to unions, many still had some sort of attachment to just knowing that they were still there, negotiating entitlement and wage standards that could flow on to non-members.

There were two other key misjudgments, both of which Howard would later acknowledge: the removal of the no-disadvantage test; and the time it would take to settle on, draft and implement the WorkChoices legislation. The ACTU took full advantage of the 12 months that passed between the Governor General's statement at the opening of the new parliament in November 2004, where the decision to go further on industrial relations reform was first flagged, and the finalisation of the package in November 2005. That it would be another four months after that before the legislation was passed only served to deepen the government's problems; all the way through, the ACTU had a clear set of concise messages highlighting the harshest elements of the policy, first in theory while the package was being finalised, and then, more solidly, as WorkChoices awaited parliamentary assent, while the government was limited to talking in generalities and adopting a permanently defensive position.

Howard has freely admitted that removing the no-disadvantage test was an error, what he calls 'the big mistake about WorkChoices'. He has also acknowledged that when he reinstated a version of the test in 2007, this was in itself an admission of how much the government had damaged its own case. 'Now, I know we tried to repair it later on, but that almost emphasised in neon lights the error that had been made.'[19] This is true as far as it goes, but it tends to gloss over what really happened: ditching the no-disadvantage test was central to WorkChoices, part of its original design. Separating out that part of the package merely confirms the unacceptability of the overall policy as far as a majority of the national electorate was concerned in 2005–07.

Clearly Howard was outmanoeuvred comprehensively by the ACTU and this counted heavily against the government, but Work-Choices was not the only contributing factor in his defeat. By 2007, the Coalition had been in power for 11 years and there was an 'It's Time' factor. Peter Costello and Howard had increasingly found themselves at loggerheads over a leadership transition, something that had been a theme of the government for most of its life but which burst into full, technicolour view only two months out from the 2007 election as panicked ministers caucused about what to do in the face of dispiriting poll numbers. This contrasted strongly with Kevin Rudd's smooth transition to the Labor leadership in December 2006.

The story of WorkChoices, however, carries a sting in the tail for the unions and Australia's workplaces. While it could be said that WorkChoices lost at the ballot box, the fact remained that it had been legislated. It was law and it was up to the incoming Labor government to replace it with its own workplace relations regime. The Rudd Government got off to an effective start: its first legislative act was to stop all Australian Workplace Agreements then being negotiated. But its subsequent actions were ineffective in vanquishing WorkChoices.

WorkChoices had a salutary and lasting effect on the Coalition parties in the post-Howard era. Since 2007, it has been gun shy of pursuing not just similar labour market reforms, but any real workplace reforms beyond laws directed at controlling specific 'rogue' unions and union officials. But that has not really mattered, because time has shown that WorkChoices moved the dial, permanently. The Rudd Government's *Fair Work Act* – its replacement legislation for WorkChoices – came into force in 2009. It did not revive the union movement, nor did it revive national wage claims. It removed some of WorkChoices' union rights-of-entry restrictions but only moderately. It did not usher in a return to collective bargaining throughout the workforce. It did not outlaw individual contracts. Wage-setting has remained decentralised for all but a small proportion of workers who are paid the minimum wage, which is adjusted by the Fair Work Commission once a year. Since 2013, wages have been stagnant, running generally at a rate that allows them only to keep pace with inflation, which itself is running at just above 2 per cent. Industrial action is increasingly a rarity. Between 2014 and 2019, the number of days lost to strikes per 1000 employees in 2018–19 has oscillated between 2 and 3 days. In the 1990s, more than 20 days was common. In 2004, when WorkChoices was first conceived, 17 days per worker were lost due to strikes.[20] The union movement is barely a shadow of its former self. In 1976, early in John Howard's parliamentary career, union membership sat around 50 per cent. Near the end of the second decade of the 21st century, it was 14 per cent, with fewer than one in ten private sector workers belonging to a union.[21]

The ACTU's ability to campaign effectively was left seriously in question after its effort in the 2019 federal election. The ACTU pulled out all stops. It spent $10 million in the lead-up to the election, including $6.5 million on advertising during the formal campaign. It worked hard to bring about a change of government but failed dismally. The campaign message was 'Change the Rules', rules that for the most part had been set by the previous Labor government. The campaign did not work; it did not deliver seats to the Labor Party. An external review concluded that it was too complex and struggled to connect with voters.[22] Since the halcyon days of 2004–07, the ACTU has never got close to recovering its campaigning mojo. Collective bargaining is going backwards. According to the Centre for Future Work, the share of private sector workers covered by enterprise agreements has halved since 2013 to just 11 per cent.[23]

The most effective and influential Australian union leader of the past 40 years, former secretary of the ACTU, Bill Kelty, has made it clear who he believes is responsible. He told a forum at Latrobe University in 2019:

What has happened since the [global financial crisis] is the ability to bargain is less because the Labor Party did a terrible job when Gillard and Rudd were fixing the right to bargain. I love the Labor Party, but if that's the best they can do to ensure unions have a proper right to bargain, that was a terrible job they did.

It is difficult to mount an argument against Kelty on this. Labor rolled back some of WorkChoices but fell far short of doing so in a transformative way. The result is that its *Fair Work Act* has been acceptable to Coalition governments through three terms of office under three Liberal prime ministers. And, more importantly, at least when compared with the public's reaction to WorkChoices in 2007, it has also clearly become acceptable to a majority of Australian voters through that time. In increasing numbers, they have drifted away from the idea that workers need strong protections and robust union representation.

John Howard might not naturally embrace the terminology, but WorkChoices worked as an ambit claim. While he did not get all he wanted, more than likely, as he surveys the contemporary industrial relations landscape, he concludes that he got quite a bit, perhaps even enough. Howard lost the battle – admittedly a pretty big battle, losing his seat into the bargain – but on workplace relations, history may judge that he won the war.

4

RESTRAINED LAW-MAKING AND UNRESTRAINED TERROR

NICOLA McGARRITY

When the House of Representatives convened on 17 September 2001, six days after the terrorist attacks on New York City and Washington DC, Prime Minister John Howard rose to give what has been described as 'one of his finest parliamentary performances'.[1] At the time of the attacks, Howard had been in Washington to celebrate the 50th anniversary of the Australia, New Zealand and United States Security (ANZUS) Treaty. During a later speech in the House of Representatives, he poignantly reminisced:

> I had been for an early morning walk. It was a beautiful
> Washington morning – there was a touch of autumn. I had
> walked past the Lincoln Memorial and many of the other
> great memorials of that great nation which stood between
> us and tyranny on one critical occasion in our history. I,
> like millions of other Australians, was deeply moved and
> distressed. I felt an enormous sense of empathy towards the
> American people who had suffered this awful deed.[2]

It is a matter of general consensus that the worst time to make laws is during or in the immediate aftermath of an emergency. The danger of law-making at such a time is that public hysteria will pressure governments to develop proposals quickly, without adequate consideration of their consistency with liberal democratic values or whether they will be effective in combating the particular threat. The 11 September terrorist attacks brought home to law-makers, however, a significant deficiency in Australia's capacity to combat terrorism. With the exception of the Northern Territory,[3] no Australian jurisdiction had any specific anti-terrorism laws on its statute books when the attacks occurred.

Although it was a matter of considerable controversy at the time, such laws are an essential part of any counter-terrorism strategy, in my view. Terrorism poses an extraordinary threat to both Australians and to the body politic. Its exceptionalism does not lie in the gravity of the harm which might be caused. In fact, terrorism poses a statistically very small threat to individuals' lives and property, and to the health and safety of the community.[4] Rather, it is the deliberate refusal of terrorists to work within the democratic decision-making framework – their strategy of using random acts of violence to terrorise the public and, through them, to coerce governments to take particular action – which differentiates them from ordinary criminals pursuing personal motives.

Regardless of one's position, compliance with international law also necessitated the enactment of new legislation after the September terrorist attacks. United Nations Security Council Resolution 1373 (adopted unanimously on 28 September 2001) emphasised the need not only to investigate and prosecute terrorists after the fact, but also to 'prevent and suppress ... through all lawful means the financing and preparation of any acts of terrorism'. With some exceptions, such as the need for measures specifically criminalising the overseas transfer of funds to terrorists or terrorist organisations, it is arguable that Australia's existing criminal law would have been sufficient to achieve the former goal. What was clearly lacking, however, was an adequate statutory framework for preventing terrorism. Amongst other things, the Parliament had a responsibility to ensure that law-enforcement and intelligence agencies had the power to disrupt terrorist attacks before they occurred.

The primary challenge that the Howard Government faced in the immediate aftermath of the 11 September terrorist attacks was to develop a comprehensive legislative package. Early in October 2001, Attorney-General Daryl Williams announced that the Cabinet had approved the preparation of legislation.[5] Five months later, on 12 March 2002, five bills of more than 100 pages in total were introduced into the Parliament.[6] On the one hand, it might be argued that this delay demonstrated that government claims of an urgent need to enact legislation were disingenuous. But given Australia's inexperience in drafting anti-terrorism legislation, the challenge of ensuring security without further inflaming community fears and anxieties, and the complexity of the draft legislation, its development in the space of less than half a year was a remarkable feat.

While this is far from an exhaustive list, the draft legislation included: a statutory definition of a 'terrorist act'; making offences of committing a terrorist act and engaging in preparatory activities; making offences of financing terrorism and a regulatory regime placing obligations on business to report suspicious transactions; making offences of targeting public places and government infrastructure with explosive devices; making organising terrorism an offence and establishing an executive power to proscribe terrorist organisations; and improving border security measures, including expanded powers for customs officers and enhanced screening procedures at airports. This was merely the first raft of anti-terrorism legislation to be introduced by the Howard Government. Indeed, less than two weeks later, the Parliament was asked to consider a proposal to give the Australian Security Intelligence Organisation (ASIO), Australia's domestic intelligence organisation, special powers to question coercively and even detain non-suspects.[7]

My admiration at what the Howard Government was able to achieve in terms of the sheer number and scope of these measures is tempered by concern about the parliamentary process by which the laws were enacted and their substantive content. This does not mean that I have a uniformly negative view of the anti-terrorism legislation enacted during the Howard era. One of the most difficult tasks, if not *the* most, in developing a counter-terrorism strategy is to define the threat itself. The scale of this challenge is demonstrated by the continuing failure of the international community to reach consensus on a definition of terrorism, despite decades of debate and the efforts of numerous working groups.[8] In contrast, at the heart of Australia's legislative regime is a definition which has been described by scholars as 'one of the best' in the Western world.[9] Initially overly broad and vague, by the time of enactment the definition had been significantly narrowed to require proof of an intention to coerce a government or intimidate the public or a section of the public; an exception had been carved out for advocacy, dissent and protest which is not intended to cause death or personal harm.[10]

My aim here is to examine not only the record of the Howard Government in relation to the enactment of anti-terrorism laws, but also its legacy. With that goal in mind, I have identified four precedents established in these formative years of anti-terrorism law-making which have proven difficult for subsequent governments to move away from. The failure of governments to learn from history has become particularly apparent in light of the legislative inflation since Islamic State declared a caliphate in mid-2014. Although early mistakes by the Howard Government might be excused on the ground of inexperience, the continued repetition of these mistakes raises 'significant questions about the capacity of government to balance its role in safeguarding civil liberties with its responsibility to protect the physical safety of Australians'.[11]

Precedent 1: Lack of historical perspective

A failure to put terrorism into historical perspective as a permanent part of the threat landscape was a noticeable phenomenon at the time. The sheer scale of the 11 September terrorist attacks, combined with the impact of the 24-hour news cycle, meant that these attacks received unprecedented attention. Global headlines reflected a sense that not only the United States, but also the whole Western world, had been attacked. Australia's close relationship with the United States meant that it was particularly affected by this perception of direct threat. Along with graphic images of the destruction, Australian newspapers described the events as 'World Terror' and 'War of Terror'. As Howard noted in his powerful speech to the House of Representatives, the perception was '[t]he world has changed. We are all diminished, we are all struggling with the concept that it will never be quite the same again.'

The reality, however, is that while the Western world might have been experiencing a new level of threat in the aftermath of the attacks, the threat itself was not new. Terrorism has always existed and, furthermore, will always exist. The refusal to acknowledge this not only heightened the community's sense of insecurity, but it also gave the government the imprimatur to take whatever steps it considered necessary to return the country to an imagined peaceful past. By this, I do not mean to imply that the Howard Government deliberately and opportunistically exploited public fear and anxiety. There is an undeniably a direct correlation between reminders of terrorism and support for conservative governments. The failure of the government to examine the nature of the threat rationally demonstrates, however, just how easy it is to lose perspective. This attitude has proven extremely difficult to move away from. For example, despite numerous instances throughout history of similar phenomena, the wave of Westerners travelling to fight in Syria and Iraq throughout the past decade has been characterised in public and political discourse as 'unprecedented'.

One consequence of the failure to place terrorism in its historical context is that Australian governments (like their counterparts internationally) repeatedly claim that the ultimate goal is to 'defeat' terrorism.[12] Such language is understandable from a rhetorical standpoint. It is obviously a far more palatable political goal than the 'mitigation' or 'management' of terrorism. In practical terms, however, the latter is all we will be able to achieve. The logical consequence of overclaiming – and we have seen this time and time again – is to perpetuate an impossible search for a silver bullet. More and more measures are laid over the top of one another, with the consequence that ever-increasing inroads are made into civil liberties for diminishing security returns.

Precedent 2: Legislation as a 'front-line response'

Legislation plays a significant role in ensuring national security. It is important not to overstate its importance, however, or to place too much emphasis upon its capacity to combat the threat of terrorism. This was famously acknowledged by the 9/11 Commission in its 'Recommendations for Reform of the Intelligence Community'. It concluded that it was not the absence of sufficient powers, but rather 'fault lines within our government – between foreign and domestic intelligence, and between and within agencies', which contributed to those attacks.[13]

Unfortunately, what became increasingly apparent during the years of the Howard Government was 'a cycle of action and reaction, of terrorist attack and legislative initiative'.[14] The Bali nightclub attacks in 2002, the Madrid train bombings in 2004, and the co-ordinated suicide attacks on London's public transport system in 2005 were all followed by strengthening of existing laws or enacting entirely new legislative regimes. My UNSW colleague, law scholar George Williams, calculated that from 2001 until November 2007, one piece of anti-terrorism legislation was enacted every 6.7 weeks.[15]

The sense that not only could terrorism be defeated, but that legislation was the best means by which to achieve this, was not limited to the Howard era. As at 15 March 2020, 85 pieces of substantive anti-terrorism legislation had been enacted federally in Australia (with a further five bills before the Parliament).[16] This does not include the countless laws which make minor or consequential amendments, nor legislation enacted at the state and territory level. This is an extraordinary figure, and has led to many commentators using the term 'hyper-legislation' to describe the Australian response to the threat of terrorism.[17]

The attraction of legislating against terrorism is obvious. It provides a quick, cheap, tangible and relatively easy means through which governments can respond – and, at least as importantly, be *seen* to respond – to international and domestic pressure. Law scholar Andrew Lynch contends that Australian governments have demonstrated a 'distinct reluctance to relinquish the political capital that comes with legislating on security'.[18] The enactment of anti-terrorism legislation is not merely self-serving, despite appearances. It also goes some way towards achieving the important goal of reinstating a sense of security at the community level. The fundamental problem with this overwhelming emphasis on legislating against terrorism is not political opportunism. It is, rather, that 'terrorism is a complex problem that transcends the disciplinary boundary of law just as it transcends the geographical boundary of the nation state'.[19] Not only did the aforementioned cycle result in a failure to draw together all of the pieces of the counter-terrorism puzzle at any particular time, leaving an overly complex and sometimes even inconsistent legislative framework, but it also meant that other non-legislative measures have tended to take a back seat.

It is understandable, given the pressures (both temporal and political) in the aftermath of the 11 September terrorist attacks, that there was limited space to be innovative about responses to terrorism. The immediate need was for a comprehensive body of anti-terrorism legislation to fill a clear gap in the statute books. To achieve this goal, it was necessary for Australian drafters to turn to other jurisdictions, and especially the United Kingdom, for a model upon which to draw. Those jurisdictions prioritised coercive (or hard) statutory measures, giving less thought to other means of responding. The use of non-coercive (or soft) measures in response to terrorism is a relatively new phenomenon, and it would be unfair to blame the Howard Government for not being ahead of the curve in developing such responses. Indeed, this government was relatively quick to recognise the role that soft measures might play. In August 2005, after a meeting between Prime Minister John Howard and other federal ministers, and Islamic community leaders, a joint 'Statement of Principles' was produced, and a Muslim Community Reference Group appointed shortly thereafter.

While any early shortcomings of the Howard Government are to be expected, what is far more concerning is the continuing failure of Australian governments to learn from experience. By experience, I am referring not only to that of Australia during the last two decades, but also the successful use of soft measures in other comparable Western democracies. To this day, soft measures such as community education, fostering meaningful cross-cultural and religious community dialogue, and addressing the genuine grievances of minority groups, continue to play only a very minor supporting role in the Australian counter-terrorism framework. Their place in this framework, as well as how they are meant to work in conjunction with firm measures, is ill-defined.

It is important to recognise that there are political and cultural limitations upon Australia's ability to move towards a softer response to terrorism. It would, for example, be unpalatable in the Australian context to adopt the financial incentives which have been used in other countries to entice people away from terrorism. Equally important, however, is that we bear in mind that coercive counter-terrorism measures are not pursued without costs. The most obvious of these are those for individuals whose human rights are directly affected or who feel a chilling effect as a result of the laws. More difficult to appraise is the sense of alienation and marginalisation generated among those community groups who feel discriminated against and disproportionately affected by the laws. It is important that we remain alive to this reality because these grievances are what terrorist organisations feed upon in attracting new recruits to their cause.

Precedent 3: Inadequate scrutiny of the legislation

It is of fundamental importance in our democratic system that draft legislation be given an appropriate level of attention in its passage through the Parliament. Careful scrutiny is particularly important in respect of anti-terrorism legislation given its frequent deviation from traditional principles of criminal justice, rejection of democratic values, and incursions into fundamental human rights. Unfortunately, insofar as the enactment of anti-terrorism laws is concerned, the Parliament has often failed to fulfil its role as a deliberative body.

In some instances, legislation was quickly drafted. To use the words of legal scholar Philip Thomas, there was typically 'an unseemly scramble amongst the legislature so that it is seen to be doing "something" … the politicians' anxiety to be viewed as resolving the crisis overrides both the established process and rational action'.[20] Even more frequently, intense pressure was routinely brought to bear upon the Parliament to approve legislation promptly by invoking the language of urgency.

The first raft of anti-terrorism legislation set a poor precedent in this regard. Daryl Williams stated that 'we cannot afford to be complacent' and called upon parliamentarians to 'direct all available resources, including the might of the law, at protecting our community', and to 'do so as swiftly as possible'.[21] The effects of this imploring were not merely rhetorical. The government's control of the House of Representatives meant that debate before the House was 'rushed and heavily criticised' and 'the government gagged the debate which lasted barely a few hours'.[22] The Opposition generally expressed in-principle support for national security legislation during the Howard era but its calls for additional time to consider draft legislation were met with criticisms that it was 'unAustralian' and accusations that it was playing politics at the expense of community safety.

One of the most striking examples is the passage of the omnibus Anti-Terrorism Bill (No 2) 2005. When this bill was introduced on 3 November 2005, the Howard Government explained that it had 'received specific intelligence and police information this week which gives cause for serious concern about a potential terrorist threat' and therefore 'would like all elements of the Anti-Terrorism Bill … to become law before Christmas'.[23] The government was successful in this goal, despite the Senate Legal and Constitutional Affairs Committee finding that the 'completely new scheme [of control and preventative detention orders which it introduced was] capable of depriving citizens and residents of their liberty and allowing far reaching intrusions into other fundamental civil liberties'.[24] That committee, which had also been required to consider the warrantless powers of law enforcement agencies and the highly controversial sedition offences, had been given an extremely short time frame in which to conduct its review. There were six days for submissions, three days of hearings and ten days to prepare the final report. Even in the rare instances where committees were allocated an appropriate amount of time, and sensible recommendations were made, there proved to be a low level of political commitment to implementing their suggestions and proposals.

This breakneck pace is a symptom of the back-to-front law-making of the Howard Government. Careful consideration of the terms and implications of legislation prior to enactment was often replaced with promises of continuing review and, in some instances, the inclusion of formal sunset clauses. The problem, however, is that *ex post facto* review is rarely an adequate substitute for careful consideration before enacting a law. Experience has shown that in practice anti-terrorism legislation is virtually impossible to repeal. Sunset clauses are renewed as a matter of course and the recommendations of parliamentary and independent reviews are frequently ignored.

Precedent 4: Sidelining of
human rights considerations

The failure to address the human rights implications of anti-terrorism legislation adequately is questionable not only in terms of its impact on the individual, but because the protection of those rights – far from being a luxury which may be dispensed with at times of emergency – is generally regarded as 'an effective weapon in the defence of democratic societies against terrorism'.[25]

The Howard Government was not unusual among Western democracies in the pressure it imposed upon the Parliament to enact legislation expeditiously. The unfortunate reality is that the risks posed by such haste were far greater in the Australian context. Rigorous pre-enactment scrutiny of legislation by the Parliament was particularly important given the limited avenues for judicial review of legislation in the absence of a constitutional human rights act. There were undoubtedly some cases during the Howard era in which the parliamentary process, especially in the Senate, was able to play an effective role in developing legislation. The 15 months of debate in relation to the highly controversial special powers of ASIO, including one continuous 27-hour period in December 2002, is particularly notable. Political scientist Jenny Hocking observed that 'few Bills have undergone [as much] scrutiny, public inquiry and renewed consideration as this'.[26] Even then, however, the debate concentrated upon specific amendments rather than the appropriateness of incommunicado detention of non-suspects by an intelligence agency which was at the heart of the regime.

An irony of living in a liberal democracy is that there is considerable pressure upon governments to mould their policies to populist demands. As the then Leader of the Opposition in the Senate, John Faulkner, deliberately misquoted St Paul in noting: 'the wages of fear are political success'.[27] This is especially so in the aftermath of an event that captures public imagination to the extent that the 11 September terrorist attacks did.

Fundamental human rights are – with limited exceptions – not absolute. It is possible to identify instances in which freedom of expression, the right to liberty, freedom of movement, the right to privacy and other rights will need to be restricted in order to protect security. I have always supported the need to enact specific anti-terrorism laws. The onus is, or, at least, should be, on those advocating intrusions into fundamental human rights to explain how they will enhance state security. In the Australian context, more often than not there has been a regrettable failure by proponents of new legislation to demonstrate their necessity. Some level of over-reaction might be excused on the basis of historical inexperience in legislating in response to terrorism. The constant ratcheting up of anti-terrorism legislation demonstrates how the 'precautionary justification for the enlargement of the scope of criminality and the diminution of civil liberties have been taken to their logical extreme'.[28]

Unfortunately, it appears that in Australia, like in many other jurisdictions, there has been a fundamental shift in approach. Law scholars Liora Lazarus and Benjamin Goold have noted that where 'constitutional and international human rights once claimed a privileged moral status, their limitation always requiring justification … claims to security now appear to receive less scrutiny than the assertion of rights that may restrict measures in its pursuit'.[29] For example, one government member, Sophie Mirabella, recalling the famous 'you're either with us or against us' rhetoric of George W Bush, stated:

Only the Australian Greens and the tiresome civil libertarians would put their distorted view of human rights ahead of justice for the victims of terrorists. Only they would try to turn into victims, people who willingly and ably volunteered to maim and kill innocent civilians, is evident throughout parliamentary debates on national security legislation during the Howard era.[30]

It is this shift which has enabled the enactment of laws which undermine some of the most fundamental principles of any liberal democracy.

As the saying goes, hindsight 'is a wonderful thing'. It is difficult for us to undo past errors or reverse previous mistakes. What we can do, however, is learn from them.

PART III
INSTITUTIONAL CHALLENGES

5

COMMONWEALTH–STATE RELATIONS

This chapter is an edited interview the editor conducted with Kate Carnell AO in October 2019. She served as Chief Minister of the Australian Capital Territory from March 1995 to October 2000, representing the Liberal Party.

Tom Frame: You were elected ACT Chief Minister in March of 1995, making you the first Liberal woman elected as either chief minister or premier in Australian history. The next month you attended a Council of Australian Governments (CoAG) meeting with Paul Keating as the prime minister. What do you recall of that meeting?

Kate Carnell: It was an interesting meeting because most of the states and territories had Liberal premiers and chief ministers back in those days, and the focus was on competition policy. Work had been done over a long period of time convincing the states and territories to sign the competition policy agreement, even though legislation had been floating around for some time. There was a level of excitement in that arena as competition policy had been achieved. I would have to say it is something of which Paul Keating should be incredibly proud. But you did not get a sense of what was next on the agenda as other policy matters like health reform and public housing reform had stalled.

TF: In terms of the relationships at that time between the Commonwealth and the states (and perhaps between the states), did you come to that first meeting believing Commonwealth–state relations needed to be reformed or repaired in some way?

KC: Definitely. That meeting certainly did not change those views. The dilemma faced by the Commonwealth Grants Commission approach is this: the states spend a very large amount of time trying to convince the Federal Government that they should get a bigger bit of the pot. The dynamics are unproductive. At one stage my team of four people were working on the ACT submission to the Commonwealth Grants Commission, with a whole floor in New South Wales of people working on the same scenarios. The dilemma with how money was carved up was very real. But the other thing that really needed to change was that the Commonwealth and state, their level of duplication was significant; efficiencies that could be achieved together being able to address a range of issues had started to be done, but had a long way to go. And it was great to see the Howard Government address a lot of micro-reform issues in a lot of different areas: environmental issues, gas reform to water – a whole range of things we are still talking about, by the way.

TF: Did it make much of a difference that you were a Liberal leader with a Labor prime minister or did Paul Keating regard the Australian Capital Territory (ACT) as not a jurisdiction that he had to be too worried about because he presumed that it would come back to Labor at the next election?

KC: I think that is probably the truth. I think the ACT is usually taken for granted by both sides for the exact opposite reason. The fascinating bit about dealing with Paul Keating was his personal approach. I recall him asking for a chat ahead of the first meeting to discuss what I would like to achieve at the meeting. He was really very pleasant. Mind you, I was his local pharmacist, so that really did break through a few barriers. One of the things that Canberra should be very pleased about was when Paul Keating rang me directly and said, 'Kate, can we do a land swap?' And I said, 'Well, I think our people have been talking about some issues'. He wanted the hospital site and was willing to give us the Kingston foreshore. That was it. We had just done the deal for the national museum to go ahead on the old hospital site and the Kingston foreshore to go into the planning stage for what we see today. It is now a vibrant hub for Canberra and a great place to live. Paul Keating was able to make decisions and make them reasonably quickly.

TF: Did you have high hopes when the Coalition was elected in March of 1996, and John Howard as prime minister?

KC: My background is small business and it always has been. The reason I went into politics is small to medium businesses in Australia need a better go. The sort of policy direction that we were taking in the ACT and that the Howard Government embraced was the reason I was in politics. It was great to hear the Howard Government talk about areas like balancing budgets, economic growth, industrial relations reform, cutting red tape, a range of those basic measures that business needs, particularly smaller business, to grow their businesses to employ people and to get economic growth happening. So, for me, this was pretty exciting.

TF: Did you get a sense at that first meeting that the Howard Government had an agenda for Commonwealth–state relations?

KC: There is no doubt the Howard Government approached

Commonwealth–state relations differently from the Labor Party. I found [Paul] Keating and [Bob] Hawke quite reasonable to deal with but the Howard Government did adopt a different approach with the states wanting to achieve great things. It was more of a collaborative approach that was a key part of micro-economic reform made in the first years of the Howard Government.

TF: Do you think the national firearms agreement made the Howard Government more ambitious than it might have been had that tragedy not occurred and that reform been made?

KC: I think so because, to be fair, it was major. Bringing the National Party on board was tough, too. Many Australians found that change difficult but the Howard Government managed to do it in a collegiate way, showing what was possible. Things went on from there in a range of different areas: industrial relations reform, environmental reform, and taxation reform. It was great to see that reform really being embraced. We have not really had too much tax reform since then.

TF: When the first Coalition federal Budget was brought down did you think the Howard Government was indifferent to your jurisdiction?

KC: I certainly do not think there was too much focus on the impact on Canberra of some of the policies in the 1996 Budget. The government was elected to balance the budget and address a $10 billion deficit. The problem was the impact upon Canberra was extraordinary because it was quite quick. Some 15 000 public servants were retrenched over a very short period of time. The *Canberra Times* published a front page filled with pictures of a traffic jam of removal vehicles running down Northbourne Avenue. The ACT ended up with three consecutive quarters of negative growth. That was a real difficulty given I had recently become the chief minister. Also, John Howard chose not to live in Canberra, and that might not seem important, but it was important to Canberrans at the time. It did feel like we had been abandoned. As a result, Canberrans pulled together, resulting in having the highest growth rate in Australia in three years. In time, Canberrans began thinking that we can do this ourselves. By not being as reliant on the Commonwealth Government, we ended up with the majority of Canberrans working in the private sector, and a community full of extraordinary and gutsy people.

TF: Did you win an unwinnable election in 1998?

KC: I thought it was going to be hard to win in 1998; mainly due to the hospital implosion at the time. That was a very real issue. It was probably the worst day of my life. Yes, we had a number of issues, but we won that election quite easily. I think the fact is Canberra wanted to set its own destiny. The election result showed that Canberra had come of age.

TF: Did Commonwealth–state relations have any kind of political cargo in the ACT?

KC: Commonwealth–state relations were always difficult because no federal government ever thinks the ACT is terribly important. We had to work hard improving the ACT's relations with the Commonwealth. On the positive side, a lot of public servants who are involved in managing Commonwealth–state relations live in Canberra. I took the 'glass half full' approach. One of the funniest bits of Commonwealth–state relations was Jeff Kennett and Bob Carr, almost with their arms around each other, trying to convince the prime minister and the treasurer to allocate significant amounts of money to the states based purely upon population. Giving large sums to the Northern Territory and Tasmania was simply too much for them. There were some amusing moments when people who you would not have thought were on the same page tried to sell the absolute unsaleable proposition to John Howard.

TF: Is it the case that political loyalties but also state aspirations cut across each other?

KC: That was certainly so. I think where that became even more front and centre was during the Goods and Services [Tax] (GST) debate. The Labor states did not supposedly support the GST at all, *except* in CoAG meetings. If you look back at the CoAG communique at that stage, the three Labor states and territories said, notwithstanding the fact that we do not support the GST, we are really positive about the proposed carving-up of the money. They were more than happy to have in-depth discussions about who got what and how that was done. Labor just wanted to emphasise that they did not really support it but could see the practical benefits were it to be introduced. And that is very much the way it works.

TF: Very early in the life of the Howard Government, the Commonwealth overturned voluntary euthanasia laws in the Northern Territory. Was that for you an indicator that either the ACT and the Northern Territory should be states or that Commonwealth–state relations needed to somehow be reformed, particularly on social matters?

KC: This was a territory issue obviously because the Commonwealth could override territory legislation. I think that just needs to change. I find it difficult to believe that it has not changed despite many forces and factors that justify change.

TF: Do you object to the Commonwealth being able to do that?

KC: It is absolutely wrong in principle and practice. I think the Commonwealth should have the right to legislate or intervene when national security is involved. But when the people of the Northern Territory or the ACT have elected a government to manage their affairs, those governments should be able to administer their jurisdiction within the confines of the law. When we were trying to run a heroin trial in the ACT the Federal Government said that they would stop us importing the heroin. So that was the end of that. That is when the Federal Government should really opt out of territory affairs where it is not about national security or national issues.

TF: Did you feel though the Howard Government on that point was more philosophically or politically inclined to say you cannot do what you say you want to do?

KC: I fully accept the Howard Government's conservative views on drug law reform or voluntary euthanasia. But they are certainly not core issues for Liberal Party philosophy, at least in my view. And they are certainly not core issues that the Howard Government took to the election. If the Northern Territory Government at the time wanted to, and they did want to legislate on voluntary euthanasia, then they should have every right to do so. The ACT should also have the right to do what it chooses to do in terms of areas like drug law reform. There are similar issues associated with the legalisation of marijuana in the ACT. It is important to let elected governments run their territories the way they think they should.

TF: Is it contrary in your understanding of Liberal Party philosophy for government to be intrusive in the ways in which you think it has been intrusive of the Commonwealth with respect to the states and the territories?

KC: I think it is totally at odds with Liberal Party philosophy. The Liberal Party has always believed that the states had a very important role in the Federation; beholding of rights and obligations to run their own deals. That has been the basis of Liberal–Coalition type policy in this space. It is not the same to say you can run your own deal if you do not upset us or if we agree with you. That is definitely not how it should work. The need for change is clear and the case for change is compelling.

TF: And in the five and a half years that you were chief minister were there changes made that were beneficial to the ACT (and perhaps also the Northern Territory and the states) in the way that funding was distributed?

KC: The health reforms that were done over the first five years of the Howard Government were quite significant. Changes in the focus of health delivery and the cost allocations around health (moving from a systems approach to outcomes-based funding) was important; as was the renewed focus on private health insurance reflecting best practice rather than continuing what was done before. Michael Wooldridge's (Minister for Health, 1996–2001) work on immunisation rates was quite stunning, requiring the states and territories to be on board. It was important that the Commonwealth worked closely with the states to stop what was truly senseless behaviour of cost-shifting between the Commonwealth and the states. The Howard Government addressed this by securing multilateral agreements including for the Pharmaceutical Benefits Scheme (PBS) and the Medicare Benefits Schedule (MBS). This was a step in the right direction, focusing on outcomes not just inputs. Now that is important stuff.

TF: With that renewed emphasis, was there less likelihood or less capacity for the Commonwealth to engage in state-based pork barrelling?

KC: You could not do it under those sorts of agreements as the payment was for activity and outcomes. The funding was tied to outcomes and to quality as well.

TF: Who was driving changes to Commonwealth–state relations?

KC: It was Federal Treasurer Peter Costello, and the Commonwealth Treasury Department generally because they paid the money. Commonwealth–state relations were fraught. It was always funny seeing the obligatory walk-out of premiers at CoAG conferences when we talked about money. There then had to be more negotiations and then the premiers would walk back in and it was all a bit silly. It is true that the role of premiers and chief ministers was to get the best deal for their jurisdiction. This created a level of tension at these meetings.

TF: Was there ever talk about dealing with problems in the Constitution?

KC: There was; and whenever there was, it took about two minutes to be thrown in the 'too hard' basket. Constitutional change is so hard in Australia. The Howard Government was focused more on micro-economic reforms that could be achieved rather than constitutional reform.

TF: Do you think that was because the Hawke Government tried it and got nowhere?

KC: That is how I saw it. The Howard Government adopted a pragmatic approach to reform. In the area of industrial relations the focus was on more flexibility in the system to allow people to employ staff more easily; introduction of Australian Workplace Agreements (AWAs), simplification of the award system, right of entry changes – all of those things business was asking for were adopted. Business wanted the Federal Government to balance the budget to control inflation and use monetary policy to stimulate growth. These were measures broadcast in the 1996 Budget. It was a pragmatic approach on what could be done, what needed to be done to really get Australia going. But the good thing about the Howard Government is it continued a large piece of work underway under Labor, like competition policy, even a range of their health reforms were actioned. Not everything was dismissed simply because they had been done under a different government. I think that is something that is important. There is no such thing as total right, total wrong in politics. Most of it is grey and in the middle.

TF: In terms of being here in the ACT surrounded by state government, did you feel there were some things that the Commonwealth might have done to improve relations between states and between states and territories?

KC: One of the things that is hard from a small state or a territory perspective is the level of competition that exists between states and territories. The amounts of money that can be thrown at projects to help grow the state budget. The dilemma we had being right in the middle of New South Wales is a whole range of New South Wales people using ACT services: hospitals, libraries and schools. With a good number of them working in Canberra and even the ones that do not work in Canberra, Canberra is the closest centre for them. The dilemma for us was negotiating directly with New South Wales, trying to get them to pay a reasonable amount of money for the services their people were using in the ACT. We did not have a whole lot of bargaining power because we were without the capacity to deny access to these services. The Federal Government could have significantly helped us. The other issue is that most services cost more in the ACT because we do not have economies of scale. The approach adopted by New South Wales was to pay us what it costs at the lower end of the scale to look after all their people. That was neither fair nor reasonable. The Commonwealth's view was clear: this was a matter the governments of New South Wales and the ACT needed to address.

TF: After 2000, you pursued a new career in the private sector leading several industry associations. How did you come to view, as an outsider, Commonwealth–state relations in the last half of the Howard Government?

KC: As an outsider, I found the level of consultation went down. I found it increasingly difficult to be involved in the early stage of policy development. Consulting less with stakeholders happens to governments that have been around for a long time. During that time, I ran the National Association of Forest Industries, and was responsible for organising that famous meeting in Launceston with the prime minister and the 'truckies', which many people say helped John Howard, in part, to win that election in 2004. At the time we thought the rally would give a political bounce, with it working like a charm in Launceston. Michael O'Connor (National Secretary of the CFMEU) was on stage with the prime minister (with his sleeves rolled up), addressing an audience of blokes in blue T-shirts and hats; these were attractive photos from a political perspective. Importantly, the messages spoken at the rally mattered to them as the prime minister argued for their jobs and their livelihoods and spoke of the impact of policies devastating the forest industries throughout Tasmania and regional Australia. The visuals of the rally were very impressive.

TF: But the Howard Government you thought was at that stage consulting less?

KC: In the early 2000s the government was good at listening; by the time I was with the Australian Food and Grocery Council we (and other groups) struggled a bit more to be heard. It just got harder to be involved in policy development and that is what industry associations exist to be doing; it is what their members want them to be doing, influencing policy in the early stages, not just when the consultation paper comes out, which is the final piece of work. The perception was there was less consulting towards the end of the Howard Government.

TF: Does it seem, though, when you are an outsider, that Commonwealth–state relations is either stopping Canberra intervening or resisting the power of New South Wales?

KC: The whole issue of Commonwealth–state relations and the CoAG agenda has gotten out of control. There is not an easy way for business or the community to input into the system. CoAG now is a bureaucracy unto itself. It did not start that way, but it is now a barrier for business and others to input into policy development. It is something that really needs to be addressed.

TF: And if you were to give the Howard Government a score out of 10 for its performance in Commonwealth–state relations?

KC: I saw it up close and personal for the first five years and thereafter from a distance. The Howard Government differed from other federal governments because it valued the states and the territories. It did not see them as an impediment to the whole approach to government. The former Labor Prime Minister, Gough Whitlam, suggested the states be abolished in favour of regional administrations. A positive of the Howard Government is that it did value the input of the states. It was always, however, a battle to secure funding. The dollars were always the issue, and still are. It is an interesting question and the answer is possibly where things really go wrong is where the Commonwealth and the states are involved in parts of the same thing, with health being one of them. Given the Howard Government worked with the states and valued their contributions, I score it a seven out of ten.

TF: Is it unclear?

KC: It is clear what the states run and what the Federal Government runs. The most pressing issue is the distribution of financial liability. By way of illustration: if I am admitted to hospital the costs are borne by either the ACT Government or the New South Wales Government, depending on where the hospital is located.

Once discharged from hospital, a consultation with my local general practitioner is paid for by the Commonwealth (to the extent of the Medicare rebate). If the doctor gives me a prescription, the Commonwealth is paying that, too. But if I was given the prescription while in hospital, the territory or state government is paying. The allocation or distribution of costs is a key issue for Commonwealth–state relations, in part because it encourages territories and states to engage in opportunistic cost-shifting exercises which run counter to the effective and efficient delivery of public services. The same observations can be made of education and vocational training. The interface between vocational training and the education systems, which are owned by the states, continues to be difficult. This is not a simple space.

TF: Will Commonwealth–state relations always be a work in progress given what the founders of the Commonwealth and the drafters of the Constitution have handed to us?

KC: It will, while the Constitution stays the way it is and while there continue to be many things that have dual responsibility at various stages in the supply chain. The challenge of offering apprenticeships into the school system – with it going well in some states and poorly in others – is a situation we do not want for Australia. We need a more holistic approach but Commonwealth–state relations makes that difficult. Arguments between the smaller states and the larger states about the carve-up of the funding pie will continue. Fundamentally, the whole system does not work well. It is neither effective nor efficient. That is the problem and it is much more practical than philosophical.

6

CONTROLLING THE SENATE

SCOTT PRASSER

This chapter examines the most controversial and perhaps the most important issue about the Howard Government's fourth term – namely that its 2004 election win, with an increased majority and especially its unexpected control of the Senate, is now regarded by most (including those within the government's own ranks, Labor leaders, academics and commentators) to have sown the seeds of its subsequent loss of office just three years later. Although celebrated within Coalition ranks at the time, and seen as an endorsement of both the Coalition's policies and its leader, John Howard, the conventional wisdom of federal Liberal parliamentarian, Andrew Robb, and some other Liberals after the 2007 election was that winning control of the Senate, historic and symbolic as it may have been, was a 'poisoned chalice'.[1] The arguments are clear.

First there was a view that, along with a renewed confidence, it also encouraged such arrogance and hubris that the Howard Government believed it could do no wrong. Uncharacteristically, the Howard Government began to neglect and misinterpret the electoral mood. It assumed its past policies were the right ones and had been fully embraced by the electorate. As political journalist Paul Kelly put it, Howard thought the electorate understood and would accept further economic reform and the expected benefits it would bring in the form of a stronger economy and more jobs, as it had in the past.[2] Meanwhile, the electorate thought Howard knew how far future reforms could go and what was most important to them.[3] These assumptions were proven wrong on both counts.

Second, the election outcome encouraged the Howard Government to return to more extensive industrial relations reform than it had intended before the election. It was thought that most industrial relations issues had been settled in Howard's first term when its first tranche of reforms were passed (Workplace Relations and Other Legislation Amendment Bill).[4] What was ignored, however, was that despite a strong electoral mandate and a landslide win, the industrial relations legislation had been severely amended by a hostile Senate.[5] The Senate continued to stymie attempts at further reforms in subsequent terms. As Kelly wrote, 'Senate resistance had turned workplace relations into a desert of lost hopes'.[6] Without a Senate majority, the government deemed further reform impossible. Consequently, the Coalition's 2004 industrial relations election platform, while promising 'more reform and increased flexibility'[7] and other proposals,[8] was constrained by this reality. This all changed when the Coalition won its Senate majority which, as Liberal Senator George Brandis proclaimed, was 'an outcome that nobody – *nobody* – expected' [his emphasis].[9] For the first time since being elected, the Howard Government was no longer constrained by an obstructionist Senate or any pre-election compromises. This opened up new opportunities. It was in these circumstances that more extensive industrial relations changes, to become known as WorkChoices,[10] was born. Because WorkChoices would eventually include not only what had previously been rejected, but also some important additional measures, some saw it as extreme and ideological.

Third, there was disquiet about how the Howard Government might use its new-found Senate majority – slim as it was. It had been more than 20 years since any government had held a Senate majority, the last being the Fraser Coalition Government from 1975–81. The general view now was that any government holding a Senate majority undermined the Senate's perceived review, inquiry and accountability functions and Australia's bicameral parliamentary democracy. As Harry Evans, Clerk of the Senate, emphasised:

> Governments use their parliamentary majorities to suppress both legislation and inquiry. Legislation notoriously is 'rubber stamped,' with no dissent by government backbenchers … Inquiries are not permitted if they cause embarrassment to government … Only upper houses not under government control actually perform legislative functions by exercising to a certain extent the legislative and inquiry power.[11]

That a Coalition government led by John Howard now had a Senate majority raised even more alarm. 'Gloom', wrote some observers, 'in something of a hysterical form, returned when the Howard Government added a very slim majority in the Senate to its substantial numerical superiority in the House of Representatives'.[12] Evans argued this was because the Howard Government was more disciplined, had fewer backbench revolts and, therefore, would be more able to exert greater executive control over the Senate than its Coalition predecessors.[13] Also, according to Evans, the Howard Government before 2004 'showed a strong interest in gaining control of the Senate by other means, either by changing the electoral system to ensure a government majority, or by changing the Constitution to allow legislation to bypass the Senate'.[14] There was also the view that having a Senate majority would be detrimental to the Howard Government as it meant that the restraining hand of the Senate, which had previously been 'Howard's best friend in terms of saving him from the electoral cost of some of his more unpopular measures'[15] would now be gone. Nothing, it seemed, could now protect Australia from the Howard Government's 'extremism' and nothing could save the Howard Government from itself.

So the conventional wisdom is that 'WorkChoices was a flawed policy and Howard … was blinded by his own ideological conviction'.[16] Winning control of the Senate meant the removal of any restraint on the Howard Government's alleged 'extremism'. It encouraged the normally astute Howard to embark on a political misadventure for which neither he, his government nor the unsuspecting public were adequately prepared. Political academic Judith Brett's post-2007 election assessment sums up the 'poisoned chalice' view:

> After he [Howard] unexpectedly won control of the Senate
> in 2004, he used his fourth term to overhaul Australia's
> industrial relations system. WorkChoices, Howard's
> industrial relations revolution, was the biggest misjudgement
> of his political career and goes a long way to explaining why
> nothing went right for him in 2007. Without the constraint
> of the Senate, he succumbed to the hubris of power. The
> reforms were not part of the Coalition's policy for the 2004
> election, they tilted the balance of power in the workplace
> decisively towards employers.[17]

Placing the Howard Government's actions in context

I seek to challenge this conventional wisdom here, placing the Howard Government's decisions to seek further major industrial relations reform in the political, historical, policy and economic contexts of the time. I contend they are not the product of hubris on Howard's part or some partisan ideological fanaticism to establish a 'new right' industrial relations utopia.[18]

Having won the 2004 election and unexpectedly gained a Senate majority (after the Coalition ran separate how-to-vote cards in Queensland and four Liberal candidates were elected), the question was what should the Howard Government now do with its renewed 'political capital' – that somewhat indefinable quality of prestige, respect, trust, style, support and influence.[19] Should it conserve its newly won political capital with the hope of a fifth term by adopting a moderate policy agenda or should it use it, in what would probably be its last term and chance to implement its long-standing industrial relations reform agenda in full? Several factors impinged on the government's decision-making and its choice of further industrial relations reform.

First, there was its 2004 fourth-term election win itself. Though not without precedent in national Australian politics, a fourth term was nevertheless a considerable achievement.[20] Moreover, the results exceeded expectations. The Liberal Party's first preference vote of 40.5 per cent was 3.4 per cent higher than in 2001, its highest since its 1975 landslide at 41.8 per cent. The two-party preferred vote at 52.7 per cent, an increase of 1.8 per cent, was not huge, but reassuring. Its House of Representatives majority rose from 14 to 24 seats. The government received swings towards it in every state. One Nation had disappeared and, although the Greens' vote increased, it was less than anticipated.[21] Most significant was the slim but nevertheless decisive government majority in the Senate with 39 of the 76 seats. This meant that previous industrial relations reforms the Senate had blocked in the government's first term could be resuscitated.

Second, there was the Liberal Party's own history. As British historian Charlotte Riley argues, 'all political movements and parties look to their past to explain their identities' and this affects their actions in the present.[22] Many Liberals and many commentators believed the Fraser Coalition Government had failed to use its Senate majority, its huge House of Representatives landslide, and its unquestionable election mandate, to reverse the excesses of the Whitlam Labor Government (1972–75) and to initiate long-lasting economic reforms.[23] These were 'years of lost opportunity'.[24] As Howard himself said, 'legions of Liberals felt that he [Fraser] had not used his massive mandates of 1975 and 1977 to effect sufficient change'.[25] Paul Kelly summed up the Liberal Party's frustration with the Fraser years thus:

> The people took Fraser at his word and gave him a great mandate: for five and a half years he had control of the House of Representatives and the Senate. In 1975 and 1977 he won the biggest election mandates in Australian history ... he was perfectly placed to implement national reforms ... But Fraser saw no imperative for reform ... The contradiction of Fraser was that this ruthless political giant-killer was a timid prime minister.[26]

For Howard, the lesson was clear: 'long years in government ... are of little avail unless the power and opportunity it brings are put to good purpose'.[27] In his fourth term, Howard wanted to avoid the perceived mistakes of the Fraser Government. He wanted to leave a distinctly different heritage for the party, the nation and possibly for himself.

Third, there was the Liberal Party's and Howard's long-term commitment to labour deregulation and industrial relations reform. While Brett reminds us that the extensive industrial relations reforms embodied in WorkChoices were 'not part of the Coalition's policy for the 2004 election', and thus the government had no mandate for WorkChoices, she misses the point.[28] These proposals went back to the 1993 Liberal election program, Fightback!, and its industrial relations counterpart, Jobsback!, that Howard had developed as industrial relations shadow minister.[29] It subsequently became, with some changes,[30] a major part of the Coalition's 1996 election platform for which they had won a substantial mandate, but which, as I have noted, were 'substantially modified'[31] by a hostile Senate with over 171 amendments 'representing a significant compromise by the government on a key policy area'.[32] Industrial relations reform was thus unfinished business for the Howard Government. They could not let the opportunity of having a Senate majority lapse. For Howard it was time to implement what he had long pioneered, promoted and supported, and to honour the very mandate on which he had first come to office, but had been thwarted all the way. Remember Howard's 1996 victory speech and the importance he placed on that mandate:

> I want to make it quite clear that although uniting the Australian people will be the cornerstone of my approach in government, we have been elected with a mandate, a very powerful mandate … We have not been elected to be just a pale imitation of the government we have replaced … We need to implement the programme on which we were elected.[33]

By early 2005 Howard announced his decision to take the initiative and to introduce major industrial relations reforms. These would have priority over Costello's tax cuts. This was not hubris. It reflected Howard's deep convictions, which Brett dismisses too easily as 'prejudices'.[34] It also signalled to the party and to supporters that the Howard Government was different to Fraser's. It was not going to abandon its principles and miss this unique opportunity to implement reforms it had long espoused. As Howard explained in a major speech early in 2005:

> We made very good progress towards a more flexible and competitive system with the passage of the *Workplace Relations Act* in 1996. But, as many of you know, important reforms in areas such as unfair dismissals and improved flexibility in agreement making have been blocked repeatedly in the Senate. But with the unexpected, but welcome and favourable election outcome in the Senate, we are now in a position to drive the industrial relations reform process further in ways consistent with our philosophy. I believe that a single set of national laws on industrial relations is an idea whose time has come. It is the next logical step towards a workplace relations system that supports greater freedom, flexibility and individual choice. Again, this is not about empowering Canberra. It is about liberating workplaces from Colac to Cooktown.[35]

Everyone within government agreed. As Howard recalled: 'the emphatic attitude of Coalition members in 2005 was that, having unexpectedly won control of the Senate ... the opportunity to further advance industrial relations reforms should not be squandered, and that the system should be made more flexible'.[36] According to insiders, this view held firm for the next three years despite the opposition that WorkChoices encountered.[37] The misgivings of some Coalition members after the 2007 election were, according to Howard, not voiced when the draft legislation was discussed at the Joint Coalition party meeting in 2005 where it received 'overwhelming backing'.[38]

What about the Senate?

The other complaint was that the Howard Government was ruthless in managing its newfound Senate majority. It 'hurried the WorkChoices legislation through parliament with little opportunity for detailed scrutiny'.[39] In addition, as one Labor senator complained, the Howard Government used 'its majority to alter the Senate rules to eliminate democratic checks and balances' which was 'a direct attack on our democratic processes and the role of the Senate'.[40] The Howard Government was 'drunk with its own power',[41] asserted another Labor senator.

These opinions, partisan as they were, and other views by parliamentary officers, reflected an exalted view of the Senate that does not match its place in the Australian system of government or historical practice. Indeed, almost from its inception, the Senate has been a prize fought over by political parties and has been heavily afflicted by partisan battles. It is where numbers and partisanship affected what legislation was passed, what committees were appointed, what topics were investigated and what questions were asked – and answered. As for being a house of review, for most of the first half of the 20th century government majorities in the Senate were the norm, with a few exceptions (1913–14, 1929–31, 1941–44), yet Australian democracy hardly seemed imperilled. Some have even argued that the Senate was originally developed to ensure such government majorities. Depending who had the numbers, the government or the opposition, the Senate oscillated between being lauded as a house of review and condemned as an outdated chamber of obstruction. Both sides expressed contradictory frustrations depending who was in office and who was out. Indeed, for a long time the Senate was seen, and used, as the reserve of party timeservers, hacks and 'meddlesome old men'.[42]

It was only with the introduction of proportional voting and the Senate's enlargement in 1948 from 36 to 60 senators that it gained some potential to exercise its review functions, because these changes made it harder for governments to win a majority, and easier for opposition parties to 'review' and thus obstruct the government. Such changes, initiated by an outgoing Labor administration, were most likely politically motivated to make it difficult for the expected incoming Menzies Coalition to gain a Senate majority.[43] If so, it worked. Menzies won office in 1949 but not a Senate majority. He subsequently called a double dissolution election in 1951 and held a Senate majority from 1951–56 and, again briefly, from 1958–61. Since then Senate majorities have become more difficult for governments to secure. It was not until 1975 that another government (that led by Fraser) secured a Senate majority. With the subsequent expansion of Senate numbers to 64 in 1975 and then again to 76 in 1984, combined with the decline in the major party vote, it was the considered view before the 2004 election that it would be 'rare for a government to control the Senate'.[44] This is why the Howard Government's success in gaining a majority in 2004 was not just a surprise, but had such a profound impact on its policy agenda. It was too rare an opportunity not to exploit.

Table 1 outlines the complaints levelled against the Howard regime in its management of the Senate, and political historian Gwynneth Singleton's assessment.

Table 1: Complaints of Howard Government's Senate Treatment[45]

Complaint	Assessment
Contested legislation-opposition amendments to legislation largely overridden and rejected.	Few amendments allowed by government.
Question Time restructured to give Labor and minor parties fewer questions and Coalition Senators more.	Fewer questions given to ALP Opposition, but the Opposition and minor parties able to ask 'double-barrelled' questions by use of supplementary questions, thus enhancing their capacity to pursue an issue in greater depth.
Questions-on-Notice – fewer answered and taking longer.	Increase in the number of questions not answered within the normal time limits – an increase from 2.9 per cent in 1993 to 15.5 per cent in Fourth Howard Government.
More use of gag and guillotine procedures to limit debate so that legislation rushed like WorkChoices and the Australian Security Intelligence legislation.	Use of gag and guillotine increased so major legislation like WorkChoices was rushed. Also, the committee inquiry was compressed; the government's 337 amendments to the Bill introduced only just before debate.
Sitting hours reduced so less scrutiny.	Fewer sitting days – 80 in 1994 (628 hours) to 58 (572 hours) in 2006 and, although number of bills fell from 351 to 340, overall less time for debate.
Fewer requested government documents produced.	Major decline from government agreeing to 53 orders in 1993–96 to 18 in 2005, 1 in 2006 and 0 in 2007.
Committee system restructured – fewer committees, fewer references, decline in response rate and delays responding to reports.	Number reduced from 16 to 8 now with all having a government chair – a return to previous Labor model. Government response rate to reports declined and timeframes reduced time for inquiries into legislation, for example, review of WorkChoices only had five days to question 105 witnesses and one day to report.
Estimates committees altered so less scrutiny.	Some days reduced, some attempt to limit topics, and public servants instructed not to answer questions on the Australian Wheat Board scandal – but there were precedents under Labor.
Dissent in the Senate from government members.	More dissent than can ever occur under ALP – Coalition dissenters rarely had impact, but National Party Senator Barnaby Joyce was successful, including blocking parts of the Trade Practices Act.

There is no doubt that the Howard Government used its newfound Senate majority to have WorkChoices and other legislation quickly passed and to control Senate procedures to minimise scrutiny, and generally to make life easier for itself. Nevertheless, Singleton concluded that this was not 'sufficient to warrant labelling the Senate a "paper tiger" … nor … render the Senate totally impotent as a mechanism for holding the government accountable'.[46] Questions continued to be asked, committees held inquiries, legislation was debated and backbench Coalition members continued to agitate occasionally, even on the floor of parliament, which would have been impossible in a Labor-controlled Senate.[47] As Singleton concluded, 'any government with a majority would have done the same. At its most basic, it is a function of having the power and using it.'[48]

What occurred under the Howard regime hardly constituted a breakdown in democratic practices. It was in keeping with the robust way parliamentary democracy, with its dominance by executive government, has long been practised in Australia.[49] After all, the Howard Government won its Senate majority democratically – unlike in some Westminster democracies where upper houses are still appointed[50] or in other jurisdictions where they have been abolished.[51] Nor should it be forgotten, as noted, just what the Howard Government had experienced with the Senate in its previous three terms. Paul Kelly explains:

> During the first three terms of Howard's government, the
> Labor Party and the Senate as an institution was highly
> effective in holding the government to account. Any
> suggestion that the government was not under intense
> pressure from the Senate is wrong. Not only were some of
> its decisive bills rejected or significantly amended, but the

Senate committee system was used to probe, to disclose and to embarrass.[52]

This is quite different to Harry Evans' assessment that the Howard Government during its first term 'had little trouble with its legislative program'.[53] It was also quite different to the 'relatively peaceful life in the Senate'[54] experienced by the Rudd Government (2007–10).

Finally, it should not be forgotten that Labor's concerns about the dangers of the Howard Government's single-seat Senate majority have a hollow ring given its long antipathy to the Senate, even including advocating for its abolition for some time,[55] as well as the actions of some state Labor administrations towards their own upper houses.[56] Labor governments, too, have expressed frustration with the Senate. As prime minister, Paul Keating attacked the Senate as 'unrepresentative swill'[57] despite his own party's representation in the chamber and claimed the 'Senate had no right to obstruct the Government in the lower house'.[58]

WorkChoices – how extreme?

Then there is the question of whether WorkChoices was as extreme and ideological as some contend, or was it just an extension of reforms and changes that had long been in train?

In summary, WorkChoices involved: creating a national workplace relations system; increased employer capacity to make individual agreements with employees; modernising the role of awards and the Australian Industrial Relations Commission (AIRC); reforming the setting of minimum wages and conditions; establishing a new Australian Fair Pay Commission to replace the AIRC; removing unfair dismissals protection for employees in businesses with fewer than 100 staff members; secret ballots before strikes; Australian Workplace Agreements no longer subject to the 'no disadvantage test' (later changed); and union rights of entry prohibited from agreements.[59]

For some individuals, WorkChoices 'tilted the balance of power in the workplace decisively towards employers',[60] reduced the protection of unfair dismissal laws, involved a 'drastic reduction in minimum conditions' and made 'almost everyone … worse off'.[61] It aroused concern even among those who were not directly affected because of its perceived adverse effects on those on lower incomes and in casual employment. Last-minute changes, reportedly imposed by Howard[62] to change unfair dismissal exemptions for firms from just 20 to 100 employees, were seen to be going too far. The 'no disadvantage' test – a key safety net of the Australian system that had been kept in the Howard Government's 1996 legislation – was repealed. Expanding the individual Australian Workplace Awards (AWAs) over collective agreements removed the compulsory insertion of unions into awards and bargaining. This was seen as Howard's most 'ideological' proposal aimed at 'weakening the privileged institutional power of the unions and the Labor Party'.[63] It was what provoked the unions to campaign so strongly and successfully against WorkChoices. For Greg Combet, Secretary of the ACTU, the package was an American-type system with employers having all the bargaining power and with many workers worse off.[64]

Others saw it differently. Combet's claims were, on any analysis, 'an exaggeration', concluded Paul Kelly.[65] Lewis suggested that, despite some aspects of the legislation reflecting the Coalition's traditional antipathy to trade unions as noted, 'the reforms were not radical or a major departure from the path of reform begun by Hawke and Keating'[66] and were required to meet Australia's changing labour market needs in an increasingly globalised economy.[67]

That WorkChoices was achieved by using the Commonwealth's corporations power, thus effectively shifting the constitutional basis for federal industrial relations law from the traditional conciliation and arbitration power to the corporations power, was not a major issue either.[68] This meant the Commonwealth could legislate directly for minimum conditions of employment and largely supplant the states in this area – criticised by some for being too centralist.[69] The legislation was validated by the High Court in 2006 and was not too different from Labor's intentions in this field.[70]

For Lewis it was not that WorkChoices was extreme or even particularly ideological that was the problem. The issue was that it was large, complex, rushed, badly drafted and poorly marketed by a government that was usually much more careful and thorough. The legislation's complexity made it hard to explain to the public. This is perhaps why the government's expensive advertising campaign failed. The potential economic benefits, a key underlying goal of the changes, were never fully promoted.

Later amendments undermined the legislation's and government's credibility. For instance, a new 'Fairness Test' introduced in May 2007 just before the election as an attempt to restore, as Howard later wrote, 'something akin to the old no-disadvantage test', looked desperate and politically motivated.[71] That some employers used the new arrangements to try to reduce workers' conditions required direct, and much-publicised interventions by the federal minister. This kept WorkChoices in the news and undermined the government's claims about its benefits. Further, the responsible minister, Kevin Andrews, was new to the field. He was not effective in promoting the program or managing the debate with the unions. He was subsequently replaced early in 2007 by the more personable Joe Hockey. The change of faces was too late. Eventually, in 2007 even the WorkChoices name was dropped because of its perceived unpopularity. As one American politician noted, 'it's not the issues than can kill you, it's the way you handle the issues' that is really important.[72]

The argument by some inside government at the time and others since was that the government should have just run with the proposals that had already been rejected by the Senate in its third term. This would have meant keeping unfair dismissal exemptions to businesses with fewer than 20 staff, maintaining the 'no disadvantage' clause, establishing a national system and avoiding a direct attack on the unions.[73]

Other factors explaining electoral loss

Although Howard admitted that the 'fear campaign on Work-Choices … hurt us deeply,'[74] he does not accept that it was the prime cause of the Coalition's election loss in 2007 nor that it should have been a more moderate package. Indeed, the importance of other factors in explaining the loss have not been given the due weight they warrant.

Foremost among these factors was the Howard Government's long incumbency of nearly 12 years. While incumbency offers many advantages, it also comes with problems. The longer government is in office, the more mistakes occur, ministerial resignations and scandals accumulate, the limits of government and budgets become more apparent, past decisions haunt current agendas, interest groups become more disgruntled, the media more critical, and the electorate becomes too accustomed and weary of a government's ploys and its personnel.

Then there was Howard's age. He was aged 65 years in 2004 – 18 years older than the new Leader of the Opposition, Kevin Rudd (elected in December 2006). It was an issue in the run-up to the election that 'just wouldn't go away'.[75] It involved not only whether Howard was still mentally and physically capable, but also whether he, and his government, had a relevant vision for Australia's future.

Underlining questions about Howard's age, capabilities and future were leadership tensions between Howard and the Treasurer, Peter Costello, that became more public at this critical juncture. Costello, long-time heir presumptive and Deputy Liberal Leader, appeared to be increasingly anxious about whether he would succeed Howard. He seemed to see himself as the solution and Howard very definitely the problem. As Costello later reflected on the government's loss in 2007, this was not because of policy failure, or even because of WorkChoices (it does not rate a mention in his memoirs).[76] Costello believed that because the 'electorate was tired of the government and of John Howard ... the way to freshen up the government, seize back the attention of the electorate is to have a new leader who can deliver a fresh message to the public'.[77] The failure of the Coalition to renew itself prior to the 2007 election, according to Costello, 'belongs squarely to John Howard'.[78]

Several incidents during this period hardly helped. They involved leaks about previous agreements made in opposition between Howard and Costello concerning future leadership changeovers; Costello's criticisms of Howard when he was Treasurer in the Fraser Government in a recently released book;[79] and reportage of Costello's 'off the record' media comments about future leadership issues. All these, noted Howard, 'produced the impression of a government unravelling ... the crumbling of a once united and impregnable government'.[80]

There were other distractions, the most significant of which was the Royal Commission into the Australian Wheat Board in relation to the food-for-oil scandal involving Iraq.[81] The issue was whether Howard or the Minister for Foreign Affairs, Alexander

Downer, were aware of the transactions. Both were witnesses before the royal commission. Although both were absolved, along with the government, from any blame, the negative headlines during the 12 months of its hearings during 2005 and 2006 raised perceptions that the Howard Government was less than honest and had been in office too long.[82] It reinforced previous concerns during its third term about the government's integrity over the MV *Tampa* controversy and the 'children overboard' affair.[83]

Perhaps Brett pinpointed the real cause of the Howard Government's downfall, although it contradicts her thesis about the primacy of WorkChoices. She concluded that the 'unravelling of John Howard began on the day in early December 2006 when Kevin Rudd was elected leader of the Opposition'.[84] Rudd became another distraction for the Howard Government as it devoted considerable efforts to attacking him and trying to find a flaw in his armour. It was to no avail. Almost from the time he became Leader of the Opposition, Rudd outpolled Howard as preferred prime minister and the Labor Party easily led in opinion polls by a wide margin regardless of what the government did.

I reject as simplistic the view that a prime cause of the Howard Government's fall from office in 2007 was because of the perceived 'extremism' of the WorkChoices reforms and its actions in relation to its newfound control of the Senate driven by Howard's hubris and arrogance following its 2004 election win. Conventional wisdom perhaps, but this view does not accord with the content of the reforms, their value and their long lineage that crossed the partisan divide, past practice concerning the Senate or Howard's character, which showed few of the usual characteristics of hubris or narcissism that have been ascribed to longstanding leaders.[85]

Because of its subject matter, WorkChoices was never likely to receive a fair and balanced assessment by the government's critics. Some critics (Brett, for example) simply found the reforms to be odious for little more reason than they were seen as part of the ideologically suspect 'neoliberal' agenda. This response was probably inevitable when most academic critics were prepared to assess the actions of Coalition governments (and Howard in particular) from a partisan perspective, in the same way that 'most interpretations of the Thatcher Government' were held to be 'partisan in character'.[86]

Suggestions that Howard lost in 2007 because he went too far with industrial relations reforms and used the Coalition's numbers too ruthlessly to push reforms through the Senate are also misguided. The Fourth Howard Government's chances of winning the 2007 poll were always very slim. Moderating industrial relations reform would not have saved it. Instead of the politics of least resistance or appeasement, Howard pursued 'grown-up' politics – seizing the opportunities that had been given him – using his numbers won democratically in the Senate to push long-sought legislation through, and delivering in full the final instalment of industrial relations reform. To do otherwise, to fudge this opportunity, would have been even more disastrous politically, economically and morally. Politically disastrous by failing to deliver 25 years of Liberal Party promises to its base, small and big business, and to the public. Economically disastrous by failing to continue with the reforms that Australia had long pioneered and still needed. Morally disastrous by failing to act in a way consistent with Howard's reputation as a prime minister committed to implementing his known convictions about what was right for the country. As Howard later remarked, failure to proceed with the whole industrial relations reform package including what was promulgated after the 2004 election would have meant that 'history would deem us policy cowards'.[87]

The real tragedy is that because the conventional view persists that Howard got it wrong, reform in this vital area has stagnated. Both sides of politics have taken the wrong lessons from the Howard industrial relations imbroglio. For the Coalition, industrial relations reform remains, as then Liberal leader, Tony Abbott, declared in 2010, 'dead, buried, cremated'.[88] It drove Labor into a Faustian pact with a declining union movement. Not only was union influence revived, it now holds Labor hostage to its power. It has also undermined Labor's credentials in economic reform. As Kelly notes, Rudd became 'the first Australian prime minister to roll back the post-1983 reforms'.[89] Subsequent Labor leaders, so much part of the union movement, have followed suit. Such reforms are now on no-one's agenda, including the current Morrison Coalition Government. Indeed, industrial relations hardly rated a mention in the May 2019 federal election.[90]

Lack of industrial relations reform partly, but not insignificantly, explains Australia's declining productivity.[91] Paul Keating in 1993 acknowledged that 'no economic reform is so central' as 'industrial relations' and it was necessary to 'accelerate the reform so that all the elements of flexibility in the economy can work in greater harmony'.[92] Keating never came anywhere close to what was needed; Labor's filial relationship with the unions hobbled him. Neither did Howard. The unions' campaign stopped him but he still advanced reform far more than anyone else. Despite Labor's attempt to turn back the clock through their *Fair Work Australia* program, it was to 'leave much of WorkChoices essentially intact'.[93]

Howard took risks to achieve greater progress in an area all agreed needed reform. He was true to his convictions that he had held since the early 1980s, while Rudd, the 'great moderniser', chose to ignore how the existing industrial relations system reduced the nation's competitiveness and productivity and threw in his lot in with the party's union backers to get elected. Howard, in the parlance of the late Austin Holmes, one-time Chief Economist of the Reserve Bank of Australia, fought the 'good fight'. It was 'the struggle to get good sense (economic rationality) into Australia's economic affairs and, more specifically, into the economic policies which influence those affairs'.[94] Howard set an example. His lead needs to be followed so that industrial relations reform can be finished, once and for all.

PART IV
PORTFOLIO MATTERS

7

INDIGENOUS AFFAIRS

TIM ROWSE

John Howard took until his fourth term to actualise his preferred approach to Indigenous affairs. As he says in his autobiography *Lazarus Rising*: 'our last year in government finally saw a paradigm change. It was as if the dam had finally burst and much of the approach which had held sway for a generation, or more was swept away.'[1] Howard is referring to taking over Indigenous affairs in the Northern Territory – known as the Northern Territory Intervention.

This package, announced on 21 June 2007 by Mal Brough, the Minister for Families, Community Services and Indigenous Affairs, included the following items: alcohol restrictions on Northern Territory Aboriginal land; controls on welfare recipients' expenditure (Basics Card); linking welfare payments to parental performance in getting their children to school; compulsory health checks for Aboriginal children; acquiring certain townships on Aboriginal land through five-year leases; increasing police presence in certain communities; new rent and tenancy arrangements for households; additional funds for housing; banning X-rated pornography in prescribed communities; ending the permit system for defined areas within Aboriginal lands; phasing out the Community Employment Development Projects (CDEP) scheme, to encourage people into 'mainstream' employment; appointing managers of all government business in certain communities. I will not revisit the debate about the Intervention. I will instead locate it in its party-political context and point to five legacies of Howard's approach to Indigenous policy.

In 1996, Howard found himself up against a policy orthodoxy that he describes in *Lazarus Rising* as 'separate development, with a heavy overlay of guilt and shame'. This orthodoxy was supported by 'the old guard of the Aboriginal leadership, the ALP' and much of the press.[2]

What does 'separate development' mean? Howard does not define it, and its imprecision leaves it open to being understood as including policy initiatives by Labor that the Howard Government continued. First, Howard did not abolish the Aboriginal and Torres Stait Islander Commission (ATSIC) until 2004, near the end of his third term, and only after the ALP announced it would abolish ATSIC. Second, the *Native Title Act* was not repealed by the Howard Government but it was amended after a strenuous struggle with the Senate in 1998. Indeed, Howard can be credited with fashioning a version of Commonwealth policy on native title only five years after the Coalition – under Dr John Hewson – had refused the very idea of a Commonwealth statute binding states and territories in their management of 'native title'. A third continuity between Keating and Howard policies was the Indigenous Land Fund, a Labor initiative complementary to the *Native Title Act*, to which every Howard budget added funds according the formula set in section 193 of the *Land Fund and Indigenous Land Corporation (ATSIC Amendment) Act 1995*.

Table 1: Amounts budgeted for Indigenous Land Fund, by year ($millions)

Year	1995–96	1996–97	1997–98	1998–99	1999–2000	2000–2001	2001–2002	2002–2003	2003–2004	2004–2005	2005–2006	2006–2007	2007–2008
$m	24.5	25.4	48.3	49.7 (23.4)	(60.0)	65.5	63.7	66.6	66.7	77.8	56.3 (actual)	40.5	21.2

SOURCE Commonwealth Indigenous-specific expenditure 1968–2008, compiled by Dr John Gardiner-Garden and Malcolm Park, *Parliamentary Library Research Paper*, 26 September 2008, no. 10, 2008–09 NB: Figures in brackets are labelled as 'accrual'.

A fourth example of continuity with what could be interpreted as 'separate development' is Howard's *Corporations (Aboriginal and Torres Strait Islander) Act 2006*, which renewed the distinct regulatory regime that had applied to Indigenous Australians' corporations since 1976. The Act sets out rules about membership, elected office-holding, meeting procedures, and record-keeping; it specifies corporate obligations about the timing and content of reports to the Office of the Registrar of Indigenous Corporations (ORIC); it is a special measure for the advancement and protection of Aboriginal peoples and Torres Strait Islanders under paragraph 4 of Article 1 of the Convention for the Elimination of Racial Discrimination and the *Racial Discrimination Act 1975*.

Conservatives such as Howard may rail against 'separate development' for Indigenous Australians, but they have pragmatically adopted territorial, legal and institutional distinctions between Indigenous and other Australians that institutionalise bipartisan policy. So is there a distinct *conservative* approach to Indigenous affairs? If there is, then being against 'separate development' does not define it.

Dealing with Indigenous Australians' demands for social justice has been a challenge for every Australian prime minister since William McMahon. In January 1972 McMahon gave insufficient thought to national symbolism when he chose Australia Day to announce a 'land rights' policy that (he was advised) was likely to disappoint Aboriginal people.[3] The National Council of Aboriginal and Torres Strait Island Women called McMahon's statement on land rights 'incompetent, uninterested and unsympathetic' and they suggested he resign.[4] A more eye-catching protest was the erection of an 'Aboriginal Tent Embassy' in front of what is now Old Parliament House. McMahon was judged to lack empathy when he visited the 'Embassy', while Whitlam – whose party was committed to legislating land rights in the Northern Territory – made his visit a public relations triumph.[5]

The lesson of these events was that a prime minister must try to align policies with whatever is the current popular concept of social justice towards Indigenous Australians. In 1972 that included conceding that some remote Indigenous Australians had a customary right to strong land title. A leader can make visible his or her alignment with emerging conceptions of just dealings if he or she can form a sympathetic public relationship with conspicuous Indigenous political actors. Such leaders have become more prominent and more numerous in public life since 1972.

Articulate and morally urgent, the Indigenous Australian demand for a fair go continues to test each prime minister or aspirant. In *Lazarus Rising*, Howard presents a vignette of his predecessor Alexander Downer's 'unnerving performance' on Indigenous policy. (Downer was Liberal Party leader from May 1994 to January 1995.) When speaking on 'native title' to a Liberal Party meeting in Western Australia and then, shortly after, to Aboriginal people in the Northern Territory, Downer had seemed inconsistent. According to Howard, his floundering 'precipitated a big fall of 17 per cent in his approval rating'.[6] Howard's anecdote suggests that he came to power knowing that he must present himself as not only consistent but also as committed to policies that passed some public test of social justice. Yet Indigenous affairs was not as important to him as economic policy, including industrial relations policy. Political scientists Paul Strangio, Paul 't Hart and James Walter write that 'His distaste for climate activists, welfare advocates and the "Aboriginal industry" hindered open-minded engagement with their claims for most of his term.'[7]

As prime minister, Paul Keating seemed to many to have succeeded in defining a policy of 'social justice', credibly establishing himself as a champion of Indigenous Australia. He won admiration for his Redfern Park speech in December 1992, telling a national story that drew on revisionist historical scholarship and that resonated with the High Court of Australia's shaming narrative in the (June 1992) *Mabo no. 2* judgment. Challenging non-Indigenous Australians to empathise with Indigenous suffering, Keating had committed the nation to repairing a damaged relationship between Indigenous and non-Indigenous Australians. After agonising negotiation with Indigenous leaders, Keating had presented the *Native Title Act 1993* and the *Land Fund and Indigenous Land Corporation (ATSIC Amendment) Act 1995* as reparative steps. No prime minister had ever had such a large opportunity to present himself as the author of a revised settler colonial compact. In a 1998 speech, Howard recalled Keating 'talking about how the native title bill was going to nourish the Labor Party for two generations'.[8] In *Lazarus Rising*, Howard is viscerally offended by the evident ideological bond – as he saw it – between the press, the Aboriginal leadership and the Keating Cabinet in the period 1992–96, and his media strategy favoured interviews with conservative radio talkback hosts.[9]

Howard scorned any assumption that Labor policies *defined* social justice for Indigenous Australia. In 1998, he dismissed what he called Labor's 'phoney claims of racism' against the Coalition's policies.[10] In *Lazarus Rising* he refers to the 'McCarthyist smear tactics' of the Keating Government.[11] He was offended by the 'vitriol' of an *Age* cartoon depicting him and Peter Reith mounted on horses and shooting Aboriginal people. He recalls the former Minister for Aboriginal and Torres Strait Islander Affairs, Robert Tickner, as epitomising 'the politically correct left of the Labor Party'.[12] In 1989, Howard had characterised the Labor Party as 'guilt-ridden'.[13] In 1995 he vowed: 'I am not going to be party to the guilt industry'.[14] In 1996, he complained of a climate of 'excessive political correctness in political debate in this country'.[15] This climate encouraged in Labor parliamentarians a belief that they 'hold some kind of monopoly of concern about the Aboriginal people of Australia'.[16] In *Lazarus Rising* he refers to 'the abjectly apologetic language so often used by the Labor Party and others'.[17] It troubled Howard that Aboriginal leaders seemed to expect a similar 'abjection' from him and his government. His refusal to apologise to the Stolen Generations signalled his distaste for this expectation. It was a position for which he was punished by the open disdain of Aboriginal leaders and many in the press. Patrick Dodson's refusal of re-appointment to the Chair of the Council for Aboriginal Reconciliation was a public rebuff. In October 1997, Noel Pearson called Liberals 'racist scum'.[18]

The problem for a prime minister wishing to position himself as a champion of Indigenous Australia was that in order to reconcile conservatives to the *Native Title Act*, Howard had to diminish Indigenous rights conferred by that Act, and he had to be seen to be doing so. On the 30th anniversary of the 1967 referendum (27 May 1997), Howard conceded that his proposed amendments to the *Native Title Act* were intended to reduce the rights of native title holders whose ancestral country was under pastoral lease. He defended this as a restoration of equality under the rule of law because 'the pendulum had swung too far' towards Indigenous rights.[19]

Presenting himself as rightly reversing Indigenous Australians' recent gains, Howard had to distance himself from One Nation, whose appeal to conservative voters included the theme of 'Aboriginal privilege'. In *Lazarus Rising*, Howard recalls this difficulty. He writes that while he and One Nation leader Pauline Hanson were in tune with 'community sentiment' when attacking 'multiculturalism, ATSIC and separatist policies for black and white Australians', they differed on whether Indigenous Australians 'were the most disadvantaged group in our midst'.[20] Howard persistently presented Aboriginal people as the deserving disadvantaged. For example, he declared his 'compassion' for Indigenous Australians in a 1995 speech.[21] In 1996 he said that Aboriginal people and Torres Strait Islanders were 'the most profoundly disadvantaged in our midst'.[22] In May 1997, he pledged to 'address the profound economic and social disadvantage continuing to be suffered by indigenous Australians'.[23]

Professing compassion gave Howard a way to align his preferred policies with 'reconciliation', which he once described as 'an unstoppable force'.[24] In 1991, the Coalition parties had voted for the bill that established the Council for Aboriginal Reconciliation; in government, Howard sought to control the meaning of that much-contested word. Howard glossed 'reconciliation' as the relief of 'disadvantage'. On 30 October 1996, he moved a motion that included that Parliament 'reaffirms its commitment to the process of reconciliation with Aboriginal and Torres Strait Islander people, in the context of redressing their profound social and economic disadvantage'.[25] In May 1997, Howard aligned his approach to 'reconciliation' with what he called 'the spirit of the 1967 referendum' which, if it 'spoke of anything … spoke of a need to remedy in a practical way the disadvantage of the Aboriginal and Torres Strait Islander people'.[26] I count 16 uses of 'practical' in ten parliamentary statements by Howard about Indigenous affairs from 1996 to 1999. In Howard's view, while there was debate on some Indigenous policy issues, there was broad agreement that, to relieve disadvantage, reconciliation must include policies that were 'practical'; this consensus meant that 'nobody has any kind of moral monopoly of concern about Indigenous people'.[27]

Showing concern about 'Indigenous disadvantage' could also be folded into Howard's carefully calibrated position on how the national story should be told. Howard's speeches in the period 1996–99 had included efforts to contain, within an overarching positive account of nationhood, the emerging scholarly view that Aboriginal people had suffered violent dispossession and harsh administration. In 1996, he employed the metaphor of the 'balance sheet': 'the balance sheet of our history is one of heroic achievement' and 'we have achieved much more as a nation of which we can be proud than of which we should be ashamed'.[28] In a speech to the Reconciliation Convention on 26 May 1997, Howard said that he felt 'deep sorrow for those of my fellow Australians who suffered injustices under the practices of past generations towards indigenous people. Equally, I am sorry for the hurt and trauma many people here today may continue to feel as a consequence of those practices.' He agreed that 'the treatment accorded to many indigenous Australians over a significant period of European settlement represents the most blemished chapter in our history. Clearly, there were injustices done and no-one should obscure or minimise them.' To 'portray Australia's history since 1788 as little more than a disgraceful record of imperialism, exploitation and racism' was, however, 'a gross distortion and deliberately neglects the overall story of great Australian achievement'.[29] This position incurred political cost. On the occasion these words were spoken, Howard had alienated his largely Indigenous audience by asserting that Parliament would not apologise for the treatment of the Stolen Generations. Televised images of this confrontation (including images of audience members turning their backs on him) 'played strongly to the view that I was at permanent loggerheads with Indigenous Australians'.[30]

For Howard to make credible his 'concern' for Indigenous Australians, he needed to form public bonds with Indigenous leaders who knew that he had cut the budgets of Aboriginal programs, diminished the property rights of native title holders, and refused a parliamentary apology to the Stolen Generations. Fortunately for Howard, developments within Indigenous political discourse in his second and third terms brought to prominence Indigenous people to whom Howard could point as being of like mind. On 3 June 1999, he noted the critique of 'welfare dependency' by Noel Pearson – 'a person who has not always been complimentary about the policies of the government I lead'.[31] On 26 August 1999, moving a motion of support for reconciliation, Howard thanked the Australian Democrats Senator Aden Ridgeway for helping him to formulate the text, mentioning Ridgeway warmly four times in his speech. He saw Ridgeway's co-operation as symptomatic of Indigenous leaders starting to meet him 'halfway'.[32] Ridgeway had first emerged as a political moderate when he was Executive Director of the New South Wales Aboriginal Land Council, credited with enforcing and modelling the council's greater professionalism.[33]

In this conjuncture the Howard Government made a gesture of conciliation by amending the *ATSIC Act* so that, from 1999, the chair of ATSIC was no longer appointed by the Minister for Aboriginal Affairs but elected by the ATSIC commissioners. The commissioners elected Geoff Clark as their chair. Clark's insistence on distinct Indigenous political rights, codified in a negotiated agreement sometimes referred to as a treaty, was sharply antithetical to Howard's insistence that reconciliation must eschew 'symbolism' and remain 'practical'. Clark's personal integrity was, however, soon widely questioned. In 2001 and 2002, Indigenous leaders such as Lowitja O'Donoghue, Patrick Dodson and Aden Ridgeway publicly distanced themselves from him and from ATSIC. As Labor's Bob McMullan conceded when voting for ATSIC's abolition in 2004, 'many Indigenous people ... feel let down by the leadership of ATSIC and, particularly, by the currently suspended ATSIC chair'.[34]

The Labor Opposition made it easier for the government by announcing on 30 March 2004 that, were it to win government, it would abolish ATSIC and replace it with an elected Aboriginal body. The government soon announced its own plan to abolish ATSIC. Ignoring a June 2004 assembly of Aboriginal leaders that called for a national representative body, in November 2004, the Howard Government appointed a National Indigenous Council, chaired by magistrate Sue Gordon. The willingness of outstanding Indigenous persons to be so selected as advisers was a political breakthrough for the government.[35]

The public disgrace of Geoff Clark in the period 2002–03 had highlighted a problem in Indigenous Australia that Indigenous Australians were increasingly open in discussing: the insecurity of Indigenous women and children in some communities. The generalised notion of 'disadvantaged' Indigenous Australians for whom a prime minister could have credible 'concern' and 'compassion' was acquiring a particular face: the battered woman, the abused child. In 2007, a report to the Northern Territory Government, *Little Children Are Sacred*, called for urgent action to end child abuse on Aboriginal communities. Seizing this exposé of Indigenous vulnerability, the Howard Government announced the Northern

Territory Emergency Response (the 'Intervention'), a package that included un-negotiated changes in Aboriginal land tenure and the management of welfare recipients' spending. Aboriginal magistrate Sue Gordon agreed to head a taskforce to oversee the Intervention, marking some Aboriginal leaders' endorsement.

In *Lazarus Rising*, Howard claims that the Northern Territory Intervention was a 'paradigm change'. At the time, he had told the Sydney Institute that his move was 'radical, comprehensive and highly interventionist'.[36] There are five lasting legacies of Howard's approach to Indigenous affairs:

Normalising native title

The most important legacy of the Howard era is widespread acceptance of native title as a negotiable Indigenous right. To be sure, those disappointed by the native title regime, from the Indigenous perspective, can attribute some of its defects to Howard's frank reversal – through the 1998 amendments to the Act – of certain advances in Indigenous rights. Critical commentary on the Act, however, also points to the original Act's framing of those rights and to the Federal Court's interpretations of the Act. The political benefit of Howard's amendments was in enabling non-Indigenous interests to feel more certain about and secure in their rights, opening their minds to negotiation with those asserting native title. The procedural innovations of 1998 are widely credited with enabling negotiation.

Normalising the supervision of the poor

The 'paradigm change' of the Northern Territory Intervention included making welfare payments conditional on the recipients fulfilling certain behavioural 'norms'. This was a big step in making more politically acceptable the state's supervision of welfare recipients' expenditure. Income Management has been accepted and normalised by the Labor Party. Responding to the Northern Territory Intervention in 2007, Shadow Minister for Indigenous Affairs, Jenny Macklin, justified Income Management for all those suffering from 'passive welfare', while arguing for additional services such as treatment for alcoholism and policies to stimulate economic development.[37] Labor also agreed that Income Management for selected Aboriginal communities could be justified as a 'special measure' under the *Racial Discrimination Act* (that is, as positively discriminatory, benefiting Aboriginal children in the selected communities). Whether Income Management was a benefit to Indigenous Australians, or a racially discriminatory curse has remained a matter of vigorous debate.

In office after 2007, Labor changed Income Management 'from a scheme targeting remote Indigenous communities to what was called a "non-discriminatory" national scheme targeting disadvantaged communities to be rolled out initially in the Northern Territory'.[38] In recent years, Income Management has been extended by non-Labor governments to locations selected on an ostensibly non-racial basis, including many remote Indigenous communities. We should not overstate the Howard Government's contribution to this shift. As political scientist Melissa Lovell has pointed out, state control over selected welfare recipients' expenditure is a development within a longer tradition of 'welfare conditionality' that includes 'an "activity test" for unemployed citizens during the late 1980s and the use of various "mutual obligation" schemes – such as Work for the Dole – in the 1990s and 2000s'.[39] 'It was the Labor Party – rather than the more conservative Liberal and National parties – that undertook to normalise' Income Management.[40]

Presuming Indigenous incapacity

A third Howard legacy is that the concept of 'disadvantage' has been politicised. The Coalition's acknowledgment of Indigenous difference placed emphasis on Indigenous peoples' socioeconomic deficits, at the expense of recognising their distinct rights and capacities. To say that Indigenous Australians were distinct not in their rights but in their needs made 'disadvantage' central to conservative rejection of 'rights-based' political discourse. Conservatives do not deny that Indigenous Australians have 'rights', such as the rights that all Australian citizens are supposed to enjoy (including property rights), but Coalition ideology has been steadfast in denying the Indigenous claim that, as Indigenous peoples, they have distinct political rights – rights to self-representation and to self-government – perhaps encoded in a negotiated treaty. There could be no better demonstration of the persistence of the conservative denial of a distinct right of Indigenous self-representation than the dismissal in 2017 by the professedly moderate Prime Minister, Malcolm Turnbull, of the proposal in the 'Uluru Statement from the Heart', that Australians be invited to amend the Constitution to enable an Indigenous Voice to Parliament:

> Our democracy is built on the foundation of all Australian citizens having equal civic rights ... a constitutionally enshrined additional representative assembly for which only Indigenous Australians could vote for or serve in is inconsistent with this fundamental principle.[41]

The conservative preference to see 'disadvantage' instead of 'rights' as the Indigenous difference relevant to public policy has elicited a critique of 'deficit discourse' – the critics' phrase for the tendency to imagine Indigenous Australians in terms of what they lack.[42] Such critics do not deny that there are measurable, aggregate socio-economic 'gaps' between Indigenous and non-Indigenous Australians. They argue, however, that deficit discourse tends to suppose *Indigenous political incapacity* to be among the many remediable deficiencies of Indigenous peoples. The effect of this supposition is that when policy solutions (for any agreed Indigenous problem) are discussed, Indigenous representations are marginalised and non-Indigenous initiative is assumed. The critique of deficit discourse demands that Indigenous people represent themselves and lead policy change.[43]

Indigenous ideological diversity

A fourth legacy of the Howard years is a more diverse and contentious Indigenous public sphere. One cannot throw a single ideological blanket over those who speak up for Indigenous Australia. Studies of the press in the Howard era have highlighted the prominence of Noel Pearson in the pages of the *Australian*. 'Pearson became an influential news source for the *Australian* during the Howard years. The newspaper also provided him with a regular Saturday column that was given prominence, often running off page 1.'[44] It is a legacy of the Hawke and Keating years that Aboriginal people were outspoken in their criticism of ATSIC from its inception (without necessarily calling for its abolition), and such criticism continued under Howard.

More distinctive to the Howard years is that the government gradually found Indigenous allies in discourse about social policy, as measured socio-economic inequality remained intractable and as Pearson's critique of 'passive welfare' resonated with many. By the time of Howard's 'paradigm change', he could be sure that there would not be a unified Indigenous response to it. To attribute to Howard or to the *Australian* the emergence of an articulate Indigenous critique of unconditional welfare and 'Indigenous rights' would risk iteration of another version of the Indigenous-incapacity theme. Conversely, there is no doubt that Howard's insistence that reconciliation be 'practical' encouraged debate about social policy and created space for Indigenous criticism of the rights-based policy ideas espoused by Labor-aligned Indigenous intellectuals.

Indigenous constitutionalism

Fifth, Indigenous constitutionalism is a direct and palpable legacy of the Howard years. The abolition of ATSIC – a joint effort by Labor and the Coalition – and the un-negotiated amendment of the *Aboriginal Land Rights Act* in 2007 reminded Indigenous Australians that their rights are weak if recognised only in legislation. As co-author in 2002–03 of thoughtful proposals for improving ATSIC, Jackie Huggins knows well what it is like to have constructive political thinking dismissed by a government too impatient to build on its experiments in Indigenous empowerment. She is not alone in tracing such vulnerability back to the 1890s, when Aboriginal people 'were excluded from the power-sharing negotiations that preceded establishment of the Australian Constitution'.[45] Even after its amendment in 1967, the 'races' power licenses the Commonwealth legislature equally to please and to disappoint Indigenous expectations.[46] Because the High Court and the Howard Government taught Indigenous Australia that the Constitution does not guarantee their rights, Australia's Constitution figures more than ever in Indigenous political thought as a charter of colonial racism. Re-writing the Constitution so that it recognises Indigenous rights has moved to the top of the Indigenous Australian agenda of reform.

8

ENERGY AND THE ENVIRONMENT

ROGER BEALE

A good way to examine energy policy from an environmental perspective in the last five years of the Howard Government (2002–07) is to look at the current situation and ask whether, if different decisions had been made, things could have been better? The major point where energy policy and the environment intersect is climate change, although the relationship between energy and air and water pollution should not be ignored.

It is a truth, universally acknowledged among energy market participants, major users, investors and analysts, that our energy and climate policies are in a mess. We have failed to develop a sustainable bipartisan commitment to an emissions reduction profile consistent with our international commitments, modest as they are. We have been unable to agree on stable mechanisms to achieve current and future emission reductions obligations required to reach carbon neutrality by 2050. Nor have we found means to motivate sustainable, least-cost emissions reductions broadly across the economy. Equally we have not been able to establish any effective linkage between grid stability, electricity market mechanisms and emissions reductions.

During the past 15 years Australia has abandoned at least five attempts to provide overarching mechanisms to address these policy concerns. There has been a failure to co-ordinate action between state and territory and national governments to avoid duplicative or competing greenhouse strategies, which is particularly worrisome in the interlinked east coast electricity grid. Ironically, in a world where there has been growing scientific confidence in the reality and anthropogenic underpinning of global warming, and the seriousness of its consequences, there is no broadly accepted public understanding of underlying climate science. Many in the community have continued to accept the views of fringe climate science sceptics.[1] Some politicians, some players in the resource sector, and some in the media, have seized on and stoked these doubts. There are echoes of the growing suspicion of 'elites', of the anti-vaccination movement, and of past efforts to dismiss the science linking tobacco smoking and lung cancer in this, at times angry, rejection of expertise.

As a consequence there is no general community consensus on the part, if any, that Australia should play in combating global warming. This means that there is also no broadly accepted strategy for sharing the costs of mitigating emissions throughout the community and between generations. It seems increasingly less likely that Australia will achieve the emissions reduction outcomes it pledged when signing the 2016 Paris Agreement – Australia agreed to reduce its emissions by 26 to 28 per cent from 2005 levels by 2030 – unless it includes the effect of over-achievement in previous periods. This would be a contentious strategy. Even with optimistic assumptions, Australia's current modest international commitment is such that we will not end this compliance period on the downward emissions trajectory necessary to play our part in limiting temperature increases to 1.5 or even 2 degrees Celsius.[2]

Furthermore, Australia's energy costs, particularly in the gas and electricity sectors, have climbed significantly for complex and inter-related reasons. Public understanding of the reasons for these increases (many unavoidable and not associated with a move toward renewable power) is limited and not assisted by what has become a strident and misleading political debate. Concerns about the reliability of power supplies, particularly during summer, have arisen as retiring and ageing generators have reduced previous capacity buffers.

While climate adaptation is less directly connected to energy policy, Australia has also not given this subject the priority it probably deserves. The global ambition to achieve a 1.5 degree Celsius limit on warming is not likely to be fulfilled. This will have considerable implications for Australia, particularly in the regions, on the coast and in the forests. The pressures it will place on drought, water and forest management policies, as well as emergency services, have already been highlighted by the 2019–20 'Summer of Fires' in Australia.

This very unsatisfactory situation is the result of a succession of bad decisions by governments and the parliament. Most of those decisions were not made by the Howard Government. But some were. Did the Howard Government miss a unique opportunity to forestall some of these subsequent mistakes? I believe so, but were there countervailing domestic and international pressures that so reduced Howard's moral and political agency that his government can be excused from any culpability?

The outlook for energy and environment in 2001

By 10 September 2001, the Howard Government would have felt pleased with its achievements in energy and climate change negotiations. Australia had made an international commitment when it signed the Kyoto Protocol on climate change to set limits on its greenhouse gas emissions. Australia had achieved all it asked for in Kyoto – a high emissions target of 108 per cent (on 1990 emission levels), flexibility mechanisms enabling it to access lower cost international abatement options, and recognition of the contribution of emissions from land clearing to its 1990 baseline. Subsequent reduction in land clearing would enable Australia to meet its target at a low economic cost.

In short, the Kyoto Protocol, and the 1990 baseline, suited Australia very well. Unsurprisingly, Australia signed the Kyoto Protocol on 24 April 1998 and commenced its domestic processes to consider ratification (which did not occur until 2007). The Howard Government had advanced the integration of the eastern states electricity markets and modernised fuel standards allowing lower-emissions vehicles. There had been a large stepwise increase in funding for greenhouse abatement and the introduction of the Mandatory Renewable Energy Target (MRET). This saw a commitment to boost Australia's renewable energy consumption by 2 percentage points (a 30 per cent increase from a low base) by 2010. Through these measures, a huge boost to programs to protect land and water quality, habitat and biodiversity under the Natural Heritage Trust, and the successful progress of Regional Forest Agreements (RFAs), the Coalition had undercut the claim of the Australian Democrats and Labor to be the only parties that could deliver environmental protection. It could argue internationally, and at home, that it was acting responsibly to recognise the January 2001 advice from the Intergovernmental Panel on Climate Change (IPCC) that:

In the light of new evidence and taking into account the remaining uncertainties, most of the observed warming over the last 50 years is likely to have been due to the increase in greenhouse gas concentrations.[3]

It had, however, three times rejected the advice of officials – which was backed in 2000 by the Minister for the Environment, Senator Robert Hill – to introduce a cap and trade system to provide a key mechanism for emissions reduction. Officials believed the government's preferred choice of purchasing emissions without an overall cap was expensive and unlikely to be very effective. This was a sign of things to come.

A disruption

On 10 September 2001, I had a brief and cryptic phone call from Washington DC. The caller was Max Moore-Wilton, then Secretary of the Department of the Prime Minister and Cabinet. Moore-Wilton told me that he thought Prime Minister Howard might have agreed with President George W Bush that Australia would not ratify the Kyoto Protocol.[4] This apparently happened at some point in a conversation that also covered global security issues, the Middle East and the possibility of a free trade agreement between the United States and Australia.

The next day, of course, brought the 11 September terrorist attacks and it is not surprising that there was no mention of climate change in the cables nor in press reporting.[5]

When the travelling party returned I was not advised, and neither was the minister, of any decision not to ratify Kyoto. No hints or suggestions were made to either the Department of Foreign Affairs and Trade (DFAT), or my own department, that we should stop the slow grind of the ratification process. There was no clear Cabinet process relating to the protocol. An election was called on

5 October 2001. Again, there was no mention in the course of the campaign of a decision not to ratify, although there was criticism of Labor's commitment to ratify by September 2002 in a media release on 18 October by Senator Nick Minchin, the Minister for Industry and Resources, while launching the $1 million program, *A Strong Future for Australia's Resources and Energy Industries.*

The Coalition Government was returned to office on 10 November. Two days later Dr David Kemp was appointed Minister for the Environment and Heritage. There was no mention of any decision not to ratify the protocol in the prime minister's charter letter to Kemp, nor was there any subsequent Cabinet process to do so. By this stage I had long since reached the conclusion that either Moore-Wilton had over-interpreted the discussion between Prime Minister Howard and President Bush, or that I had misunderstood Moore-Wilton's call.

The tenth anniversary of the *World Summit on Sustainable Development* was scheduled for Johannesburg in August 2002. Climate change was again a central focus, with the European Union (EU) and several developing nations applying pressure on the United States. On World Environment Day (5 June 2002) David Kemp and I were in Bali where Kemp was leading the Australian delegation to the Preparatory Conference (PrepCon) for the Summit. Japan and the EU had just announced their ratification of the protocol to coincide with the PrepCon. We were stunned to hear that Prime Minister Howard had used a question without notice in the House of Representatives to announce that Australia would not ratify the protocol.

This decision cast a shadow across the Howard Government's domestic energy and climate policies for the remainder of its life. It also reduced the public's faith in multilateral action in the one field where it was essential. Given that Australia had received all it sought at Kyoto and was committed to achieving its targets, irrespective of ratification, how and why did this happen?

Domestic and geopolitical issues

Through the late 1990s and into the new millennium, Australian ministers, officials and commercial interests had been negotiating closely with China to close a deal which would underpin further development of the north-west of Western Australia's shelf gas field and confirm Australia as one of the top global LNG exporters, to mirror its position in thermal and coking coal. John Howard had become personally involved in these negotiations. When Howard announced his decision not to ratify the protocol on 5 June 2002, this $25 billion deal was on the cusp of being agreed. It was finally announced on 8 August.[6] The export liquified natural gas (LNG) sector lobbied strongly against incurring any greenhouse obligations that could inhibit its commercial viability.

Similarly, the coal, aluminium and cement sectors, and existing coal-fired power generators, lobbied powerfully against ratifying the protocol through the Australian Industry Greenhouse Network (AIGN) and the Mining Industry Council. They argued that any endorsement of the protocol could place them at a long-term disadvantage in competition with regional competitors without greenhouse obligations. Many companies in the finance, insurance and services sector, on the other hand, supported ratification. There were considerable tensions at the most senior levels within the Business Council of Australia (BCA). The resources sector won the debate with Howard but not within the BCA; it acknowledged it could not reach a position either firmly in favour of or against ratification.

The environment (including climate) was not a major issue in the 2001 election. The focus was instead on irregular boat arrivals and border control. The Coalition was strengthened in its view that it had established its environmental credentials and did not need to enhance them further. Clearly, George Bush's electoral victory in December 2000 had changed the international scene enormously. Here was a president of the United States who supported free trade and who, in spite of a campaign pledge to seek carbon caps for the energy sector under his Clean Skies program, had abandoned that pledge within months and started the process of withdrawing the United States from the protocol.[7] There was now no risk of American trade intervention to exert pressure on Australia on climate change and it was unlikely that the EU would act alone.

The Republican Party victory came hot on the heels of Australia's leadership of the INTERFET taskforce in East Timor. While the tensions over East Timor, and the palpable risks of a clash with Indonesian armed forces, seemed to have little to do with climate change, the deployment had underlined serious gaps in Australia's military capabilities and the importance of American diplomatic, logistical and deterrent support. Howard had always been a firm supporter of Australia's alliance with the United States. After East Timor, the 11 September terror attacks and Australia's involvement in the October 2001 invasion of Afghanistan, the importance of synchronicity with the United States to underline the alliance became even more pronounced. This synchronicity echoed through all spheres of Australia's international engagement.

The withdrawal of the United States from the protocol, and the failure, over close to four years of tortuous negotiations, to secure an agreed path forward for China and the leading developing nations to take on emissions reductions obligations, meant that the protocol was only capturing a minority of total global emissions. This combination of factors – a huge slate of carbon-intensive resource investments that would stimulate economic growth, aggressive lobbying by segments of industry, the heightened importance of the United States alliance, the belief that the environment was no longer a key negative for the Coalition, and the flaws within the protocol – can explain what was an important symbolic 'Captain's Call' by Howard not to ratify.

After the 'Captain's Call': 2002–2004

David Kemp responded quickly to the prime minister's decision not to ratify Kyoto. He pointed out that it was important for Australia to maintain its international credibility. The most effective way of doing so was to acknowledge the fairness of our Kyoto target and, accordingly, to commit to meeting the target while revitalising our domestic strategy. Following brief negotiations just one week after the announcement of the LNG deal with China, Kemp and the Minister for Foreign Affairs Alexander Downer issued a joint press release approved by the prime minister, setting out the path forward domestically and internationally on climate change.[8] The key elements of the forward strategy were:

- Australia will strive for an effective global response to climate change.
- Australia will position itself to maintain a strong and internationally competitive economy with a lower emissions signature.
- Domestic policy settings will balance flexibility and certainty, and emphasise cost-effectiveness.
- Australia will anticipate adaptation needs.[9]

Two elements of this statement were new. The emphasis on adaptation was fresh and, more particularly, there was openness to explore options on domestic policy other than simply reinforcing 'renewable power and plantations'. The emphasis on increasing flexibility and reducing investment uncertainty at least cost was code for emissions trading.[10] The statement also recognised the fundamental importance to our economy of the trade-exposed resource- and energy-intensive sectors. There followed an intense period of consultations with industry and environmental groups. Again, the Business Council was far from unified.

In July 2003, five ministers brought a submission to Cabinet recommending the phased introduction of an emissions trading scheme excluding the agricultural and transport sectors. It was supported by extensive modelling done by the Treasury and the Australian Bureau of Agricultural and Resource Economics (ABARE) under the instructions of the departmental secretaries' committee on greenhouse policy. The modelling showed that the costs of the proposed scheme were modest.[11] Guy Pearse, a former speechwriter to Robert Hill, the former Minister for the Environment (1996–2001) and Defence (2001–06), claims in his book on Howard's environmental policies *High and Dry* that the proposal was submitted by Peter Costello (and his Treasury Assistant, Joe Hockey), David Kemp (Environment), Ian Macfarlane (Industry), Warren Truss (Agriculture) and Brendan Nelson (Science).[12]

While industry groups had not been shown the Cabinet submission (which would have been a serious breach of Cabinet confidentiality) they had clear knowledge of its contents. There was a concerted lobbying effort and, Pearse reports, after consultation with selected industry groups and ABARE, Howard returned to Cabinet with revised modelling by ABARE on scope and parameters that were different from those previously agreed by the Secretaries.[13] The submission was then formally rejected. Focus then shifted to preparation of the long-promised energy white paper.[14]

Howard released *Securing Australia's Energy Future* on 15 June 2004. It marked a shift in emphasis from any consideration of emissions trading toward technology development.[15] The most significant announcement was establishing a fund 'to generate at least $1.5 billion in investment to demonstrate low emission technologies to reduce greenhouse gas emissions from our energy sector'.[16] Most of that expenditure was directed at the fossil fuel sector, primarily carbon capture and storage for coal- or gas-fired generation, but with a considerable sum also to assist with commercialising promising renewable technologies.

The expectations of early yields from carbon capture and sequestration (CCS) were partly based on wildly optimistic advice. I was present at a meeting with the prime minister where he was advised by industry sources and associated scientists that the cost per ton of carbon dioxide (CO_2) abated by CCS could be as low as $10 per ton. A number of officials, me included, argued that this was hugely optimistic. Our intervention was not welcomed. In fact, the cost has turned out to be $100–$150 per ton, although there are hopes the cost can be reduced. It is an important medium-term option but it is proving much harder to reduce the costs than some in industry thought. Nevertheless, the emphasis of the white paper on reducing the emissions footprint of our major exports made sense.[17]

The Mandatory Renewable Energy Target (MRET) of 2 per cent was confirmed and the scheme was extended to 2020. In effect, as it was likely that the 2 per cent target would be reached by 2006–07, meaning in the absence of emissions trading, no new investment in renewable capacity was likely after that date. The developing industry would simply fall off a cliff. This was in spite of a government-commissioned review lead by former Country Liberal Party Senator, Grant Tambling, recommending an increase in the target to 20 per cent by 2020.[18]

The White Paper recognised three factors that would loom larger in the future: first, the likelihood of future energy price increases as new generation, transmission and distribution capacity replaced old, fully amortised assets, and demand increased; second, the need for a stable and predictable policy framework to support energy asset investment; and, third, intermittent renewable sources such as solar and wind would place pressures on grid stability unless effective storage mechanisms were developed.

The first point has been forgotten, or rather pushed aside, in the political argy-bargy over climate policies and electricity cost increases. In pushing for an emissions trading system with a capacity to develop a futures market, it was exactly that stable and predictable policy framework that officials were hoping (fruitlessly) to create at what would have been a low initial price. Finally, while the White Paper commendably gave the development of the national energy market a boost and recognised the risks of intermittent power, it failed to anticipate that there would be a future need to integrate mandated intermittent sources, with very low marginal dispatch costs, into the very centre of the market's pricing mechanisms.[19] But then, so did we all.

Howard went to the 2004 October election feeling very confident that energy and climate were not election issues. His government was spending more on climate mitigation and adaptation than could have been imagined a decade earlier; he had established an effective defence to the decision not to ratify Kyoto; Australia was in striking distance of achieving its Kyoto target courtesy of a reduction in land clearing, which had happened without any significant action by the Commonwealth; energy prices continued to be low and Australia was beginning to ride a huge energy resources boom. In brief, there was nothing to worry about here.

The election was fought and won on other issues. Security had moved to the fore and the only time the environment appeared in the election was when Mark Latham made a pledge to unwind the Tasmanian Regional Forest Agreement (RFA), with disastrous consequences for his own party.[20]

Hubris followed by panic?: 2004–2007

The Howard Government won the 2004 election, securing a majority in the House of Representatives and, unexpectedly, in the Senate as well. The Coalition felt it had a mandate for radical change – in this instance, not in the energy and climate sphere, but in the labour market. That would lead to future electoral problems which are only of concern to this story, to the extent that they later led to anxiety to clear other issues off the plate – climate and energy included. In the energy and climate sectors, all seemed well. Australia would likely meet its Kyoto targets, there appeared to have been no electoral backlash against non-ratification, and Australia's international focus on building the Asia-Pacific Partnership on practical greenhouse projects was well in place.

Emerging from the background was drought. 1996 and 1997 were low rainfall years throughout eastern Australia. 1998 was Australia's hottest year on record, but nothing appeared to be unusual given the variability of its weather.[21] Then the winter rains continued to fail into the new century, 2001 and 2003 being among the driest years on record. The drought continued and was widespread from south-east Queensland through the entire Murray–Darling Basin to Adelaide. As 2005 began, there was still lower than normal rainfall and the first signs of the possibility of water shortages in all the eastern capitals emerged.

Climate scientists were properly cautious in linking the drought with climate change, but noted that it was not inconsistent with many climate models suggesting a progressive drying of south-east Australia as had already happened in the south west. Others were less cautious. In 2005, scientist Professor Tim Flannery published *The Weather Makers*, which won the New South Wales Premier's Prize and became a minor bestseller.[22] Al Gore, the former vice-president of the United States, was campaigning actively on climate change and participating in the production of a 'documentary' film about the risks of climate change – *An Inconvenient Truth* – released early in 2006 and attracting large audiences. Suddenly climate change had moved from the pre-problem stage of the public issue attention cycle, where mostly only the experts and vested interests were concerned, to the second stage, characterised by Anthony Downs in his classic study as 'alarmed discovery and euphoric enthusiasm' by the general public.[23] By 2006, the Lowy Institute for International Policy reported that 68 per cent of their polled population supported the proposition that 'global warming is a serious and pressing problem. We should start taking steps now even if this involves significant costs.'[24] Only 7 per cent of those polled said that 'until we are sure global warming is really a problem, we should not take any steps that would have economic costs'.

This is the stage in the public issue attention cycle where governments can act with broad support, enacting policies and structures, or risk being punished for failing to respond to suddenly heightened concerns. The 'policy wonk' shorthand for this is 'never waste a crisis'. Failing to act can lead to lost opportunities. This phase of the cycle lasted until 2008, with 60 per cent still anxious to act and prepared to accept economic loss.

In the third stage of Downs' issue cycle, the public realises that solving any great problem usually involves significant costs for some, or many, in the community. Corporations, unions and regions whose interests are particularly threatened entrench their opposition. The willingness to allow a mandate for action diminishes. In the fourth stage, some of those who strongly supported action become discouraged. Others find it uncomfortable to think about the issue and either refuse to do so or reduce their cognitive dissonance by rejecting the underlying science and data or embracing conspiracy theories. Action becomes harder still.

In the final stage the issue becomes accepted as the new normal, with awareness of it quickly spilling on to the front pages of newspapers once more if there are precipitating events. While Downs was writing in the early 1970s in the context of the first blossoming of interest in the environment and a renewed push for civil rights in the United States, his analytical structure remains persuasive today.

From 2005, the failure to ratify the Kyoto Protocol became a symbolic issue, and an increasingly significant proportion of the public began to see the government's domestic climate responses as weak. The Commonwealth was no longer seen as leading on the issue and was unwilling to exert its potential constitutional power (ratifying the protocol would have strengthened its scope for 'covering the field' in emissions reduction strategies). The Australian states initiated a process to develop a state-operated national emissions trading scheme (NETS) and progressively set in place a series of overlapping renewable subsidy and feed-in programs outside any national co-ordination or integration with grid management and market rules.[25]

The Commonwealth response to increasing community anxiety was to form a House of Representatives Standing Committee on Industry and Resources in March 2005 chaired by the former Minister for Small Business and Consumer Affairs Geoff Prosser. Its charter was to inquire into, and report on, the development of the non-fossil fuel energy industry in Australia. One of the reasons for Australia's relatively massive per capita carbon emissions was that, unlike virtually every other major economy, it had no nuclear power in its energy mix. The Prosser Committee stated that it had no 'in principle objection to the use of nuclear power in Australia', noting that there 'would be clear greenhouse gas emission and other technological and potential economic benefits from doing so'. Recognising that nuclear power would not be cost-competitive in Australia, the committee believed that nuclear energy should be able to access the government incentives available to other low-emission technologies.[26]

The next stage of the evolving Howard energy policy was motivated by other concerns. There was considerable international anxiety about nuclear arms proliferation, particularly in the Middle East, but a recognition of the legitimacy of ambitions to develop nuclear power for peaceful energy purposes. The United States developed a proposal for it and partner nations to lease processed uranium to these nations and then retake these fuel rods and reprocess and store the waste. It also announced a major drive on fourth-generation nuclear power plants designed to address cost and safety concerns. This was raised by the United States Energy Secretary, Samuel Bodman, in a meeting with Prime Minister Howard on 15 May 2006. In a subsequent press briefing, Howard was careful not to rule Australia in. He did, however, leave open the possibility that Australia should be able to examine processing, nuclear energy and storage in the future should it advance the national interest.[27] Moving quickly, less than three weeks later Howard announced that a prime ministerial task force would review uranium mining, processing and nuclear energy in Australia. It would be led by former Telstra chief executive and nuclear physicist, Ziggy Switkowski.

The report[28] concluded that Australia was:

well positioned to increase production and export of uranium
oxide to meet market demand. It also saw an opportunity
for Australia to be a participant in the wider nuclear fuel
cycle given international confidence in the quality of
our production processes, our sophisticated technology
community … and the strength of our commitment to non-
proliferation.[29]

The report also saw nuclear power as a practical option for Australia's long-term low-greenhouse power mix, but noted the very long lead time of 15 years for its development. The prime minister responded to the report in these terms:

In light of the significance of global climate change and as
the world's largest holder of uranium reserves, Australia
has a clear responsibility to develop its uranium resources
in a sustainable way – irrespective of whether or not we end
up using nuclear power … I am announcing today a new
strategy for the future development of uranium mining and
nuclear power in Australia … [involving] … a number of
actions that can be taken immediately.

With the election due in November 2007 it was far too late to develop a communications strategy informing Australians of what needed to be done and why. For any pursuit of nuclear power to succeed it would have had to be based on a full-throated endorsement emphasising the importance of the medium-term climate challenge facing Australia – and that had been missing for some time.

While the Prosser and Switkowski reports were being formulated, the so-called 'Millenium Drought' was deepening. Australia's capital cities were considering de-salination plants. Anxiety was rising in the government about how to handle the politics of climate.[30] As WorkChoices was proving controversial for the government and unpopular with the public, it was important to take climate off the table as another issue on which the government was lagging Labor in the public's mind. The government called its public service advisers together. In his book *Triumph and Demise*, political journalist Paul Kelly describes the moment Howard realised he would need to consider emissions trading:

[The Secretary of the Department of Prime Minister and Cabinet, Peter] Shergold reached the bullet point advocating an ETS [Emissions Trading Scheme], Howard asked: 'What's that doing there?' It was the decisive moment; the next exchange was a classic in the advisory art. [Secretary to the Treasury, Ken] Henry said: 'Prime Minister, I'm taking as my starting point that during your prime ministership you will want to commit us to a cap on national emissions. If my view on that is wrong, there is really nothing more I can say'. It was a threshold moment. 'Yes, that's right', Howard said cautiously. Henry continued: 'If you want a cap on emissions then it stands to reason that you want the most cost-effective way of doing that. That brings us to emissions trading, unless you want a tax on carbon'.[31]

This discussion led to the establishment on 10 December 2006 of a joint government business prime ministerial task group on emissions trading. It was to report by 31 May on a workable global emissions trading system and the steps Australia might now take to prepare for it.[32] The task group, which brought together industry heads and senior officials under the chairmanship of Peter Shergold, produced a number of recommendations. They embodied a thoughtful reiteration of previous studies and extended advice the government had now received from officials for a decade:

> scaling up the extensive suite of existing, predominantly non-market, interventions to a level that would support long-term, sustained deep cuts in emissions is unlikely to be viable from either an economic or environmental perspective and would be unlikely to resolve investment uncertainty.

> There are two distinct policy questions here for the Government: whether to announce a cap on post-2012 domestic emissions ahead of a more comprehensive post-Kyoto global agreement; and if so whether to implement a domestic emissions trading scheme in order to achieve that cap.

> On balance, the Task Group believes that it is appropriate for the Australian Government to set an explicit constraint on Australian emissions beyond 2012. The Task Group considers that an emissions trading scheme is necessary to achieve such a cap at least cost.[33]

This was the proposal that Prime Minister Howard took to the November 2007 election. By October that year, drought and climate change had so marked the public psyche that the Australian Broadcasting Corporation (ABC) television mini-series, *Rain Shadow* (with its haunting theme music), became an instant hit with its viewers.

Howard had acted too late to reverse public cynicism about government energy and climate policy. Inactivity on both issues contributed to the loss of his own seat of Bennelong and the federal election.

The Howard premiership is noted for its huge achievements in energy policy. It laid the foundation for the resources boom through cultivating strategic links with China. Australia moved to be the world's second biggest exporter of LNG (with some benefits to global climate) and coal (which, by increasing supply and somewhat decreasing price, possibly had the opposite effect). It modernised Australia's fuel standards, enabling the upgrade of Australia's vehicle fleet. It rationalised the excise treatment of most fuels. It further progressed integrating Australia's electricity market and established the key regulatory agencies for electricity and the transmission of gas. It won a deal at the Kyoto Conference that achieved all the government had hoped for. Australia was well on the path to meeting its Kyoto targets, albeit principally through a reduction in land clearing.[34] But in politics and in policy timing is everything.

When the window of opportunity opened to establish an overall emissions cap and trade system, and the possibility arose to build lasting institutional links between climate policy and the energy market, Howard failed to act early enough. Similarly, his decision not to ratify the Kyoto Protocol became symbolic of his government's failures to act resolutely. Had he ratified the protocol and claimed maximum constitutional reach, it is very likely that the overlapping, ill-conceived renewable schemes developed by the states might have been avoided. Such action could have helped a smoother and more integrated transition to renewable power. His government bravely raised nuclear power but soon realised it was electoral poison. It was not forthright in its support of the mainstream climate science. These policy failures, and other factors, cost it dearly in the November 2007 election. But they cost the country more.

As prime minister, Kevin Rudd also failed to sense that the window of opportunity for a community consensus on climate was beginning to close. Instead of quickly endorsing the Coalition's emission trading scheme (ETS) policy and an emissions cap, Rudd instituted a time-wasting inquiry and used the issue to stoke divisions among his Coalition opponents. By their intransigence in blocking the legislation, the Greens made the perfect outcome the enemy of a good result. The Global Financial Crisis, which began in mid-2007 and ended in early 2009, then swamped all other considerations. By then, public support for early action, even at some cost, had slumped to below 50 per cent and, by 2011, it was level pegging with the view that any steps to deal with climate should be gradual and low-cost.[35] A disaster for rational climate and energy policy ensued and continues to this day.

9

INTERNATIONAL AFFAIRS

This chapter is an edited interview the editor conducted with Alexander Downer in November 2019. Downer served as the Minister for Foreign Affairs from 1996 to 2007.

Tom Frame: Was there a Coalition approach to foreign affairs that you pursued after March 1996?

Alexander Downer: I became the minister after being a career diplomat. For the previous year I had been the shadow minister for foreign affairs. Through my life I had had plenty of time to think about our approach. It can best be summarised this way: as a government we were focused very much on the national interest. We saw foreign policy, including trade policy, as a tool of promoting the national interest. I would contrast our approach with the Labor Party thinking, which was much more ideological. Gareth Evans remains more multilateralist, using expressions like 'good citizenship', as a foundation objective of foreign policy. I don't want Australia to be a bad citizen but I do want to promote the national interest. The whole concept of foreign policy being about the promotion of our national interest – defined as our security interests, our economic interests and the protection and promotion of our values – was at the heart of our foreign policy from when we were in opposition (and I was the Leader of the Opposition, 1995–95) to when we came into government. We knew what our core objectives were going to be in the foreign policy sphere and we knew what events we would confront. Most importantly, we knew how to get there.

TF: Was departmental reform needed after two long-serving Labor foreign ministers in Bill Hayden and Gareth Evans?

AD: After 13 years of a particular foreign policy paradigm, the department inevitably took some persuading to embrace change. Prime Minister and Cabinet (PM&C), Treasury, and the Department of Foreign Affairs and Trade (DFAT) are the most professional government departments in Australia. There are a lot of very clever and very able people in DFAT. They serve as distinguished public servants and they effectively carry out the policy of the government. They naturally provide some advice.

In government, the Labor Party had talked very much about engagement with Asia and emphasised that Australia's destiny was in the Asia-Pacific region. I used to wonder why they talked in these terms so much because those things seemed obvious. You only had to look at where Australia was on the map of the world to know that we are a significant, although not a great, power. Australia first had to secure its economic and security destiny in its own broadly defined neighborhood. Before 1996, DFAT and the Labor Government were fawning in their approach to Asia, almost begging to be accepted as part of the region. Whereas my view was this: we *are* part of the region and we had something to contribute. This is true of all human relationships; people are not going to take much notice if you do not have much to offer. Going to the Indonesians or the Thais or the Chinese and begging them to take Australia seriously, and then turning up and describing our geography to them, this seemed weak to me. It was far better to demonstrate Australia's worth to our neighbors through things like the strength of our economy, the proficiency of the Australian Defence Force, and the soft power that Australia can deploy. These things are substantial when combined. After 1996 our neighbours came to understand and to appreciate what Australia could and did bring to the Indo-Pacific region. They grew to respect us more. Not only was my approach right from the beginning, it was an approach that worked incredibly well in the Coalition's pursuit of the national interest.

TF: Did the Howard Government begin with a 100-day plan for foreign affairs?

AD: It was never our intention to address the National Press Club and explain what we had achieved in the first three months of Coalition rule. Foreign policy is more serious and has greater substance than that. We had a foreign policy that we released before the 1996 election. As the minister, I certainly had a clear sense of how Australian foreign policy should work. We would use events to implement that foreign policy.

There were two important conflicts we needed to address. The *first* was Bougainville. Four times as many people were killed in the Bougainville civil war than died in the Northern Ireland 'troubles' from 1969 until the Good Friday Agreement was signed in 1998. This was a very bloody and difficult civil war, draining the resources of Papua New Guinea (PNG) and humiliating the PNG Defence Force. Australia shares a border with Bougainville, and an Australian mining company operated the Bougainville mine around which the conflict revolved. Gareth Evans and the department (DFAT) had tried as best they could to resolve the issues in dispute but they had not succeeded. In my view, we had to deal with this continuing problem. A lot of people in DFAT thought the conflict was intractable and Australia's involvement would produce serious unintended consequences. But we did achieve a satisfactory resolution. I realised quickly that we needed to work with New Zealand. Some of the Bougainville Revolutionary Army's leaders thought they were not only fighting Papua New Guinea; they were fighting Australia as well. We were their enemy too. I had to placate them. The New Zealanders played a really important intermediary role. Working with New Zealand, we ended the Bougainville civil war and brought peace.

The *second* conflict was East Timor. In and of itself, East Timor was not such a big issue but managing our relationship with Indonesia was. The foreign policy establishment held the view espoused by the former Prime Minister, Paul Keating, that Indonesia was the main game and we ought not be worried about East Timor. The department tried unsuccessfully to persuade me to adopt this view and it never really agreed with the contrary views that I held. I understand how important Indonesia is to Australia and its interests. This relationship was, however, always going to be hostage to problems in East Timor while they continued. So how do we address the East Timor problem? The department's resolute view was it must remain part of Indonesia. We must support the Indonesians in maintaining East Timor as part of Indonesia while giving them lectures on human rights every so often when complaints about the conduct of its officials and military attracted media attention. When I discussed these matters with their Foreign Minister, Ali Alatas, or with President Suharto, they told me Indonesia wanted to give East Timor wide-ranging autonomy. I did not think this approach would work. In reply, I told them I would confer with the East Timorese on whether they thought autonomy was acceptable. The East Timorese leadership said they did not think so; they wanted an act of self-determination. After the 1998 election, the so-called 'Howard Letter', originally drafted by the Departmental Secretary, Ashton Calvert, was sent to the newly installed President BJ Habibie.

These were two conflicts that demanded our attention. There was a view in the department that each involved problems that could not be resolved. The solutions were not easy but they were effective.

One other point needs to be remembered. The Howard Government did something very important in 1998 which is completely forgotten. In that year the Asian economic crisis spread across the region and our neighbors 'hit the wall'. Indonesia lost 14 per cent of its GDP in one year. The crisis involved some huge problems. The effort that we made, and Treasurer Peter Costello deserves to be singled out for praise, in helping Indonesia, Thailand and South Korea with our support for the IMF's financial packages of a billion dollars each had significant and lasting implications. It was a clear demonstration that Australia is a huge country with a small population but it is a stable and successful nation that enjoys peace and prosperity. While the so-called 'Asian tigers' hit the wall economically, Australia did not. Australia was strong. Our economy remained strong. We did not go into a recession. Further, we had resources that could be deployed to help those countries. The 1998 crisis had a cathartic effect on how those countries viewed Australia. We did not have a prime minister and a foreign minister claiming Australia was part of Asia and pleading for acceptance at regional summit meetings. To have done that would have made Australia look weak. In turning up with a billion dollars to help Indonesia at a time of crisis, Australia demonstrated strength and commitment to the relationship in a manner that our regional neighbours had never seen.

TF: How did the Asian economic crisis in 1998 influence Australia's role in East Timor in 1999?

AD: Put simply: Australia's voice now mattered. It mattered to President Habibie; it mattered to Ali Alatas, then the foreign minister;

and it mattered to General Wiranto, then Indonesian military chief. What Australia thought mattered to these people because we were a significant country with influence. Australia brought strength to negotiating tables through its economic capacity and through its alliance relationships. There is no country in the Asia-Pacific region which has closer relations with the most powerful country in the world, the United States, than Australia. The fact that we could call on the Americans based on a close and continuing alliance relationship made a huge difference to the way the region perceived Australia. We cannot dismiss the abiding importance of the American relationship, although some on the political left argued we should focus more closely on our relations with Asia and less on our ties with America. But it was our relationship with the Americans that gave us added muscle in Asia, and which gave us value to Asians and made us more acceptable to their governments. Through the strength of our economy, through the alliance relationship with the United States, through our creative application of soft power and through our diplomatic networks around the world, Australia was a country whose opinions were regarded with respect. When the 'Howard Letter' was finally read by President Habibie and read out at a meeting of his Cabinet, the Indonesian Government realised that Australia had changed its policy towards East Timor and that, as a consequence, Indonesia was going to change its policy as well. Not a single foreign policy commentator has noticed this extraordinary exercise of Australian power. Nor have I noticed anyone in East Timor saying: 'Thank you, Mr Howard' for sending that crucial, policy-changing letter to President Habibie and, in so doing, creating a pathway to our independence as a country.

TF: Were you surprised by the extent of Australia's influence?

AD: I was surprised we were so influential and equally surprised by President Habibie's reaction. We had suggested they implement wide-ranging autonomy for a number of years and thereafter have a referendum to see whether the East Timorese were content with the arrangement continuing. But Habibie had another view. He said: 'We are going to consult them straight away and then we will decide what to do'. We then spent some weeks persuading them that they should have a referendum under United Nations supervision, which they agreed to. We persuaded the UN to do some good and useful work.

The United Nations actually did a superb job in East Timor led by the Secretary-General, Kofi Annan, who was, in my judgment, the last significant secretary-general. We built a good relationship with him throughout this period. It was yet another demonstration of Australian capability. The violence in East Timor associated with the referendum was appalling. We were very usefully told by the Australian political left that we should invade East Timor and end the violence. I suppose they then would have said: we did not conduct the diplomacy right, we just went to war with them. I was not willing to countenance war with Indonesia. Not then, not ever. That is an exceptionally poor idea.

With some difficulty, we eventually persuaded President Habibie to increase domestic security across East Timor and, finally, with the help of President Bill Clinton and the United Nations, he was willing to authorise what became known as INTERFET. This was a further demonstration of Australian strength. We were able to exercise significant influence over the American president, who was initially very reluctant to act. After we 'roughed up' the Americans, including in the media, we managed to get Washington to provide tangible support. We also managed to get the entire Security

Council, including the Russians and then the Chinese, to support the resolution establishing INTERFET. In these efforts we started off modestly with New Zealand before drawing in Britain, Singapore and Thailand. Eventually we got Jordanians. It was a remarkable outcome achieved quickly and efficiently. This was a crucial exercise of Australian power which again gave us still more prestige in the region. We brought peace to East Timor and we left it in peace. We provided billions of dollars of support for Asia during the Asian economic crisis. We helped Indonesia through its transition to democracy. We helped President Habibie deliver independence to East Timor. Australia really counted as a player in the Asia-Pacific region. We really mattered. We had become an important country.

TF: What were the differences you noted following the election of the Bush administration? What was the main contrast between the Clinton years and then the Bush years, and your experience as the foreign minister?

AD: Our personal relationships were in the main warmer with President Bush and his colleagues. That is not to diminish the relationships we built up with the Clinton administration. I remain in contact with Madeleine Albright and many others from that period. We were very friendly with Condoleezza Rice, Colin Powell and Stephen Hadley and enjoyed a great personal bond with them. As an aside: if only Condoleezza Rice had wanted to be the president of the United States; she would have been fantastic.

TF: Was having the trade minister from another party ever an issue?
AD: Tim Fischer and Mark Vaile were very easy to work with as the ministers for trade. The arrangements were, in one sense, quite odd.

As leaders of the National Party, Tim Fischer and Mark Vaile were also the deputy prime ministers. In the national hierarchy they were more senior than I was. But within the portfolio hierarchy, I was the portfolio minister and therefore senior. I had overall responsibility for things like the departmental budgets. It all worked fine and it was never a problem.

TF: Did the constant change in defence minister create difficulties for you with continuity of policy or practice?

AD: No. That there were five defence ministers in 11 years meant that I was able to exercise more influence than I would otherwise because new defence ministers had a lot to learn. It was a complex portfolio involving complicated public administration questions. By 2001, I had been the foreign minister for quite some time. I knew people in Defence and I had worked with them. We had had adventures together in places like Bougainville, East Timor, Afghanistan and Iraq. This helped to create a harmonious relationship between the two departments.

TF: Did you ever contemplate changing portfolio?

AD: Any portfolio, other than the Treasury, would have been a demotion. It was in my head that should Peter Costello either resign in a moment of pique or become prime minister, I would be the best person to take his place. I had an economics degree and was the shadow treasurer at one stage. I have an interest in economic issues. Becoming the defence minister, for instance, after being the foreign affairs minister, would have been a step backwards. To become social security minister or the health minister – I did not have any interest in those domestic portfolios.

TF: Was the prime minister as closely involved in your portfolio as he appeared to be in Defence?

AD: He was not too involved in my department, leaving foreign policy to me. When it came to an important matter, like the 'Howard Letter' on East Timor, he focused his mind substantially on the details and any 'whole-of-government' implications. We also had a National Security Committee of Cabinet where major issues were canvassed. The broader strategy was usually devised by me.

Of course, a prime minister must spend a lot of his or her time on internal party management. It is a very important issue because you have to be good at that in that area to remain the prime minister. John Howard had a great affection for the Australian Defence Force (ADF). When we were putting together INTERFET we had a National Security Committee of Cabinet meeting to discuss force structure. We were taking the advice of the Chief of the Defence Force (CDF), Admiral Chris Barrie, and the Chief of Army, Lieutenant General Frank Hickling. I recall being advised that sending 5000 troops would stretch our military capacity to the limit. We also learnt that Australia did not have the heavy lift capability needed to transport troops. We simply did not have the modern equipment required for operations in our region. John Howard and I looked at each other in astonishment. From that moment, John Howard was determined to modernise and re-equip the ADF. The government increased sailor, soldier and airman numbers; we spent a huge amount of money buying C-17s; built ships; bought tanks, new generations of tanks; we did amazing things. Prime ministers are fond of taking credit for everything that happens during the life of their government. I would say that this great build-up of the ADF was driven by John Howard.

TF: Did those you faced as shadow spokesmen for foreign affairs – Laurie Brereton, Kevin Rudd and Robert McClelland – oblige you to think or act differently?

AD: Laurie Brereton and Robert McClelland were worthy opponents. I only focused on them when parliament was sitting. They did what you would expect them to do. They attacked the government and asserted that everything the government did was wrong. We did not expect them to endorse anything the Coalition said or did. My staff and I would come up with lines to attack them and their party. Beyond parliament, they were largely ignored. Kevin Rudd was different in that he was completely unprincipled. There was no principle that would stand in the way of Kevin's ambition.

TF: Was the Coalition destined to lose the 2007 election?

AD: Polling showed that the public thought well of the government's security, economic and trade policies. We were not in any way in trouble when it came to almost any policy. Our 2007 Budget was perhaps the most popular budget in Australian history. Domestically and internationally, Australia was going very well. We introduced popular initiatives to deal with Indigenous challenges (the Northern Territory Intervention); we had the $10 billion Murray–Darling initiative at the beginning of 2007, which was a very necessary decision that was widely welcomed; we were wrestling with climate change while WorkChoices was far from popular. In the end it was not any of those things. The voters were tired of us. They had had enough of the Coalition. In any event, by 2007 we had run our race.

Early in 2007, John Howard came to my electorate for an event related to the Murray–Darling Plan. Afterwards, he and I had lunch in a local cafe in Goolwa. He said to me: 'I don't know, look at these polls, they're just terrible. Even private polling's the same. The public are happy with what we're doing, but we're going so badly. What do you think we should do?' I said: 'Well, we need to have a great fight with the Labor Party'. Because Kevin Rudd kept saying, 'Whatever the government does, I'll match … I'm a fiscal conservative'. As we know, he turned out to be completely reckless with money. But he claimed he was a fiscal conservative. I said to John Howard in the end we really needed to have a great fight. We need politically to go to war with Labor. We need some breathtaking initiative that they cannot support to demonstrate our continuing energy and our fight. He said to me: 'The trouble is we have kind of done everything that we wanted to do'. And I replied: 'Yes, that is a problem'.

Even after deregulating the labour market, introducing the GST, balancing the budget and paying off government debt, resolving previously intractable foreign policy problems, building up the ADF, strengthening the economy and making reforms in areas like health and education, it was not enough. We did not achieve as much as in retrospect as we could have but we had led reforms in all these areas and the country was going well. We might have made it look too easy and the people just got sick of us.

PART V
NEW CHALLENGES

10

HEARTS AND HEADS: THE CHALLENGE OF WELFARE REFORM

PATRICK McCLURE

Australia's income support system costs the taxpayer $150 billion annually in government spending. It is a complex system of payments and supplements that inadvertently entrenches disincentives for people to work. It has failed to adapt to the changing employment market of part-time and casual work, higher skilled jobs, more women in the workforce, and linking training and skills to industries where there are jobs.

There is also now a public expectation that people who have the capacity to work do so, or should be engaged in some form of training.[1] The goal of welfare reform for any government must be to provide an adequate level of income support, operate a simple and sustainable system of payments and supplements, and provide incentives and obligations for people with capacity to get into training and jobs. This requires the balancing of hearts (incentives) and heads (obligations). My chapter explains the genesis of welfare reform initiated by the Howard Government.

Background

In September 1999, the Minister for Family and Community Services, Senator Jocelyn Newman, authorised release of a Green Paper entitled *The Future of Welfare in the 21st Century*. A 'Green Paper' is usually a discussion document that outlines a series of issues of concern to a government and what it believes are the possible courses of action available in addressing them. It is something akin to a combined discussion and options paper.

Newman was to speak at the National Press Club and explain what the government was proposing and why. The paper listed a series of questions in relation to imposing obligations on people with disabilities, sole parents and long-term unemployed. The paper's contents were leaked in advance to the media. The Opposition raised questions in the Federal Parliament and there were media reports critical of the punitive approach to what was termed 'welfare dependency'. As a result, the minister cancelled her speech and a public controversy gained momentum. The Prime Minister's Office intervened by asking me to lead an independent Reference Group on Welfare Reform. I agreed to participate.

On 29 September, the prime minister announced to the parliament that the government was commissioning the Reference Group. Its task was to produce a comprehensive Green Paper on Welfare Reform with an Interim Report due early in 2000 and a Final Report by June 2000. The next few days involved negotiations between me and a range of senior ministerial staff and policy officials including the late John Perrin, the Prime Minister's Social Policy Adviser; Rod Nockles, Chief of Staff to Minister Newman; and Wayne Jackson, Deputy Secretary of the Department of Family and Community Services. The terms of reference and membership of the group were finalised and promulgated. The focus of our work included six guiding principles:

- maintaining equity, simplicity, transparency and sustainability
- establishing better incentives for people receiving social security payments, so that work, education and training are rewarded
- creating greater opportunities for people to increase self-reliance and build capacity, rather than merely providing a safety net
- expecting people on income assistance to help themselves and contribute to society through increased social and economic participation in a framework of mutual obligation
- providing choices and support for individuals and families with more tailored assistance that focuses on prevention and early intervention
- maintaining the government's disciplined approach to fiscal policy.[2]

The Reference Group members included talented people with community service, economic, management and social policy backgrounds.[3] Having worked throughout my career with disadvantaged groups, I was determined that any proposed welfare reforms would recommend a mix of incentives and obligations that most Australians would agree were fair and reasonable. We had a huge task ahead.

Public consultations

I insisted there be a transparent process for the review. A program of consultations with key interest groups was put in place. The Reference Group called for public submissions and posted them on a customised website. We invited expert speakers to address us on social and economic issues, the roles of Centrelink and the Job Network, and the interface of business and community sectors. We received 362 public submissions and conducted 25 consultations with peak business, government and community organisations. Additionally, there were focus groups with income support recipients.

Conflicting paradigms

In the early months of the process, the task was made difficult by conflicting paradigms between the group's community representatives and its public servants. The focus for the public servants was on adopting their department's priorities, including a relatively narrow interpretation of mutual obligation which had formed the basis of Minister Newman's original paper. The community representatives sought a broader conceptual framework for welfare reform. My role was to broker a path through the conflicting approaches, ensuring the group remained collaborative and productive. It was a challenging task. Pressure was placed on the public servants to meet fiscal constraints and their minister's advocacy of mutual obligation. There was also commentary in the media by representatives of the Australian Council of Social Service (ACOSS) and the National Welfare Rights Network that 'draconian obligations' were going to be imposed on vulnerable Australians. Our subject matter ensured vigorous discussion within the group and ideas were constantly tested and gradually changed. This process led to an expanded concept of social obligations, resulting in a shift in emphasis from negative welfare dependency to positive social and economic participation and opportunities for training and jobs.

Research

The final report was based on research and evidence. Group members studied the approaches of other Organisation for Economic Co-operation and Development (OECD) countries. They examined papers on welfare reform, labour-market programs, financial incentives, social enterprise and community capacity-building in the United Kingdom, Canada and the United States. There were presentations by departmental specialists and university researchers on issues including Australia's income-support system, the interface of taxation and income-support systems, labour-market programs, demographic trends, patterns of income-support reliance, financial incentives, labour market shortages, corporate governance and sustainability, and small and medium-sized enterprise as well as focus groups on community attitudes to mutual obligation.

Case for reform

The Reference Group members articulated a case for fundamental reform based on several major issues: the growing divide between 'job-rich' and 'job-poor' households; and strong employment growth in some areas and high rates of joblessness in others. Additionally, 860 000 children were living in households with no parent in paid work; labour-market trends have changed, with more part-time and casual jobs rather than permanent, full-time jobs; female participation in the workforce has increased; there are now new jobs in finance, construction, retail and human services in place of jobs in manufacturing and primary industries; and over the past 30 years, there has been a steady increase in the proportion of working-age people receiving income support and other supplements. Of special concern is the proportion of the population that depends on income support for most of their expenditure; and job opportunities for less skilled workers have stagnated or declined, while the demand for highly skilled workers has increased as a result of technological change and globalisation. This has resulted in a widening distribution of earnings.[4]

Without appropriate action, Australia risked consigning large numbers of people to an intergenerational cycle of joblessness. Australia already has one of the highest levels of joblessness among families with children in OECD nations. Evidence suggests that children in families where parents are unemployed are more likely to be unemployed as they grow up.

Economic and social disadvantage has negative consequences on individuals, families and communities. Lack of paid employment during the prime working years and consequent reliance on income support reduce current and lifetime incomes. In addition, participating in paid employment is a major source of self-esteem. Without fulfilling work, people can fail to develop or become disengaged from family, employment and social networks. This can lead to physical and psychological ill health and reduced life opportunities for parents and children.[5] Our working group identified shortcomings in the system: service delivery was fragmented and not focused on employment; categories of pensions and allowances were complex and rigid; incentives for work were inadequate; and social and economic participation were not recognised.

Objectives

The Reference Group members argued that the nation's social support system must be judged by its capacity to help people participate socially and economically, as well as the adequacy of income support payments. The goal of welfare reform is to minimise social and economic exclusion, and Australia's success in doing this was to be measured according to the following three key outcomes: a significant reduction in the incidence of jobless households; a significant reduction in the proportion of the working-age population that relies heavily on income support; and stronger communities which generate more opportunities for social and economic participation.[6]

Participation

The Reference Group stated that the concept of participation is central to welfare reform:

> Australia's social support system must do more than provide adequate levels of income support for people in need. It must ensure that people are actively engaged socially and economically, including in the labour force, to reduce the risk of long-term disadvantage for themselves and their families.[7]

The group introduced the principle of social obligations to broaden the concept of mutual obligation. This was a major change from what Minister Newman had originally proposed. It took the emphasis away from a narrow punitive obligation on individuals. Social obligations are reciprocal and extend throughout society, not only between government and individuals. These obligations extend to businesses and trade unions: businesses have obligations to their customers, employees, society and shareholders; trade unions to their members and society.[8]

The Final Report of the Reference Group outlined five features of the proposed Participation Support System. Each feature was integral to the vision of a Participation Support System.[9]

Individualised service delivery

The model incorporated a number of key design principles: integrating income support and other services through the gateway agency, Centrelink; streaming individuals into different types of services based on assessment of their needs and capacities; providing a range of broker activities to help disadvantaged individuals access training and jobs; and linking services, brokers and assessment in ongoing assistance to the individual. The report also stressed the need for individuals to be able to access childcare, public transport and affordable housing.

Simple and responsive income-support structure

The key recommendations were to maintain an adequate income support system responsive to individuals' changing circumstances. The complexity of the current system of payments and the need for a simple and responsive system was recognised. We acknowledged, however, that this would be costly, and divided the recommendations for change into initial steps and medium- to long-term actions. The report proposed an integrated payment structure over the long term. It would consist of a standard base rate of payment; add-on modules for the cost of children, childcare, housing, disability and travel in remote areas; and a participation supplement to cover the costs associated with training and job search.

Financial incentives

The report stressed that an effective participation system must send strong positive messages about the benefits of work. In the extant system there were disincentives for some people to enter the workforce. The report outlined the need to improve incentives for all paid work, including for part-time and casual work. It canvassed options such as In-Work Benefits, which included the Earned Income Tax Credit (EITC) and Return to Work Benefits such as the Participation Supplement and a Transition Bank. We also recommended reducing the Effective Marginal Tax Rates (EMTRs).

Mutual obligations

The Reference Group supported a broad interpretation of the concept of mutual obligation, underpinned by the concept of social obligations. We contended that businesses, communities and individuals are held together by mutual expectations and obligations. As we stated in the report:

> The Participation Support System will involve a greater commitment of all parties – government, business, communities and individuals – to generate opportunities for social and economic participation and to ensure more active engagement between service providers and individuals, particularly those most affected by social exclusion.[10]

> Governments have a responsibility to manage the economy to enable economic growth, long term environmental sustainability and the well-being of communities.[11]

> The obligation of business is to generate wealth for shareholders, act in the interest of customers and contribute to taxation. This involves integrating social, environment and governance strategies (ESG) into the business plan.

The report also considered community expectations on individuals receiving income support. It argued that people of workforce age with the capacity to work and in the appropriate circumstances will attempt to find work. It also recognised that people with caring responsibilities already fulfil their obligations, for example, caring for young children, people with a disability, and frail aged or chronically ill people. Additionally, people with significant disabilities already fulfil their obligations.

Social partnerships – building community capacity

The report identified four processes through which government, businesses and communities can build capacity: by investing in economic development and infrastructure; by creating community business partnerships involving national, state or local businesses working with communities to provide training, jobs and services; by social entrepreneurs developing businesses with a social purpose that can revitalise communities; and by micro-businesses, often run by women, young people and mature-aged people, generating jobs and services in local communities.[12]

Launch of the Interim Report and response

The Reference Group's Interim Report, *Participation Support for a More Equitable Society*, was launched at a press conference on

28 March 2000 at Parliament House in Canberra. There had been 36 drafts in the lead-up to the report. There was nationwide publicity for our findings. The *Daily Telegraph* hailed the recommendations as being a 'brave new plan to get welfare recipients involved in the community and learn skills to get jobs'. The *Sydney Morning Herald* credited the Reference Group with preparing the ground for the most radical restructuring of Australia's social welfare system since the mid-1980s, when the Hawke Government reformed the welfare system, and stated it provided 'a strong case for change and suggests the broad direction change should take'. The *Australian* commended the report as being 'a bold approach to reforming the nation's welfare system' and 'valuable because it points out the failings of our old solutions and outlines innovations for the future'.

The Reference Group developed a feedback questionnaire published on a customised website and distributed to all organisations and individuals who had made a submission. There were focus groups of income-support recipients as well as consultations with community organisations, peak bodies and government departments. I participated in media interviews and addressed conferences and forums throughout the nation. The report generated great community interest and debate.

Public launch of the final report and responses

In July 2000 the Reference Group presented the Federal Government with the final report. Federal Cabinet formally accepted the report on 16 August 2000. There was another press conference. Plainly, the media were interested in our work and the government's proposed reforms. The final report contained 65 short-, medium- and long-term recommendations which received significant media coverage. The 'McClure Report' was the lead story in national and state print and electronic media. The major political parties and media praised the report's findings. According to Media Monitors, the coverage and reception was 92 per cent positive in favour of the report's directions.

In receiving the report, Prime Minister John Howard remarked:

It is an excellent document. The Government endorses the broad thrust of the goals outlined. We will be giving a detailed response. We will examine all of the recommendations and I repeat the assurances previously given that the social security safety net will remain.

The Leader of the Opposition, Kim Beazley, and the Shadow Minister for Family and Community Services, Wayne Swan, were equally complimentary in their comments: 'A government with a fair mind and a good heart will find opportunities in this report to take social policy forward'. The Leader of the Australian Democrats, Senator Meg Lees, thought 'this is a report we could support if the thrust of the package is adhered to in the Government's response'.

The media were similarly generous in their appraisal of our work and the initial political response. Political journalist Michelle Grattan wrote in the *Sydney Morning Herald*:

Mission Australia's Patrick McClure has scored a trifecta. Government, Labor and Democrats all had positive things to say about the inquiry's blueprint for welfare change … The strength of the McClure report is that it is not driven by a narrow Right or Left ideology. Indeed, if you ask whether this report comes from the Right or the Left in its approach, the answer is both.

Political analyst Tony Walker, writing in the *Australian Financial Review*, observed:

> Rare is a report on such a vexed issue as welfare reform which draws support from across the political spectrum and business, and yet that is what Patrick McClure appears to have achieved.

Lessons drawn from the process

There are a number of lessons to be drawn from the experiences of the Reference Group. It was a new way of developing social policy. The Chair of the Reference Group was the CEO of non-government organisation Mission Australia, not a senior public servant. Members were chosen from community, academic and business organisations as well as the public service. They contributed new ideas and independent thinking. I was able to broker a significant change in the organising paradigm, from the narrow punitive model proposed in Minister Newman's original Green Paper to a broader framework of social and economic participation. The process showed how community representatives can be engaged in partnership with public servants in developing good social policy. The independence of the Reference Group was an important factor in the broad acceptance of our recommendations.

The involvement of community representatives in such a commitment over nine months involved a significant investment of time and resources for both individuals and their organisations. It also led to criticism from the sector that we were working too closely with government. It is, however, the responsibility of third-sector leaders to be involved in developing social policy with government to ensure the interests of disadvantaged groups are represented at the table.[13]

The government response

The government's response to our report was disappointingly slow. The implementation process appeared to lose momentum. In the ensuing months, Jocelyn Newman retired from politics. She was succeeded as Minister for Family and Community Services by Senator Amanda Vanstone. The new minister did not provide the leadership needed to implement all the reforms we proposed. In the absence of ministerial initiative and energy, a new Welfare Reform Consultative Committee was formed comprising community representatives and public servants. Its aim was to develop a plan of implementation – something the minister and her office should have provided.

On 22 May 2001, the Federal Government finally released its response: *Australians Working Together: Helping People to Move Forward.*[14] The package was the centrepiece of the Howard Government's sixth Budget, with the Coalition committing $1.7 billion over four years as the start of a ten-year reform program. The package included: a Working Credit and Literacy and Numeracy Supplement, budgeted at $526 million; Job Search Training, Intensive Assistance, Work for the Dole, Literacy and Numeracy, Transition to Work, and Training Credits, budgeted at $324 million; a Personal Support Program with improved information technology, budgeted at $143 million; helping parents return to work, budgeted at $251 million; increasing childcare places, budgeted at $16 million; helping mature-age people, budgeted at $146 million; employment and training for people with a disability, budgeted at $177 million; community building, employment and training for Indigenous people, budgeted at \$83 million; and community–business engagement, budgeted at \$22 million.[15]

In response to the Budget announcement, I welcomed the government's commitment to welfare reform and much of the new package. I expressed concern for the shortfall in provision. We had suggested an upfront \$1 billion investment. We noted that major expenditure had been left until later years. At the time I remarked: 'I would like to see the major investment in the first year and the return on investment will be getting people into jobs'.

My main concern was the risk of losing momentum over the four years. The recommendation to align the levels of pensions and allowances was not implemented in 2001. This was a major mistake. The increasing difference between levels of pensions and allowances has led to increasing inequity between pension and allowance levels over the following decades.

Recent reforms

In 2014, I was asked by the Abbott Government to chair the Reference Group on Welfare Reform and report to Kevin Andrews, the Minister for Social Services. I was familiar with Kevin Andrews and I looked forward to this new challenge. Our final report, *A New System for Better Employment and Social Outcomes*, was launched in February 2015.

The report proposed four pillars of reform: a simpler and sustainable income support system; building individual and family capability; engaging with employers; and building community capacity.[16] The key recommendations included: simplifying the complex and inefficient system of 20 payments and 55 supplements to five payments and four categories of supplements; a priority investment approach with early intervention services focusing on groups most at risk of lifetime welfare dependence; developing a social purpose capital market and social impact bonds addressing social problems; and a new information and communications technology system driving efficiencies in the income support system.

The Priority Investment Approach (PIA) is a new way of addressing welfare dependence. It involves actuarial analysis to identify groups with the highest future, life-time cost of welfare dependence. Funding of early intervention strategies with these disadvantaged groups achieves better outcomes for them and saves billions of taxpayers' dollars in future costs to the nation.[17]

The actuarial model predicts the future income support use of the Australian population. People are grouped into 12 broad welfare classes: six for income support recipients; three for people receiving payments but no income support; and three for the rest of the population. Each year the model is enhanced to take account of changes to the economy and the unemployment rate. The statistical evidence illustrates that young teenage parents, youth on disability support and young carers are three groups with the highest average future lifetime welfare costs.

The Commonwealth Government under Minister Christian Porter invested $100 million in the *Try, Test and Learn Fund* funding early intervention projects for young carers, young parents, working aged carers, students, mature-aged people, at-risk youth and refugees. The latest PIA baseline data for future lifetime cost of welfare shows a 10 per cent reduction between 2015 and 2018 with future, lifetime savings of $700 billion. From 2014 to 2019 there has also been a significant reduction in the number of people on the Disability Support Pension, Parenting Payment, Youth Allowance and Family Tax Benefits A and B.[18]

The challenge of welfare reform continues but a good start was made during the Howard years. Securing bipartisan support for reform remains a hurdle. The income support system involves $150 billion of government spending each year. It is a complex system of payments and supplements. Reform is hard work and it is a balancing act of ensuring an adequate level of income support, simplifying a very complex system, funding early interventions to prevent lifetime welfare dependence, and providing pathways for people to access training and jobs. As we were able to show in 2000–01, it is possible to balance hearts (incentives) and heads (obligations).

11

THE HOWARD GOVERNMENT AND THE RISE OF THE AUSTRALIAN GREENS

NICK ECONOMOU AND ZAREH GHAZARIAN

The 2004 election marked the beginning of the last term of the Howard Government, although the election result itself was a triumph for the Liberal–National Coalition. In addition to defeating Labor and its recently installed leader, Mark Latham, the Coalition benefited from particularly strong Senate results in Western Australia, Victoria and Queensland and thus secured a rare majority in the upper house. This fact was lost somewhat amidst changes occurring to the Australian party system in which new minor parties were starting to secure Senate representation. In the 2004 half-Senate contest, for example, the Greens party won two seats while a Family First senator won a seat in Victoria. In the meantime, the Australian Democrats, who had positioned themselves as defenders of the balance of power in the Senate, motivated by the mantra of 'keeping the bastards honest', failed to win a seat and commenced their descent to oblivion.

The extent to which the Howard Government was responsible for the rise of the Australian Greens in national politics, especially during the 2004–07 period, is worth close consideration. Our argument is that the Howard Government contributed to the rise of green politics in Australia between 2004 and 2007 primarily because of the way it managed debate on environment policy. At the time, the Howard Government had to respond to the demand for action arising from key stakeholders, especially in the Murray–Darling Basin, who were dealing with the persistence of a particularly severe drought. Indeed, public authorities such as the Bureau of Meteorology (BOM) officially referred to this drought as the 'Millennium Drought'.[1] According to the BOM, it had begun in 1996 – the same year John Howard defeated Paul Keating. The way the Howard Government sought to co-ordinate a national approach to managing water allocation in the basin soon included consideration of a national climate policy based on an emissions trading scheme. This occurred alongside the rise of Malcolm Turnbull as the Environment Minister. Both the minister and the policy would affect Australian politics for many years after the Howard Government's defeat in 2007.

The Howard Government's responsibility for the rise of the Australian Greens party is not as obvious as its legacy in the policy debate, however. Indeed, there is a lack of any empirical evidence to suggest an immediate link. If the 2004 half-Senate election was remembered for anything, it was the election of Family First's Steve Fielding in Victoria, notwithstanding that the ticket polled a primary vote of only 1.5 per cent. The Greens ticket in Victoria, by contrast, did not win a single seat despite polling a primary vote of 6 per cent. The reason for this had little to do with the Liberal or National parties (although a strong vote for the Coalition ticket in Victoria had directed some surplus to the Family First ticket). Rather, it was the decision of the Victorian branch of the Australian Labor Party (ALP) to direct its preferences to Family First that helped Fielding win the seat while denying the Greens' John Ristrom. The Tasmanian Labor Party had employed the same tactic in its Group Vote Ticket (GVT), and this nearly prevented the Greens candidate, Christine Milne, from securing a seat despite polling over 9 per cent of the primary vote. In the end, the willingness of many more Tasmanians to cast their own preferences instead of relying on the Labor GVT delivered the seat to the Greens.

The bitterness expressed over the Family First success in Victoria was a matter for the Greens and Labor. The Liberal and National parties, on the other hand, could rejoice in gaining a majority in the Senate. Three years later, the political situation changed. The Howard Government lost the 2007 election, although the swing against it in the contest for House of Representatives seats meant little for the Greens. The national swing to the Greens in the lower house contest was 0.6 percentage points and the party failed to win any House of Representatives seats. The result was a little stronger in the Senate, where the swing to the Greens was 1.4 percentage points and the securing of three seats was a net gain of one seat on the 2004 result.[2] The Greens now had a solid block of five upper house seats, but the combination of Greens and Labor seats came to 37 and was thus short of a majority. South Australian independent Nick Xenophon would be the powerbroker after the 2007 election.

Green parties in Australia

Parties that focused on ecology, peace and disarmament were a feature of the national parliament well before the Howard-led Coalition first won office in 1996. For example, in 1984 the newly formed Nuclear Disarmament Party, which advanced anti-nuclear policies, succeeded in winning a Senate seat but soon experienced internal divisions which ultimately led to a split.[3] Nevertheless, the party was successful in winning another seat in the Senate in 1987 but, by the early 1990s, had disintegrated. By this stage, the Western Australian Greens (WA Greens) was gaining momentum and won Senate seats in the 1990 and 1993 elections.

The election of the Howard Government, however, coincided with the election of the Australian Greens to the Senate. Led by Bob Brown, the nascent Greens party had national ambitions. Brown had developed a high public profile, especially during his time as Director of the Tasmanian Wilderness Society, when he was involved in opposing plans to dam the Franklin River in the early 1980s.[4] While Brown campaigned on environmental conservation matters in the party's early years in parliament, issues concerning foreign policy and national security were prominent in the political debate and during the 2004 election campaign.

This provided opportunities for the Greens in parliament to raise the party's profile. This was most clearly evident when Bob Brown and fellow Greens Senator Kerry Nettle were ejected from parliament for interrupting a speech by the President of the United States George W Bush late in 2003.[5] The Greens also underwent significant organisational reforms in preparation for the 2004 poll. And after remaining as a separate party since its creation, the Western Australian Greens finally joined the Australian Greens confederated structure in 2003.

Expectations were high that the Greens' adversarial approach, as well as its more resolved organisational structure, would lead to stronger electoral results at the 2004 election as part of a seemingly inevitable 'upward trajectory'.[6] As has already been noted, the problem for the Greens was that in 2004 there was a swing to the political right in the broader electorate which allowed the Howard Government to claim a majority in the Senate – a rare feat in post-war Australian politics. As a result, the 2004 to 2007 period was one in which the power and influence of the Greens in the Senate was marginalised. The party did not hold the balance of power and consequently its capacity to shape national policy was diminished. This did not mean, however, that green issues would disappear from Australian politics; policies concerning natural resources and the environment were prominent during the last term of the Howard Government.

Green politics 2004–2007: the policy debate

By 2007 the national electorate was ready to change the party of government. Industrial relations dominated the 2007 campaign, although it was also the case that the recently installed Labor leader, Kevin Rudd, placed climate change as one of the key issues that Labor would pursue vigorously if elected to government.[7] This approach reflected the Opposition's long campaign of trying to cast the Coalition as being divided over the issue of climate change.[8] This was despite the fact that the Howard Government had actually been responsible for a number of policy initiatives designed to address the need to reduce carbon emissions. Prime Minister Howard was also to appoint the newly elected member for Wentworth, Malcolm Turnbull, to a number of positions within the government in which he would have some responsibility for water resource management as well as climate change. By 2007, Turnbull, a strong advocate of the need to take climate change seriously, was Minister for the Environment. This was a legacy of sorts as well; Turnbull would eventually lead the Liberal Party twice (once as prime minister).

Labor's accusation that Howard and his Coalition colleagues were climate change deniers was based on the Howard Government's steadfast refusal to complete a process seeking to have nations agree to an international approach to greenhouse gas emissions reductions. The international approach had been co-ordinated by the United Nations, under whose auspices a conference had been convened at Kyoto in 1997. At Kyoto, a large group of nations (presently 192) promised to ratify the protocol by which they would reduce their greenhouse emissions in an effort to address global warming. Some nations, including the United States, refused to sign up to this agreement.[9] It was Howard Government policy to sign but not ratify the Kyoto Protocol, partly because ratification could be to the detriment of Australia's economic interests, given the link between greenhouse gas mitigation and reduced dependence on coal, and partly to align Australian policy with that of its major ally, the United States.[10] Labor and the Greens seized upon the Howard Government's refusal to ratify the Kyoto Protocol as proof of the Coalition's lack of interest in the 'green' agenda, thereby reinforcing the political situation in which the government and the movement were implacable antagonists.[11]

In reality, however, the Howard Government between 2004 and 2007 was much more accommodating of aspects of the environmental agenda than its political opponents were prepared to concede. The persistence of a severe drought throughout eastern Australia influenced the Howard Government's approach to two issues in particular – first, the management of water in the Murray–Darling Basin and, second, the government's approach to climate change policy, notwithstanding its stated intention not to ratify the Kyoto Protocol. As the drought persisted, pressure began to build on the Coalition to lead a national policy response. The urgency of water management was amplified by the political significance of the Murray–Darling Basin to the Coalition. The basin, with its strong National- and Liberal-voting towns and with an economic profile dominated by irrigation-dependent agriculture, was (and still is) a core Coalition constituency. Here emerged an interesting tension underpinning the debate, especially with respect to how water resources were to be allocated, between agricultural interests on the one side, and ecologists on the other.

In its intergovernmental relations with New South Wales and Victoria, the Commonwealth Government placed renewed emphasis on bringing water-saving technology to the basin's irrigation systems.[12] This was the basis for co-operation with state governments, notwithstanding their different party-political persuasion, and the farming communities in the Basin, who were also supportive. The problem for the Howard Government, however, lay in competing ecological demands seeking to secure water allocations to contribute to 'environmental flows'.[13] These demands focused on arguments about the basin suffering a major ecological catastrophe that was symptomatic of a bigger crisis (in this case, climate change). The government, the ecology lobby argued, needed to go beyond simply using the Council of Australian Government (COAG) to get the states to cover their irrigation channels. As a major metropolitan newspaper opined:

> The outlook for Australia makes for bleak reading. The report predicts a hotter climate, more droughts, violent storms, agricultural losses and serious environmental damage in 30 to 50 years … all means must be employed if we are to halve emissions by mid-century, to ensure climate change remains manageable.[14]

As the drought continued, this narrative increasingly resonated with electors in major metropolitan centres. The Howard Government responded accordingly. First, it re-organised the former Murray–Darling Basin Commission as a means of reinforcing the Commonwealth's leadership on water resource management. In 2007, the government announced a $10 billion National Water Security Plan and placed the re-named Murray–Darling Basin Authority (MDBA) at the centre of a process designed to cap water usage and determine water allocations in the Basin. Passage of a new piece of legislation – *The Water Act 2007 (Cth)* – provided a statutory framework by which the MDBA could advise the Commonwealth minister on water allocation. The legislation aimed to ensure that all aspects of water resource management would be covered in the decision-making, including water quality (important to the communities that depended on the Basin for drinking water), salinity management, and the need for water to address environmental demands.

Meanwhile, a shift in position occurred in relation to climate policy. In 2006, the Secretary of the Department of the Prime Minister and Cabinet, Dr Peter Shergold, was appointed to investigate policy options the government could pursue to lower carbon emissions in Australia. Shergold's report was delivered in 2007 amid much fanfare and a sense that this was to be the Australian equivalent to Britain's Stern Report – the major study of the economics associated with climate change commissioned by the British Government. By this stage a Prime Ministerial Task Group on Emissions Trading had also been established and it became clear that a carbon emissions trading scheme was to be the centrepiece of the government's climate change policy.

In November 2006, the government announced it would create a National Climate Change Adoption Research Facility, in yet another tacit acknowledgment that climate change was relevant to the domestic policy debate. Indeed, in the lead-up to the commencement of the 2007 federal election campaign, John Howard declared that, if it was re-elected, his government would legislate to establish an emissions trading scheme.[15] The only thing the government would not countenance was a retreat from its initial decision not to ratify Kyoto.

The rise of Malcolm Turnbull

The sense of shift associated with the Howard Government's approach to these aspects of the environmental debate can be further appreciated by tracking the Liberal personnel who held, or exercised some influence over, the environment portfolio between 2004 and 2007. The rapid rise of Malcolm Turnbull from the backbench to become the Minister for the Environment (in less than one parliamentary term) was the most significant development during this time. He was first elected to the House of Representatives in 2004 after wrestling Liberal pre-selection for the seat of Wentworth from the incumbent member, Peter King. As a former activist on behalf of the Australian Republic Movement, and known to hold socially progressive views on matters ranging from marriage equality to climate change, Turnbull might have been considered to have been a little too moderate for the quite conservative outlooks of the prime minister and many in the Cabinet. On the other hand, inclusion in the ministry is one method by which a prime minister can seek to exercise control over a high-profile and ambitious parliamentarian.

Whatever the reason, Howard initiated Turnbull's ascent in 2006 by appointing him Parliamentary Secretary for Water. At the time, Senator Ian Campbell was the Minister for Environment. In 2004, Senator Campbell was locked in a conservation dispute involving a proposed wind farm at Bald Hills in the south Gippsland region of Victoria. The project had state government approval but was opposed by a small but noisy group of local residents and conservationists who claimed the wind farm would pose a danger to the threatened orange-bellied parrot. The opposition group had the backing of local Liberal member for the electoral division of McMillan, Russell Broadbent. Soon after the election, Senator Campbell used the *Environment Protection and Biodiversity*

Conservation Act 1999 to refuse Commonwealth permission for the project, thereby indicating that, if the political circumstances were considered favourable, conservation outcomes could be secured – a sign, perhaps, of a willingness on the part of the Howard Government to be flexible on other matters on the agenda, including the climate change debate.

In the meantime, Turnbull was given oversight of the newly created Office for Water Resources. This unit was answerable not to the environment ministry but to the Department of the Prime Minister and Cabinet (PM&C), although Turnbull was technically an assistant minister to Campbell. The series of water initiatives mentioned previously was announced soon after. Then, in early 2007, the prime minister announced a ministerial reshuffle as part of a cabinet 'rejuvenation' ahead of the federal election due later that year. In the reshuffle, Senator Campbell was reassigned to Social Security and his former subordinate, Malcolm Turnbull, became the new minister. Armed with the Shergold plan and with the prime minister's approval, the new minister outlined a new policy to mitigate greenhouse gas emissions by instituting an emissions trading scheme. This proposal was not to be realised, as the Coalition lost the 2007 election.

John Howard's prime ministership ended with the November 2007 election. The consequences of his choice of Turnbull as the standard-bearer for a modified Coalition approach to water resource policy and climate change would reverberate for at least a decade. Turnbull would ascend to the Liberal leadership twice – once as Leader of the Opposition in 2008 and once as Prime Minister in 2015. On each occasion, the politics of climate change were central to his political demise. On the first occasion, he contemplated giving the Rudd Labor Government parliamentary support to get its emissions trading scheme a majority in the Senate. The second occasion was ahead of the 2019 election, when he tried to formulate an energy policy (the National Energy Guarantee or NEG) based on reducing carbon emissions. This also coincided with a growth in voter support for the Australian Greens, which had retained a seat in the House of Representatives since 2010 as well as holding the balance of power in the Senate for a time after the 2010 election. It would seem that the Howard Government's impact on green politics was felt in public policy long after its electoral defeat in 2007.

The Howard Government formulated significant environmental policy between the 2004 and 2007 elections, mainly in response to community demands for a national approach to the challenges emanating from the 'Millennium Drought' that affected eastern and south-eastern Australia. Water resource management, especially in the Murray–Darling Basin, and climate change were the two most important issues of this period, although there was also the matter of delivering on the commitment to stop the Bald Hills wind farm made to Russell Broadbent and his constituents in McMillan during the 2004 campaign.

These conservation initiatives did not, however, impress the nascent Greens. The Howard Government would soften its position on the idea of an emissions trading scheme and the sympathetic Malcolm Turnbull would ascend to the environment ministry. But the Kyoto Protocol would not be signed and this gave Labor and the Greens something symbolic on which to campaign in 2007.

Was the Howard Government responsible for the rise of the Greens? Given that the Greens party comprises part of the left-of-centre in the Australian party system, and tends to take members, supporters and voters primarily from the Labor Party, the Coalition's culpability for the party's rise is limited to indirect contributions. The Coalition's geostrategic support for the United States in both the 'war on terror' and on the matter of the Kyoto Protocol put it in direct opposition to the Greens. By inducing such a polarised debate, the Howard Government might have caused some Liberals to re-align with the Greens. On the other hand, pragmatism abounded in the Howard Government's approach to conservation issues. Wind farms could be stopped, money for climate change and water allocation initiatives could be found, and Malcolm Turnbull could be promoted as environment minister and promise an emissions trading scheme if the political conditions demanded such responses.

These concessions to the conservationist agenda were significant developments, but it is not clear to what extent it helped the Greens consolidate as a component of the Australian party system. The advance of the Australian Greens really occurred at the election after the Coalition's defeat in 2007. The climate change debate, on the other hand, was something the Howard Government made a major contribution towards, and the Howard legacy would resonate long after the government's 2007 defeat. Given the talismanic status of climate change to its contemporary manifestation, this is the policy area where the Howard Government gave succour to the Greens, notwithstanding the Coalition's increasing pragmatism on this matter the longer the drought went on. Attempts by subsequent governments – both Labor and Coalition – to institute pragmatic policy solutions to tackle climate change have failed as a result.

PART VI
THE BEGINNING OF THE END

12

A VIEW FROM EDEN-MONARO

GARY NAIRN

In retrospect, the Coalition's final term in government was one of highs and lows, especially for me personally. The 2004 election, my fourth consecutive win, was extremely satisfying, resulting in an increased margin from the 2001 election (0.5 per cent swing). I recall developing strong support from a wide cross-section of the community. The type of support that comes from certain individuals voting specifically for you, and not the party you are representing. Contrary to some other analyses of election results, the local member can make a substantial difference, one that tends to build over subsequent elections.

The second high was my elevation to Parliamentary Secretary to the Prime Minister following the October 2004 election. I admit to being disappointed in not being promoted after the 2001 election so the opportunity to work closely with the prime minister was exciting. I was eager to demonstrate that I had more to contribute as part of the Howard Government. My responsibilities for the National Water Initiative and the National Water Commission added to my excitement.

The highs of an election win and promotion were quickly overrun a few weeks later when my wife of 31 years was diagnosed with terminal cancer. She died 21 weeks later. In hindsight, my roles as the Federal Member for Eden-Monaro, Parliamentary Secretary to the Prime Minister and ultimately, early in 2006, eight months after her passing, being promoted to Special Minister of State, were life savers. Being extremely busy was of great benefit to the grieving process. My children and I greatly appreciated the support of the prime minister and my party-room colleagues.

While the weeks leading up to my wife's passing were difficult, they were made more so as they also coincided with the start of a determined personal attack by some extreme elements in my electorate. For example, my office received a number of offensive phone calls; an apparent box of chocolates mailed to my office was in fact a box of faeces; I received unwelcome phone calls at home during the early hours of the morning; and an anti-forestry campaigner forged my letterhead and signature to write to a small business in the forestry industry informing the owners the government was withdrawing a previously announced grant. The actions of this individual were galling and heartless. The small business owner was aware that he had qualified for the grant as part of the Australian Government's Forest Industry Structural Adjustment Package (FISAP). The government was assisting the industry to be more efficient, thus allowing more sustainable logging. I had announced the grant a couple of weeks previously and he was looking forward to receiving the funds promised. When he opened what he honestly thought was a letter from me saying it was not happening, his distress was apparent, and he phoned me after receiving it. The letter was a hoax. The culprit, identified by the Australian Federal Police following an investigation, was Harriet Swift. She was referred to the House of Representatives Privileges Committee by the Speaker of the House, David Hawker. After an exhaustive inquiry that took until 2007 to complete, its chairman, the Member for Blair, Cameron Thompson, moved:

> That the House agrees with the recommendations of the
> Committee of Privileges presented on 31 May 2007 about
> allegations of documents fraudulently and inaccurately
> written and issued in a member's name and: (1) finds
> Ms Harriet Swift guilty of contempt of the House in that
> she undertook conduct that amounted to an improper
> interference with the free performance by the Member for
> Eden-Monaro of his duties as a member; and (2) reprimands
> Ms Swift for her conduct.

The motion received unanimous support but this basically amounted to a 'rap over the knuckles' for Swift. Incredibly, she had previously received similar treatment from the Senate Privileges Committee in 1981 when she harassed Senator Brian Harradine, coincidentally when his wife was being treated for cancer.

Personal attack and intimidation continued at an intense level, particularly during the final year or so leading up to the 2007 election. This was the beginning of the organisation GetUp!. Eden-Monaro was one of its first targets. Its campaigning coincided with the unions' 'Your Rights at Work' and these two organisations, along with the Labor Party, developed a well-coordinated campaign against the government and me in Eden-Monaro.

GetUp! first came into the public view within Eden-Monaro with a planned debate its members organised in Narooma. Some of them really believed they were just part of a genuine community-based group without any political allegiance. The fact that the National Secretary of the Australian Workers Union (AWU), Bill Shorten, later to become Leader of the Labor Party for a time, was a founding director of GetUp! seemed to be overlooked by many.

The debate was promoted widely as the first political debate that would be the subject of a podcast. Nothing special now, but it was in 2007. They had also organised for journalist George Negus to be the moderator as he was related to one of the Narooma GetUp! organisers. The Liberal Party advised me not to participate as they believed it would be a total set-up. While I accepted that would be the case, I took the view that I had to take part in it, for two reasons. First, it was gaining substantial publicity through the media and as I was the sitting member it would have been very easy for my detractors to portray me as running away from a significant public debate. Second, and more importantly, as this was a first for podcasts, as Special Minister of State, I was the minister responsible for advancing the digital economy. Not participating would have appeared hypocritical. I participated, as did all other candidates. Yes, it was a set-up, no doubt there. Each time I attempted to speak I was booed by audience members. Each time my Labor rival, Mike Kelly, started to speak, he was cheered. This went on for the entire debate. It was so blatant that when the debate closed, George Negus, feeling quite embarrassed by the audience's behaviour, asked them to give me a special round of applause. I doubt I lost any votes attending the event. Perhaps I retained some and maybe gained a few by turning up and dealing with the GetUp! bias.

Throughout that final year I had the uneasy experience of a certain individual showing up at almost every event I attended, displaying various protest and anti-government and anti-Nairn signage. We were clearly being followed and were forced to go to great lengths to lose them. After the election, I was reliably told the unions had paid my antagonist to 'pester' me for 12 months.

In my view, the most difficult issue to deal with during the final term was the government's workplace relations policy, WorkChoices. In hindsight, it was a bridge too far for my electorate to accept, but only in political terms. We had made progress since coming to office, but the electorate saw the additional step as unnecessary. WorkChoices allowed our opponents to distort the facts, creating concern in the community, and the government's handling, timing, and marketing of it did not help us.

In the lead-up to an election, often it is side issues that dominate the media, overtaking important policy matters. In my case, just two months out from the election, it was a series of questions Julia Gillard, then Deputy Leader of the Opposition, asked me at the beginning of Question Time. The dominant policy issue then, except for WorkChoices, was Labor's taxation policy. Earlier that day on radio, Kevin Rudd had made a botch of answers relating to Labor's proposed tax policy. Then, in answering a question later at a media doorstop in Queanbeyan, he could not nominate existing tax rates and thresholds. This became the big issue of the parliamentary sitting week, with media attention squarely on the Leader of the Opposition. Labor was looking for a distraction and, unfortunately, I was the target. The first question at Question Time that afternoon was from Gillard:

> My question is to the Special Minister of State. I refer the
> Minister to a community meeting last week in his seat which
> Labor candidate and decorated soldier Colonel Mike Kelly
> addressed. I refer the Minister to a question posed by his
> chief of staff, Peter Phelps, to Colonel Mike Kelly asking if he
> compared his military service in Iraq to that of Nazi guards
> at the Belsen concentration camp. Does the Minister endorse
> his chief of staff's conduct and what will he do about it?[1]

While I was aware my chief of staff, Peter Phelps, had attended the meeting, he had not told me about this exchange with Kelly. Instead of briefing me fully on what was discussed, he simply said he had 'a robust debate' with Kelly. I was blindsided by the question.

I am aware that a former military lawyer who is standing for the seat of Eden-Monaro invited people from the public – in fact I got an invitation at home as well – to attend a forum. I think that it is only appropriate that individuals in their own private capacity, when invited to attend a forum, go along to that forum and participate in the debate. Certainly, Dr Phelps was there. He went in his personal capacity and participated in debate at that forum, as I understand it and as passed on by my chief of staff the day after it occurred. As he was invited he decided he would attend and he participated in the debate.

My answer did not satisfy the Opposition. Gillard asked another question:

I refer to the following exchange with Mike Kelly, a former colonel, at a community meeting in his electorate. Mike Kelly said: 'No, I was a soldier, and I did what I was ordered to do'. The Minister's chief of staff, Peter Phelps, then said: 'Oh, like the guards at Belsen perhaps? Are you using the Nuremberg Defence?' Does the Minister believe the words that were used are acceptable to be used by anyone in any circumstance, public or private? Given that the words were said by the Minister's chief of staff, does he endorse them; and, if he does not endorse them, what will he do about it?[2]

I replied:

As I said in my earlier answer, I was not in attendance at that particular forum. My chief of staff did not attend that forum at any direction from me. He was not at that forum as my chief of staff. He attended as a citizen of Queanbeyan who had received an invitation to attend the forum. I cannot particularly comment on whether or not those words were said, because I was not there. However, clearly, I would not agree with any comments that might compare the work of Australian soldiers with the work of those in Nazi Germany.[3]

Gillard asked a third question that exemplified political side tracking. The issue dominated the opening half hour of Question Time in the House, and the Opposition used it to good effect. Oddly, the previous Saturday I had attended a function with the Labor candidate and his wife in the electorate, where neither one of them mentioned the exchange involving my chief of staff. The political imperative was strong, as this was to be the last week of Parliament sitting prior to the election.

The final election result in Eden-Monaro was a swing away of more than 6 per cent. My margin had been 2.5 per cent after the 2004 election. The 2007 election result might have been much closer, or I could even have held on, had it not been for the Australian Electoral Commission (AEC) undertaking a contentious redistribution of boundaries. Following the 2004 election, due to population growth in Queensland, the number of electorates in New South Wales was reduced by one, thus a redistribution was required. Interestingly, the 2004 boundaries for Eden-Monaro still contained the correct number of voters required by the redistribution quota. But due to the methodology the redistribution committee used in determining the boundary changes, a section of coastal Eden-Monaro, including Bateman's Bay and its surrounds, was transferred to Gilmore. Those numbers lost from my electorate had to be made up by expanding the electorate westerly over the mountains, for the first time including Tumut and Tumbarumba, and other nearby towns that came within Eden-Monaro. This was disappointing. Bateman's Bay was a reasonably strong area for me, where I had nurtured support progressively over each election since 1996. Tumut and Tumbarumba were dominated by the timber manufacturing industry, an industry with very strong union control. A completely new area quite separated from Eden-Monaro's traditional area, a unionised workforce, replaced a significant Bateman's Bay population that had been voting in Eden-Monaro since Federation. Additionally, Tumut and Tumbarumba had been shifted between the electorates of Farrer and Riverina several times during the past decades, upsetting some locals who regarded themselves as 'redistribution pawns'. While a redistribution is totally independent of government, the people took out their frustration on me, a member of the government.

I mention this process in detail as, between 2007 and 2010, another redistribution in New South Wales occurred, reverting the boundaries of Eden-Monaro to virtually the 2004 boundaries. The people of Tumut and Tumbarumba were again 'pawns'. At the time of the 2007 redistribution, the boundary changes made no sense to me, and it was frustrating to see the boundaries revert to 2004 boundaries again in 2010. If I had fought the 2007 election on the 2004 or 2010 electorate boundaries, I know the result would have been so much closer. But whether close enough, we will never know. Ironically, as Special Minister of State, I had ministerial responsibility for the Australian Electorate Commission (AEC) but obviously, and rightly, was unable to influence the redistribution committee's decisions.

What I was able to influence was a trial of electronic voting. In November 2006, I introduced the Electoral and Referendum Legislation Amendment Bill 2006. The bill included two trials to take place during the 2007 election, one for blind and vision-impaired people, and one for Australian defence personnel serving overseas. Blind and vision-impaired people had never been able to submit a secret ballot as they always required someone to assist them in casting their vote. A computer-based system was the basis of the trial and it was conducted at 30 pre-poll voting centres located around Australia. Voters seated at a computer and using headphones were prompted to select their preferred order of candidates. A paper ballot paper was printed and then included in the normal counting of votes. While it was effective and very well received by visually impaired voters, it was also costly on a per-vote basis. With Defence personnel serving overseas at the time of an election, it had been estimated that up to a third were not able to have their vote counted due to the time it took to receive an absentee vote and to respond. This meant that possibly some 1500 voters were disenfranchised. The trial provided those personnel with the option of voting electronically via the Defence Department's secure network. I was proud to introduce both reforms.

The dominance of WorkChoices, and the Coalition's lengthy time in office, resulted in a somewhat complacent electorate, making the decision to 'let the other mob have a go' somewhat easier. Rudd, often portraying himself as 'Howard lite', gave the electorate confidence that nothing much would change except that there might be a few new ideas to add to the great stability they had experienced over the previous almost 12 years. As we now know, the ensuing 12 years have been ones of instability, including during the Coalition's time in office after 2013.

The mood for change was evident throughout my electorate over the final six months of the year. I was often given the 'cold shoulder' by electors when attending community functions and when door-knocking homes. It was not so much that people were angry with me, they were simply ready for a change, sensing the country was about to change the government. Therefore, as had occurred at the previous 14 elections since 1972, the people of Eden-Monaro would ensure they had their member as part of the new government. Losing the election on 24 November 2007, while very disappointing, did not come as such a big surprise to me.

13

A VIEW FROM FORDE

KAY ELSON

As a proud member of the 'Class of 96', I was privileged to serve throughout the duration of the Howard Government. The people of my working-class electorate of Forde epitomised the 'Howard battlers' – from the struggling but aspiring suburbs in Logan City, to the regional townships on the outskirts of the Scenic Rim with farms and ageing communities facing real and protracted economic challenges. Nearly a year before the 2007 election I made the personal decision that I would not be seeking another term. This meant that I had both an insider's perspective on the way the Coalition Government operated in its final term and, by working closely with my local Liberal candidate, an observer's perspective on how the 2007 campaign was conducted.

While there was an 'it's time' element within the electorate, I believe it is fair to say that the roots of our demise in 2007 were actually sown in our somewhat unexpected 2004 victory. First, Labor learnt the lesson of courting defeat with an inexperienced and erratic leader (Mark Latham) who made the electorate feel less than 'relaxed and comfortable'. So much so that by 2007 they packaged Kevin Rudd as John Howard 2.0 – a younger, cooler version but still 'an economic conservative'.

Second, having won a third 'unexpected' victory, we complacently went into the 2007 election recycling the same prototype campaign that had previously produced results. It was apparent at the time that 2007 called for a much more creative and innovative approach. Third, gaining a majority in the Senate in 2004 meant that, as a government, we no longer had the pressing political imperative of winning our policy arguments with the weight of public opinion. We 'had the numbers' and it fundamentally changed how the government had operated since 1996.

I will address each consideration in more detail but a few points need to be made clear. The public were not 'waiting with a baseball bat' for John Howard, as they had been for Paul Keating in 1996. They were waiting sheepishly to hand him the proverbial gold watch and send him into the retirement they had heard so much speculation about in the media. The 2007 election was not about voting out a government that had not performed or delivered. On the contrary, John Howard had been such an exemplary leader and delivered so much that he had made government seem almost easy. Debt paid back: tick. Budget in surplus: tick. Borders controlled: tick. Too easy. Anyone could do it.

In fact, there is an argument to be made that the apparent ease with which John Howard had carried the prime ministership, and the overall success of our government, was a catalyst for the revolving door of prime ministers that was to come: when each successive prime minister could not deliver similar (or even close) results, it was characterised as a personal failing rather than a case of unrealistic expectations. I am not arguing for a minute that there were not personal failings aplenty in those prime ministers who followed. But I think the public have now been shocked into realising that government, and especially economic management, is not simple and easy. It is a testament to John Howard, Peter Costello and the Howard Government generally that the Australia people ever believed it was.

Before 2004 the Howard Government had a history of seemingly impossible policy achievement, despite (or perhaps because of) not having control in the Senate. Privatising Telstra, changing the tax system and introducing the GST, legislating Work for the Dole, stricter gun laws, offshore detention for asylum seekers, tougher national security in the wake of 9/11, and changing the waterfront industrial relations policy. All achieved by 'bringing the Australian people along', as Howard often described it. Explaining why change was needed, building our case, selling our message and making the point at every opportunity. Winning public sentiment was crucial to applying the pressure to get the votes from either Labor or the cross-bench in the Senate.

After 2004 that political imperative no longer existed. Whether consciously or not, the way we had conducted government shifted. Public consensus was nice, but no longer imperative. We had stopped bringing people along – and it was reflected in internal processes and attitudes as well.

WorkChoices was a case in point. Despite a massive media advertising campaign, it was staggering how little material was produced for parliamentarians to distribute early in 2007 to counter the union campaign. While local members were hearing angry words in their electorates, the central campaign provided very little to help rebut the scare campaign, creating a vacuum that Labor happily filled. Instead, so many parliamentarians were told that 'WorkChoices isn't an issue'. In 1998, by contrast, the views of local members were sought and they were consulted about the problems of selling the GST to an anxious and sometimes confused electorate. In the many months leading to the 2007 election there was very little urgency or sense that we needed to persuade people to stay onside.

I will not argue the policy merits – they are either sound or 'over-reach' depending on your point of view. But our political approach to this important reform was indulgent and arrogant. And I do not believe we would have found ourselves in that position if we had needed to convince the Senate, via the public, to legislate crucial changes to industrial relations. We would have had to argue the case, and ultimately the legislation itself would have been tempered. The public did not understand WorkChoices and, from the outset, and in the subsequent early 2007 vacuum, Labor and the unions were the only ones 'explaining it' to them. In my electorate people could not comprehend that the same prime minister who had been the battlers' champion now wanted to cut their wages. To them, it was proof that the government had lost touch and had been in office too long.

In Canberra, there was also a perceptible shift in the emphasis that the prime minister and ministry placed on actively consulting the backbench. Since 1996, it had been a hallmark of our government, and regularly included intimate dinners with backbenchers to sound out the mood in the electorates. The discussions were respectful and robust and were focused on how to tackle issues that were biting outside Canberra. Those dinners became fewer and far between. It was harder to meet with ministers and the prime minister – minders now took their place as go-betweens. Our government became one further step removed from the Australian people. It is human nature that complacency inevitably creeps in with time – in relationships, in jobs and in governments. Our numbers in the Senate just made it worse.

At the same time, in the public arena, two of our key strengths were apparently crumbling – leadership stability and keeping interest rates low. Our own members clumsily fuelled speculation about a 'succession' in the media. It became a spectacular own goal and undermined the strength and certainty the prime minister had always represented, especially after 2001. Despite exceptional economic management, continuing balanced budgets and the establishment of the Future Fund, the increases in interest rates (six times in two years) put a question mark over our credentials. This meant our massive poll advantage over Labor on this key issue narrowed dramatically. Leadership uncertainty, interest rate rises and WorkChoices all raised anxiety in the electorate. Australians were no longer 'relaxed and comfortable'. With hindsight, it is all relative, given the destructive chaos that was to ensue in the coming decade.

Having the high-profile journalist and television presenter Maxine McKew contesting the prime minister's own seat added to the perception of erosion. This was gleefully reported by an increasingly hostile media that had become bored and had shifted their focus to climate change and more activist issues. The perception of a dying government was not helped by the number of Coalition parliamentarians choosing to retire – 12 in the House of Representatives (including me) and five in the Senate. Labor capitalised by portraying Kevin Rudd as a safe pair of hands, capable of doing exactly what John Howard had done for so many years. He was John Howard-lite (to quote Tony Abbott) but with a more caring emphasis on health, education and the environment. How wrong those depictions of him proved to be. I am still amazed that the 'BS-meter' of the Australian people never moved before the election, although those who knew him were well acquainted with his shortcomings. That it took his own party removing him from the prime ministership for the Australian people to belatedly see the real Kevin Rudd remains surprising to this day.

At an organisational level, our federal campaign did not do enough to point out the risk of turning to Labor. On the contrary, we did the opposite. I believe our campaign slogan, 'Go for Growth', displayed a terrible tin ear. What did that mean to people in my electorate who were worried about their jobs and rising interest rates? Their translation was, 'Helping big business cut your pay so they can make bigger profits'. It provided further 'evidence' that our focus was not on them, but on money. This actually fed into Labor's WorkChoices scare and their overall narrative. How did that slogan in any way explain the economic risks to a whole generation of young voters with no adult knowledge of how bad the economy had been under Keating? 'Go for Growth' was incomprehensible at best to Howard's battlers, and elitist and uncaring to those who worried about health, education and the environment. It was a further sign that the Coalition was out of touch and needed to be moved on.

Even putting aside the worst possible slogan choice, I believe our 2007 campaign was not nimble, creative or forceful enough to counter the flash of 'Kevin 07' and the cash of the unions' advertising campaign (by most estimates, well over $30 million). As someone looking in – not a candidate – I saw a re-hash of old methodology, old graphics, old campaign tools and old approaches. It looked tired. We looked tired.

In contrast, Kevin Rudd harnessed the beginnings of a new wave of interest in social media activism. The youthful and positive image of young Australians in their 'Kevin 07' T-shirts being engaged and interested was a positive balance to the unions' scare campaign about the real and personal impact of an 'out of touch and out of date' government. Hindsight always provides greater clarity. History has certainly shown that the vast majority of Australian people now regard Prime Minister Howard and the Coalition Government he led very highly. I am still stopped regularly in local shopping centres by those who recount the Howard years with admiration and longing for those days to return. We achieved some tremendous things for our country. In the post-Menzies era, there has only been one four-term government with the same prime minister throughout. It is a testament to John Howard's character and political skills that he was able to work so successfully, and also so closely with our National Party colleagues, to keep a steady leadership team in place through some very turbulent times, to introduce tough and necessary policy, and to peak at the right time for four successive elections, if not a fifth.

Some have said that many factors in the 2007 election delivered a perfect storm that helped sweep Kevin Rudd to power. But quite a few of those factors were of our own complacent making. We certainly did not even attempt a modern and creative re-telling of our successful and inclusive 'For all of us' campaign that helped bring the Australian people along with us for so many years. That the electorate was not waiting with baseball bats suggests that, as a party and a government, we could and should have done more. People tend to forget that Labor's victory in 2007 was not the landslide that 1996 had been for the Coalition. John Howard's first government had a 45-seat majority; that enjoyed by Kevin Rudd's government was only 27 seats. That said, it felt like it in Queensland where 10 per cent swings in some booths were common.

Looking back, there were measures we could have taken as a party organisation and a government to ensure that the prime minister was able to decide the timing and circumstances in which his stellar political career came to a close. To me, the 2007 election was a sad final epitaph for a strong, caring, inclusive, diverse and productive government that always had the national interest at the front of its mind.

14

A VIEW FROM DEAKIN

PHIL BARRESI

The Coalition Government's comprehensive victory in 2004 would, in part, influence the Australian political discourse for more than a decade; even beginning perhaps the most controversial period in Australian political history. From a marginal seat member's perspective, the election win and subsequent three-year period in office can best be described by paraphrasing Charles Dickens' classic line, as the 'best of times and the worst of times'.

Members of parliament, Liberal and National candidates, and their families, staff and supporters were all anxious on election night. As the count progressed there was a distinct early voting trend away from Labor, with the aggressively toned Mark Latham at the helm. The Australian people were settling on what they knew and respected – a Howard Government was safe and secure, and one with which the electorate felt comfortable. In Deakin we gained a 3.5 per cent swing to the government, the first time in decades we had secured victory without having to rely on preferences. Popular opinion was that the Goods and Services Tax (GST) reform we fought for two elections was now gone and the electorate was comfortable with the government. The economy was being managed well, prosperity could be seen, and voters were relatively happy.

Coming into the 2004 election we had a proven strong leadership team – Howard, Anderson and Costello, and a Cabinet brimming with talented performers. But it was not just the leaders and the front bench: the Coalition backbench was united and supportive of our leaders and any potential disunity that crept out was quickly managed. These were the best of times. On reflection, these were also the genesis of the worst times, as we became complacent and never seriously considered the future with any political strategy for what life would look like beyond a Howard-led government.

Throughout history, it is commonplace to see examples that demonstrate the after-effects of resounding victories on the battlefield – be they political or otherwise. Such victories can evoke hubris, feelings of invincibility and overt dominance toward the vanquished. I recall that early euphoria within the party room in 2004, the illusion that our newly gained victory and electoral margin was akin to a cloak of invincibility. The feeling was further extended when the Labor Party re-elected Kim Beazley to replace a seemingly troubled Mark Latham. Our view was that Beazley was beatable and Howard was his controlling nemesis. Little did we realise this change of leader would trigger further the leadership troubles within the Labor Party, which would ultimately work in its favour.

During the Howard Government terms, we had discussed the continuing challenges of intergenerational growth – the three P's: population, participation and productivity. The latter two would lead us to a policy pathway for our eventual defeat. Many of our cheer squad in the media and some in the party room were under the illusion that with a majority in the Senate for the first time in 20 years, we could now revisit contentious policy that we had previously discarded. Some called for us to remedy the failings of former conservative governments, which in their time had strong mandates in both Houses yet avoided difficult policy reforms such as industrial relations.

These policy musings by our Liberal and National Party supporters were underpinned by the fact we had developed a reputation as good economic managers under the stewardship of Howard and Costello, supported by exceptional ministers in Richard Alston, David Kemp, Peter Reith and Nick Minchin, to mention a few. The Howard Government had already delivered significant changes in tax, waterfront, asset privatisation such as the Telstra sale, new trading agreements, and taking control of Australia's borders.

At an electorate level we could evidence the reforms through the popular initiative to bring back vocational education at the secondary school level. The much-anticipated Automotive Manufacturing and Technology Skills Centre was established on the grounds of Ringwood Secondary College as a partnership between several local schools and the two levels of government – these reforms and more were part of our continuing quest to make a difference to the nation and to be re-elected.

Howard's government increasingly provided a stark contrast to the mismanagement of previous governments. As political history demonstrates, however, when money is safe and secure, people's minds drift to non-economic policy issues that concern the 'relaxed and comfortable' voting public. From 2004 these issues became more prominent and the public began to question the direction of the government on other matters. The nation's lengthy enjoyment of sustained growth had created a thirst for more cutting-edge political reforms, providing a reassured electorate of an even lengthier period of prosperity. Paradoxically these were the twin forces working against us and we did not recognise it or, indeed, respond in a manner that satisfied the electorate during this final term. Let me explain this in terms of strategy failure.

I recall early in my political career contrasting strategy with the hierarchy of human needs theory as set out by renowned American social psychologist, Abraham Maslow. The theory has at its base the core non-negotiable human needs – physiological needs such as food, shelter, air and clothing. These are followed by safety needs, namely security, order, law and freedom from fear. If these core human needs are not met, individuals and society become nervous and seek protection elsewhere.

In the three years to the 2007 election, what the government strategists could not see was that a perfect storm was developing around the most basic of human needs. The Howard Government was perceived as threatening the community and their comfortable lives. We failed to realise the impact of our decisions until it was too late. We were convinced that what we were doing was right for the country.

In modern society a person's security, identity and future rely on financial security. How much money they accumulate, the access they have to it, how they can use it, and the manner in which they earn their money all play a part in their personal security. If their financial wellbeing is threatened, then so is their overall security, and anger, resentment and resistance will set in. At a community level this was exemplified by one specific policy initiative – industrial relations reform.

WorkChoices was born on the back of the industrial fights of the 1970s and 1980s. To some who fought those battles there was unfinished business, especially in the Keating Government's introduction of unfair dismissal laws. To some, these laws had evolved into an easy earner for those seeking 'go away' money. Stories of extreme cases of unfair dismissal where criminality was a reason for termination were being reversed by the courts or requiring the employer to make a significant payment to the sacked worker motivated some in the government to seek change to legislation. The response from our side was simple: 'We have the numbers in the Senate, let's use them'.

The controversial bill was passed, as we believed we were providing employers and workers with an equitable, rebalanced industrial relations system. The backlash was immediate and emotional. According to the advertising blitz by the unions and anti-government forces such as GetUp!, workers would have no job security and would be made to work hours that did not consider families. It was brutal, and their messages were being heard. We failed to consider the severity and strength of this feeling. When thousands marched in the streets, filled town halls and sporting fields like the Melbourne Cricket Ground, the message was clear. And yet, even at that point, it was not too late to make the necessary adjustments.

Security of workers' rights

In my electorate of Deakin, concerned residents were expressing their anxiety for their children and grandchildren, questioning why the government wanted to attack families. We did not. But that was the message they could hear. Late in the fourth term I chaired the taskforce asked to review and recommend changes to the legislation following community-wide consultation conducted with Minister for Workplace Relations Joe Hockey. After a series of meetings in Melbourne with the retail and hospitality sectors, Hockey and I both realised that we were in deep political danger. We were confronted with example after example of Australian Workplace Agreements (AWAs) that did away with basic rights. Templated agreements were being written up *en masse*. The much-anticipated employer industry campaigns in support of the government never materialised. Many preferred to go to ground rather than have their members exposed in parliament for breaches of conditions and wages. Parliament was used day after day to highlight illegal abuses, and newspapers ran stories of young people being exploited. We made amendments but the perception was already taking hold that Howard was attacking family security.

Neighbourhood street meetings were often hostile. Highly conservative regions of my electorate – Blackburn, North Ringwood and Heathmont – were increasingly venting on social issues: the plight of asylum seekers and reduced ABC funding, but none more than on labour reforms.

During this period our credentials as sound economic managers were being questioned by the public. John Howard proclaimed during the 2004 election campaign that interest rates would always be lower under a Coalition government and, until that point, it had been the case. Prosperity was rising and investment into the housing market was easier than at any other time in recent history – the best of times. Soon after the 2004 election the Reserve Bank began to increase interest rates to spike prosperity demand in fear of the impact of inflationary pressures on the economy. The additional threat to the other basic human need – shelter, as evidenced by the family home – was beginning to have an influence.

The promise Howard made in 2004 of low interest rates was now seen as a yoke around our neck and the government was now blamed for each increase, adding to the perception that the government was threatening people. First their jobs, now their homes. Reinforcing the negative perception further, on Melbourne Cup Day during the 2007 election campaign period, the Reserve Bank raised interest rates to an 11-year high.

At this point we can add in another national development threatening the basic needs of life – the 'Millennial Drought'. As far back as 2006, at a function in my electorate, Howard raised growing public concern about water shortages and water management. The drought was affecting our crop and cattle and sheep regions. It was very dry throughout 2006. The likelihood of drought-breaking rain was a distant hope. Overlay this desperation with the new developments in climate change science and the debate about climate impacts was becoming white-hot politically. The perception was that Howard was a 'climate change denier' and this term was then used about others within the government, developing a perception we were not up for the challenge and our government was out of touch. No matter the language or the actions of the prime minister, we could not shake the idea that we were not supportive of the Kyoto Protocol, which was completely false, as we were acting and meeting our targets.

Politics, very often, has nothing to do with reality; it is frequently about manipulating perceptions. The way the perceptions of climate change denialism were being manipulated by Labor, GetUp! and supportive media was dangerous for the government.

Voters were frustrated with the government and they wanted something different, something new, some hope to address the list of threats to their wellbeing. The change of momentum came when Labor turned on the always steady Kim Beazley and went to highly ambitious Kevin Rudd. Here was a man who was purported to have been plotting toward leadership, briefing the media and working the numbers, for many years. His moment had arrived. With the change of Opposition leadership came the popular opinion that Howard had Rudd's measure. The self-confident Queenslander, who had never held ministerial office, would be seen as too inexperienced for the job.

Coalition leadership tensions ultimately became an openly discussed issue some months before the election, when Peter Costello was seen as jockeying to replace John Howard. It culminated in the open canvassing of a leadership push on the eve of the Asia-Pacific Economic Cooperation (APEC) summit with meetings among some Cabinet ministers taking place at Kirribilli House, the prime minister's Sydney residence. As a backbencher fighting for survival, I can affirm that these manoeuvrings were conducted without our participation, let alone our knowledge. We were trying to win the battle on the ground. For many backbenchers, the last thing they wanted was leadership tension and party-room chaos. As an orderly transition was never on the table, many members were convinced a coup was, therefore, off the table. As many backbenchers owed their political survival to both Howard and Costello, they would not accept the unceremonious removal of one half of the duo during the last weeks of government.

While I am sure the discussions on a possible leadership change did not have a significant impact on voting intentions, it did give rise to the argument that the government was tired and needed renewal or replacement. On reflection, the horse had already bolted and any late push only confirmed we were out of touch with modern Australia. Sadly, to this day, political parties of all persuasions fail to learn the lesson from the corporate world: build a succession plan into your future for continuing survival. It is a prudent investment in continuing effectiveness.

Although Labor had experienced a coup, leadership change happened mid-term and resonated with the public. They seemed to think Beazley's time had come and gone. What better replacement, many thought, than the man who sounded like a younger version of Howard – a Labor economic-lite. The electorate warmed to the likeable, energetic, moderate-sounding and younger-looking leader. Rudd pitched himself as an economic conservative. It did not take the electorate long to realise they had been badly misled, but by then he had won the election.

The branding of Rudd as 'Kevin 07' was catchy and fresh. It had appeal especially to the under-30s, who had never known a Labor government and thought Howard was unable to talk to their demographic. 'Kevin 07' was well supported through Labor's creative use of the new social media channels. It was obvious our campaign team were yet to comprehend the power and influence of campaigning in this new medium. Labor targeted the tech-savvy generation with messages of freshness, job security, continuation of economic prosperity and attentiveness to their social values. In contrast, the Howard Government campaigned on 'more of the same' – good as it was. The national vote showed that the campaign excited no-one, especially not in the marginals. Many people took for granted the national prosperity in which they had an increasingly large share.

A number of humiliating human rights issues were raised, which added to the feeling of a government that was harsh and cared little for people in distress. The controversial immigration cases of Cornelia Rau (an Australian permanent resident with mental illness who was detained after claiming she was a German tourist), Vivian Solon (an Australian citizen wrongfully deported to her former country of origin, the Philippines) and Dr Mohamed Haneef (who was falsely accused of assisting terrorists and had his Australian visa cancelled) together with the mandatory detention of asylum seekers were features of our immigration regime that attracted substantial criticism. The community, along with some members of our own backbench, began to contest the humanity of Coalition policies. It was difficult to develop an effective counter-narrative.

In Deakin, immigration was only one of the policy issues that was bombarding my office daily. Early in our final term of office I arranged with the Minister for Immigration, Senator Amanda Vanstone, to visit the Baxter Detention Centre in South Australia.

Along with two colleagues, Bruce Baird and Petro Georgiou, we were the first parliamentarians to be given access to the facility. Asylum-seeker issues continued to run hot in the electorate, even to the point where a human rights lawyer was threatening to launch lawsuits against me personally. I was keen to see for myself the conditions under which asylum seekers were held, and then to report to my constituents in an informed way, especially concerning the welfare of one particular asylum seeker who had been in detention for more than six years on the grounds of being stateless – Peter Qasim. My intention was to demonstrate that compassion in immigration policy is possible without compromising the integrity of our border control policy.

In the end this issue, along with others, such as ABC funding, Indigenous affairs, youth unemployment and climate change, paled beside the potency of the union movement's well-organised, and orchestrated, Your Rights at Work campaign. Unions worked as a co-ordinated group along with activist group GetUp! to establish well-resourced and paid electorate campaign teams. Campaign workers drawn from within and external to the electorate included nurses, firefighters, teachers and ambulance employees: highly respected professionals door-knocking and letter-writing to the electorate advising voters they would lose their jobs unless a Rudd Government was elected to repeal the WorkChoices legislation. It was a very simple, yet clever campaign.

I knew I was now fighting for political survival. Deakin was earmarked as a key electoral battlefield in Victoria, alongside the seats of Latrobe, Corangamite and Dunkley. In my view, we distributed enough material to the electorate and expended an unprecedented amount on advertising to convince voters to support us for another term. As the sitting member I could not have done any more in the electorate to support that message. But we could never match the millions of dollars the unions and GetUp! were spending to support the Opposition's cause.

The party's response to the massive Your Rights at Work campaign was to fight at a local level. Sitting members were directed to highlight their electoral achievements and personal affinity with their community, and to emphasise that they would fund the local issues of greatest importance to their neighbourhood. The aim was to demonstrate 'the local MP who listens and acts'. This was a strategy that had made a positive difference in the past. Despite the warnings, I remained optimistic that, at least, I would be re-elected even if the government lost office.

The notorious No Tolls on Scoresby campaign, blackspot funding, and removal of level crossings in the electorate resonated strongly with voters in my area. In fact, traction was being made on one key election promise – the undergrounding of the rail line at the Springvale Road bottleneck in Nunawading. Labor would never support it. The Shadow Minister for Transport, Martin Ferguson, had previously made his views about federal funding for suburban transport infrastructure well known. The impact of this one project was significant. With two weeks to polling day – in spite of the fierce union campaign – I remained confident of success on 24 November. Labor then announced it would match the Coalition's funding commitment, ending the momentum towards the government.

It was clear that no amount of spending promises could convince the electorate to switch on to our message and, when it did, Rudd matched any and every pledge and promise. Our tactic ultimately undermined our own electoral advantage – being good economic managers. Rudd claimed that the spending promises were the result of a Coalition government in a state of desperation. Although he matched them, the Australian people agreed with Rudd. The government looked desperate and willing to throw fiscal restraint to the winds in order to retain power.

The rising engagement of community action groups effectively working against the government was gaining significant traction in Deakin and influenced the voting preference of those who would normally have supported me. Non-conservatives who respected my grassroots work in the electorate, and welcomed the many improvements I had brought to the community, decided to join the growing movement against the government. At one private business roundtable dinner, Howard proclaimed to the business leaders present that if he went, so would the member for Deakin. A sobering reminder of the fragile situation faced by marginal seat members.

Whenever an official campaign is announced, political strategists aim to seize the momentum as early as possible, to win the first week and build a base of support for the following weeks. During this first week a significant health policy was to be launched in Deakin, giving me the presence of the entire leadership team, their spouses and other local members and senators. The national spotlight for one day would shine on Deakin.

It did, but not in a positive manner. Due to a series of unfortunate problems in scheduling his travel, the Minister for Health Tony Abbott arrived late for a controversial National Press Club debate on health policy with his Opposition counterpart, Nicola Roxon. They had a minor verbal altercation when he finally turned up. It did not look good. Nor did the negative publicity we attracted from a run-in between Abbott and the critically ill mesothelioma sufferer, Bernie Banton. The week got worse. These incidents, along with the Lindsay electorate campaign brochure fiasco (involving the candidate's husband and mischievous, false claims about Islamic extremists supporting the Labor candidate), put us on the back foot, adding weight to the question: 'Is it time for a change to a more disciplined and conservative-looking Opposition?'

As the polls closed on 24 November 2007, early results indicated a substantial swing against the government. We lost 22 seats in the House of Representatives and, in the electorate of Deakin, we endured a swing away of 6.2 per cent. We suffered a staggering loss of 6000 votes. These voters eventually returned to the Coalition in 2013. Deakin remains a solid Liberal seat, although it is still considered marginal according to technical definitions.

On a personal level, an overwhelming feeling of disappointment and dejection took hold, particularly for the many hundreds of people who had supported the campaign. To witness the dirty tactics of union heavyweights against our ageing and loyal supporters at the polling booths, shouting through megaphones, tearing down bunting and generally being intimidating, added a further depressing note to the day.

On television, I watched John Howard concede defeat. I was deeply impressed. He was a statesman to the end. The moment reminded me, too, that I was a servant of the Liberal Party, which had extended to me the privilege of serving the community in which I lived. I retain pride in the work I did representing the Deakin community in the Federal Parliament.

Howard was highly respected by his colleagues and by the community as well. This respect was not universal. But the electorate knew what they got with John Howard – he was the ultimate conviction politician. Come the 2007 election, they no longer shared his convictions. In the electorate of Deakin, the difference between success and failure came down to the intensely personal WorkChoices campaign driving the perception that the government was heartless, unconcerned about the impact of its policies on workers' financial security and individual wellbeing. Feelings of being secure, relaxed and comfortable were becoming a distant memory. The mood was for change. Very soon, many of the Howard battlers came to regret their decision. Labor did not deliver the future it promised and Rudd was not the man they thought they knew when deciding he should lead the country. Whereas no-one regards the 'Rudd era' with any affection, the Howard years attract more respect as every day passes. It was an honour to have contributed to its effectiveness and its longevity.

15

A VIEW FROM BRADFIELD

BRENDAN NELSON

'Transition' was the word that stalked the Howard Government increasingly and relentlessly through its final term. When would the transition from Howard to Costello occur – and how? Pundits, commentators, and political scientists questioned only the timing and circumstances. But for most of us within the government, it was both complex and simple. It would be entirely in John Howard's hands. It would be his decision and his alone.

While it may seem strange to admit, I did not really know Peter Costello until after the election loss on 24 November 2007, nearly 12 years after coming to the parliament as the member for Bradfield in 1996. Along with my colleagues, we had seen his brilliance. We had marvelled at his tactical and strategic dominance of the House of Representatives and his ability to demolish his political opponents. We saw him mature as he crafted and delivered 11 budgets, guiding the nation's finances through thick and thin.

I had also clashed with him on matters of detail in the Expenditure Review Committee. His grasp of statistics and things like economic growth rates was phenomenal. But most of us did not really know Costello, the man. The intensity of parliamentary sittings was such that the only night free for dining with colleagues outside the parliament was Wednesday. He had a dozen fellow Coalition parliamentarians with whom he socialised and whose company he enjoyed and courted. It was a tight group. After the loss, I was finally introduced to him and the depth of his character. I discovered a man of rich intelligence, decisive, witty, deeply committed to his wife and family and imbued with solid values. But I also observed a man paradoxically somewhat shy and, perhaps, even risk-averse.

There was a widely held assumption that Costello would be the next Leader of the Parliamentary Liberal Party. This assumption had persisted for well over a decade as John Howard remained the man most able to deny Labor office. On the morning of 14 March 1993, Labor's political maestro, Graham Richardson, appeared on Channel 9's *Sunday* program with Laurie Oakes. Richardson's party had seen off John Hewson the day before as the man who had lost the 'unlosable election'. Oakes asked the triumphant Richardson who he thought should lead the Liberal Party. His voice acquiring a more sombre tone, Richardson replied, 'There's only one person in the Liberal Party that would come within a bull's roar of worrying us, and that's John Howard'. And so it would be. Howard returned to the leadership in January 1995 through the seamless, generous good grace of Alexander Downer. I 'stayed' with Howard and remained loyal. While Costello's emissaries would occasionally 'feel me out', my continuing commitment was to Howard. After the 2004 election, more than a few of my constituents would ask me when we would 'retire John Howard'.

Three experiences with John Howard as prime minister explain my loyalty to him. I had resigned myself to a long career on the backbench while Howard remained our leader. But after John Moore's unexpected retirement from parliament late in 2000, my phone rang as I sat in the local Bob Jane franchise waiting for the tyres on my car to be replaced. Howard telephoned and asked me to take up the position of Parliamentary Secretary to the Minister for Defence. I later learned it was Peter Reith, the incoming Defence Minister, who had persuaded Howard to give me an opportunity. As with everything, I threw myself into it. Almost a year later, following the 2001 election victory, Howard called me again. He asked if I would come into the Cabinet as the Minister for Education, Science and Training. Of course I said, 'Yes'. He then said:

> Brendan, while I am on the phone there are a couple of things I would like to say to you. After the 1998 election, two of your colleagues in New South Wales were promoted and you were not (Tony Abbott and Joe Hockey). Instead, I gave you the worst job I could give anyone, chairing the Sydney Airport Community Forum working on aircraft noise. You must have been angry and disappointed about that. But you just got on with it, never complained and did the job.

Howard went on with understatement and wisdom:

> I have had a few disappointments in my life, but how people deal with disappointment says much more about them than dealing with success … The other thing I want to say, Brendan, is this: you and I have different views on some issues. But I want you to bring your views to the Cabinet.

After the call and amidst my excitement, I reflected on the qualities of leadership to which I had just been exposed.

On Sunday 3 October 2004, I arrived in Launceston to address a large audience, campaigning for the election the following Saturday. Shortly before the dinner event, my mother called from

Adelaide to say that my father had just died. Knowing I physically could not get out of Launceston, I composed myself and did what I was there to do. I had phoned my campaign team back in Bradfield to let them know of my father's death, but I would continue.

That Sunday night was also the Rugby League grand final. John Howard had attended. I had just fallen asleep in my hotel room close to midnight when the phone rang. It was Howard. He called to express his condolences and offer comfort. He spoke about his own father, and the conversation lasted a good ten minutes. The prime minister, five days out from election day, was taking the time to call me. You do not ever forget those things.

The third experience that explains the loyalty that I, and most of the parliamentary ranks of the Liberal Party, had for Howard dates from early in my tenure as Minister for Defence. Private Jake Kovco had been killed in unclear circumstances in Baghdad. His was Australia's first death in the controversial Australian deployment to Iraq. Realising that the family were 'battlers' and the body was to arrive by private carriers in Melbourne at midnight, I arranged to go with the Chief of Army on the prime minister's Royal Australian Air Force (RAAF) jet to Sale, Victoria and pick them up. About to board the aircraft in Canberra, we learned that the wrong body had been placed on the plane from Kuwait. Going to RAAF Base Sale to tell them myself seemed the only responsible thing to do. Shortly after take-off, I called John Howard at the Lodge. Having told him of what had happened, he said, 'You're doing the right thing, Brendan. Don't hesitate to call me if you need to.'

In Sale, Jake's widow, Shelley, was deeply distressed and demanded to speak to the prime minister. I decided that she should. Five minutes of extremely robust things were said to Howard by an incredibly angry widow. She passed the phone back to me. John Howard said, 'Brendan, do you think I could have a conversation with you away from the Kovco family?' I stepped out on to the tarmac, expecting a dressing-down for having disturbed the prime minister in this way. Instead, he said, 'Brendan, what you are going through there is the hardest thing imaginable. If you need to call me at any time through the night, please do so.'

These experiences with John Howard were shared by ministers and backbenchers alike. As always, it is about character. Transcending his position, power, intellect, and other personal qualities was the character of the man, revealed to us often in unexpected, extraordinary circumstances.

As had happened with a degree of frequency, in mid-2006 a public spat erupted over the leadership and Peter Costello's possible ascension. On this occasion, however, a contemporaneous note emerged, written by former parliamentarian and Minister for Defence Ian McLachlan. The note had been written on a small piece of paper after a meeting between Howard and Costello late in 1994. Howard had apparently agreed to 'hand the leadership over' to Costello after a term and a half in office, should the Coalition win in 1996. Costello and his supporters tried to force Howard's hand. He said he would stay if his party wanted him to do so. Costello did not have the numbers. He did, however, have a choice. In fact, he had two choices. He could remain as Treasurer, praise Howard's leadership of the government and offer himself to the party room as leader if a vacancy for the leadership should come. In doing so he would pay respect to his own colleagues, whose decision it is to choose the leader.

Alternatively, Costello could have chosen to say words to the effect of, 'It has been a privilege to serve as Australia's Treasurer for a decade, but you have decided to remain as prime minister. I am going to resign and head to the backbench' to Howard, but did not. Instead, Costello did as he had done before. He huffed and puffed, metaphorically stamped his feet and, in doing so, galvanised support behind Howard.

In my view, Howard, knowing more about politics than most of us and sensing where it would end, would have done a deal. Howard would have arranged to vacate the Lodge by Christmas 2006. If he had not, Costello would have bled Howard from the backbench and been prime minister by March 2007, certainly before the budget. From my observation, he was not like Keating, who was willing to take a risk in his efforts to depose Hawke in 1991.

There was one notable leadership change in December 2006. The Labor Party replaced Kim Beazley with Kevin Rudd. Howard had – correctly, in my view – believed that he could beat Kim Beazley. He had a well-founded conviction that Beazley was not 'hungry' enough or aggressive enough for the top job. We will never know. Rudd certainly was. When Kevin Rudd positioned himself as an 'economic conservative', the electorate heard Tony Abbott describe Rudd as a 'younger version of John Howard'. The voters thought that was exactly what they were seeking.

The year 2007 would be our political demise. A truism in politics is that disunity is death. Just months into the year, Costello remarked to me, 'Have you noticed we're getting leaks?' I agreed, but I was certainly not the source. He named a recently appointed member of Cabinet. I knew we were on track to lose at two junctures in 2007. Peter Costello's 2007 Budget was his best since 1996, concentrating on families, home ownership, iron-clad fiscal consolidation and sovereign wealth funds. Yet the nation's most authoritative public poll, Newspoll, in the last fortnight of June when the budget had 'washed through' the electorate, gave Labor a 10-point two-party preferred lead.

Then it can be the little things. At a mid-year Cabinet meeting, I listened incredulously as debate concluded with agreeing for the

Commonwealth to take over the Burnie hospital in Tasmania. This vain attempt to hold the federal seat of Braddon would signal the government was serious about both health and regional Australia. It nonetheless violated the principles upon which the government had stood. I thought at the time, 'It's over'. But our fate was sealed on WorkChoices.

The Cabinet met three times to consider the wide-ranging reforms, which I supported. Collapsing a myriad of workplace relations awards into a streamlined number and further consolidating workplace agreements and flexible individual agreements to increase productivity made sense. I recall at the final meeting saying, 'We are not here for the sake of being here. We are here to do what is right for the country.' The failure to uphold the 'no disadvantage' test was a fatal error.

The Asia-Pacific Economic Cooperation (APEC) forum was held in Sydney in September 2007. Newspoll recorded Labor holding a 14-point two-party preferred lead over the Coalition, published on the eve of the leaders' gathering. Alexander Downer called. With Howard's agreement, he was organising an informal gathering of Cabinet ministers to canvass their views on the situation and specifically, if Howard should go. Except for Tony Abbott, Helen Coonan and Mal Brough, all came to Downer's hotel room on the Thursday night. Costello had not been invited. Downer, having already canvassed the three not present for their views, asked what should be done. He said that Howard wanted to know what we thought. I asked Downer two questions: 'Does John Howard believe we can win the election?' Downer said, 'No'. I then asked, 'Does John Howard believe he can hold his own seat?' With hesitation, Downer replied, 'No – but it depends what day you ask him'. The consensus, not agreed by all present, was that Howard should go. There was one critical proviso: only if he chose to do so himself.

I was among those who believed the Cabinet should not ask him to go. If he wanted to stay, then I would respect and support his decision. I told him this personally early the following week.

At the Sydney Opera House prior to the APEC leaders' dinner on the Saturday night, Costello asked me outside so we could talk away from the drinks and canapés. We walked alone around the perimeter of the building. He opened by saying that Howard's situation was hopeless and we now needed to change. Having canvassed the backbench, he was of the view that I had majority support to be his deputy. The election could be pushed into early 2008, and he and the new government could reposition on several key issues to give it a fighting chance of re-election. While agreeing that the proposition had merit, I told Costello that I would not be party to Howard being pushed from the prime ministership. His rusted-on devotees would be outraged by any such action and a worse electoral outcome would eventuate. If he went of his own accord, then yes, I agreed to stand for the deputy's position.

It is a matter of record that John Howard chose to stay and fight. As Janette Howard later said of her husband, he had never walked away from a fight before and would not do so then. The die was cast and our fate was sealed.

The messy, dogged issue of transition carried into the campaign. Tony Abbott contributed unhelpfully by suggesting during a media interview that if the government was returned, John Howard would serve for a year, then Peter Costello for two (or, perhaps, Howard for two years and Costello for one). The voters were even less impressed with that than with the multitude of spending promises. Australians had lost faith in us and nothing we were saying was changing their mind. During campaigning in Queensland, I had been booked to announce $500 000 for a set of traffic lights with Ross Vasta in the electorate of Bonner. Hours before the event I was told I was no longer needed, as the prime minister was going to do it. These were desperate days.

On election day as I made my way around the polling booths in Bradfield, the former Liberal Party Federal President, Tony Staley, telephoned. He asked me if I would stand and serve as Peter Costello's deputy in the event of the inevitable election defeat. Taken aback by the call, I told Tony that I simply wanted to get through the day. In the event that we did lose, I would be honoured to put my name forward for consideration as Peter's deputy.

I did election coverage for Sky News that night. As the parliamentary seats of colleagues and friends were declared lost, one Liberal member was returning to the House of Representatives with an increased majority. Malcolm Turnbull's election night event was an upbeat affair and he projected an air of great self-confidence in the electorate of Wentworth. Howard later told me that as he was being driven across the Sydney Harbour Bridge to the hotel event at which he would concede defeat, Turnbull called to detail his plans for the future. Howard told me that he simply said to Turnbull, 'Now is not the time'.

The morning following the election, I sat in the kitchen of our Sydney home with my wife, Gillian, and my most loyal confidant, the New South Wales Liberal Party Vice-President, Rhondda Vanzella. We discussed nominating for the deputy leadership and what it would mean for us, our lives and our family. I decided I would do it. I was literally speaking to Joe Hockey on the telephone just before midday about my decision, in the knowledge that he and several others would also likely nominate. Suddenly, Joe stopped and said, 'Costello's just announced he won't run for leader'. We were both silent, stunned. The Liberal Party, like all of us, was blindsided. We were unprepared for a future without either John Howard or Peter Costello. A short time later Malcolm Turnbull announced his candidacy for leader.

I was thrust into considering a tilt at the leadership. Many urged me to do so. Others felt that whoever led the party at that point would not be the next Liberal prime minister. A common theme I encountered was: 'Brendan, we have to have the Malcolm experiment. We have to get him through the system and out of here. Let him be leader now and be done with it.' There was an assumption that he would not succeed as leader. The sooner this happened, the better. While I could see the argument, I relied on my instinct. In life, you have to have a go. I had also seen enough to worry me about Malcolm Turnbull that year and did not want his influence to spread or be prolonged.

We were a party without Howard, Costello, and, effectively, Downer as well. We were about to go through a period of deep grief, anger and infighting. We needed a leadership style that would heal, embrace, and hold on to the Howard legacy while articulating a vision and setting markers for the future. In my view it needed to be an inclusive, consultative leadership. It would be important coming out of government to allow the surviving parliamentarians to have their voices heard and to let off steam in the party room and not in public. I also had to accept that former ministerial survivors, now Opposition frontbenchers, were exhausted. They were convinced the Coalition had years in Opposition ahead. Defeat had been delivered for three principal reasons.

The first was longevity. I read some focus group research from December 2006 conducted in the electorate of Mayo. Labor had just switched Beazley for Rudd. One female participant had said, 'I respect Mr Howard and what he has done, but I am over him'. In my opinion this reflected a national attitude. It gave most Australians no joy to effectively put down the much-loved family pet, but they had to. This is what they did. The second was overreach on workplace relations. The electorate thought we had gone too far into ideology unconstrained by the Senate majority unexpectedly delivered in 2004. The third was climate change. In refusing to ratify the Kyoto Protocol, we had been monstered on the symbolism around action on climate change, standing alone with President George W Bush. That the nation was in drought effectively escalated the importance of this issue.

Within a month of assuming the leadership, I concluded that Kevin Rudd was not the 'real deal'. He was not the man in the pamphlet who had come to the voters' letterboxes in 2007. I told my leadership group in January 2008, 'Australians have bought a Holden every year for 11 years. They have agonised over it and have now bought a Ford. It will not be until they find the tenth defect that they will throw their arms in the air and proclaim they were wrong. It will be a while, but this will turn. And it will turn quickly when it does.' Some listened, but others simply would not. They and most of the media and commentariat were shocked, unwilling to accept that I had been elected leader instead of Malcolm Turnbull.

New leaders of the opposition coming out of government usually get a reasonable chance to settle into their role. Nonetheless, they also become a lightning rod for criticism of the previous government and its flaws and failings. Just months into the job, I remarked to the Federal Director of the Liberal Party, Brian Loughnane, that while I knew it was going to be hard, nothing had prepared me for this. Brian proffered, 'Brendan, Kevin Rudd has just taken politics into the entertainment space and you are a player in it'.

It was a perfect storm. Rudd was the most popular Australian prime minister in modern polling history. Costello, while strongly supporting me, should have been the leader but did not want to be. Then there was Turnbull's unstoppable ambition. I had never encountered personal ambition of such depth and breadth, and doubt I ever will again.

In this messy, brutally gut-wrenching transition, a member of the public – a regular 'punter' – summarised it best in a way the professionals never could. I was standing in the queue for breakfast at the McDonald's at Sutton Forrest early one morning, on the way to Canberra a week after the national apology to the Stolen Generation. As I waited, Newspoll broadcast across Channel 9's *Today Show*: 'Preferred PM (Prime Minister) – Rudd 75 per cent, Nelson 15 per cent'. The man behind me proffered an assessment, 'Brendan, just because we like Kevin Rudd does not mean we do not like you. We just put the guy in.' He went on, 'But I will tell you one thing: I reckon this government is like the set of a western movie. Fake walls with sticks holding them up at the back. You wait and see.' When the 'sticks' fell down late in 2009, the Liberal Party galvanised behind Tony Abbott. The unplanned transition was complete, and another election was in sight.

PART VII

LEGACIES

16

THE SUCCESSION THAT WASN'T

TOM FRAME

John Howard and Peter Costello forged one of the most effective and enduring political partnerships in Australian history as prime minister and treasurer between 1996 and 2007. Not unlike the initially close relationship that existed between Prime Minister Bob Hawke and Treasurer Paul Keating, or before them, John Curtin and Ben Chifley, Howard and Costello shared a commitment to fiscal discipline and economic reform, especially in taxation and industrial relations policy.

Costello was ambitious and Howard's obvious successor, although the prime minister showed no signs of slowing down or relinquishing the post after five years in office. Labor made the Howard–Costello succession an election issue in the 2001 campaign, claiming the more popular Howard would retire in favour of the less popular Costello during the term of the coming parliament. In 2006, Labor concluded that Howard would never retire and made its own leadership decisions, replacing Kim Beazley (who had twice failed to defeat Howard in a national ballot) with Kevin Rudd.

During the November 2007 election campaign it was impossible for the Coalition to deny its senior leadership team was fractured. It was also difficult to deflect Labor's charge that the Liberals had no long-term plan for Australia because they lacked a long-term leader. The consensus view among critics is that Howard 'fumbled the leadership succession and lost control of two issues which, like the leadership messiness, were to damage him in the 2007 election: WorkChoices and climate change'.[1] Political commentators Wayne Errington and Peter van Onselen thought Howard 'made the one mistake in politics that he wouldn't be around to learn from – misjudging his optimal retirement date'.[2]

While personal disputes and professional rivalries are the essence of political drama and are much loved by commentators eager to inject colour and texture into their stories, only two questions of substance need to be considered. First, did the succession have a bearing on the government's performance in parliament and its conduct of public administration? Second, was the electorate so concerned about the squabbling that they switched their votes from the Coalition to Labor? After briefly examining the history of prime ministerial successions, the effects of the protracted speculation that Howard would retire sometime after the 1998 election, and the ways in which the prime minister and the treasurer both contributed to the persistence of disruptive tension, I will consider these two key questions. And I will conclude by suggesting that Costello's decision not to contest the leadership of the Liberal Party after the November 2007 election defeat was among the most significant for the Coalition and the country in the decade that followed the demise of the Howard Government.

Longevity and succession

For the first 50 years of Australian nationhood, a period when most people stayed in the same job for extended periods, none of the prime ministers served long enough for there to be talk of succession. The longest serving incumbents prior to Robert Menzies, who started his record incumbency of 16 years in 1949, were Billy Hughes, Stanley Melbourne Bruce and Joseph Lyons. Hughes was prime minister for a period of seven years and 105 days from 1915 to 1923, involving two changes of party allegiance along the way; Bruce served for six years and 255 days from 1923 to 1929 before losing office and his seat in the House of Representatives, the first and only one of two prime ministers to do so (the other being John Howard); and Lyons died in office after seven years and 91 days, serving as prime minister from 1932 to 1939.

Menzies' long incumbency was accompanied by occasional speculation about when he would retire and who would succeed him. In February 1961, an opinion poll revealed that 39 per cent of voters thought he should retire; 30 per cent of Coalition supporters thought his time was over. But his popularity rebounded in 1962 and 1963. Just before his 69th birthday, he was preferred by 79 per cent of Coalition voters, with the deputy prime minister, John McEwen, securing 2 per cent and the deputy Liberal leader, Harold Holt, being preferred by 1 per cent. When asked to nominate their preference for Menzies' successor, half said they had no idea. Only 21 per cent wanted Holt, 19 per cent wanted McEwen and only 3 per cent wanted the Attorney-General and Minister for External Affairs, Sir Garfield Barwick.[3]

Despite some historians claiming he deliberately despatched potential rivals to distant diplomatic, administrative and legal posts, leaving only the dutiful Harold Holt to wait his turn, Menzies never spoke publicly of succession plans or gave hints about retirement. Having achieved a record number of election victories, including by the narrow margin of one seat (after the election of the Speaker) in 1961, as the founder of the Liberal Party Menzies effectively managed a smooth departure at a time of his own choosing. He spoke with a few friends and colleagues before Christmas 1965 about retiring but did not discuss the matter with his deputy. He informed his Cabinet colleagues on 19 January 1966 and issued a very personal public statement the next day:

> Though I still work long hours, I can no longer sustain the very long hours of work which once delighted me. In short, I am tired; my pace has slowed down; I could not properly continue in office for very much longer and at the same time do justice to the growing problems of the nation.

Not to remain for at least two years after the election would be, he explained, 'unthinkable and electorally deceptive'. He was also conscious of what would follow:

> Our people have become accustomed to me, for better or worse, for so many years that it would be grossly unfair to my successor to give him insufficient time to make his own mark in his own way. I am sure that the right thing for me to do is to make way now.

Aged 71, he announced his decision suddenly and it took the press and the public by surprise.

Menzies anointed no-one to take his place and the party faithful were uncommitted. The transition to Holt was seamless, although more Coalition voters actually wanted McEwen, leader of the minority Country Party. (Menzies appeared to prefer Paul Hasluck as deputy party leader, having recommended his appointment to the Privy Council in the hope of raising his standing above that of William McMahon, who was, in fact, elected as Holt's deputy.)

The Coalition then won the November 1966 general election with a substantially increased majority – an unexpected result which significantly boosted Holt's credibility as prime minister. Bringing a different tenor to the prime ministership, Holt managed to create the impression that his government was different to the one led by Menzies despite there being no change in the ruling party. Having been complicit in Menzies' removal from the prime ministership in August 1941 and regretting it for the rest of his life, Holt was Menzies' ever-loyal deputy. He was content to wait until the leadership came to him a decade after he was elected Deputy Leader of the Liberal Party in August 1956. In being patient, Holt was rewarded with the respect and the loyalty of Cabinet colleagues when he became prime minister.

Those who followed Holt over the next ten years – John McEwen (who held the post briefly until the Liberals elected a successor to Holt, who drowned on 17 December 1967), John Gorton, William McMahon and Gough Whitlam – were in office for such brief periods that succession speculation did not begin, let alone gain momentum. Gorton faced a leadership challenge after the October 1969 election (the only re-elected prime minister ever to face such a challenge) and another in March 1971. The latter was resolved by Gorton resigning following a tied party-room ballot. He had been prime minister for three years and two months. Although Malcolm Fraser was prime minister for more than seven years from 1975 to 1983 and provoked an unsuccessful leadership challenge from Andrew Peacock in April 1982, he showed no signs of slowing down or retiring when he lost the March 1983 election. There had been no succession planning in anticipation of Fraser's departure at the age of 52. Indeed, Fraser told journalists early in 1983 that he only needed to win one more election after the present contest to be prime minister during the Australian Bicentenary.

After resigning the party leadership and deciding to leave parliament, Fraser let his colleagues know that 'Andrew Peacock would make a better leader than John Howard'. He later claimed that he preferred Peacock because, 'on the core liberal values, I had learned to have confidence in Andrew's attitude. I had come to be not so confident in John's.'[4] As Fraser was from Victoria and Howard from New South Wales, state loyalties predisposed him to supporting his Victorian colleague, Peacock. Fraser also viewed Howard's free market inclinations and social conservatism with suspicion.

Peacock and Howard contested the party leadership, with Peacock becoming leader and Howard his deputy. Fraser believed they would complement one another with the full spectrum of abilities and aptitudes needed for effective party leadership. Peacock and Howard saw things differently. Suspicion and distrust were never far from the surface of their interactions. The tension between the two men continued for a decade, with Howard replacing Peacock as leader in 1985 and then Peacock ousting Howard in 1989. Fraser later remarked that 'if he had known they were going to fight each other for the next ten years, he might have decided to stay in parliament himself, sought the leadership and contested the next election against Hawke'.[5] This was a reasonable assessment of the disastrous Howard–Peacock rivalry and its electoral consequences but an overly generous view of his prospects of attracting popular support and regaining the prime ministership.

As Peacock and Howard struggled for supremacy within the Liberal Party, Paul Keating's leadership ambitions within the Labor Party were being thwarted by Bob Hawke, who had been prime minister for more than five years and seemed determined to continue for five more. Hawke had become prime minister at the age of 53 (he was one year older than Fraser); Keating was 14 years his junior but had been in parliament for a decade before

Hawke was elected. Keating was impatient for his opportunity. In November 1988, Hawke reluctantly agreed on a succession plan at a brief meeting held in Kirribilli House (the prime minister's Sydney residence). Keating had asked for the meeting after Hawke had said his treasurer was not indispensable, a comment that deeply offended Keating, and insisted that their mutual friends, Bill Kelty, the Secretary of the ACTU, and businessman Sir Peter Abeles, attend as witnesses. Hawke would hand over to Keating before the 1993 election, assuming Hawke won in 1990 (which he did). In September 1990, Hawke told Keating he would retire after the Commonwealth Heads of Government Meeting scheduled for October 1991.

After Keating delivered an address to the Canberra press gallery in December 1990 in which he referred to himself as the 'Placido Domingo of Australian politics' and derided the prime minister's leadership, Hawke accused Keating of treachery and reneged on the agreement. By this time, Hawke's approval rating had fallen significantly. He was no longer one of Australia's most popular prime ministers. Late in May 1991, incensed that Hawke had cynically (as he saw it) used the agreement at Kirribilli to extract two more years as prime minister, Keating told the political journalist Laurie Oakes about the agreement and accused Hawke of failing to keep his word. Keating hoped that both his parliamentary colleagues and the public would turn against Hawke, although the existence of a deal that bypassed the will of the people and the Labor Caucus did not look good from any angle. The Leader of the Opposition at the time of the pact, John Howard, later observed:

> The two of them really had no right to make that agreement
> in the first place. They don't own the leadership of their
> party; it is a gift of the caucus. I was vaguely offended that it

was done in the presence of a corporate representative and a union leader. It was the apogee of the corporate state.[6]

Keating eventually toppled Hawke and became prime minister in December 1991. This was the start of a bitter and enduring feud that diminished both men over the ensuing two decades.

The tensions between Hawke and Keating and, to a lesser degree, Peacock and Howard, reflected the absence of formal procedures regarding leadership challenges in the rules of the major parties. Until recently, party leadership has been determined by the parliamentary party room and not by the wider membership. In this respect Australia was different to many similar countries, including Britain and Canada. It took the deposition of Kevin Rudd by Julia Gillard in 2009 and the resignation of Malcolm Turnbull in 2018 to prompt the adoption of new rules to make it much more difficult for incumbent prime ministers from either major party to be toppled.

Succession speculation

John Howard became prime minister when he was 56 – an age many people think is the prime of life. It did not take long, however, for succession speculation to begin. Given his age (which happens to be near the average age for incoming Australian prime ministers), some Liberals may have seen Howard as an interim leader whose essential role was to lay a firm foundation for Costello who, being 18 years younger, would provide long-term leadership of the party and the nation. The first time Howard mentioned leadership succession was on 22 February 1997. Reflecting on his first year in office, Howard spoke of a '10-year leadership transition'. He remarked: 'while my health lasts and I've got my marbles and I'm delivering good leadership and political success, you stay. But when that changes, you don't.'

Five months later, as the government prepared for an early election to gain a mandate to introduce a new tax system featuring a consumption tax, Costello raised the question of the party leadership for the first time. He claimed that his Liberal colleagues had asked him to replace Howard. He said: 'Look, bear this in mind, I helped John Howard become leader and I did that because I thought he was the right person to lead the party and he has my full support'. Howard responded, 'I think people are always after the top job in politics – nothing unusual about that. I'd be the last person to decry ambition.' This was the first of many casual references to the Liberal leadership made by both Howard and Costello, and early signs that it would become a source of tension.

On the eve of his 60th birthday (26 July 1999), Howard told journalists: 'I don't have any intention of retiring'. When asked two months later: 'Mr Howard, do you see Peter Costello as your successor as prime minister?', Howard replied: 'I am not thinking of any successions, I am thinking of winning the next election and remaining prime minister'. Yet a year later (on his 61st birthday) he told broadcaster Philip Clark that after the 2001 election, 'obviously one has to recognise, I'll then be in my sixty-third or sixty-fourth year … and nothing is forever'. On 15 October and with the election campaign underway, Howard talked openly of succession. He remarked: 'If I go, Peter Costello will become the leader'. He went on: 'You shouldn't assume I will retire. But I am being very upfront that it's something two years into my term I'll decide: whether I'm going to run again. We have no witnesses. We don't even have a deal.' The significance of the latter two statements was not apparent to voters at the time. Nor the import of the mixed messages the prime minister was sending to the treasurer. He would go in good time but at a moment of his own choosing.

Having secured a third election victory and responding to further questions about the leadership, Howard replied on 12 April 2002: 'The question of my successor will be a matter for the parliamentary party, if and when there's a vacancy and there's no vacancy'. Five days later he was asked: 'What do you think your heir apparent, Peter Costello, will be like as prime minister, eventually?', he responded: 'It's a purely hypothetical issue'. He then added: 'Nobody's immortal but when you are in a job and enjoying it and I hope, without sounding in any way presumptuous, doing it tolerably well, I won't put it any more strongly than that, you don't start talking about who might be doing it in the future'.

The succession was not raised again until 28 November 2002, when both Howard and Costello confirmed there had been a private discussion. The prime minister said: 'We have private discussions about a lot of things'. Asked whether he wanted to succeed Howard, Costello commented, 'Let's see what happens next year'. The *Australian* reported on 2 January 2003 that Howard was under pressure to remain prime minister until after the 2004 election from Coalition parliamentarians concerned about their prospects of retaining marginal seats. Two months later, in response to a comment that he had been hinting at retiring mid-term, Howard was now 'going to go straight through to the next election'. The key issue was Iraq, with Howard pledging to 'see this issue through'. Notably, Hawke had invoked the 1990–91 war in Kuwait to delay his departure. On 3 June 2003, Howard told the Liberal party room that he would continue as prime minister for as long as the party wanted him. Costello later mused: 'It wasn't my happiest day'. When the matter was raised again on 8 March 2004, Howard persisted with the same response. He would 'remain Leader of the Liberal Party for so long as the Party wanted me to and while it remained in the Party's interest that I should'.

Frustrated by the delay, for the first time Costello's supporters raised the prospect of a leadership handover after the election. Senator George Brandis commented on 7 May 2004: 'I think most people expect that if we win the next federal election there will be a peaceful, harmonious transition from Howard to Costello'. On 24 August 2004, Howard commented on his own political longevity, telling an audience of retirees: 'I think people should continue in the workforce for as long as they want to and as long as they're making a contribution and age is irrelevant'.

Possibly hoping to end speculation, Howard was interviewed by the *Australian* on 30 April 2005 in Athens. He declared: 'I'm not going anywhere … I still have got plenty of ideas and there are lots of things I want to do. I am not planning my post-prime-ministerial life.' The next day Costello was asked about Howard's so-called 'Athens declaration' and refused to rule out a leadership challenge. He told journalists: 'I don't think the events of the last 24 hours have helped the government or the Liberal Party'. An opinion poll published in Fairfax newspapers showed Costello trailing Beazley, who had returned to the Labor leadership in January 2005, as a potential prime minister – and Beazley continuing to trail Howard by a considerable margin. Labor's Treasury spokesman, Wayne Swan, remarked: 'I don't know how this farce will unfold but I can't see him [Costello] being there in six months' time'. Labor frontbencher Stephen Smith commented that 'everyone knows that Costello doesn't have the bottle to challenge Howard'. In a doorstop interview at Parliament House, Costello told reporters: 'I promise you I'm going to be around for a long time … I've been in politics a long time and there's still so much work to be done that I want to make a contribution.'

Three months later (30 August 2005), Costello told the Nine Network, 'I feel in a sense that I do lead in this country'. Costello's remark sounded like an echo of Keating's claim that he, rather than Hawke, had effectively led the Labor Government in the 1980s, particularly when the prime minister was dealing with family issues. When launching my biography of Harold Holt earlier the same month, Costello drew attention to the experience of an earlier member for Higgins. After noting that 'the passing of the mantle from Menzies to Holt lifted support for the Liberal Party', he praised Holt for 'reconsidering options that had previously been considered and rejected' and giving 'the Liberal Party an opening to modernise in response to changing social and economic factors at work in Australia'.[7] These were the very things that Costello wanted to do as prime minister if given the chance. Plainly, Costello was hoping to get at least 12 months in the top job before facing the voters. This would place him in a similar position to Holt four decades earlier. Howard was virtually being told he needed to retire in mid-2006 to give Costello sufficient time to persuade voters that his government was different to the one led by Howard and that it was one worthy of re-election.

On 7 October 2005, two days before the anniversary of his fourth election victory, the 66-year-old Howard again insisted that he was not thinking of retiring. Costello, realising he still did not have anywhere near the party-room support to succeed, publicly rejected any prospect of a leadership challenge. On 7 December 2005, he committed himself to delivering the 2006 Budget. By then, Costello and his supporters realised that Howard would not and could not be cajoled into retiring but thought that, after he celebrated a decade as prime minister in March 2006, there was a chance he might consider retiring. After all, Costello's supporters were entitled to think, Howard could not hope to win a fifth straight election. They thought Howard would want to leave office a winner, emulating Sir Robert Menzies, by departing at a time of his own choosing. But by mid-2006 and with the window Costello needed to establish himself as prime minister rapidly closing, a new approach was needed.

The McLachlan note

In 2001, journalist Paul Kelly of the *Australian* asked Howard whether he condoned 'Kirribilli-type' deals to ease the tensions that frequently accompany leadership successions and whether he had such a deal with Costello. Howard replied: 'Not when it involves misleading the Australian public. No, I don't. We have no witnesses. We don't even have a deal. We have nothing of the kind.' This was not the view of the former Minister for Defence, Ian McLachlan. He was present at a discussion between Howard and Costello about the long-term leadership of the Liberal Party when it was clear that Alexander Downer's leadership was in terminal decline in December 1994. McLachlan believed an undertaking had been given and received.

McLachlan had written himself a note detailing the essence of the conversation between Howard and Costello to which he had been party, a note he carried in his wallet for the next 12 years. McLachlan was unequivocal: Howard had given an undertaking to make way for Costello one-and-a-half terms into a Coalition government in return for Costello agreeing not to contest the party leadership should Downer resign. This was in many respects a strange undertaking, potentially making Howard a very short-serving prime minister. Although he had not sought undertakings from Howard in 1994, Costello, who had been elected Deputy Leader in 1994 and did not face a ballot for his position in 1995, certainly thought such an undertaking had been given. He evidently believed Howard was duty bound to honour what he considered a personal commitment, most probably in 1999 or 2000.

Howard, however, recalled the conversation differently. He thought it was neither a promise nor even a firm commitment. It was little more than an indication of intent that might change as circumstances changed. McLachlan reminded Howard of his obligation to Costello when he (McLachlan) decided to retire from politics in 1998. Howard did not feel himself obliged to make way for Costello, who made no mention of the December 1994 'undertaking' in any conversation with Howard at that time. Howard thought that McLachlan 'gave an inflated significance to the discussion because he was involved in it'.[8] McLachlan had also supported the ill-fated 'Joh for PM' campaign in 1987, which did much to derail Howard's chances of becoming prime minister that year.

The December 1994 'agreement' remained confidential until July 2006 when its existence was revealed in a newspaper article by journalist Glenn Milne, who sensed a deal might have been done, a suspicion confirmed when he raised the matter and received a 'no comment' response from McLachlan. Milne heard about McLachlan's note from a third party, probably a businessman, sympathetic to Costello. Liberal parliamentarian Alex Somlyay confirmed that McLachlan had made a note of the conversation, which was 'to make sure there was a peaceful transition' from Downer to Howard. In the media flurry that followed, Costello said there was an undertaking; Howard said there was not. Superficially, this looked like a re-run of the Kirribilli agreement between Hawke and Keating, although it was very different in that Howard was neither prime minister nor even leader of his own party. Howard was adamant: 'the situation is very simple – there was no deal made ... there were lots of discussions at the time, including one in which Mr McLachlan was present. That did not involve the conclusion of a deal.' Costello was asked whether the prime minister was lying:

> I'm telling you what happened. I'm not making any
> allegations against anybody. I am telling you what happened
> and look, you can interpret whatever you like. That is what
> happened and people are entitled to know what happened,
> and so I will tell you what happened.

In his autobiography *Lazarus Rising*, Howard revealed that several senior ministers (Brendan Nelson, Malcolm Turnbull, Alexander Downer and Mal Brough) urged him at that time to remain leader, with Turnbull arguing vehemently against Costello taking his place. Howard said Costello 'completely misread both my temperament and my personality' in imagining that 'I would succumb to the sort of rank amateur pressure placed on me through media briefings'. Had Costello deflected questioning or deflated its significance, Howard claims he would have retired before Christmas 2006, just as Kevin Rudd seized the Labor leadership from Beazley. Howard blamed Costello for this 'tragedy': 'Peter's handling of the December 1994 incident [published by Glenn Milne in July 2006] had created a situation where I had no alternative but to announce when I did that I would stay'. Resisting pressure to retire had become a matter of character and an issue of principle for Howard, although it could hardly be said that Costello was applying much 'pressure'. Costello had not mentioned the 1994 agreement publicly or threatened to challenge for the leadership. The only pressure that existed came from the mixed messages Howard was giving to journalists and their obvious response: 'so, when are you going?'

One year later (July 2007), political commentators Wayne Errington and Peter van Onselen released their 'definitive biography' of the prime minister. It referred to Costello's continuing insistence that a succession deal existed and noted his obvious disappointment that Howard had not honoured it. The new book also featured Costello's criticisms of Howard's performance as Treasurer in the Fraser Government. Costello also told the authors about his objections to undisciplined government spending at election time. This was the nearest thing to Keating's 'Placido Domingo' moment. With the latest ACNeilsen poll showing the Coalition trailed Labor 42:58 and leadership division only likely to make things worse, Howard responded by describing Costello as the nation's best treasurer. In wanting to defuse a situation that was plainly not working in his favour, Costello praised Howard as the nation's best prime minister, with the possible exception of Menzies.

The story took a new twist in August 2007 when the ABC journalist Michael Brissenden reported on a dinner he had attended on 5 March 2005 with Peter Costello and two other journalists, Paul Daley and Tony Wright. The three journalists kept extensive notes of their conversations with the treasurer and seemed to have the same recollections. Brissenden recalled that Costello set April 2006 as the absolute deadline for Howard to stand aside. It would be one month after Howard celebrated ten years as prime minister and it was mid-term for the government. Ironically, there was a spike in Howard's personal approval rating following his tenth anniversary in office. But, were Howard to refuse to stand aside, Costello would challenge for the leadership and, if he were unsuccessful, head to the backbench. Just as Keating had done in 1991, he would 'carp' at Howard's leadership and 'destroy it' until he won the leadership and then defeated Beazley at the 2007 election. He boasted that Howard could not win 'without me'.

The three journalists believed they could report the story, only to learn shortly afterwards that Costello had changed his mind.

When the essence of these remarks appeared in a *Bulletin* story early in August 2007, Costello denied the comments attributed to him: 'I don't know where the *Bulletin* got that from, certainly not from me'. This denial led Brissenden to report his recollection of what was said. The incident did not enhance Costello's stature. Either he had to challenge or accept that his moment would come whenever Howard decided to go.

The treasurer's supporters, principally Bruce Baird, Christopher Pyne and George Brandis, faced one perennial issue: Costello was always less popular than Howard. In May 2007 the *Bulletin* published a survey showing that while a majority of voters thought Howard should have retired, only 17 per cent thought Costello would be a better prime minister.[9] By the second half of 2007, however, the prime minister seemed to be losing touch rapidly with the Liberal Party's traditional support base. They were wearying of him and even strong supporters like Newscorp columnists Andrew Bolt and Janet Albrechtsen wanted him to go. Howard's decline did not facilitate Costello's rise, however. The leadership tension served only to distract voters from what the Coalition had done, and might do, if given a fifth term in office. In September 2007, Howard asked Alexander Downer to canvass the mood of Cabinet on whether he should go. The Asia-Pacific Economic Cooperation (APEC) Summit was then being held in Australia. It was, by then, far too late for him to retire. The only beneficiary would have been Kevin Rudd. Howard later conceded this gesture was a 'serious mistake'. While most of Cabinet (excluding Costello, who was not consulted) wanted him to go, Howard now insisted that the Cabinet own their decision and ask him to go publicly. That was not going to happen. Howard had consulted his family and decided he 'would rather go down fighting than desert on the eve of battle'. He would rather be a loser than a quitter.

The hitch for the Liberals was that the prime minister would not commit to a full term after 2007. Howard did not want to make such a pledge and appear to be like three contemporaneous state Labor premiers, Steve Bracks, Peter Beattie and Bob Carr, whom he felt had been dishonest in promising to serve a full term and then abruptly resigning mid-term. Howard offered no firm commitment to the electorate and, consequently, according to Labor, no long-term plans.

The Liberals' pollster Mark Textor believed mismanaging the succession had electoral consequences. Voters thought Howard was untruthful and Costello was weak. The government's senior leadership had been severely tarnished and its re-election qualifications traduced. This was a glib view but pollsters are employed to deal with appearances and not actualities. A united team was certainly more attractive than a divided one but no amount of close collegiality would have reversed the general trend of polling in 2007: the people wanted a change. The Kevin Rudd-led Labor Party achieved a swing of 5.44 per cent (two-party preferred) and Labor gained 23 seats. The Coalition looked destined for six years (two parliamentary terms) or more in opposition.

Howard had led the Coalition to a devastating defeat and accepted full personal responsibility. He hid behind nothing and no-one. The Coalition's WorkChoices legislation had been blamed for a large part of the defeat and Howard had personally championed the reforms. Would the Coalition have done any better in the November 2007 election with Peter Costello as leader? It is very difficult to say. We only know that staying with Howard meant it suffered a heavy defeat. Had Costello, who was only six weeks older than Rudd, become prime minister in mid-2006 and done some of the things that Howard would not countenance (such as apologising to the Stolen Generations and ratified the Kyoto Protocol), he might have nullified Rudd's growing appeal and Labor's efforts to exploit Howard's age and conservatism. Costello might have promoted a younger Cabinet and embraced some bold policy initiatives to let the electorate experience a new and energised government.

In sum, he *might* have hoped for the Harold Holt effect – same party, new leader. I am inclined to think the election outcome might have been different with Costello campaigning as prime minister but it would have needed a good many stars to align for the Coalition to retain power. As each month passed in 2006 and 2007, the scope that existed for reinvigorating a Coalition government rapidly diminished. When electoral defeat appeared very likely in August–September 2007, turning to Costello then would not have made any difference. Costello was ready to accept the challenge for the sake of the party and its future. It was too late.

The personal dimension

Howard did not manage the succession well from the start. Hindsight reveals that enduring problems were created by his offer to stand aside for Costello at some point in the medium term when discussing the party leadership in December 1994. The conversation led to an expectation on Costello's part (and evidently McLachlan's too) that at some point in the future, and well before electoral defeat was inevitable, Costello would have his chance. While there were obvious benefits in returning to the leadership unopposed, Howard would easily have won a leadership ballot against Costello and gone on to win the March 1996 election. In sum, talk of succession in 1994 was unnecessary and, indeed, premature. Howard was determined not to miss this entirely unexpected opportunity to resume party leadership, but he went one step too far in pursuing a smooth transition.

Having won the 1996 election with a huge majority, Howard could have made it clear to Costello and his parliamentary colleagues when questions were first raised about his future in 1997 that only electoral defeat would end his prime ministership. Notwithstanding the inevitable media interest in the leadership succession, Howard could have shut down the guessing with a blank refusal to canvass the matter. Labor could claim, as it did during the 2001 election campaign with the help of some injudicious remarks from Tony Abbott, that a vote for Howard was really a vote for Costello. This unproductive speculation gave the impression that the senior leadership of the Liberal Party was divided when it was actually very united. No useful purpose – none – was served by Howard talking continually about the future in a manner that kept people guessing. He was merely stating the obvious when telling journalists he would stay for as long as the party wanted him. He also knew that he enjoyed considerably greater support in the party room than Costello – and always had. He could and should have made his position clear: the voters had elected his government and he would stay until they elected the Opposition. For such an experienced politician who made a virtue of staying on message, Howard drew attention away from the government's legislative program and its policy development with more than 20 veiled hints of retirement that left everyone guessing. Talk of leadership succession neither bolstered Howard's standing in the party room nor won him any favours with the electorate. It was counterproductive.

If there is anything to be taken from Howard's role, it is the folly of making pledges about the future when what lies ahead, especially in politics, is usually so uncertain and often utterly unpredictable. Undertakings to retire are not legally binding and the conditions associated with them are often unspoken and liable to misconceptions. The people want those they elect to push the public interest and to promote the common good. They are distrustful of 'career' – meaning 'professional' – politicians who are too attentive to their own interests. The voters only wanted to know whether John Howard would continue to serve until their choice fell on someone else. The electorate was largely unconcerned with his retirement plans nor did they give him their vote because he might serve for only half a term – they wanted and expected a full term in 2001, 2004 and 2007. If Howard decided to leave for whatever reason, the public would cope with his decision and accept his successor – or not. In an already uncertain world, speculation was unsettling.

Conversely, Costello should have spoken directly with Howard about succession in 1998 if he believed a firm undertaking had been given. He did not communicate this view for another eight years. That the December 1994 conversation was neither mentioned nor addressed directly until 2006 appears to have given Howard the sense that he was not under any continuing obligation. Instead of making the point once, and once only, that Howard had reneged on an 'undertaking', and accepting the reality that Howard would probably stay until the Coalition was defeated, Costello appeared sullen. One of his own staffers, Nikki Savva, thought he looked like a 'sook'. A physically strong and young man looked uncharacteristically weak in not challenging the physically smaller and older Howard and this detracted from the treasurer's standing and stature. If he believed the job ought to have been his, by virtue of a prior undertaking or because he had the potential to lead the Coalition to election victory, he should have challenged and dealt decisively with the matter.

By way of obvious contrast, Paul Keating wanted the prime ministership, believed Hawke had reneged on a deal and thought he could do a better job – and was determined to prove it. He challenged Hawke and accepted the opprobrium that usually accompanies such a decision. Hawke was not immune to challenge. He moved against Bill Hayden unsuccessfully in July 1982 and successfully in February 1983. Keating moved against Hawke while, in his judgment, he had enough time to establish himself as prime minister before the scheduled 1993 election. No leader is immune to having their support tested. Keating was successful on the second attempt in December 1991 and no-one was left wondering about the kind of prime minister he would make. He did win an unwinnable election in 1993; something the pollsters had said Hawke could not do.

There are rival assessments of who was to blame among commentators. Political commentator Peter Hartcher thought the problem began with Howard but was exacerbated by Costello:

> Howard, as leader, bore responsibility for failing to manage
> an orderly succession. But Costello bore responsibility for his
> response to Howard's failure. He committed a fundamental
> misjudgement. This was not a morality play – this was a
> power play. Howard went into the confrontation as prime
> minister, with four election victories to his credit, a solid
> majority of the party behind him, and an iron determination
> to crush this challenge to his credibility. Costello went into
> it with a pout, a moral pose, no plan and perhaps 25 votes,
> representing less than a quarter of the party room.[10]

Given that Costello lacked sufficient support in the party room to seize the prime ministership (and noting his justifiable dislike of destabilising campaigns despite apparently being willing to contemplate one), he might have done more among his colleagues to attract their goodwill and perhaps their vote in any leadership ballot. It is unlikely that Costello would ever have secured more than 30 votes in the party room. Howard was able to retain collegial support because he was substantially more popular in the electorate than Costello – something Labor was always keen to exploit. Instead of hoping (or assuming) the polling would improve once he became prime minister, Costello might have considered ways to increase his profile and improve his appeal while treasurer.

Although there was never a time when Costello was more popular than Howard, Costello might have argued that Holt's standing improved dramatically after he became prime minister in January 1966 and Keating's likewise after December 1991. But 1966, 1991 and 2006 were very different. When gaining and holding power is critical to political success, giving Costello a 'turn' because he deserved it never resonated with his parliamentary colleagues. Winning elections was vital and that was where Howard had a track record.

Costello's own supporters noted that he never worked the party room to secure support at Howard's expense. He did not ring the self-interested or the waverers. He loyally supported Howard and never plotted against him. But his frustrated leadership ambitions had damaged the government and hurt the Liberal Party. The more he lamented Howard's intransigence about retiring the less likely he was to succeed him. Many thought Costello was impetuous and this precluded him from attracting further party room support. Howard's chief of staff and later Liberal senator, Arthur Sinodinos, agreed. It looked like bullying and 'elements of the party didn't like the way it was done'.[11] Costello saw it differently. He had not raised the succession publicly and had tried to avoid the existence of McLachlan's note being reported. He believed in loyalty and insisted he had never been disloyal. It was Howard who raised the spectre of retiring and then tried to dissipate the interest he had aroused.

Would Howard have gone in the second half of 2006? Howard says that was his intention. Costello concluded he would never make way. Commentators were mixed in their judgments: about half thought he would have emulated Menzies and retired, another half thought he would remain until eventual electoral defeat. There were few concrete signs he would depart at the end of 2006 although Howard believed setting a firm timeline would weaken his authority – as happened when Tony Blair relinquished the British prime ministership in favour of his long-serving Chancellor of the Exchequer, Gordon Brown. Whatever his intentions, Howard suffered the fate that Paul Keating prophesied awaited prime ministers: 'We all get taken out in a box'. Costello concluded his account of the leadership succession that wasn't by noting that 'leadership is not only about winning; it is also about departing'. After noting that Menzies knew when to go, Costello wrote, 'Howard never managed a transition. He did not accomplish generational change.' The Liberals lost in 2007 because 'we failed to renew. We mismanaged generational change. We did not arrange the leadership transition. The electorate did it for us.'[12]

There were, however, two aspects of this matter that deserve positive comment. First, knowing that Costello wanted his job ensured that Howard kept in close touch with his backbench. They were engaged and energised by his attention and acknowledgment of what they could achieve in their electorates, in parliamentary committees and in the debating chambers. Plainly, Howard had learned from his first experience of being Leader of the Opposition and this helped him to lead a more united team.

Second, there is nothing to suggest that the leadership tensions adversely affected the government's performance. Despite the tensions, the Howard Government functioned effectively and the electorate never suffered. In contrast to the paralysis that plagued the

Rudd–Gillard–Rudd governments as a consequence of infighting, Costello continued to perform the duties of treasurer effectively and efficiently. He did not resign his office or engage in counterproductive leaking to the press. He continued to deliver budget surpluses and promote the government's economic program. Costello was never a wrecker and believed in putting the interests of the party, the government and the nation first. To his enduring credit, he never set his own aspirations ahead of the public interest or the common good.

The abiding consequence

Despite lacking the level of party room support that Howard had enjoyed since his return to the Liberal leadership in January 1995, Costello was the obvious candidate to succeed Howard whenever he decided to retire. He had the rank, the standing and the experience. Costello was an exceptional parliamentary performer and commanded the respect, although not the affection, of colleagues. Alexander Downer was never in contention after his brief and unsuccessful time as Opposition leader in 1994–95. Among the other senior ministers, Tony Abbott, Brendan Nelson and Malcolm Turnbull were possibilities but they were well behind Costello, who was without peer in terms of his standing within the party and with the public.

When he declined nomination following the electoral defeat, the Liberals were confronted with a problem they had never considered. The assumption was that Costello would lead the party and do so for an extended period given he had only recently turned 50. The Liberals had faced a similar situation when Holt drowned in 1967. There was no obvious successor, other than William McMahon, who was unacceptable to the Country Party. The party selected Senator John Gorton, who first had to be elected to the House of Representatives before struggling to maintain the support of his colleagues. It was not until Malcolm Fraser became leader in 1975 that the Liberals had a leader who enjoyed a security of tenure.

In December 2007, the Liberals elected Brendan Nelson to the party leadership. He defeated Malcolm Turnbull, who made it plain his leadership ambitions were far from exhausted. Turnbull replaced Nelson within a year before he himself was defeated by Abbott in a leadership spill on 1 December 2009. Labor claimed to have learned from the past when it came to leadership succession. The new Treasurer, Wayne Swan, noted that he was older than Rudd and had no prime ministerial aspirations. Julia Gillard, Rudd's deputy, disclosed that:

> My working assumption is that I will be deputy prime
> minister and Kevin will be prime minister and the only way
> the arrangement will be terminated will be on the day that
> the Australian people decide to terminate it.

She and Rudd had never talked about succession. But when the Labor Party's research showed that the government was doing badly in the polls, Rudd agreed to stand aside for Gillard if electoral defeat looked likely. Rudd said he told Gillard: 'I will at that point resign the prime ministership and offer an uncontested succession to you'. The two even shook hands to seal the arrangement. But after conferring with colleagues for just ten minutes and learning she had the numbers, Gillard told Rudd she would be challenging him at a party room meeting the next day. Gillard denied a deal was made but conceded she had given Rudd 'false hope'. Rudd has made much of her reneging on the deal he thought they had made. Someone with initially strong public support but weaker party support (Rudd) had been replaced by someone with always weak public support but consistently stronger party support (Gillard).

Despite securing a very substantial swing to Labor at the 2007 election and setting new popularity records, Labor performed poorly at the August 2010 election. It lost 11 seats while the Coalition, now led by Tony Abbott, gained seven. The Labor Party, led by Julia Gillard, was dependent on the support of three independents to form government.

In 2008, the Parliamentary Liberal Party was not ready for a future that included neither John Howard nor Peter Costello. It is not unreasonable to contend that had the Liberals been led by Peter Costello (especially given doubts about the government's handling of the Global Financial Crisis), the Coalition could have been returned to power in 2010 and Costello might have led a government that enjoyed greater unity under a stronger leader and avoided the leadership turmoil that saw Abbott replaced by Turnbull, who was later replaced by Scott Morrison. It seemed that Nelson, Abbott and Turnbull lacked sufficient standing in the party to protect them when the polls were against them. The succession that wasn't destined the Liberals to more than a decade of instability.

17

THE DEAD BOUNCE BUDGET

ANDREW BLYTH

Peter Costello delivered his 12th and final budget on the evening of 8 May 2007. The second-longest serving federal treasurer was announcing a record tenth budget surplus. No previous serving treasurer in Australia's political history had achieved such a feat, nor since.[1] While standing at the ornate wooden dispatch box given to Australia by King George V, Costello showered the electorate with populist spending, especially tax cuts, while revealing a substantial cash surplus.

Costello's statement continued his practice of hard decisions and tough choices in the public interest. A firm hand remained on the nation's economic tiller with a steely eye focused on the pending federal election by year's end. Proclaiming the country was now debt free and living within its means, he left nothing to chance. This budget was part of a political strategy crafted to win office and to position Costello as heir apparent. Costello's 'best budget' was also one that the electorate noticed the least when it counted. After 11 years and six months of 'economic sunlight',[2] the electorate was indifferent. They had never had it so good nor taken effective economic management so much for granted. Costello's last budget may go down as the most overlooked in Australian history.

Budget media coverage

This chapter surveys print coverage of the 2007 Budget and evaluates its effect on the subsequent federal election. This coverage was extensive in both national and state-based newspapers with substantial editorial critique in the four broadsheets, News Corp's *Australian*, and Fairfax Media's *Australian Financial Review*, *Sydney Morning Herald* and the *Age*. The News Corp tabloids *Daily Telegraph*, *Herald Sun*, and the *Advertiser* also devoted many column inches to explaining what the budget meant and how it would affect most Australians.

Australian

Peter Costello has crafted a budget that is rich in politics and pregnant with the promise that dividends from the boom will be used to transform Australia. This year's budget is responsible in its use of the forecast $10.6 billion surplus, the substance and timing of income tax cuts and its provision to lock away surplus funds to secure long-term prosperity. Mr Costello will be hoping this budget will be seen as the turning point that put the Government back in the electoral game.[3]

Australian Financial Review

As a pre-election budget, federal Treasurer Peter Costello's budget is better than it might have been, but only just. As a tactical measure, it is as shrewdly pitched as we've come to expect from a Howard government now seeking a fifth term after 12 years in office. Once again the Treasurer and his officials have been standing in a blizzard of $100 notes, trying to work out how to spend them in a fiscally responsible way. This reflects past success and good luck in managing the economy through a boom with the Reserve Bank having to slam on the brakes.[4]

Age

A $10 billion surplus has allowed the Treasurer to play Mr Responsible and Santa Claus in an election year. The great fear for this election-year budget was that the Federal Government would sacrifice the future for the present. But on any reading of the figures, it has balanced, well-measured investment in the country with an ample splash of electoral gifts. There has not been a war chest like it, and yesterday the Government opened the lid.[5]

Sydney Morning Herald

For a pre-election budget from a government behind in the polls, Peter Costello's 12th was surprisingly responsible. After 15 years of uninterrupted growth, helped by competent and responsible management of the economy, there is plenty of money the Government could give away.[6]

Herald Sun

The rise of Labor under Kevin Rudd demanded a Budget that would make the electorate less keen for change. Empowered by a $13.6 billion surplus for this financial year, Mr Costello has responded generously. But this is a responsible, and for an election year, almost sober Budget. Clearly the Government is leaving itself room to offer more in what will surely be a white-hot election campaign. Overwhelmingly it reinforces the Government's economic credentials.[7]

Advertiser

Treasurer Peter Costello yesterday placed great faith in the electoral potency of his twelfth Budget, purely because of its economic merits. For a Budget designed to save the Government's electoral skin, it is a document with plenty of appeal. Mr Costello has now framed a critical electoral test for the resurgent Labor Opposition, which is yet to prove its economic credentials. Mr Rudd will have to find money for bold and innovative election promises, without damaging the Budget's popular aspects. This will be a challenge. Mr Costello's measured and balanced Budget has put the Government on the front foot.[8]

Budget commentary

The *Sydney Morning Herald* political commentator, Peter Hartcher, provided a useful budget summary. He made the point that the most notable aspect of the federal budget was something that did not happen: Peter Costello and John Howard did not panic. Hartcher argued that despite trailing Labor in the polls, the government did not lose its nerve. Further, he explained that maintaining its economic credentials saw the government deciding not to run the budget surplus down to zero or into deficit, and choosing not to spend everything at once in tax cuts and new spending. While there certainly was 'populist' spending, the 2007 Budget was considered responsible and restrained: 'this keeps intact the Government's single most valuable electoral credential – its claim to be a better economic manager than Labor'.[9] With the Howard Government having a record of using election-year budgets to turn around its political fortunes, and the Budget preserving the government's perceived strength of economic management, Hartcher pondered, 'Can it do it again?'

The government was entitled to be encouraged by media commentary and editorials. Reading that the 2007 Budget was considered 'measured and balanced', 'responsible … almost sober', and containing 'plenty of appeal' would have no doubt pleased the treasurer. Having spent months crafting an economic and political strategy to turn around the government's fortunes, Costello knew the public would take some convincing. It would be only a matter of time for the government to find out whether it was successful.

Kevin Rudd's reply

Two days after Costello delivered the budget, the Leader of the Opposition, Kevin Rudd, delivered an address in reply in the House of Representatives. Rudd focused on the economy, the environment and national security:

> I believe Australia faces three core challenges to secure
> its future: first, to build long-term economic prosperity,
> beyond the mining boom, by rebuilding productivity growth.
> Second, to deal with, rather than avoid, the great challenge
> of climate change and the water crisis before the cost of
> inaction becomes too great. Third, to make sure the fair go
> in Australia has a future, not just a past – both within the

workplace and beyond the workplace as well. And beyond these three great challenges is the underlying challenge of remaining vigilant on our national security in an increasingly uncertain and threatening world – which is why budgets need to be about the next decade, not the next election.[10]

In showcasing Labor's economic credentials, Rudd insisted he would not try:

> to outspend the Prime Minister and I have not. Instead I offer an alternative plan for Australia's future. I believe if as a nation we rise to the great challenges I have outlined tonight we can build a better and more secure future for our families and for our country. So many Australians are depending on us to do so: our farmers and their families battling the drought; pensioners and carers struggling to make ends meet – notwithstanding the one-off payments they have received; working families under financial pressure, for whom tax cuts are always welcome, together with child-care relief. All this, however, depends on building a strong economy into the future. All this depends on us now seizing the day on revolutionizing our approach to education. All this depends on us seizing the day on climate change and water. And all this still depends on ensuring that, in this great country of ours, Australia, the fair go has a future, and not just a past.[11]

Rudd had set out his plan for office. The election starting gun had been fired.

The former British Labour Prime Minister, Harold Wilson, once remarked that 'a week is a long time in politics'. This would be true for Peter Costello and John Howard as they waited for polls conducted over the weekend following the Budget. The news was mixed. Leading with the headline on 15 May, 'Most popular budget on record, but no bounce', the *Australian*'s political reporter Dennis Shanahan observed:

> Peter Costello's 'masterclass' budget was the best-received on record but has failed to immediately lift the Howard Government's fortunes and has left Kevin Rudd and the ALP in an overwhelmingly favourable position. Voters have given the budget the highest rating for economic management in the 11 years of the Howard Government – 60 per cent – and say it is the best time for their own pockets, with 36 per cent saying they were personally 'better off'. According to the latest Newspoll survey, taken last weekend exclusively for the *Australian* after Tuesday's budget, Labor's primary vote rose from 48 per cent to 50 per cent and the Coalition's was virtually unchanged on 36 per cent.[12]

Shanahan thought that on economic management, the public rated the 2007 Budget the best since 1992, exceeding the tough budget of 1996 when the government 'slashed spending and got 59 per cent for being "good for the economy"'. Significantly, the polling showed strong endorsement across all age and income groups with even 49 per cent of Labor supporters saying the Budget was good for the economy.

When asked later that morning for his thoughts on the polling result while visiting marginal seats on Queensland's Gold Coast, the treasurer claimed he was against instant poll gratification:

> Budgets are brought down with an eye to the future of the country. They are not brought down for short-term reasons.

I am looking at where the country has to be in decades to come. That is my focus and that is what the Budget was designed to do.[13]

When speaking on commercial radio, Costello explained it could take a couple of months before positive reactions to the Budget would be reflected in the opinion polls, noting that tax cuts commenced on 1 July. In a display of one-upmanship, Labor's Wayne Swan responded on Australian Broadcasting Corporation (ABC) television news by spinning the polling result in Labor's favour: 'there's a very positive reaction to Kevin Rudd's Budget reply'. A new level of confidence was now evident among Labor's senior leadership group.

The *Australian* editorial that same day, headed 'Dead Bounce Brings Danger of Spendfest', warned that the well-received Budget was yet to register in Newspoll, reinforcing the conclusion that the government needed to work doubly hard in getting its message across to voters:

If there is a positive glimmer for the Government, it is that a majority of voters clearly still see the Coalition as the best custodians of the economy. Asked if Labor could have done a better job of the budget, 31 per cent said 'yes', 44 per cent 'no' and 25 per cent were undecided.

But without clear evidence of a turnaround in the Government's fortunes soon, the real danger is in Mr Howard launching an unseemly spending assault in an attempt to buy his way back into office. The message in the Newspoll reaction to the budget is that voters are waiting with open arms, and wallets.[14]

In post-election analysis of the 2007 campaign, political scientist Marian Simms thought the May Budget contained few surprises. It was a mixture of solid infrastructure expenditure alongside more populist initiatives, especially tax cuts. Simms observed that, in political terms:

> previous Coalition budgets had created a poll bounce on the two-party preferred figures, partly based on the perception of the Coalition as a better economic manager than Labor. This time the polling boost was barely noticeable.[15]

The message from polling was clear: while voters still trusted the Coalition as financial managers, they were increasingly ready to trust Rudd and Labor with the economy. With no hint of deep-seated anger or escalating disillusionment with the Howard Government apparent in the polls, voters appeared to take surpluses, tax relief and future funds for granted. The economy was not relying on the Coalition Government to produce growth or stimulate investment. The problem may have been that Costello made fashioning effective budgets look too easy. A poll recovery by mid-June was needed if the Coalition was to make the kind of comeback it had achieved in 2001 and 2004.

Election 2007

On Sunday 14 October 2007, John Howard announced a federal election would be held on Saturday 24 November. The campaign would run for 39 days. This would be the fourth time the Coalition Government sought a renewed mandate from the people. With polling over the last six months confirming Labor dominating the two-party preferred vote — and Coalition strategists aware that many voters were no longer listening to the government's messages – Costello greeted the announcement of the election campaign with a sense of urgency:

> This is an important election for Australia's future. It will determine whether we go forward with prosperity and more jobs, whether our businesses are strong and whether we have the economy which we require to build the healthcare system and the education system that we want for the future. And I am focused on opportunities for Australians and I want to see Australia be stronger than it is now. And that is going to take a lot of work but I am very focused on that challenge.[16]

This urgency was met with an announcement the following morning of fresh plans to recast the Australian income tax system. Costello and Howard announced a package aimed at reducing the tax burden on low-income earners while promising to reduce the top marginal tax rate for higher income earners. In addition to the $34 billion in taxation relief announced the previous financial year, Costello declared this additional suite of measures as being ambitious and good for the country and the economy. Having quickly drafted a major tax policy on the first day of the campaign, Melbourne 3AW radio personality, Neil Mitchell, asked Costello: 'Is this a rabbit or have you got more left in there?'[17]

The Coalition had fired its one remaining shot in the locker. Two days later, Labor announced it would match the package, with minor changes. Costello was left flummoxed. There was nowhere now to go.

Newspaper endorsements

Halfway through the campaign, newspaper editorials and political commentary were offering some hope for the Coalition even while Labor enjoyed a clear lead in the polls. By election day, most newspaper editorials were endorsing Rudd and Labor. Despite two state-based newspapers and one national newspaper telling their readers that the Coalition deserved a fifth term in office, the remaining broadsheets and tabloid newspapers favoured change. Rudd had demonstrated his leadership credentials and Labor was fit for government. The following extracts convey the prevailing mood among the editorialists.

Advertiser

There are many issues which are important in this election. None are more important than a resilient economy. Whether led by Mr Howard or Mr Costello, the Coalition should be returned to power.

Herald Sun

The *Herald Sun* believes the Coalition deserves another term in office. In saying so, we put performance ahead of potential, achievement ahead of promise, certainty ahead of uncertainty. Mr Rudd has not made a compelling case for change.

Australian Financial Review

A switch to Labor would be a switch to an untried team which has only recently converted to economic conservatism after years of obstructing reform … despite our reservations about the Howard Government's energy and vision, it remains better qualified to plot a safe passage through choppy seas.

Sydney Morning Herald

The Coalition has served Australia well [but] appears unwilling to respond to the new and growing challenges Australia faces. We believe this country must, for now, look elsewhere for that response – to Kevin Rudd, and the Labor Party.

Australian

Mr Howard and his team have a proven track record but, to us, they have run out of energy. Their campaign is a signal of their torpor. There is much detail missing from Mr Rudd's promised reform revolution, especially in education and health, but we believe he has the administrative experience to manage constructive change. We recognise that no change is free of risk, but we recommend a vote for Mr Rudd.

Daily Telegraph

We believe Australia has been lucky to have been led by John Howard for the past 11 years. But we now believe Mr Howard has reached his use-by-date if for no other reason than he almost believes it himself.

Courier Mail

Kevin Rudd is a man for his times: outward looking in a world where our circumstances will be increasingly shaped by events we do not control; intellectually capable in a climate that demands considered responses to rapid change; and in touch with popular sentiment … He deserves the popular sentiment … He deserves the public's support. And he has the support of the *Courier Mail*, only the second endorsement we have given federal Labor since the newspaper was established 74 years ago.

Mercury

There is no better time to change. Australians are in the mood for it and there is confidence in Labor to do the job and confidence in Mr Rudd as a conservative and cautious helmsman very much in the Howard mould. Labor deserves the chance.[18]

After an election campaign some commentators thought had been underway for 12 months, it was now for the voters to determine Australia's future.

Election result

On 24 November 2007, the Australian electorate voted for change. The morning after the election defeat, Peter Costello held a press conference in his electorate attended by reporters from the national media. With his wife Tanya at his side, and having had little sleep the night before, Costello congratulated Kevin Rudd before thanking his family, ministerial and electorate staff, and party supporters for their enduring efforts. What he said next sent shockwaves through the Liberal Party. Costello would not be seeking the leadership of the Liberal Party. He was done. Reflecting on his period in office – and of his need to repay his wife for her selfless support – Costello reminded voters (and perhaps his colleagues) of what he believed they had forsaken:

> I think the achievements of recent years have been absolutely outstanding. I have personally been the longest serving Treasurer in Australia's history. I have brought down 12 federal budgets. The incoming Treasurer will not inherit a situation that I did with a $10 billion deficit and $96 billion worth of [net government] debt. The incoming Treasurer will have a balanced budget. There will be no Commonwealth debt, we are saving $9 billion a year in interest payments alone. We have reformed the tax system and introduced a broad base consumption tax; 2.2 million more Australians are in work and young people have a better opportunity for work than they have in a generation.

Fearing a potential raid on the Future Fund, Costello warned:

> Do not let an incoming government raid that Future Fund. Because once that Future Fund is opened for any purpose, it is open for all purposes. This is something that is much more important than politics for the long-term interests of this country. I have great belief in Australia and its people. I want to see this country be everything it possibly can be and for me it has been a privilege to play my part in making this a better country.[19]

Concluding his press conference, the theme of retrospectivity continued:

> You can look at our record and you can compare it to any other government in Australian history. I think it will compare well. You know, don't take it from me, but you know what the Budget is like, you know what debt is like, you know what inflation is like, you know what unemployment is like, you know what the tax system is like, you know what growth has been. Compare that to any other government in Australian history and I invite you to draw your own conclusions. Nobody actually said to me at any stage during the campaign, you've done a bad job. In fact, quite the reverse. But you did pick up, from time to time – you've done a good job, maybe it's time for a change. I don't think they quite knew what they were getting. I don't think, to be frank with you, even Mr Rudd knows what they are going to be getting, but they'll find out soon enough.

In his memoirs, Peter Costello recalls a Cabinet meeting held in July of 2007 appraising new policy proposals.[20] Ideas submitted by ministers were debated, their merits assessed and several policies stood. The goal was to deliver a fresh message to the public. While the year featured many policy announcements (ageing, water security, defence, the Northern Territory Intervention, disability assistance, tax relief) the government never drew level with Labor in polling. Rudd had been ahead of Howard as preferred prime minister since February. The problem, according to Costello, was not of policy inertia but public indifference: 'We've got policy coming out our ears. The problem is, no one is listening.'[21]

Drawing on the lived example of Paul Keating and his government before the 1996 election, Costello argued bluntly the electorate had grown 'tired of the Government and of John Howard'.[22] This argument had been put to Howard the previous year. By the second half of 2007, an opportunity for leadership renewal had passed. Costello believed a new political strategy was essential in defending marginal seats in the hope of limiting Coalition losses. He wanted to raise doubts about Labor's lack of ministerial experience, oblige the media to scrutinise Labor's policies more closely and to illuminate the economic risks associated with changing the government.

In contrast to the Coalition's waning fortunes, nothing was going wrong for Labor. In its favour was the Canberra press gallery. The commentators advocated change. They did this by going easy on Rudd, giving him the benefit of the doubt. With the economy 'practically running itself',[23] and notwithstanding disciplined economic management with budget surpluses, eliminated public debt and accumulated capital in sovereign wealth funds, Costello was no longer being heard. Voters were captivated by Labor's promise of fiscal conservatism with the prospect of progressive social change. After four terms, the Coalition had lost the public's attention. They were bored.

Costello fought hard but his last budget produced a 'dead bounce'. The 2007 Budget was meant to be a new start in the Coalition's campaign to defeat Labor – again. But Costello's budget made no difference. It did not produce a turnaround in the polls. There was, in fact, nothing in the budget that Labor opposed. Economic management, once a strong suit for the Coalition, no longer impressed the electorate. Despite low inflation, low unemployment, low interest rates and low growth in wages, it was the perception that the government was stale and its leaders stodgy that hurt the Coalition most. Voters thought that either party could manage the economy well. They were willing to overlook the Keating years. Labor had learned from past mistakes.

Costello was wearied by the need to restrain his more spend-thrift colleagues. He had attracted neither their affection nor their party room support. They did not want him as their leader in government; he was not willing to be their leader in opposition. The extent of his achievements was not then known. He had placed Australia on the path to prosperity, giving it some resilience in the face of future economic headwinds. Australia did better than most nations in withstanding the 2008 Global Financial Crisis because of Costello's many legacies. But much of his work was soon undone as budget deficits and government debt returned. They remain a feature of the Australian economic landscape.

He had warned the Australian people but they were not listening to him, either.

18

JOHN HOWARD: CONSERVATIVE, LIBERAL, OR WHAT?

GREGORY MELLEUISH

The question of whether Prime Minister John Howard is best understood as a liberal or a conservative is a vexed one. For some of his critics, including academic Robert Manne, and journalists Donald Horne and Guy Rundle, Howard was not worthy of being granted any such lofty appellations. Rundle saw him purely as an opportunist.[1]

John Howard sought to establish the principles on which the Liberal Party is founded. He claimed that the Liberal Party is a 'broad church' that brings together the liberalism of English 19th-century empiricist philosopher John Stuart Mill and the conservatism of Irish 18th-century politician and philosopher Edmund Burke.[2] There are a number of dimensions to this claim. Is it a serious intellectual attempt to elucidate the foundation principles of the Liberal Party and its policies? What exactly is meant by the terms 'liberal' and 'conservative' in the Australian context, and why are those terms represented by an English and an Irish thinker? Can terms such as 'liberal' and 'conservative' be applied to the actions of a politician, political party or government, or are they just elements of a rhetoric designed to create an attractive public image?

Adoption of the idea of the Liberal Party as a 'broad church', as the party of John Stuart Mill and Edmund Burke, can be seen as a response to the changed political landscape created by both the reforms of Hawke and Keating in Australia and the demise of communism in the Soviet Union and eastern Europe. The Liberal Party could no longer describe itself, in these new circumstances, as being defined by anti-socialism. It is worth recalling that it was the fourth prime minister of Australia, George Reid, who first described the then Liberal Party as an anti-socialist party in 1906 as he attempted to bring protectionist and free trade liberals together in opposition to the emerging Labor Party.[3] For Reid, liberalism mattered. In his 1906 election speech the word 'liberty' appears eight times, more than in any other election speech, with the exception of 1917 when Billy Hughes used the word ten times in defence of conscription.[4]

Defending liberalism as the opponent of socialism made sense in the decade of the 'Australian Settlement' but it no longer resonated in the 1990s. A sort of lazy liberalism that defined itself in terms of what it opposed was no longer possible given the proclamation by the American historian, Francis Fukuyama, of the 'end of history' and the triumph of liberalism. One of John Howard's great achievements was, in these circumstances, to create a new image of the Liberal Party by stamping it as the party of John Stuart Mill and Edmund Burke. Howard was not the first Liberal figure to use Burke and Mill in this way. In 1988, Malcolm Fraser also described the Liberal Party referring to Burke and Mill but in a quite different manner.[5]

Howard used the names Burke and Mill in a number of speeches but nothing indicates a very deep philosophical engagement with either figure. The usage is largely rhetorical, designed to resonate with the party faithful. The circumstances were complex. With the coming of Whitlam, the Labor Party slowly shed its conservative skin in its quest to become a socially progressive party. It can be claimed that Whitlam sought to appropriate the socially progressive elements of Mill for Labor. Howard instinctively understood that if the Liberals could put on that 'conservative' skin, they could also attract those who were repulsed by the more socially progressive elements of Mill as appropriated by Labor. However, as Mill, and particularly *On Liberty*, have long resonated in Australian political life, including being quoted in Menzies' *The Forgotten People*, Howard could not dispense with Mill as a symbol of liberalism.[6]

There is an irony here. Menzies had expanded the universities in the late 1950s in part because he believed that he was creating an additional white-collar constituency for the Liberal Party. The accidents of history, including Arthur Calwell's narrow loss in 1961 and the coming of Gough Whitlam as a Labor 'messiah' in 1972, allowed Labor to cast off its ingrained social conservatism and to become the party of progressive liberalism. Calwell was perhaps the most socially conservative political leader in Australian history. As I have argued elsewhere, this set of circumstances enabled Whitlam to become an apostle of progressive liberalism.[7]

Howard's 'broad church' formulation allowed the Liberal Party to reclaim Mill as a liberal but with his progressive and radical elements shorn off. By pairing Mill with Burke, Howard was able to formulate what is essentially a form of 'liberal conservatism'; an approach invented in 19th-century British colonies such as Australia, where there were no real conservatives, only a need to distinguish between moderate and progressive liberals and radicals. Given the circumstances of the Liberal Party in the early 1990s, such a move was essential.

The formulation of the 'broad church', however, was not meant to be a statement of how the Liberals would govern, such as John Hewson had attempted with Fightback! or in Malcolm Fraser's invocation of Burke and Mill. Fraser saw Burke and Mill as providing complementary advice to aid in the art of governing. Fightback! was a radical libertarian plan for transforming society and the economy in Australia. It failed because it was too dogmatic, setting out what looked like a radical plan designed to create a new Australia that could be very easily portrayed as an attack on Australian values.

Howard's response to this situation was to develop the idea of the Liberal Party as a 'broad church' that encompassed both social conservatism and economic liberalism. As I have argued elsewhere, Howard misuses the idea of the broad church as it originated within the Church of England; the broad church was just one group within the church.[8] Nor does he mean that the Liberal Party is a *via media*, a middle way between extremes. Rather, the conservatism of Burke and the liberalism of Mill are held together in a constant tension, but it is unclear if that tension allows for more creative political thinking and action or if it is more like a meeting of the synod, in which the various groups constantly plot against each other.

Invoking Mill and Burke gave the Liberal Party a good pedigree, even if it came from outside Australia. It made it appear to be a party based on sound, thought-out political principles. Most importantly, the 'broad church' sought to keep the various fractious elements of the Liberal Party all under the same umbrella. In the longer term, this formulation was linked to the creation of a new narrative for the Liberal Party that sought to connect Howard with Menzies as the two titans of the Liberal Party.[9] This narrative involved two things. One was preventing the original Liberal Party created in 1909 from having any importance, primarily, one suspects, because the Reid 'free trade' versus Deakin 'protectionist' issue is too divisive even in the early 21st century. In reality, the Liberal Party remains the party of fusion, of Reid and Deakin, but no one will admit this to be the case. The second was the banishment of Malcolm Fraser from the pantheon of Liberal gods, despite the fact, as will be shown, that Menzies, Fraser and Howard shared common values.

This is somewhat at odds with many traditional understandings of liberalism in Australia. Wishing to be seen as conservative was really something quite new in Australian politics. No former non-Labor party leader ever referred to conservatism in a positive fashion in an election speech. Both George Reid, the original catalyst behind the formation of the original 'fusion' Liberal Party, and Sir Robert Menzies, the founder of the current Liberal Party, only mentioned conservatism in disparaging terms in order to emphasise their genuine liberal credentials and the necessity for Australia to be a country based on liberal and democratic principles.

It has always been unclear what being liberal in Australia actually means. At various stages it has largely been associated with notions of good government. For much of the second half of the 19th century most Australians viewed themselves as liberals. They held John Stuart Mill in very high regard, but then so did Billy Hughes in *The Case for Labor*.[10] Mill is the only liberal thinker invoked by Sir Robert Menzies in *The Forgotten People*. The only political thinker in Australia who consistently cited Mill was Bruce Smith, who can be considered a failed politician because he was too ideological. Smith also cites Burke about 50 times in *Liberty and Liberalism*, including on the title page.[11]

Leaving aside Smith, liberalism in Australia has found very few systematic expositions and is often mixed up with a number of other ideas and beliefs. For example, in his *Reflections of an Australian Liberal*, politician Sir Frederic Eggleston sees liberalism in terms of the transformation of communities into brotherhoods.[12] One can see the nebulous nature of Australian liberalism quite clearly in the debates of the Constitutional Conventions during the 1890s when many of the participants, who would happily identify themselves as liberals, went out of their way to avoid being accused of theorising. Many of them, including Alfred Deakin, often sound like Burkean conservatives, which simply reflects their backgrounds in the Common Law.[13]

Menzies may refer to Mill in *The Forgotten People* but this work is far from being based on the ideals of theoretical liberalism. Its most striking aspect is its invocation of the ideal of 'home'. Menzies also wrote an essay on politics as an art,[14] and his liberalism, like that of the Federation Fathers, was founded on a combination of a powerful appreciation of political practice and an idealisation of England.

Given the relative absence of liberals with a theoretical bent in Australian history, it is not surprising that Australian political leaders rarely discuss their political beliefs in terms of abstract political ideas. Invoking Mill and Burke as the twin poles of the Liberal Party was really without precedent and, as has been argued, was fundamentally a rhetorical gesture. It does little to explain the actual ideas and beliefs that motivated Howard. For these, we need to look deeper.

With Menzies, and most other earlier liberals, there is a set of embedded and implicit ideas and values, values that often go under the radar when discussing the role of political ideas in Australia. These implicit ideas are clearly manifest in such places as the Constitutional Conventions of the 1890s, where there is a rejection of natural law, and in the stress placed by Menzies on the word 'home' in *The Forgotten People*. The particularity of the use of political ideas and words is too often overlooked by commentators in their desire to push the ideas invoked by politicians into ideological boxes, even if the fit looks awkward and inappropriate.

The argument I am putting here is quite simple. If we are to understand what has been described as John Howard's 'liberalism' and 'conservatism', there is little value in attempting to use those abstract concepts as a way of understanding his words and ideas. We need to appreciate what can be described as 'subterranean' values, the sorts of values and beliefs that are embedded in Howard's patterns of thought. Terms such as liberalism and conservatism tend to obscure such values under an abstract universality.

As with Menzies, Howard's speeches are difficult to understand if a liberal and/or conservative template is imposed on them. The two speeches that I would like to examine are the 2004 and 2007 election speeches.[15] The key liberal word 'liberty' does not appear in either. This is not unusual for a modern Liberal leader, none of whom is a liberal of the George Reid variety. The word 'freedom' appears seven times in the 2004 speech but not at all in 2007. Freedom was also Menzies' preferred term in *The Forgotten People*, and in the earlier 1940 election speech he spoke of the 'freedom of the soul'.[16]

'Individual' as a noun appears in both speeches but generally in conjunction with the word 'family'. The word 'family' appears in both speeches while the word 'home', which appears 21 times in Menzies' *Forgotten People* speech,[17] is used by Howard 15 times in 2004 and 23 times in 2007. In his 1980 election speech, Malcolm Fraser stated that 'the family is the focus of Australian life'.[18]

The liberal constellation of 'individual', 'liberty' and 'freedom' is either not found, or found very sparsely, in these two speeches, while 'family' and 'home', terms that hearken back to former liberal leaders, appear quite frequently. At the same time, it is true that Howard did refer to 'free individuals' in *The Australia I Believe In* in 1995 but he also wrote that he valued 'the central role of families in the lives of individuals' and stated that he believed 'in an Australia in which the family is recognised as the central, stabilising and cohesive unit of our society'. He also advocated policies to make life easier for single-income families.[19] In the 1988 manifesto, *Future Directions*, there is an appeal to the individual but also a recognition of 'the basic institutions of home, family and community' as crucial to the wellbeing of the country.[20] Why should this be so?

A clue can be found in those passages of the speeches where there are also some interesting connections between family, home and small business. Consider the following from John Howard in 2004:

A belief that the family is the greatest source of emotional support and inspiration that an individual can ever have. As the son of a small business owner an unshakeable belief in the role of dynamic small business as an engine of economic progress and personal self-fulfilment. A passionate belief in flexible workplaces free of rigidity in the industrial system and unwanted union interference.

Our commitment to small business is strong, consistent and enduring. But so, of course, is our commitment to the Australian family, an unshakable belief that it really is the centre of the life of this nation and a belief that the role of government is not to tell parents how to bring up their children, not to tell parents where they should be educated, not to tell parents whether one or other should be at home full time when the children are young.

Small businesses are the heart and soul of the Australian economy. There are 1.2 million of them, employing almost 3.5 million Australians. They are dynamic. Many new small businesses are started by women. Many operate from home.

They represent the new face of innovative Australia. The new face of entrepreneurial Australia.

This is a fascinating passage, as Howard moves seamlessly from his own background to idealise small business as 'an engine of … personal self-fulfilment' and then on to his 'commitment to the Australian family' and the right of parents to stay at home with young children. Then the following paragraph brings together small business, home, women and innovation. Again, it is worth noting that Howard had stated that he particularly valued the role of small business, in particular in 1995. Howard's vision of innovation contrasts with the model of innovation based on the alternative triad of university, government and big business, such as was expressed in the 'clever country', Bob Hawke's recasting of Donald Horne's depiction of Australia as the 'lucky country'.

Contrast these sentiments with those of John Howard in 2007:

Families are the building blocks of a good society and
the policies that we've developed over the last eleven and
a half years, the family tax benefits, the baby bonus and
many others, have supported families at every stage of life
expanding the horizons of their choices.

Evidence from around the world shows that a culture of
saving and home ownership, even among families on modest
incomes, is associated with an orientation towards the future:
household stability, stable marriages, steady employment,
educational attainment, healthy lifestyles and local civic
involvement. This is the essence of the opportunity society
I want Australia to become, where people are encouraged to
work hard, save and look after their families and contribute

to their communities. In addition, capital gains tax will
be removed for Australians who share equity in a family
member's first home. The home being an almost sacred part
of the Australian Liberal creed stretching back to Menzies'
memorable evocation of homes material, homes human
and homes spiritual in the forgotten people speech of 1942.
And what unites our creed of optimism is the belief that the
Australian people do not need governments instructing them
about virtue. They are more than capable of charting their
own course towards a good life for themselves and for their
families.

As I noted earlier, Menzies referred to home, not the family, in *The Forgotten People*. Here, it is clear that Howard's invocation of family is meant to be equivalent to Menzies' idealisation of the home. The home is described as 'almost sacred'. The individual and the family are connected together so that the whole basis of a person working hard is to 'look after their families and contribute to their communities'.

Howard was absolutely correct to make the connection between his vision of a small-business Australia that revolved around the family with Menzies' forgotten people. This linkage between family, home and a desire to be self-sufficient and not dependent on anyone else has a long history in Australia. It is a desire that has deep roots in what might be termed the Australian dream of a republic of small property owners. It makes perfect sense to anyone who has been brought up in a family that owned and ran a small business.

There is a contrast here between the rhetoric of the 'broad church' largely pitched at the level of rhetoric and ideology and the 'subterranean' set of political values that motivates someone like

Howard. *The Forgotten People*, a work to which Howard and Fraser both looked back, is not a work of political philosophy but a statement of the values that have motivated Liberals from Menzies to Howard. Those values placed great emphasis on self-reliance and personal effort but also on the role of the state to provide the conditions under which that self-reliance could flourish. What Howard advocates can be described ideologically as social liberalism. Howard's chapter on his welfare measures in *Lazarus Rising* indicates his social liberal orientation.[21]

The situation created by the results of the 2004 election, whereby the Coalition had control of both houses of parliament and Howard possessed more authority as prime minister than had hitherto been the case, meant that he was in a position to unleash what is best described as the utopian side of these values in the shape of WorkChoices. Howard admits that control of the Senate granted to his government in 2004 was unexpected, an accident of history.[22] Fortune had smiled on him. He had a once-in-a-generation opportunity to do something. Not only that, but it could be construed that providence had granted Australia the great gift of prosperity.

I have argued elsewhere that there have been three 'utopian moments' in Australia: the move to re-distribute land in the 1850s and 1860s through free selection; the Deakinite settlement of the early 20th century with its emphasis on a 'new province for law and order' and 'modest comfort'; and what can be described as the 'education revolution' of the past 30 years.[23] It is now possible to draw a series of interim conclusions.

First, in seeking to deregulate the industrial relations system through WorkChoices, Howard stood in direct opposition to the second utopian moment of Deakin and Henry Bournes Higgins. He opposed the Deakinite moment because it institutionalised union power through its use of the courts to create industrial peace. Courts were necessary to impose order by Deakinite liberals because, following David Syme, only some sort of state-sponsored power could impose order in a world composed of corrupt human beings.[24] Liberal critics of industrial arbitration, such as Elton Mayo, disliked it because they believed it suppressed organic relationships between employer and employees and reduced all conflict within a workplace to a matter of wages and conditions.[25] Underpinning such critiques was a belief that artificial state-backed interventions into society do not allow for the development of natural and harmonious relationships between people. Howard's belief that families and their members are the best judges of what they should do indicates that he believed more in natural harmony than state-imposed harmony.

Second, Howard was not a supporter of the 'education revolution' form of Australian utopianism. He did not think that university education would lead to the creation of a more prosperous and just society. This is unlike Sir Robert Menzies, who believed strongly in the capacity of education to create a better world.[26] Educational utopianism, which focuses heavily on universities and which has permeated much of Australia, has the creation of a tertiary-educated elite to run the country as its goal. It has been largely appropriated by the Labor Party. Howard's utopianism is that of family and small business.

Third, the utopianism expressed by WorkChoices goes back to the sorts of impulses that led to the various Land Acts of the colonial period. The dream of the Land Acts was a social order of small producers who would live together in villages composed of families and create a harmonious social order. A similar vision inspired Bob Santamaria and his dream of an Australia composed of rural Catholic villages nearly 100 years later.[27] It also informed the Australian suburban dream and the desire to be independent as the owner of a small business. It is not opposed to the ideal of community but views community as something built up from below, not imposed from above, and involves the principle of subsidiarity.

Fourth, Howard's version of this utopian impulse can be described ideologically as a sort of social liberal distributism. The role of government is to establish the framework and conditions under which families and small businesses can thrive. Understood in this way, WorkChoices makes perfect sense as the removal of those impediments that hinder the natural operation of human relationships, with those relationships being understood more in terms of family and home than the abstract individual.

What does this mean? Imposing a liberal and conservative template on Australian political thought can be somewhat misleading, especially if these modes of politics are viewed through an American, and/or English, lens. The ideas that have driven Australian politics are not primarily derived from the icons of political theory such as Burke or Mill. There are other sorts of ideas, many subterranean, that have also influenced politics in Australia. These include distributism, traditionalist republicanism, and a faith in what is best described as 'rough justice'. One can see these sorts of ideas at work in Australian political history, including both the so-called Australian settlement and in Menzies' *The Forgotten People*. Howard inherited and developed these ideas.

My firm conclusion is that the terms 'liberal' and 'conservative' have their uses both in political rhetoric and for academics seeking to reduce complexity to simple models. But they also tend to obscure the sorts of values and impulses that lead to action in the real world. Also, we all have utopian impulses, even those of us who claim the mantle of conservatism. In the somewhat extraordinary circumstances following the 2004 election, the opportunity arose for John Howard to put his utopian impulses on display. I feel that they are far more revealing in explaining his actions than anything to do with the idea of the 'broad church'.

In many ways, Howard can be considered to be the last Menzian. True, he did not take on Menzies' view of education and the university. But in terms of his emphasis on individual, family and personal responsibility, there is a connection running from Menzies to Fraser to Howard.

Despite Howard's desire to re-invigorate the Liberal Party through his rhetorical vision of the 'broad church', he remained a Liberal who was shaped by these traditional political ideas, which were best expressed in his actions.

19

THE HOWARD GOVERNMENT AND MINISTERIAL STAFF

MARIA MALEY

The role of ministerial staff in Australia's political system has grown steadily since the election of the Whitlam Labor Government in 1972. Today Australia's ministerial offices are large, politicised and powerful. Among the more than 400 ministerial staff working for federal ministers there are chiefs of staff, policy and political advisers, media staff, office managers and receptionists. Here I focus on the work of the policy and political advisers and the chiefs of staff within these offices, discussing the legacy of the Howard Coalition government's use of ministerial staff. Structural changes, professional experience and decisions made during that time fundamentally changed our ministerial staff system. The Howard period exerts a continuing influence on ministerial offices, Cabinet processes and political-administrative relationships.

The development of the ministerial office

To trace the development arc of the ministerial staff system we need to understand the foundational decisions made in the early 1980s. It was the Whitlam Government which first brought large numbers of people from outside the public service into ministers' offices, and this was continued to some extent by the Fraser Government. The structures that we still have today were created, however, in 1984 with the passing of special legislation to govern the employment of ministerial staff: the *Members of Parliament(Staff) Act 1984*, by the Hawke Labor Government. It was in 1984 that the crucial decisions were made, which established ministerial advisers as a separate category of staff who were political appointees, employed personally by ministers outside the public service and not bound by a requirement to be impartial.[1]

There was bipartisan support to expand the ministerial staff system at this time. In an internal review of the Fraser years known as the 'Valder Report' (after its principal author, John Valder), the Liberal Party favoured substantially increasing the political support staff for ministers to help them gain greater control over the apparatus of government.[2] Labor's plan was to place politically appointed staff inside the public service, but this was fiercely resisted by the leading public servants of the day, in particular Sir Geoffrey Yeend, the head of Department of the Prime Minister and Cabinet (PM&C).[3] While Yeend supported many of the public service reforms that Labor was making at the time, he was implacably opposed to the idea of placing political staff inside the public service. Yeend saw this as certain to destroy the Westminster public service Australia had inherited, which was based on an impartial public service. In the end Labor compromised, and did not place political staff inside the public service. It created a separate structure for political staff, outside the public service, so that departments remained impartial. This separation of the political staff from the impartial public service is the fundamental structural characteristic of Australia's ministerial staff system and it has had a number of consequences.

One is that there were no constraints on its growth, and over the next 20 years the politicised ministerial office flourished. The move to the new (permanent) Parliament House in 1988 created space for the burgeoning staff numbers. Spacious offices now accommodated increasing ranks of ministerial advisers, who worked with ministers in the secluded and separate ministerial wing of the building. This meant ministers no longer mixed with members of parliament, the media and others walking the corridors, intensifying the relationship with their staff and increasing their influence. In the Hawke and Keating periods, the role of ministerial advisers grew significantly.

Ministerial staff under Howard: structural legacy

This is the context in which the Howard Government came to power in 1996. The newly elected Coalition maintained the staffing structures Labor had created. John Howard was initially critical of the size of ministerial staffs and reduced the numbers by around 20 per cent. Over time, the numbers swelled beyond what they had been under Labor. In May 2007 there were 437 ministerial staff, a number that was not exceeded until October 2019 when it reached 441 staff.[4] The most dramatic growth in the Howard years was in the size of the Prime Minister's Office (PMO), which grew from 30 staff under Paul Keating to 50 under John Howard. In 2020 the PMO had 57 staff members.[5]

The Howard Government went on to entrench and elaborate the ministerial staff system it inherited from Labor, especially by reorganising the PMO to be more focused on political management and executive co-ordination.[6] There was an increased role for political actors and political considerations in government decision-making. In their study of the chiefs of staff to Australian prime ministers, political scientists Anne Tiernan and Rod Rhodes describe the staffing of John Howard's office as the 'triumph of the political'. Political considerations moved to centre stage.[7] Under Paul Keating the PMO was very powerful and it played a strong co-ordinating and policy advising role. Its authority was, however, largely informal. This led to some rare, but damaging, mistakes. One was the 1994 woodchip licence decision, where little restraint was exerted over warring ministers.[8]

When the Howard Government came to power it introduced some important innovations to the structure of the PMO, strengthening its capacity to exert control over ministerial offices and the management of government business. The PMO became critical to Howard's centralised control of political and policy direction.[9] Initially it was not as effective, and early stumbles culminated in the resignation of two of Howard's most senior staff, in the wake of the Travel Rorts Affair.[10] Arrangements stabilised after 1998, with Arthur Sinodinos in the role of chief of staff and the restructuring of the PMO, which now included a large media unit.[11] Sinodinos' personal and professional qualities were critical to the effectiveness of the PMO. Later PMs, and even Labor political staffers, have said he set the 'gold standard' for how to run a PMO.[12] (His 'gold standard' was used to criticise a later occupant of the role, Peta Credlin.)

Howard broke with longstanding practice and installed a political adviser as Cabinet Secretary, Michael L'Estrange, who had worked for him in the lead-up to the 1996 campaign.[13] Since 1949, this role had been filled by the secretary of the PM&C. Now a political actor was put in charge of managing the operation of Cabinet, its documents and its meetings, although PM&C staff still provided support and administration. The wording of Cabinet decisions – which are always important, contentious and have consequences – was in the hands of a political operator, not a senior public servant. This was because Howard believed Cabinet was essentially a political operation.[14] There was initial frostiness between L'Estrange and PM&C, and the Cabinet Secretary moved from the department to an office in the ministerial wing of Parliament House. Over time, however, this became a crucial relationship for ensuring centralised political control and steering.

Working under the Cabinet Secretary was a new unit known as the Cabinet Policy Unit, which was small – fewer than seven members – but proved to be effective.[15] The Cabinet Secretary and Cabinet Policy Unit formed part of a 'sophisticated infrastructure of advice and support for [Howard] and his Cabinet'.[16] The Cabinet Policy Unit provided Howard with independent advice on matters coming before Cabinet. It enabled political management of the Cabinet process and more strategic thinking, because of its role of keeping an eye on long-term agendas, so often obscured by the need to respond to short-term crises. Senior public servants had suggested the idea of Cabinet 'retreats' for ministers to focus on policy co-ordination and the big issues. At least once a year the Cabinet Secretary asked all department heads for ideas and issues to be discussed at these Cabinet retreats. Mirroring this initiative at the administrative level, all of the department heads met annually at the HC Coombs Centre in Kirribilli, across the street from the prime minister's residence in Sydney. John Howard attended. He was open in talking about his priorities for the year ahead, followed by an extended question and answer session and then drinks.

The Cabinet Secretary and Cabinet Policy Unit worked with ministers, ministers' offices and department heads on the tricky matters of what could be brought to Cabinet, when and how. This freed the prime minister's chief of staff to focus on day-to-day issues, providing personal advice and, importantly, managing the prime minister's relationships.[17] The Cabinet Secretary also worked closely with the secretary of PM&C and with a new unit created in

2003, called the Cabinet Implementation Unit.[18] This was a departmental unit whose remit was to monitor how a select group of the top priority programs arising from decisions of Cabinet were being implemented. They produced reports giving ministers and departments a traffic light rating – green, amber or red – depending on their progress in implementation. This kind of centralised tracking made ministers nervous at times but it also increased discipline throughout the government. It was an early warning system, alerting the prime minister and the government to potential problems.[19] In this way, new structures in the PMO provided the potential to marshal bureaucratic and political resources in steering policy towards political objectives. This steering capacity was enhanced by strong political authority over the bureaucracy.

Despite initial tensions between the Howard Government and the public service (after one-third of departmental heads were sacked and public service numbers slashed in 1996), departments generally became highly responsive and attuned to government objectives.[20] Appointed in 2003, the Secretary of PM&C, Peter Shergold, provided the prime minister with a confidential document every week called 'Horizons'. This two- to three-page document made Howard aware of upcoming matters at the political and bureaucratic level that he 'should be alert to'.

All these mechanisms formed part of an interlocking system of political and bureaucratic co-ordination at the centre of government. How well the mechanisms worked in practice varied, depending on the individuals involved. But these structural innovations made it possible to achieve centralised political control over the ministry and the public service. It was also helped by the unusual stability of the senior staff around John Howard and the consistency of the prime ministership, with only one incumbent over a period of nearly 12 years. This contrasts with the volatility of subsequent governments, where both prime ministers and their staff have churned rapidly.

The Rudd and Gillard Labor governments did not follow Howard's model, and dispensed with the Cabinet Policy Unit and assigned the role of cabinet secretary to a minister. When the Coalition returned to power in 2013 under the leadership of Tony Abbott, it replicated the structure that had been developed during Howard era, reinstating the Cabinet Policy Unit (now called the Cabinet Office) and, with one exception, the Cabinet Secretary was again a political staffer.[21] In the Morrison Government the role of the Cabinet Secretary has grown even further. Their authority now includes giving ministers approval to bring items to Cabinet, finalising the agenda, and approving meeting attendees and ministerial absences.[22] In this way, the Howard Government created a model for subsequent Coalition prime ministers in how they would structure and organise the PMO and the Cabinet.

Legacy of experience

There was a more direct legacy flowing from the Howard Government to subsequent Coalition governments. Australia has one of the biggest ministerial staffs in the world. Staff turnover is high. Over its long life, the Howard government employed many people as political staff. Some of them became significant players in subsequent Coalition governments, including the Morrison Government. Of the 30 Coalition ministers in office during March 2020, eight – that is, one quarter – worked as political staffers in the Howard era. Greg Hunt, Alan Tudge, Josh Frydenberg, Matthias Cormann, Paul Fletcher, Dan Tehan, and Linda Reynolds have brought their experience as advisers between 1996 and 2007 to their work as cabinet ministers in the Morrison Government. Since 2013, four of the five cabinet secretaries have previously worked as political advisers in the Howard Government.[23] Prime Minister Morrison's Chief of Staff, John Kunkel, worked as a political staffer for Tim Fischer, Mark Vaile and John Howard (as speechwriter) and was also employed in the Cabinet Policy Unit in the Howard period. The continuing influence of the Howard Government is apparent in the presence of its former staff now filling key political positions. Its influence is also felt in the senior ranks of the bureaucracy. Phil Gaetjans was a ministerial staffer for ten years in the Howard Government and now heads PM&C.

Ministerial advisers are sometimes denigrated as 'wet behind the ears', 'the kindergarten' or 'the teenagers'. The head of PM&C, Martin Parkinson, lamented in 2018 that ministerial staff, like politicians, receive no prior training:

> before taking up positions that are central to democracy. ...
> [They receive] no training on the operation of government,
> their personal roles and responsibilities, or the separation
> between the apolitical public service and their own, correctly,
> political roles.

He said 'it can be hard for staffers ... to know how to work properly and most effectively with the public service to implement their agenda'.[24] Most of the training advisers receive is on-the-job.[25] Often they bring to the job little in the way of practical experience, institutional memory, and understanding of the public service or government processes. What they do bring is political loyalty, personal ambition and eagerness to learn. It is therefore important that some staff bring experience to the position and provide a counterweight to the 'boy scouts in the office'.

I researched the group of political staff recruited for the first

Abbott Government in 2013, when the Coalition came to power after six years in opposition. At the time, the media reported the government was seeking 'grey hairs', people with previous advisory experience, to join ministers' offices. I found that 27 per cent of the policy advisers and chiefs of staff recruited at this time had previously worked as ministerial staff in the Howard Government. Many returned to work as ministerial staff again after working in other careers.

Almost 70 per cent of chiefs of staff in early 2014 were formerly political advisers in the Howard Government. Most did not stay very long. Nevertheless, they formed a cadre of seasoned political operatives in the first period of Coalition rule. We think of the public service as providing the crucial continuity in our political system. It appears that some continuity of political personnel may be emerging in our system, because of the large staff structures that now exist. A small political cadre can have experience spanning different governments and time periods, bringing knowledge gained from advising one government to the service of future governments. This is a positive development, providing a bedrock of experience in a workforce that is often young and constantly churning.

Legacy of accountability and transparency

The more negative aspects of the Howard Government's legacy for ministerial staff relate to accountability and transparency.

During this period there was an intense focus on the role and accountability of ministerial staff. The Senate Committee which inquired into the 2001 Children Overboard affair noted that ministerial staff played a worrying role in the events.[26] Amplifying these concerns, the Howard Government did not allow its staff to appear before the Senate Committee. Commentators, such as academic

Patrick Weller, began referring to ministerial staff as 'junk yard attack dogs' and the 'hard men and the hit men' of the political system. Weller described them as 'convenient scapegoats who will take the bullet for their ministers and protect them from political fallout'.[27]

This was not the only catalyst for the deep questioning that began at this time. Pushing to the surface were anxieties about how the role of staff had developed and grown since 1984, with no regulation and scant attention to its broader impacts, which were now being felt. There were calls from many quarters to reconsider the roles, structures and practices that had evolved over the previous two decades and to better define the employment of ministerial staff in the future.[28] The Howard Government did not step into that conversation.

In 2003 a new senate committee was established specifically to examine the role and functions of ministerial staff, how they could be held accountable and the adequacy of their employment framework. It was called the *Inquiry into (Staff) Employed under the Members of Parliament Staff Act 1984*. Its report was tabled at the end of 2003. Among other things, the committee recommended a code of conduct be developed for ministerial staff, which would clarify their role and its boundaries. The code needed to state that ministerial staff could not direct public servants and could not make executive decisions. The committee recommended there be an annual report on ministerial staff for greater transparency and to bring them into line with information provided on the public service. It also recommended that ministerial staff be allowed to appear before parliamentary committees in certain limited circumstances.

The government senators on the committee rejected all of the recommendations. They argued it was unnecessary to have a code of conduct and that any regulation of staff could undermine the role of ministers and the confidential processes of government. The Howard Government never formally responded to the committee's report. This was a lost opportunity to have a bipartisan debate about the appropriate role of ministerial advisers and the restrictions that ought to be imposed on their conduct.

When Labor came to power in 2007 under Kevin Rudd, it introduced a code of conduct for ministerial staff and an annual report on their arrangements. The Rudd Government announced that it would allow its staff to appear before committees in some limited circumstances, although that policy has not yet been tested. On returning to office in 2013, the Coalition maintained the code of conduct under a new name (the *Statement of Standards for Ministerial Staff*), and added a new standard – that staff must not post online commentary or publish books or articles expressing their personal views about policy. It abolished the annual report.

The wording of the current *Statement of Standards* is weak. It states that advisers must 'acknowledge' they are not authorised to direct public servants and 'recognise' that executive decisions are the preserve of ministers and public servants. Writing from the vantage point of academia following his retirement from the public service, Peter Shergold argues that more explicit directions about what staff 'may not' or 'must not' do would be more effective.[29] Enforcement of the standards is private and secretive, in the hands of the PMO and the Government Staffing Committee, a body internal to the government which does not report publicly on its meetings.

In 2019 the Independent 'Thodey' Review of the Australian Public Service recommended that the government establish a statutory code of conduct for staff, with 'appropriate' mechanisms of enforcement (for 'appropriate', read 'independent').[30] The Morrison Government rejected this proposal. Many commentators continue to believe that accountability mechanisms for ministerial staff need to be improved. Developing strong systems of accountability is not a straightforward task. This remains unfinished business in our political system.

Perhaps the most powerful and enduring legacy of the ministerial staff system in the Howard era is the loss of transparency. Until 2001, the names of ministerial staff were published in the Commonwealth Government Directories, alongside the names of senior public servants. This practice changed in the Howard Government's third term. In the 2002 Directory, the names of ministerial staffers were removed. They have not been in the public domain since. In most other countries, the names of ministerial staff are published. At a time when there were calls for greater accountability for ministerial staff, the Howard Government moved in the opposite direction. The shutters came down. Ministerial advisers moved into the shadows and remain there. It is not clear why this decision was made. The government provided no justification or explanation. While this period was marked by security concerns in the wake of the 9/11 terror attacks, it also coincided with the Children Overboard scandal, where the conduct of ministerial staff was under intense scrutiny. The most plausible explanation is that it was a decision to shield staff from the media and to limit parliamentary scrutiny of their conduct. It is a decision upheld by subsequent governments of all parties. Ministerial staff play a vital role in supporting ministers to be effective in their jobs. To recognise this, senior ministerial staff should have their names published in the online government directory alongside those of senior public servants.

Legacy for minister–department relationships

To assess the legacies of past decisions, the influence of ministerial staff on the public service must be considered, and especially their impact on the relationship between ministers and departments. In 1983, Sir Geoffrey Yeend opposed the idea of creating a separate institution for political staff under the *Members of Parliament (Staff) Act*, which he referred to as forming 'a separate political service'. He predicted this would divide ministers from their departments, cause departments to become 'more remote', and it would reduce ministers' attachment to their departments. In his brief to Prime Minister Bob Hawke, he warned this could threaten the entire political-administrative system as 'it is the minister's relationship with his or her department that is quite fundamental to our system of administration and our system of government'.[31]

As ministers rely more on their political staff for policy advice and as the locus of policy-making shifts increasingly towards ministerial offices, government departments face many challenges. Ministerial advisers are third players in the minister-department relationship. They are gatekeepers and intermediaries between the minister and the department. All documents pass through their hands and they have the power to prevent departmental advice from reaching the minister. If departments cannot work effectively with ministerial offices, they risk disconnection from ministers and from policy-making on key issues.

Some former senior public servants argue that since the end of the Howard period there has been a decisive shift in the policy-advising role towards ministerial offices. In his history of the Treasury, long-time official Paul Tilley describes how in the post-Howard period ministerial staff took on a prominent policy role, 'usurping a substantial part of the core policy role at the expense of the public service'.[32] He recounted that at one point Treasury stopped providing written policy advice on contentious issues, providing only factual information:

> The balance of policy advising was shifting to the ministerial offices, where issues were seen more through a political lens. Treasury allowed itself to be manoeuvred out of the policy advising space to become more of an information provider. The ideal situation for the offices was for Treasury to provide the factual material and they would put the policy advice over the top. There was no policy partnership here.[33]

The Sports Rorts scandal of 2019–20 provides an extreme example of the supplanting of departmental advice by that of ministerial staff. At one stage the Board of Sport Australia was told not to send its endorsed funding recommendations to the minister as the minister's office had already developed its own list of proposed grants, using a different set of criteria. It did not submit its own recommendations for two funding rounds.[34] There is widespread concern about these trends. A 2018 survey of public servants revealed a large number felt uncertainty about the role of the public service and feared its role might be usurped by political staff.[35] Former Public Service Commissioner Andrew Podger argues there are serious problems in political–administrative relations today; he describes relationships between ministers and departments as changing 'from a partnership to one often more akin to "master-servant" where the "master" is not just the minister but also the minister's chief of staff and other advisers'.[36]

These trends may be a product of the febrile and politically chaotic environments that followed the Howard years, and the heightened political pressures now faced by ministers and governments.

However, changes made in the Howard period laid the groundwork for the developments: the growth of the ministerial office, its greater importance in political management, the dominance of political considerations which characterised the governing style of the period, and the demand for heightened responsiveness from the public service. These changes provided the preconditions for the increasing influence of ministerial offices in governments which followed, under arguably less capable leaders who faced more fraught political environments. As the Sports Rorts scandal demonstrates, these shifts continue to be features of our political–administrative landscape. As Australia's ministerial staff system continues to evolve, we need to ensure that policy advice from the public service is considered and can gain purchase in ministers' offices. Relationships between ministers' offices and departments need to be close partnerships, in which the professional, non-partisan expertise of the public service is respected.

The nearly 12 years of the Howard Government was an important period in the development of our ministerial staff system. Innovations, structural changes and decisions made at the time have left a powerful legacy that subsequent governments have built upon. It continues to influence the professional lives of some Morrison Government ministers, bureaucrats and key advisers, who learned foundational lessons about ministerial work during the Howard era. The most transformative change was the shift of ministerial staff from the public domain to a hidden arena that is accessible to few. This complicates and constrains attempts to increase their accountability. The amplification of political resources in the Howard period, which delivered centralised political control and greater steering capacity to ministers, laid the groundwork for possibly unintended consequences. In the periods which followed, ministerial offices have become a prominent element in Australian political–administrative relationships. This creates a risk that their growing influence will displace the professional, non-partisan expertise of the public service. We must pay careful attention to this development, ensuring that critical relationships between ministers and departments remain strong and close, and that the independence and integrity of public institutions remain protected.

20

PREPARED FOR OPPOSITION?

MARIJA TAFLAGA

The Federal Liberal Party of Australia entered opposition on 24 November 2007 after almost 12 years in government. John Howard's government had been characterised by strong internal stability, significant policy achievements and its share of policy failures and scandals. At the beginning of 2007, the election was considered a tough, but not impossible task.[1] Howard had won victories from behind in 1998, 2001 and 2004, and he faced the untested Kevin Rudd and an Australian Labor Party (ALP) that had lost four consecutive elections. Ultimately, Rudd proved deft at using the government's own longevity and strengths against it and the Australian people politely but firmly dismissed the government. The 2007 election saw the end of Australia's second-longest serving government, the second-longest prime ministership, and for only the second time since Federation, a prime minister who lost his seat. Returning to opposition brought with it memories of 13 years of leadership turmoil, ideological contestation and personal rancour that had plagued the party from 1983 to 1996. Would the party meet a similar fate in the 2010s?

At face value, asking whether a government is prepared for opposition seems a silly question. Much of Westminster parliamentary politics is bluster and theatre. In this confidence game, planning for what ought to come after is a morale-sapping admission of defeat. Particularly at a time when colleagues, party activists and volunteers must sustain their faith in the possibility of victory and must work hard to limit electoral losses. Too much forward planning could be seen to tempt fate.

Yet political parties' preparedness for opposition can be assessed beyond formal planning. Political parties are institutions with their own formal structures and rules, informal norms and cultures. These formal and informal features establish the 'rules of the game' within parties, but also structure possible actions for party members and officials and even shape their capacity to imagine what is feasible or desirable in terms of party reform. Moreover, parties operate within an adversarial parliamentary system that shapes how political parties will interpret the role of opposition – where do parties balance 'constructive' opposition with the aim of destroying and replacing the government? Likewise, the different operating procedures and norms within the Australian House of Representatives and the Senate produce different patterns of opposition, even within the same party.

All political parties are made of three dimensions or faces.[2] First, the party in public office (i.e. parliament), which comprises elected members and senators. This includes institutions such as the party room, the leader's office and the (shadow) cabinet. Second, the party in central office, which is responsible for fundraising, running election campaigns and administering candidate selection. For the Liberals, this comprises the Federal Secretariat located in Canberra, and the state divisions, which hold considerable independent powers that include candidate selection and managing election campaigns within their state. Third, the party on the ground: the party's membership base spread across electorates throughout the country. Liberals tend to think of the membership as part of the organisational wing. These 'grassroots' are the bottom rung in a hierarchical organisational ladder. Until the advent of social media, local branch membership was a key way that parties connected with ordinary citizens.[3]

While no political party in power actively prepares for opposition, I will examine the Liberal Party's transition to opposition in terms of its stability, its capacity to organise itself as an opposition, conduct internal policy debates, and assess the party's preparedness as an organisation to adapt to the rigours and strains of opposition, before broadly considering Howard's legacy.

Stability and party leadership

The Liberal Party is leader-dominated, particularly when compared with other parties in Westminster systems. The parliamentary party elects the leader – not the party executive or members. Because they are elected by their colleagues, Liberal leaders have the power to hire and fire their cabinets. Leaders are given significant authority to set a policy agenda and are expected to act as the corporate figurehead of the party, with their philosophical and ideological views matching the consensus of those within the party room at the very least.[4] But this authority is only fully granted to proven winners – the Liberal Party is famously intolerant of electoral losers. Throughout the democratic world, expectations on party leaders have increased. As politics has become more 'presidentialised' or 'personalised', party leaders have gained more authority and resources, but also a greater weight of responsibility to make the right decisions.[5] The broad political and media environment, which promotes this kind of personalised politics, has only intensified this longstanding trend, reinforced by the Liberal Party's internal organisation and its preference for strong and dominant leadership.

This pattern is further complicated when in opposition. It is not for nothing that commentators like to say that the opposition leader's role is 'the worst job in the country'. Opposition leaders have less influence than prime ministers and fewer spoils to share. They also have the unenviable job of motivating a group of politicians, many of whom who are demoralised or mourning the loss of power and status. Indeed, Liberal leaders must try to foster co-operation within their party without the disciplining power of government and without the public service. Opposition then adds an additional level of complexity for Liberal leaders – they have less personal authority to get their own way. During opposition, the Liberal party room has typically been less willing to acquiesce to leaders on contentious policy issues. Additionally, while opposition leaders have more resources than in the past (staff, travel budgets or the parliamentary budget office), they concurrently carry a greater individual responsibility for decisions made. This makes Liberal opposition leaders (and increasingly, even prime ministers) vulnerable.

Thus, when John Howard lost his seat in 2007, and Peter Costello announced a day later that he would not seek the leadership, the Liberal Party was thrown into disarray.[6] Campbell Newman, the Mayor of the Brisbane City Council, was the party's highest ranking public office-holder. Commentators speculated that Labor might govern for a decade. For Howard, losing his seat relieved him of serving out part of his term and it also meant one less by-election to fight on top of the wave of retirements of former ministers. Costello's refusal to take up the leadership (he was clearly the heir presumptive to Howard) and the departure of many experienced Coalition figures such as Alexander Downer and Mark Vaile, shocked those remaining in parliament and presaged rapid generational change. This increased the likelihood of internal party instability. (See chapter 16 in this volume on leadership succession.)

The party was fortunate that the loss in 2007 was not devastating compared with Labor's defeat in 1996, which decimated its parliamentary ranks. Three men put themselves forward to lead the Liberal Party: Tony Abbott (who withdrew before the leadership ballot), Malcolm Turnbull and Brendan Nelson. Only Abbott had any – albeit brief – experience of being in opposition. Within three years, the party would see three leadership changes and each of the three challengers would become leader. While Nelson was successful in the first contest, he remained leader for only nine months, at which point he was successfully challenged by the ambitious Turnbull.[7] Turnbull lasted until December 2009.

Turnbull was deposed in tumultuous scenes as the Liberal Party was unable to resolve an internal party dispute over climate policy. Abbott emerged as an unlikely leader – his aggressive political persona and erratic post-election behaviour had seen many write him off as a serious contender. As leader, his belligerence on climate policy wrongfooted Labor and contributed to its ill-fated decision to depose Rudd as prime minister in 2010.[8]

At the 2010 election, Abbott brought the Labor Government, now led by Julia Gillard, into minority. While Abbott was unable to secure confidence and supply from crossbench members, his electoral success, Labor's weakened position and his relentless, negative political tactics instilled the Liberal opposition with a new confidence and discipline, effectively ending the party's downward spiral of internal instability for the remainder of its time in Opposition.[9] Julie Bishop, the Liberals' most senior woman, never chose to make a bid for the leadership. Instead, she went on to work with all three men as Deputy Leader of the Liberal Party, primarily in foreign affairs.

Organising Parliamentary opposition and internal policy debates

Opposition is a time to reassess the party's policy direction (though usually, not its broad philosophical principles) and to allow more internal party debate. How the opposition chooses to organise itself includes both procedural questions and questions of style. A party's approach to opposition influences how internal policy debates evolve. Both weaker party leaders and looser party discipline facilitate a wider debate. This is normal for a party in opposition and a healthy level of internal party debate is desirable, despite what media commentators might say about discord and division.

The opposition's role is long-institutionalised in Australia, so many decisions about how to organise itself are routine. The structure of the shadow cabinet mimics the government: party leaders allocate portfolios and decide how to deploy the team's ministerial experience. The greater challenge is adjusting to the reality of opposition where scope to lead debate or to *do something* is limited. Most of an opposition's work is reacting to the government's agenda and less time is spent developing policy. The opposition's impotence is exaggerated in the House of Representatives, where governments usually hold majorities. This contrasts strongly with the Senate, where the opposition is influential and able to draw on significant scrutiny, investigative and legislative powers.[10] Indeed, senators, particularly backbenchers, report that opposition often offers more meaningful and engaging work than government.[11]

Oppositions face the dilemma of how to interpret the role of opposition as *political parties*. The solidification of the party system in the 19th century changed the way parliament operates and the result is that *political parties*, not individual elected representatives, interpret and enliven the role and functions of oppositions.

Decisions are taken through a party, rather than a legislative, lens. Older conceptions of how oppositions ought to behave, articulated by parliamentary legends such as Winston Churchill and Robert Menzies, emphasised the opposition's foremost duty is to oppose. These objections were made at a time when the primacy of parliament was more significant, and the tradition of the independently minded MP was stronger.[12] However, as the role of government has expanded and party discipline become stricter, parliamentary scholars have emphasised the importance of alternation – that today's opposition is tomorrow's government.[13] The official opposition, once returned to office, will have to implement its promises and live with the consequences of its actions in opposition. Therefore, the opposition must behave responsibly when making promises to voters and when interpreting and practising the norm driving behaviours of the legislature – lest they reap what they sow.[14]

The truth lies somewhere in between, because the role of party-opposition is conflicted. On the one hand, the opposition has absorbed most responsibilities of elected MPs who are not ministers (the executive). This includes both scrutiny and constructive amendment functions. On the other, the opposition is not only critic-in-chief, but *legitimately* seeks to destroy and replace the government. Historically, the Liberal Party has tended to follow Menzies' dictum and emphasise the combative dimension of opposition. John Hewson was a rare exception, where policy was placed centre stage, and Howard, particularly during the 1980s, considered policy development more important than did most Liberal opposition leaders.

In 2007, the Liberal Party had to decide what kind of opposition it would be. This choice was shaped by two major debates that dominated the party's opposition years. First, defining the Howard government's legacy and why the party lost. Second, how to respond to the government's agenda and particularly climate change. Bickering over why the party lost power may seem beside the point, but establishing a consensus about where the party went wrong is directly related to where the party should go next. It is forgotten now, but the Howard government's legacy was open for debate internally. The moderates, led by George Brandis, argued that Howard's leadership had been too narrowly focused on the 'mainstream' and had failed to come to terms with either Indigenous or multicultural Australia, and was too cruel toward refugees, too focused on culture wars and, uninterested, ignored the environment.[15] Kevin Rudd's apology to the Stolen Generations – his first act in parliament – underscored this critique when Brendan Nelson was booed after repeating Howard's formula that Australians need not feel guilty for actions taken 'with the best of intentions'.[16] However, the opposition – briefly and cautiously – supported the dismantling of the Pacific Solution, and a younger generation of front bench Liberals began the process of softening the party's rhetoric on multiculturalism.[17]

But the moderates were unsuccessful in defining Howard's legacy. The dominant explanation, despite the shadow cabinet's continued moderate dominance, was the conservatives' argument that electoral defeat could be explained by policy overreach, particularly on the industrial relations policy, WorkChoices, and the government's longevity.[18] In Rudd, voters had found a youthful version of John Howard, who promised a conservative economic agenda, but with more compassion for the vulnerable and more concern for the environment. Ultimately the Liberals did not demur from repealing WorkChoices, despite a few notable protests (see chapter 3 on WorkChoices). Confining the reasons of electoral loss to WorkChoices and an 'it's time' factor reduced pressure to revisit other policy domains.

The Liberals' first term of opposition was dominated by supporting, and later critiquing, Australia's response to the Global Financial Crisis (GFC) and the dilemma of reacting to Rudd's Carbon Pollution Reduction Scheme (CPRS). For the Coalition, the politics of the GFC was relatively straightforward – it played to its strengths on economics as an issue domain. However, climate policy was significantly more challenging. The split was (and continues to be) difficult to manage because it divided Coalition partners and ruptured the party on its fundamental approach to the role of the state. Pricing carbon – that is, properly accounting for the cost of economic activity on the environment and human health – requires a significant re-organisation of the economy with far-reaching consequences for the way citizens, the economy and the state all relate to each other. As oppositions are the prisoners of ascendant governments' agendas, it was not a policy debate that the opposition could avoid or define in a less provocative way, as the current Coalition government has attempted to by discussing 'energy security' as distinct from the climate emergency. Some members of the party room, particularly those in the Senate, where they were more engaged with the policy detail and did not have electorates to manage, were deeply focused on the policy implications; for others it was a matter of political management. Unlike social issues, such as same-sex marriage, it was not practical to resort to a free vote to resolve the issue. The party, which had deferred action in government, was now forced into making a decision in opposition.

Like other Westminster conservative parties, the Liberal Party grants its parliamentary party supreme authority in policy making. However, the Liberals have poor policy dispute resolution mechanisms and lack formal factions that could facilitate decision brokering. Moreover, the party's remaining policy bodies, such as the party room and the backbench committee system, have declined over time.[19] It is because the party is leader-dominated and invests authority in the parliamentary party to set the policy direction that it becomes vulnerable when it has a weak leader who cannot assert or accommodate the party's policy preferences. In effect, for intractable policy conflict, leadership change becomes the mechanism to resolve the issue.

Malcolm Turnbull faced such a situation in 2009. As Roger Beale argues in his chapter on the environment (chapter 8), the fourth Howard Government relinquished the opportunity to frame and implement a policy on its own terms. It was reactive, not creative. That Howard had gone to the 2007 election promising a price on carbon was important for Turnbull's position. However, his opponents countered that all policies were subject to review in opposition. He could not, and should not, presume the party room supported carbon pricing. Turnbull was unable to dominate his newly resurgent party room and some colleagues resented his driving ambition and high-handed style. Turnbull lacked the experience and political management skills to shepherd the policy through – though he came close. Importantly, Turnbull was bereft of the party machinery that could help resolve the issue without the party resorting to leadership change to force an outcome by proxy. Moreover, the tactics adopted by the Rudd Government, which sought to place maximum political pressure on Turnbull's standing as leader, while hoping to secure the Liberal Party's support to pass the CPRS, proved too much. Both men miscalculated.

Tony Abbott was successful in reducing the Labor Government to minority status at the 2010 election. Labor's vulnerability quelled the Liberals' internal instability as they focused all their energies on bringing down the government on the floor of parliament. Specifically, Abbott's approach to climate policy precipitated the conditions for the Coalition's return to government in 2013.

The Liberals' narrow focus and tight discipline also unleashed an onslaught of negative politics that saw a change in the way parliament is used in conducting Australian democracy.[20] Australia is no stranger to negative and ferocious opposition. In the postwar era Gough Whitlam's attack on Gorton, particularly the 1970 budget, or Billy Snedden and Malcolm Fraser's incessant attacks on the Whitlam government's legitimacy, anticipated Abbott's relentless, and at times juvenile, attacks on the minority Gillard government. As I have argued above, oppositions have a right to negativity – after all, they are in the business of replacing governments. But there are costs. Whitlam would have to confront his own arguments when the Senate attempted to block his budget; Snedden demanded an election in 1974, after which he humiliatingly and ridiculously claimed 'we didn't win, but we didn't lose all', and Fraser never shook off the shadow of illegitimacy that surrounded his ascension to power via the dismissal. The 2010–13 minority parliament was characterised by incessant squabbling, petty politics and hypocritical behaviour on all sides, but the government's inability to control procedure meant that the opposition's negativity was extraordinarily effective and continued unchecked. This spectacularly poor performance was a co-production between Abbott's Opposition and the Gillard Government that saw Australians' trust in politicians and parliament collapse. A change of government in 2013 failed to restore voters' faith as it had in the past and trust in politics continues on its downward trend to this day.[21]

Tony Abbott also came to regret his negatively framed agenda, which constrained his actions in government. Many of the policies opened for debate in the immediate aftermath of defeat in 2007, remained unresolved when the Liberals returned to office – climate change, same-sex marriage and the size of government. Instead of resolving these issues in the relative safety of opposition, they were deferred until they became impossible to ignore in government. As prime minister, Abbott struggled to move beyond being an opposition leader. When Abbott attempted a new direction, embodied by his infamous expenditure-reducing 2014 Budget, his government and his own approval ratings went into freefall. In the last days of his premiership, Abbott was at war with his own party as the decisions of his government became increasingly incoherent.[22] He was replaced as prime minister in 2015, by Malcolm Turnbull. Abbott's difficulties in government are in part related to his failure to engage in policy debate and argue for a positive case for Australia in the 21st century during his time as opposition leader. This failure in part explains his government's thin legacy. In the case of climate change, Australia still has no pathway forward. The wrong lessons were learnt by all from this period of opposition. Shortly after Labor's return to opposition, one senior Labor figure was reported as saying, 'part of the task in opposition is learning that you can bag the shit out of something and still wave it through'.[23] Hardly a good outcome for Australians.

Organisational capacity, reform and renewal

Cut off from the resources of government, parties in opposition must turn to their own central offices for political and policy advice. Today, oppositions are significantly better resourced than in years past. Shadow ministers receive additional salaries, political advisers, travel allowances, and access to expertise within the Parliamentary Library. Since 2010, the Parliamentary Budget Office (PBO), has facilitated the opposition's access to accurate policy costings – though the Abbott-led Opposition had misgivings about the PBO and were slow to utilise this resource.[24] Finally, there are more think tanks and policy groups willing to offer policy advice. Nonetheless, party organisations and their central offices remain important to the smooth running of the parliamentary party.

As Howard's biographer, Wayne Errington, has argued, the Howard years, particularly the fourth term, were a wasted opportunity to tackle long-overdue party reforms.[25] Like parties across the democratic world, the Liberal Party has its share of difficulties including declining and narrowing membership, the corresponding decline in parties' effectiveness as democratic linkages, and continuing debates over internal party democracy.[26] The Liberal Party's strong decentralisation of power presents particular challenges to implementing nationwide reforms, as the painstaking but ultimately modest organisational reforms in 1994 demonstrate. More recently, debates over internal party democracy within New South Wales or the merger of the Liberal and National parties in Queensland demonstrate that reform is challenging at any level of the party.[27]

In 2005, the Liberal Party's retiring Federal President, Shane Stone, warned the party against complacency. In his farewell address, Stone argued for greater centralisation of fundraising and candidate selection, hinting at the destructive influence of factionalism, stating: 'I know that will not sit well with some people who revel in the control they exercise in their local patch and who have largely lost sight of their real political opponents'.[28] This was not a new observation. The party's structural flaws and cultural frailties were documented at the national level in 1983.[29]

Many of the party's problems such as declining party membership, atrophy of the party machine, difficulties in communication and co-operation across state divisions, a lack of productive ways for members to participate in policy discussion, moribund branches, uneven fundraising and funding arrangements, insufficient training for candidates and staff, and problems with formally co-ordinating policy development across the party were raised again by former Federal President, Tony Staley, in his review of the 2007 defeat.[30] In addition, the Staley Review noted that the party was struggling to come to grips with the digital age, both for campaigning and communication. The review mirrored Stone's sentiments by calling for greater powers for the Federal Secretariat. He also illuminated a lack of overall co-ordination, proposing that the Federal Executive should meet at least four times each year. The review argued for more democratic ways of selecting candidates via plebiscites, which some divisions did experiment with in the years following 2007.[31] Notably, the growing problem of factionalism remained unaddressed.[32]

A modest number of changes were made, such as increasing the number of vice-presidents on the Federal Council. Most reforms still needed to be enacted at the state level. Several attempts at reform in the wake of the 2007 defeat ultimately failed, with Brendan Nelson unable to bring his authority to bear on factional power blocks within state divisions.[33] The difficulty was underlined by the Reith Review, which made the same points about party reform in 2010.[34]

An area where the Liberal Party – like most Australian parties – has struggled is in the descriptive representation of the Australian population. Women's under-representation is particularly serious, but was not raised in the 2007 review. The reason for this is explicable. In the mid-2000s, the Liberal Party was making steady, albeit modest, progress at selecting and electing women to office. In a first for the Liberal Party, it elected a female party president, Chris McDiven, in 2005. McDiven was one of several pioneering party activists who had worked tirelessly and without payment to increase women's capacity as candidates in the previous decade. While women's representation was declining at the federal level in the Howard Government's final term, it was increasing at the state level.[35]

With the benefit of hindsight, the Liberal party failed to lift women's representation beyond 25 per cent – at best. In the mid-2000s the party had cause to believe their strategy would continue to bring improvements, but its weaknesses were exposed with defeat in 2007 – many women elected in 1996 were in marginal seats. Part of this was a product of a successful electoral strategy. As Liberal politician Margaret Fitzherbert notes, Howard particularly valued female candidates in marginal seats because of their social skills and ability to connect with the community.[36] But, as critics noted, they were less likely to be promoted to the ministry and their careers were truncated by changing electoral cycles. These concerns prompted calls for the introduction of a quota system.[37] As the Liberals were able to return to office in 2013 without addressing women's under-representation (which is different to 1996), this debate within the party continues to drift. In recent years, the Coalition has responded by selecting more women for Cabinet positions and has reinvigorated efforts to offer women training as candidates.[38] Only time will tell if this strategy proves successful at moving the share of women elected beyond 25 per cent.

Many of the Liberal Party's organisational problems stemmed from its extraordinary electoral success at the federal level and the party's organisational structure remaining largely unchanged since its founding in 1944. Typically, far-reaching reviews only happen in the wake of defeat. Most issues identified in reviews were also present when the party won elections. Internal party reform is difficult because it means taking on entrenched power within one's own organisation and is often described as self-indulgent by the media. Therefore, it is unsurprising that the appetite for reform is low in opposition, when leaders are weak; and low in government, when the party has the pressing task of governing. Party reform is usually undertaken as a way of signalling a willingness to modernise – and often then only as a last resort. Governing parties rarely feel the need to acknowledge that there may be anything amiss within their own organisation.

Whether John Howard would have been able to effect the successful implementation of significant organisational reform throughout the federal organisation or even in the New South Wales division, given the cultural premium placed on federalism and independence of the state divisions within the Liberal Party, is difficult to answer. However, given Howard's authority within the party after the 2004 election, it is difficult to argue that anyone else would be more successful without requiring the party to suffer successive defeats as it had done in the 1990s. As Stone noted in his memoir, Howard resisted calls for some members to retire, seeing this as the purview of the organisation.[39] Howard well understood how the Liberal Party worked and part of that meant respecting the party in central office to carry out its own affairs on its own terms. Perhaps this reluctance is precisely why the party has failed to reform itself over the decades. It is not an accident that ex-party leaders, including Howard and other senior ministers, tend to be at the forefront of reform efforts, knowing full well what is needed. Yet most failed to use their parliamentary authority to push for organisational change when they were at the height of their influence.

Readers might ask: why call for change when the party has won three elections since 2013 (albeit by very small margins on two occasions)? The federal Liberals have been much more electorally successful than Labor. As senior members of the party continue to caution, the present organisation faces significant internal pressures and is losing its vitality, but it is still an organisation that wins elections. The party's long run of success suggests that perhaps these issues are only of concern to political scientists. But the overall decline in how well political parties represent (or reflect) the electorate worldwide is probably linked to a decline in levels of trust by citizens in government.[40] Parties no longer function as democratic linkages. Howard himself has lamented the ever-narrowing pool of candidates, a pool which was already shallow, of Australians to stand for office. This dilemma extends well beyond the Liberal Party, and even beyond Australia. It is a difficult problem facing political institutions throughout the democratic world.

Howard's legacy

With his victory in 2004, John Howard cemented his place in the pantheon of Liberal greats. If the Liberal Party's opposition years between 1983 and 1996 demonstrate anything, it is that the strength of Howard's formula for political success and the party he crafted during his prime ministership proved to be durable. Howard remains an important and respected elder statesman of the party, with only Menzies, the party founder and longer-serving prime minister, casting any shadow over his achievements. Howard's formula of invoking a 'relaxed and comfortable' Australia remains the recipe for electoral success. As does his approach to many pressing policy issues of the day, such as climate change. While Howard missed an opportunity to undertake substantial, effective organisational reforms, the Liberal Party curiously continues to win elections – or is it that Labor still manages to lose them?

PART VIII
CLOSING REFLECTIONS

21

THE HOWARD GOVERNMENT:
A PICTORIAL REVIEW

ELIZABETH LUCHETTI AND DAVID FOOTE

Introduction (Elizabeth Luchetti)

The Australian Government Photographic Service (Auspic) is the official government photographer. It was established in 1988, coinciding with the opening of the new and permanent Parliament House by Her Majesty, Queen Elizabeth II. Auspic takes official photographs for parliamentarians undertaking official business, and photographs of significant events in the life of the parliament. Auspic has been the responsibility of a number of Commonwealth agencies since 1988. The management and preservation of and access to these images are currently the responsibility of the Department of Parliamentary Services.

The Department of Parliamentary Services recognises that Auspic images are unique and valuable assets. To ensure they are managed to a high standard, are preserved for long-term access, and can be easily discoverable to potential users, a project is underway to curate, catalogue and incorporate the selected images into a digital asset management system.

The Auspic Content Migration Project has categorised the photographs into the following groupings:

- parliamentarians' official portraits
- parliamentary proceedings including opening and closing of parliament, state occasions and other ceremonies, speeches and Question Time
- ministry and Cabinet business and group portraits
- the House of Representatives, Senate and Joint House Committees
- the swearing-in of parliamentarians and ministers
- the Australian Parliament House building including construction, maintenance, architecture and gardens
- special events including the Parliament House Open Day, election campaigns and presentations
- visits to Australia by foreign dignitaries and overseas visits by the prime minister, as requested by the Protocol and International Visits Branch[1] in the Department of the Prime Minister and Cabinet (formerly the Ceremonial and Hospitality Branch).

The Auspic collection has historic significance as it is a valuable record of the life and work of the Australian Parliament. The images are also a valuable record of Parliament House as a working building and an icon of Australian democracy.

The Auspic archive consists of both analogue film and digital files. The creation of 'born digital' content began in 2000; however, the generation of both analogue and digital images co-existed in many instances until about 2007. From 2008, all images in the archive have been born digital. The digital archive consists of approximately three million images and grows daily. Images for inclusion in the digital asset management system are selected on the basis of photographic merit (that is, excellence in image composition, content and quality) and/or historical significance and their uniqueness. Many duplicates or derivatives are removed. The project aims to curate, archive and incorporate into the digital asset management system more than 50 000 images from this historic collection and commence curating, cataloguing and archiving new photographs on the day the photograph was taken.

To date, the project team has focused on preparing images from the following categories for incorporation:

- official photographs of parliamentarians dating back to the 35th Parliament (July 1987)
- a 'best of' selection for each year (based on the Auspic photographers' own preliminary curation)
- images of parliamentary committees
- selected international visits by Australian prime ministers
- images of newly sworn ministries and significant group portraits of parliamentarians; and
- the 'best-of' individual prime ministers.

The Auspic project is an exciting opportunity for the Department of Parliamentary Services to preserve these valuable assets and make them easily discoverable to potential users. It will showcase the workings of Parliament House, the senators and members who have served there, and detail important historic events. Aspects of this collection will be shared with the Australian public to enhance research and study into the life and work of the Australian Parliament.

Two seconds of time (David Foote)

I have been invited to nominate ten Auspic photographs capturing the Howard era. What a dilemma trying to narrow down a few representative images from among 3.5 million. Should I go for my own images or my favourites taken by former Auspic colleagues? Ultimately, the selection was down to my favourites and a few from 2004 to 2007, the period covered by this volume. What follows is a brief reminiscence of some of the events I have covered, drawing on images from the Auspic Collection.

I joined Auspic in 1992 and covered the 1993 Federal Election. In 1996, I followed the Leader of the Opposition, John Howard, on his campaign to become prime minister – flying across Australia, often covering several cities in a day, culminating on election night at the Sheraton Hotel in Sydney. Little did I know he would become part of my life for nearly 12 years. We continue to cross paths. Prior to 1996, Auspic only covered events in Parliament House. In 1996 we moved to the Department of the Prime Minister and Cabinet, and started to follow Prime Minister Howard on his visits abroad. During the next 20 years I covered more than 60 overseas visits with six prime ministers. Back in 1996, the news cycle consisted of the morning newspapers and the evening television news. There was no social media and we did not have the constant news cycles we have today. Those were the days of film cameras and basic mobile phones.

I first visited Washington DC and New York City in September 2001. The first night in Washington, Ambassador Michael Thawley hosted a dinner with the Secretary of State, Colin Powell; the Secretary of Defense, Donald Rumsfeld; and Vice President Dick Cheney among the guests. The next day we went to the naval yard where President George W Bush presented the bell for the recently

Howard passes the Lincoln Memorial.
David Foote, Auspic – DPS

Congress building through Police Do Not Cross ribbons.
David Foote, Auspic – DPS

decommissioned warship, USS *Canberra*, to the Prime Minister of Australia. The president and prime minister then travelled to the Oval Office for further talks. As the leaders sat down, I walked backwards, re-positioning for a different photograph. The way behind me was clear as I started to walk backwards; a split second later, I felt something under my foot, and then a hand on my shoulder. Turning around, I found that the toes and hand belonged to the Secretary of State, Colin Powell.

The next day was far different to what I could ever have imagined. I always think of Mr Howard as a walker, as my day always started with covering his morning walk. That day he stopped in front of the White House for a photo with staff and the travelling photographers. Later, while I was eating breakfast and watching the news, there were reports of a plane crash in New York – at the Twin Towers of the World Trade Center. I went to the office, where the staff were watching the live news, in time to see the second plane crash into the second tower. A short time later, as Prime Minister Howard spoke to the travelling Australian media, the Secret Service said a bomb had gone off at the Pentagon and smoke could be seen from our accommodation, the Willard Hotel. The press conference finished and the Prime Minister quickly departed with his Secret Service squad. The Willard Hotel is close to the White House and the area was immediately closed down. We walked to the Australian Embassy and sat there for the rest of the day, watching the shocking events on the large screen.

It is fascinating to see today's news become tomorrow's history. When I spoke recently with Tony O'Leary, Prime Minister Howard's long-serving press secretary, we confirmed that neither of us have any images of Prime Minister Howard from that day. There was always the concern that if we took photos, the media would publish them. If you do not take them, they can't be distributed.

The use of images has a number of pros and cons, depending on the issue. I can think of numerous images taken by press offices over the years that were never released.

As we had travelled to the United States by commercial flights, and all flights were now grounded, the most pressing question was how were we to get home? Fortunately, Prime Minister Howard was offered Airforce Two to take him home. We travelled as far as Hawaii, where a Qantas Boeing 747 was to take us back to Canberra. As we arrived over Canberra, just before dawn, fog rolled in so we couldn't land. Instead, we diverted to Sydney and arrived to the announcement that Ansett Airlines had just collapsed.

Some events have connections that continue to reverberate. On Boxing Day 2004, the Indian Ocean earthquake and tsunami occurred. The epicentre was the west coast of northern Sumatra, Indonesia, and its capital Banda Aceh was especially badly affected. In early February 2005, Prime Minister Howard visited Banda Aceh to observe the Australian Defence Force and civilian aid teams at work. The best way for the Prime Minister to view the devastation was from the Royal Australian Navy Sea King helicopter N16-100, code-named 'Shark 02'. Two months later in April 2005, 'Shark 2' crashed while on relief operations on Nias Island, Indonesia, with the loss of nine lives.

The deceased were returned in a ceremony at Sydney Airport on 5 April 2005. Their families were joined by the Governor General, Major General Michael Jeffery; the President of Indonesia, Susilo Bambang Yudhoyono; and Prime Minister John Howard. Hiding behind my cameras, my eyes watered as I photographed the Governor General, President Yudhoyono and Mr Howard placing medals on the flag-covered coffins. I knew the partner of one of the lost crew and could feel her loss acutely. Autofocus has given me sharp images of many of the sad events I have covered.

Prime Minister Hon John Howard steps from
the Sea King 'Shark 2', Banda Aceh, Indonesia.
David Foote, Auspic – DPS

Governor General of Australia, Major General Michael Jeffery; the President
of Indonesia, Susilo Bambang Yudhoyono; and Prime Minister Hon John
Howard place medals on the flag-covered coffins from the 'Shark 2' crash
disaster.
David Foote, Auspic – DPS

In 2007, Sydney hosted the Asia-Pacific Economic Cooperation (APEC) forum. The Prime Minister's Office asked me to photograph all his meetings and events. I had covered numerous APEC visits over the years and was familiar with where the media pools would be positioned prior to pic-facs. This time I was given free range to follow the Prime Minister. Sydney was in APEC lockdown with fences and security everywhere. In 2007, the Prime Minister's Sydney office was in the Commonwealth Office Block, 70 Phillip Street. The place was a hive of activity, with world leaders coming in and out for bilateral conversations, known colloquially as 'bilats'. The workmen on a Phillip Street building site must have been surprised to see the President of the United States, Prime Minister Howard and Deputy Prime Minister Mark Vaile walk by as they headed to the nearby Intercontinental Hotel for a joint press conference. After the press conference, President Bush and Prime Minister Howard cruised Sydney Harbour. The cruiser was surrounded by teams of armed security in small fast boats and jet skis. My phone was on silent and kept vibrating; it was one of the Australian press photographers sending me obscene messages because I was appearing in his pictures as he shot the leaders from a media boat. Sometimes it was difficult not to become part of the event I was recording.

Leaders at APEC customarily don the host country's traditional wear. I followed Prime Minister Howard to the front steps of the Sydney Opera House where the leaders were grouping for the traditional APEC leaders group photo. They were given Driza-Bone coats and Akubra hats. Unfortunately, the hats had to be removed as they would cause shadows over their faces. Canada had presented stylish leather bomber jackets. I remember seeing Mr Howard wearing the jacket some time later but I never saw

**President of the United States George W Bush and Prime Minister
Hon John Howard on Sydney Harbour.**
David Foote, Auspic – DPS

**APEC leaders in Vietnam 2006 wearing traditional Vietnamese 'ao dai'
tunics.**
Peter West, Auspic – DPS

**Prime Minister Hon John Howard and Jamie Fox have
a second attempt at opening an APEC umbrella.**
David Foote, Auspic – DPS

him with the traditional attire presented by other countries, such as Vietnam and South Korea.

Over many years I have come to believe that some events demand to be recorded. On this occasion Mr Howard, advisers and security were walking from the Sydney Opera House to Government House when it started to rain. Prime Minister Howard was given an APEC umbrella that failed to open properly. His second umbrella also failed to open; fortunately the rain stopped.

For the years 2004 to 2007, the following are among my favourites in the Auspic collection.

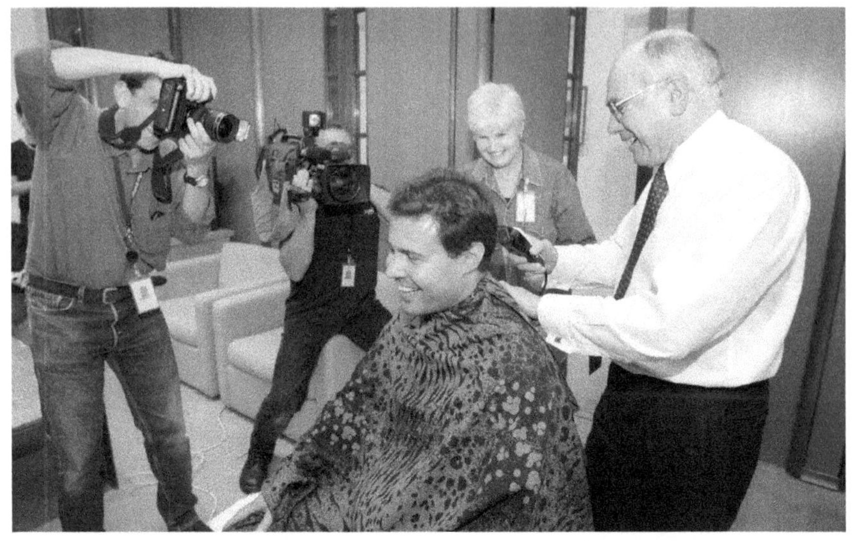

At a fundraiser, a young Josh Frydenberg, then a staffer in the Prime Minister's Office, has his hair cut by John Howard.
David Foote, Auspic – DPS

Meeting with the Governor of California, Arnold Schwarzenegger, Los Angeles.
Michael Jones, Auspic – DPS

With the Leader of the Opposition Mark Latham at St George Leagues Club, Sydney, for a NRL Grand Final Breakfast during the 2004 election campaign.
David Foote, Auspic – DPS

Her Majesty Queen Elizabeth photographed with the 2006 Ministry during her visit to Parliament House, Canberra.
David Foote, Auspic – DPS

The Queen's Official Reception, Parliament House, Canberra.
Michael Jones, Auspic – DPS

Prime Minister Howard's morning exercise was his daily walk. Often on visits abroad the only way to see the city was on his morning walk. During elections, the walks continued, attracting even more security, media and, on occasion, protestors as well.

These images are each of one or perhaps two seconds of exposed time from Howard's 12-year career as prime minister, yet they convey so much.

John Howard seems to have a peaceful walk, passing under the Sydney Harbour Bridge as he returns to Kirribilli House. Often the photographers, camera crew and security would create 'clear' photos of just the Prime Minister.
Michael Jones, Auspic – DPS

What it really looked like. The Prime Minister walks under the Sydney Harbour Bridge surrounded by security, media and protestors.
Michael Jones, Auspic – DPS

**Leaving the Sofitel Wentworth following the
Coalition's defeat by the Labor Opposition.**
Michael Jones, Auspic – DPS

22

REFLECTIONS ON RETROSPECTIVES

JOHN HOWARD

The principal achievements of the Howard Government have been thoroughly canvassed in this series of retrospective volumes. It is commonly agreed that economic reform and prosperity, together with gun control legislation, and the liberation of East Timor are in the front rank. While I won't attempt anything like an exhaustive list, I want to mention two other areas which have received less prominence than they deserve. They are our approach, both in Opposition and Government, to the privatisation of former government enterprises, and the development of an integrated family policy.

The Coalition's approach to privatisation was a classic example of taking a strong policy position in Opposition, maintaining it in the face of regular Labor ridicule and criticism, observing and supporting the Labor Government's adoption of the Coalition's approach and, finally, in government itself, completing the process to implementation.

As Leader of the Opposition in the middle 1980s I argued for the privatisation of Qantas, Australian Airlines and the Commonwealth Bank. I was attacked by both Prime Minister Bob Hawke and Treasurer Paul Keating for embracing what they described as a 'mad Thatcherite slash and burn exercise'. Our policy, as a federal Opposition, was exploited during the South Australian state election of 1985 – which was won by the Labor Party. These attacks caused unease among Opposition members but we held to our position. The Liberal and National parties did not buckle because the policy was soundly based. Although the success of the Thatcher Government's privatisation program in Britain was something of a role model, there were good home-grown reasons for our approach. We knew that Government-owned enterprises, however well run, lacked the competitive efficiencies of the private sector. Privatising government businesses would also provide opportunities for private share ownership, particularly if preference were extended to employees of the enterprise.

Having 'squeezed the lemon dry' with unrelenting political attacks, the Hawke Government then abruptly changed course. It would privatise Qantas, Australian Airlines and a portion of the Commonwealth Bank. Naturally, the Coalition supported these moves, seeing the newfound attitude of Labor as a vindication of policies it had frequently derided. It was the policy of the Keating Government at the 1993 election that the government should retain majority ownership of the Commonwealth Bank. This was no more than a short-term political expedient. To compete effectively, the bank had to be in full private ownership. Union pressure had forced this unworkable commitment on the Labor Government. Economic realities overwhelmed the Keating Government as the May 1995 Budget, which would be its last, rapidly approached.

I well remember the then Finance Minister, Kim Beazley, calling me late in the afternoon of Budget day to inform me that privatisation of the Government's majority ownership would be included in the budget to be delivered that evening. In many ways it was to be the fiscal centerpiece. Beazley asked whether it was still the policy of the Coalition to support the full privatisation of the bank. I confirmed that it was. He replied that the Labor Government would need Coalition support in the Senate to pass this foundational component of its budget, as the crossbench senators, such as the Australian Democrats, were opposed. There was much poetic justice in this development. Having a decade earlier ridiculed the Coalition, the Labor Party was reduced to pleading with us to maintain the consistency of our policy in order to pass its budget. The necessary legislation was passed and full privatisation of the Commonwealth Bank of Australia began. The process was completed by the incoming Coalition Government in 1996.

Telstra remained government owned. The Coalition committed to partial privatisation of the corporation in the 1996 election campaign. Having shamelessly reversed its policy in government, the Labor Party reverted to type in Opposition and constantly stood against the Coalition's partial privatisation of Telstra and, ultimately, its full privatisation after the Liberal and National parties secured control of the Senate at the 2004 election. There was no logical justification for the Labor Party to support privatisation of the Commonwealth Bank in the early 1990s, yet in Opposition to be against any public ownership of Telstra. It was pure political expediency.

The other area deserving special mention is the development of family policy. Our initiatives went beyond the raw elements of new tax benefits and the often derisively styled 'baby bonus'. These and other specific policies were based on a broad and truly liberal philosophy of freedom of choice, and a recognition of the fundamental reality that the most important social responsibility we have is to raise the next generation. Inevitably, this responsibility carries with it the additional cost burden of providing for children's needs. Long before I became prime minister in March 1996, I articulated the view that a taxation policy which did not recognise the additional cost of raising children lacked a social vision.

A crucial element of our approach was, to the maximum extent feasible, to provide parents with freedom of choice about caring arrangements for very young children. Some elected for both parents to return to work as soon as possible. Others opted for one parent to remain out of the paid workforce so as to provide full-time care for a young child or children. Our policy sought to provide, both through the tax system and with childcare subsidies, broadly equivalent support for either choice. The parent who stayed at home sacrificed an entire income. When both parents re-entered the workforce, childcare costs were involved.

The baby bonus replaced previous maternity payments. It was non-means tested, making it readily understood. This initiative had the added virtue of being a lump sum payment associated with the birth of a child, was the equivalent of several months maternity leave, and provided flexibility for parents in deciding if and when both would return to the full- or part-time workforce after a birth. A combination of these measures helped to account for the increase in Australia's fertility rate in the early 2000s. It was certainly not the only reason but it contributed substantially. The fact is, however, through a combination of a low fertility rate and a sharp drop-off in migration, Australia's population growth is now at its lowest point for a century.

In different ways this integrated family policy approach was dismantled by successive governments. There is now an absolute premium on female workforce participation. This phenomenon is both desirable and understandable but it should not occur at the expense of freedom of choice about the caring arrangements for young children. Low- and middle-income families who choose to have one or other parent care for a young child full-time deserve adequate assistance through the tax system.

23
POSTSCRIPT

TOM FRAME

After the defeat of the Howard Government in November 2007, more commentary was devoted to identifying the reasons for its election loss than assessing its performance over the previous three years. Other than analyses of WorkChoices and the Northern Territory Intervention, little of substance has been written about the Coalition's final term of office. I have argued elsewhere that the four Howard governments need to be considered separately if their successes and shortcomings are to be properly assessed. Each had a mood and a mindset of its own, professing different objectives and facing different opposition. This postscript briefly assesses what was written about the Fourth Howard Government during its term in office and in the aftermath of Labor's victory.

It was not until the Coalition looked destined for a third election victory in the second half of 2001 that the First and Second Howard governments became the subject of extended assessments from academics, journalists and commentators. Most accounts went well beyond disapproving; they were hostile. Led by former La Trobe University academic Robert Manne, the Coalition's critics attacked not only the government's policies but its conduct of national affairs, alleging that it was mean-spirited and untrustworthy, indifferent to the demands of human dignity and disdainful of the conventions that had undergirded Australia's place in the world. The detractors, many labelled 'Howard haters' by conservative commentators, wrote articles and published books that dominated the reading lists of Australian political studies courses from 2001 to 2004. Most of these titles were canvassed within my introductory chapter to *Trials and Transformations, 2001–2004: The Howard Government, Volume III*.[1]

The first volume to praise the Howard Government appeared in March 2006, marking the tenth anniversary of the Coalition's election victory. *The Howard Factor: A Decade that Transformed a Nation* consisted mainly of medium-length (4000-word) essays written by journalists working at the *Australian*.[2] Edited by Nick Cater, the book was intended to address what Cater considered the biased political commentary of the previous decade. Unlike earlier works which were meant to hinder the re-election of the Coalition in 2001 and in 2004, *The Howard Factor* could reasonably claim to be more even-handed and less polemical. It was not published during an election campaign and included contributors who were not associated with the Coalition; nor were they necessarily sympathetic to its policies.

Cater claimed that 'no newspaper is better equipped for the task of producing a work of this nature than the *Australian*'.[3] The idea for the book originated with Dennis Shanahan, the newspaper's Canberra-based political editor, who 'persevered with his proposal until he got the answer he wanted, then he worked tirelessly to ensure that it became a reality'.[4] The cover blurb explained that:

John Howard's federal election victory over Paul Keating in 1996 was the start of a quiet revolution that changed

Australia forever. His critics told us he was a white-picket-fence conservative, Little Johnnie, Lazarus with a triple bypass. Instead, Howard has driven a decade of reform, reinventing conservative politics and redefining the national debate. In this long-overdue assessment of the Howard years, some of the *Australian*'s leading commentators chart the seismic shift in politics, society, workplaces, culture, the economy, trade and foreign affairs. They describe how Howard has redrawn the political map, turning the conservatives into reformers and forcing the progressives to defend the status quo.

Cater explained that 'apart from a few bilious tracts written by Howard's opponents, there has been only one attempt at a biography and that book, by David Barnett [and Pru Goward], hardly scratches the surface'.[5] By way of contrast, he noted that 'four books have been written about Mark Latham and one on Kim Beazley, neither of whom has won an election'.[6] In a combative preface, Cater was critical of Paul Keating's complacency as prime minister and asserted that the three Labor leaders who followed him (Beazley, Crean and Latham) were 'enemies of change'. He went even further in contending that 'the conservatives have stolen the mantle of reform and the progressives have become the new conservatives' largely because Howard 'has established a new political orthodoxy'.

Cater's collection is laudatory in places. It marvels at Howard's personal resurgence after being rejected by his party and the public, and the government's ability to expose divisions and exploit the fissures in opposition parties. There are few direct criticisms of the prime minister or the Cabinet. The approach appears to preference observation over disapproval, with comparisons and contrasts softening the assessments of most contributors. For instance, Mike

Steketee thought that the Commonwealth Government's reach into the community increased rather than receded under the Coalition, particularly in welfare, family assistance and workforce participation, where reform was inconsistent and achievements were modest. This theme continued in the chapter by George Megalogenis who believed the Howard Government had seriously under-performed on taxation reform (despite the introduction of 'A New Tax System' in 2000, which included a consumption tax) and that by Brad Norington who concluded that the Coalition's industrial relations program was a work-in-progress. In other words, it had not yet gone far enough.

Essays on 'Hansonism', immigration and Indigenous affairs managed to be neither critical nor complimentary, emphasising the pragmatism of the Howard Government's approach instead of offering a critique of its philosophy, which often took a back seat. In foreign affairs, defence and national security, this particular panel of writers was prepared to award points to the Howard Government before the effects of many policies were known or the consequences of some decisions could be adequately assessed, such as the decision to participate in the invasions of Afghanistan in 2001 and Iraq in 2003.

On other matters, the contributors employed quotes from Labor figures to say things they seemed a little disinclined to say themselves, while noting that the Coalition was helped by Simon Crean's lack of appeal in the electorate at the beginning of his time as Opposition Leader, and Mark Latham's attraction of hostility at the end of his time as Opposition Leader. In essence, it was asserted and not really argued that the Coalition was given a good run because Labor was not an effective opposition. The most biting criticism was actually offered not by a journalist but by the controversial cartoonist, Bill Leak, who later admitted an admiration for Howard and his government. Leak claimed that:

Howard has reshaped Australia to conform to his own vision. We love the inflated feelings of international self-importance he has given us and we don't seem to care about all the things he has taken away. Happy to live in an economy instead of a society, we might as well also accept that we are all Little Johnnies now. Smaller, meaner and less attractive, we're looking more like monkeys every day.[7]

The most enduringly helpful feature of the book was a 100-page inventory prepared by Cater's wife, Rebecca Weisser, of the major news stories relating to the Howard Government appearing in the *Australian* from March 1996 to December 2005. The inventory was followed by a series of tables measuring Australia's performance against a series of key economic indicators compiled by George Megalogenis, who concluded:

> The report card, while mixed, is generally very good. The Howard years have been recession-free, which is a boast no other long-term prime minister can make, not even Howard's hero Robert Menzies. But if you look closely enough, you can see the seeds for the next slow down. They are the imbalances in the household debt and the current account. Sooner or later, our borrowing binge will have to end, and with it the warm buzz of the nation's longest boom.[8]

This more even-handed assessment took a decade to appear, although it said little about the Fourth Howard Government and its re-election prospects which, in 2005, were still fair. The Coalition's polemical detractors were, by way of contrast to its admirers, never idle.

The left-leaning publisher Scribe released Russ Radcliffe's edited collection of political cartoons *Man of Steel: A Cartoon History of the Howard Years* in 2007.[9] Radcliffe made no secret of his disdain for John Howard and most of his ministers. The introduction begins:

> Man of steel or lying rodent? Among the playful metaphors employed by Australia's political cartoonists, variations on these two themes have come to define the parameters of popular opinion about John Howard. Take your pick. I'm sure that the latter is the more passionately held view for, despite his electoral success, Howard is not a politician who has inspired popular devotion – except perhaps among grateful backbenchers who owe him their political careers.[10]

According to Radcliffe, Howard is unworthy of any credit because, he claimed, 'domestically, he reaped the benefits that flowed from the Keating reforms; internationally, the war on terror allowed him to adopt a tough, statesman-like pose'. He accused Howard of 'presiding over a nation, that far from being relaxed and comfortable, has been divided and ill at ease'.[11] Radcliffe asserted that the 'most dubious legacy' of the Howard years was the 'decline and fall of notions of accountability and responsibility' with 'dishonesty and dissimulation' having no apparent political consequences. The Coalition won in 1996 because the electorate wanted a change; it won in 1998 because Kim Beazley's campaign was 'lacklustre'; it won in 2001 by 'beating up border protection and the "threat" imposed by refugee boats', it won in 2004 'subliminally conflating international insecurity with domestic issues, particularly interest rates'.[12] The campaign theme – 'Trust' – that carried the Coalition to a fourth election victory was 'shameless' while the electorate was unwilling to gamble on the unpredictable Mark Latham. The electorate was manipulated, timid, anxious or uncaring when it voted for the Coalition. But with the rise of Kevin Rudd, Radcliffe thought 'Howard's final powerwalk into history, eyebrows to the breeze and bottom lip all aquiver, can't be far away'.[13] Radcliffe was soon granted his wish.

The Coalition's election demise promoted a number of works that were, perhaps inevitably, more descriptive than analytical. The *Quarterly Essay* series commissioned Judith Brett's *Exit Right: The Unravelling of John Howard* in December 2007.[14] Drafted within days of the election, it was a speculative assessment of events whose causes and consequences could not yet be even-handedly or even reasonably assessed given the political dust had not yet begun to settle. More substantial accounts were produced by Peter van Onselen and Philip Senior, who published *Howard's End: The Unravelling of a Government* in August 2008 and Peter Hartcher, whose *To the Bitter End: The Dramatic Story Behind the Fall of John Howard and the Rise of Kevin Rudd* appeared in May 2009.[15] Both books were focused on the 2007 election campaign and its immediate aftermath. Neither book looked in depth at the Fourth Howard Government nor offered an overall assessment of Coalition rule from 1996.

In addition to his collaborative work with Senior, van Onselen also edited a collection of essays, *Liberals and Power: The Road Ahead*, in November 2008.[16] He promoted the view that the Liberal Party lacked vision because it was without values, and that prolonged estrangement from public office was likely. Van Onselen repeated what had become routine criticism that Howard 'did not prepare his party for life after his departure', thus leaving behind a political movement 'at its lowest ebb intellectually and competitively'. After allowing Robert Manne and Tony Abbott to present what were contrastingly critical and celebratory perspectives with conclusions that were not unexpected, George Brandis – who supported Peter Costello's leadership aspirations – offered a thoughtful and nuanced appraisal of his former leader's political philosophy. Although he treated the four Howard governments as a unity and noted that Howard was 'a bundle of contradictions' (implying that most people are not, when experience suggests they are), Brandis thought that Howard was 'most disappointing when he allowed his social conservatism to get in the way of his Party's traditional commitment to individualism'.[17] His final comment is heavily laden with contemporary significance: 'A great government though it was, the Howard Government would have been a greater government still if it had been more consistently true to the Liberal Party's liberal values'.[18]

Other works drew comparisons between the incoming Howard Government in 1996 and the newly elected Rudd Government in 2007. Australian National University academic Norman Abjorensen claimed in 2008 that 'Rudd's first year could not have been more different from Howard's':[19]

> Generally, the Rudd government has been seen as sound, cautious and unspectacular (very much like the prime minister himself). Interestingly, this first detailed review of Rudd Labor comes as the Howard years are being put under the microscope on ABC television, which means that a useful comparison can be made of the first Howard government (1996–98) and Rudd's first year. Quite simply, Howard's government got off to a terrible start; Rudd's, by contrast, has so far been untroubled.[20]

The principal deficiency in Abjorensen's account is not that he was too harsh on Howard but that he was too generous to Rudd – and far too soon.

The election of the Rudd Government did not prompt a substantial revision of the second edition of George Megalogenis' assessment of the Howard Government, *The Longest Decade*, published in May 2008.[21] Megalogenis explained his approach to political commentary when introducing the later edition:

> This book looks at Keating and Howard together as part of a bigger Australian story, with a bias towards their terms in the Lodge … I want to tell two intertwined stories, the political and cultural, and pose the question that taunts our age: how did the Keating-Howard economy take us from growth to greed?

He interviewed both Keating and Howard extensively and invited them to criticise one another.

In what the publisher's endorsement claimed was a 'non-partisan analysis of the forces shaping Australia today', Megalogenis argued that 'treasurer Keating cleaned up the mess that treasurer Howard had made of the economy at the start of the 1980s; Howard as prime minister was given a mandate to repair the society that had been divided by his predecessor, Keating, in the 1990s'. He also notes there was a good deal of consistency in their approach and that both 'changed Australia; yet, for each reform they imposed, the nation snapped back, forcing them to adapt before dismissing them both'.[22] Although there is some merit in making Keating and Howard synonymous with the principal tensions that persist in Australian politics, the approach Megalogenis takes draws attention away from the achievements of their respective governments. The preceding two decades certainly featured a battle of strong-willed men engaged in a vigorous struggle for supremacy but the focus was often on power and not on policy. Howard has been more willing than Keating to concede that there was substantial commonality in their visions for the nation's future.

With the end of the Rudd Government's political 'honeymoon' – and this period lasted longer than most new governments enjoy, owing to Rudd's initial popularity and the electorate's high hopes for his success – leading Coalition ministers offered their own treatment of the Howard years in the context of where and how they felt Labor was 'squandering' the Coalition's legacy. Their main focus was the economy, which was experiencing the GFC – the 'Global Financial Crisis' – an upheaval that began in the United States in the second half of 2007. These treatments were highly generalised.

In 2008, Peter Costello produced a memoir in collaboration with his father-in-law and former New South Wales Liberal leader, Peter Coleman.[23] Its commentary transcended the Howard years, outlining the former Treasurer's views on a range of policies in addition to his views on the Liberal leadership and the succession that wasn't. *The Costello Memoirs* have not been widely quoted in general assessments of the Coalition's time in office.

Tony Abbott published *Battlelines* in 2009. It was a snapshot of how the world looked to one former Howard Government minister prior to his elevation to the Opposition leadership in December of that year.[24] Much of his commentary on the Howard Government had appeared in van Onselen's 2008 edited collection. Abbott assessed 1996–2007 in the context of explaining what his party needed to become in seeking re-election, a remote prospect when the book appeared. *Battlelines* moved from the past to the present and the future – sometimes in the same sentence – with greater interest in the latter years of the Howard Government when

Abbott served as a senior minister. He dealt with the entire period of the Howard Government from the vantage point of 2009 when claiming that the Labor Party was still mimicking the Coalition on many policy fronts. Keating had previously said the same thing of the first Howard Government. But Abbott was critical of the extant literature:

> If Labor is mostly considered the 'sexy' side of politics, one reason is the overwhelming preponderance of books by Labor politicians or about them. In the eleven months he was opposition leader, there were two biographies of Kevin Rudd. By contrast, until the last year of his prime ministership, there was only one biography of John Howard. The relative scarcity of books about the conservative side of politics could prompt the conclusion that we have little worth saying. Most of the people describing conservative politics in Australia are unsympathetic to it – even the more perceptive academic writers, such as Judith Brett.[25]

While this might have been a fair assessment of biographies, it was less true of general assessments of the previous 20 years. Indeed, by 2009, much more had been written of the Howard Government than of the Hawke and Keating governments combined – an observation that still stands.

To highlight the enduring differences that exist between Labor and Coalition national governments, a triumvirate associated with *Quadrant*, Keith Windschuttle, David Martin Jones and Ray Evans, edited a series of essays entitled *The Howard Era*.[26] Published in 2009 and readily acknowledging the wisdom of hindsight, the editors were candid about their intentions:

Given that the Labor Party and its epigone treat Australian
political history and foreign policy since Gough Whitlam's
administration as their personal fiefdom, there is a pressing
need for commentators of a realist or conservative disposition
to define the enduring legacy of the Howard era, trace the
evolution of the Howard Government over time, its successes
and failures, as well as identifying the principles that
informed its practice.

The editors were concerned about the 'self-appointed academic
guardians of Australia's progressive future' to explain away the
philosophical credentials of the Howard Government, reducing
these years 'to some temporary and inconvenient aberration on the
road to a post-Western, multicultural utopia'. Windschuttle and his
colleagues praised the Howard Government's achievements before
claiming it:

> became complacent in power, lost sight of the principles that
> had ensured its early success and captured popular hearts
> and minds. As it tergiversated over policies as varied as
> emissions trading, workplace reform and the socialisation of
> the Australian mind, so it lost its authoritative voice.

This was also the first volume to canvass some of the previous works
on the Howard Government. It noted the emergence of commentaries from 'across a political spectrum from extreme loathing to
measured admiration'. Margo Kingston's two works, *Not Happy,
John* and the follow-up, *Still Not Happy, John*, which were published in 2004 and 2007 respectively, were examples of the former.[27]
David Martin Jones described them as 'little more than politically
correct rants against both Howard and the nescient constituencies

that returned him at successive elections'. He argued that 'such works evince the paranoia that embraces great swathes of the Australian commentariat rather than any attempt at informed insight or empirical assessment'. Jones thought that Manne's *The Howard Years* was 'equally acerbic but somewhat more measured'.[28] This was a curious summation. Was he implying the collection was polemically biased but not to an excessive or egregious degree? Or that it was damning but did not seek to demean its subjects? As for commentaries that offered 'measured admiration', there was not much beyond Cater's *The Howard Factor*.

The contributors listed the Coalition's successes and failures, outlined any mitigating factors before concluding with a similar judgment: on balance, the Coalition did reasonably well in most areas of public administration. The editors obviously worked hard to ensure the authors avoided hubris or 'cheap shots' at commentators whose forecasts had proved to be inaccurate. There were times, the contributors noted, when Howard personally or the government collectively was weak or frightened, misguided or opportunistic, confused or conflicted. In some fields of policy, particularly those with well-defined measures of effectiveness, the Coalition deserved to be judged harshly for reckless action or fickle attitudes that hindered growth or squandered opportunities. On a few issues, the government clearly failed to impress some of the more conservative commentators, who were scathing of Howard and his ministers when they caved in to either sectional interests or special pleading.

Although this collection also lacks a closing summary that might have provided a balance sheet of the Howard Government's performance, there is nothing to suggest the contributors felt the need to redress an imbalance in the extant scholarship by veering deliberately in the opposite direction. On the contrary, the reverse is actually true. These chapters are critical and, in some respects, condemnatory. But they attempt to give credit where it is due and, in this sense, they are responding to earlier works that found nothing of merit in anything the Howard Government did or tried to do.

There were no further substantial assessments of the Howard Government until *The Reith Papers* was published in 2015.[29] This book was significant in that it provided a contemporaneous commentary on the first five years of Coalition rule with brief reflections written more than a decade later. It had much less to say about the Fourth Howard Government, as Reith was, by then, a private consultant and media commentator. The diaries were actually notebooks (that numbered more than 120 in total) in which the former Workplace Relations and Defence minister recorded the proceedings of meetings he attended, drafted preparatory notes for coming meetings, weighed the pros and cons of any proposed policy or action, reflected on people he met and places he visited, and outlined his evolving views on a range of subjects. He kept these notes thinking, 'one day I might write a regular column', which he later did. He did not plan to 'publish my journal entries in memoir form' but was encouraged by former Deputy Prime Minister, Tim Fischer, to produce a book 'on the grounds that Coalition MPs don't write enough about what really happened on the inside during those years'. Faced with the quandary of what to include from the notebooks more than a decade after they were produced, Reith explained:

> At times, I was surprised by my comments and I have wrestled with the issue of making public some personal comments. But in the end I decided I couldn't write a memoir based on diary entries if I excised the bits that some people may not appreciate.[30]

The Reith notebooks and diaries have since been donated to the Howard Library at UNSW Canberra. They are a treasure trove of insights into Australian political life between 1996 and 2001, and they include some of the more caustic personal comments Reith decided against quoting in his book.

Most assessments of the Fourth Howard Government published between 2006 and 2009 dwell on two things. First, the Coalition's final term in office was neither better nor worse than the second or third terms. It was certainly better than the first if measured in political leadership and policy competence. It was not a bad government. In fact, it was an effective one in many areas of public administration. Although there are very few treatments of the Fourth Howard Government that are not at least tinged by interpretations of the November 2007 election result, none of the more moderate commentators thought its performance justified its removal from office.

Second, the same commentators thought the Coalition's final term in office also revealed the government was losing touch with the electorate and lacked the capacity for internal renewal. When Kevin Rudd replaced Kim Beazley as leader, the Labor Opposition looked and sounded more caring and compassionate. Referring to himself as a 'fiscal conservative', Rudd was committed to preserving the rate of economic growth and providing the political stability that had made the Howard Government appealing to voters. Rudd had ideas and energy, coupled with passion and determination. He promised a number of symbolic gestures, such as ratifying the Kyoto Protocol on the environment and offering a national apology to the 'Stolen Generation', that were designed to make the Coalition look reactionary and Howard appear to be heartless.

Rudd's performance as Leader of the Opposition was outstanding. He sounded like an alternative prime minister and Labor looked like an alternative government. Nothing the Howard Government had done in 2006 or was trying to do in 2007 was working in terms of lifting the government's standing in the opinion polls. It is doubtful that a late change to Peter Costello as prime minister would have changed the electorate's mind. The electorate had simply had enough of the Coalition and voters were clearly in the mood for change.

Published accounts of the Fourth Howard Government all come to a similar conclusion about its fate. When campaigning began in October 2007, none of the commentators believed the Coalition would even come close to retaining office. Unlike 1996, the Coalition could not rely on the electorate's enduring antipathy to Paul Keating nor on residual fears of Labor's economic management credentials. Unlike 2001, there was no international crisis, not even a looming global financial crisis, with sufficient gravity to persuade the electorate to maintain its faith in the Coalition. The voters had simply stopped listening to John Howard. They knew he would not see out a fifth term and they were yet to be convinced Peter Costello was the leader they wanted. There were, many voters thought, few apparent risks in giving the other side an opportunity to run the country. The Fourth Howard Government defied a long-standing tenet of Australian politics: oppositions do not win elections, governments lose them. In 2007, Labor had clearly won.

With hindsight, what might the Coalition have done to avoid defeat? It might have exposed and then exploited the deep flaws in Kevin Rudd's character. These flaws were evidently so severe that his government was terminated not by the voters, but by his own colleagues, in June 2010. The Coalition might have also done much more, much earlier, to renew its leadership. Peter Costello should have been invited as early as 2005 to raise his standing within the party room and improve his approval rating within the electorate.

With more time to prepare, the Treasurer might have been able to persuade the electorate that he could combine the legacies of the past with the aspirations of the future to provide demonstrably different government. In 2007, the electorate did not want either the Howard they knew or the Costello they had not yet seen.

Once he decided to stay and fight the 2007 election, Howard faced the prospect of losing his own seat in the House of Representatives to the high-profile Labor candidate and former ABC television presenter, Maxine McKew. When she secured enough votes to become the new member for Bennelong, Howard joined Stanley Melbourne Bruce as only the second prime minister to lose both an election and his seat. Julia Gillard, who had deposed her predecessor and had now been deposed herself, received some ironic consolation from Paul Keating, who had also deposed his predecessor, Bob Hawke. Keating told her: 'we all get carried out in a box'.

In one sense, this observation was also true of John Howard. His departure was swift and there was no lingering presence. Unlike Paul Keating, who retained his seat but quickly resigned from parliament to deal with his bitterness, Howard accepted with good grace that this parliamentary phase of his political life had come to an abrupt end. He soon realised the loss of Bennelong, which made no difference to the overall election result, might have been a blessing in disguise. He would not be sitting on the green benches of the House of Representatives for another three years, facing an inevitable barrage of taunts from Rudd and the possibility of unnerving his successor as Liberal leader. Howard left parliament with dignity and would continue to be a notable public figure. He had followed Menzies in so many things but had not discerned the right time to relinquish the burden of responsibility. He had stayed one year too long.

Like most defeated governments, the Liberal Party was not well prepared for opposition. Few governments ever plan for their own demise, at least publicly. Doing so would look defeatist and deplete morale. Against the odds, when the next election came in less than three years, the Tony Abbott–led Opposition nearly regained office in 2010. To survive, Prime Minister Julia Gillard was obliged to form a minority government with the support of three independents. The Coalition formed government in 2013 with a substantial majority on the floor of the House of Representatives largely because the Labor Party descended into factional in-fighting, as it often does. The Coalition's wilderness period could and should have been much longer. When it regained power, the Abbott and Turnbull governments expressed their esteem for the Howard Government without emulating its foremost attribute – discipline. The Howard Government may have made sound administration and party cohesion look far easier than it ever is.

APPENDIX 1:
THE FOURTH HOWARD CABINET AND MINISTRY

ANNETTE CARTER

On 9 October 2004 John Howard led the Coalition to their fourth victory in the federal election, winning a 14-seat majority. It was the first time that the Howard Government gained a majority in the Senate. It was also the election when Malcolm Turnbull, future Prime Minister of Australia, entered the House of Representatives. The swearing-in ceremony of the fourth Howard ministry took place on 26 October 2004, 17 days after the election.

John Howard's Cabinet remained unchanged from the one he took to the polls. He stated that 'while there will be some changes in ministerial responsibilities, the performance of individual ministers and the changes to the Ministry over the last year did not suggest a need for more extensive changes'.[1] This was partly because significant changes had been made within the year prior to the election. David Kemp, Member for Goldstein; Daryl Williams, Member for Tangney; and Chris Gallus, Member for Hindmarsh, had made the decision to leave parliament at the 2004 election. John Howard made changes when they made their announcements, about six months prior to the election, allowing the government to 'maintain the sense of forward looking and continuity of the Government' if the Coalition were to be re-elected.

The first new appointment was Helen Coonan, Senator for New South Wales, as Minister for Revenue and Assistant Treasurer. She was the first woman to hold a Treasury portfolio since Federation. The other appointment was Ian Campbell, Senator for Western Australia, as the Minister for the Environment and Heritage. John Howard believed these appointments would 'further strengthen and invigorate and refresh the Federal Ministry'. It was speculated that Ian Campbell's appointment would help bolster the Western Australian representation and challenge Kim Beazley's votes.[2]

Three of those appointed into roles following the movement of Helen Coonan and Ian Campbell were from marginal seats, which some believed was a way to attract more votes. Fran Bailey was the Member for McEwen, a seat that had changed hands between the same Labor and Liberal candidates several times since 1984. Jim Lloyd, the Member for Robertson, and Teresa Gambaro, the Member for Petrie, were both from bellwether electorates. Appointed as Parliamentary Secretaries were Bruce Billson, the Member for Dunkley, and Mal Brough, the Member for Fisher.

Peter Costello and Alexander Downer continued in their long-held senior ministries; Costello as Treasurer and Downer as Minister for Foreign Affairs. When the Coalition eventually lost to the Labor Party on 24 November 2007, Costello and Downer had held those offices for 11 years and 267 days. Previously, the longest serving Treasurer and Foreign Affairs Minister had been Sir Arthur Fadden, Treasurer for eight years and 355 days in the Menzies Government and Richard Casey, who was Minister for External Affairs for eight years and 283 days. Other senior cabinet posts that remained unchanged were Tony Abbott in Health, Brendan Nelson in Education and Robert Hill in Defence.

Three new ministries were created to 'improve the delivery

of government services and to implement the Coalition's welfare promises'.[3] Joe Hockey was appointed to the new job of Minister for Human Services, overseeing six agencies including Centrelink and the Child Support Agency. This ministry was created to 'overcome a lack of focus on the efficient delivery of government services'. Two other new ministries were focused on getting more people into the paid workforce. Gary Hardgrave became Minister for Vocational and Technical Education and Peter Dutton, the youngest member of the ministry at 33, became Minister for Workforce Participation. Dutton said that he was 'proud and pleased to be taking up his first front bench position in such an important portfolio'.

The Nationals' De-Anne Kelly from Queensland was advanced to the ministry at the expense of Danna Vale from New South Wales. When Howard was questioned by journalists about why Danna Vale had not been appointed, he answered, 'Look, she did a very hard working job. She hasn't been included. I want to thank her for her services. She remains a very good friend and a very good colleague and, can I say, a very spectacular converter of marginality into safety when it comes to political contests.'[4]

The main difference between the first three Howard Governments was the majority it had in the Senate. When discovering the outcome of the Senate, Howard stated:

> I'm naturally very pleased that the Coalition will have
> a majority in its own right in the Senate ... It's a truly
> remarkable victory for our two parties in Queensland to win
> four out of the six Senate seats in that State. It's a result that
> few people expected ... But I want to assure the Australian
> people that the Government will use its majority in the new
> Senate very carefully, very wisely and not provocatively. We
> intend to do the things we've promised the Australian people

we would do but we don't intend to allow this unexpected but welcome majority in the Senate to go to our heads.[5]

The Senate majority allowed the Howard Government to have its controversial industrial relations reforms, which had previously been stalled by a combination of Labor and cross-bench opposition, to be enacted.

There was substantially greater female representation in the fourth (and final ministry) than in the first. Four women were in the ministry when Howard led the Coalition parties to power in 1996. In contrast there were nine women in 2004. On the point of women in the ministry, Howard stated:

> The fourth Howard Ministry will simultaneously be able to point to the largest number of women in the Cabinet since Federation as well as the largest number of women heading Government departments. The number in the case of the latter will go from two to six and if you look at the appointments in the public service area. They've all been promoted on merit, we don't have quotas, we don't believe in them. But I think it's just worth drawing attention to that meritorious double. And it is quite an important and significant development.[6]

Changes in public service posts included the appointment of four new women as departmental secretaries. Joanna Hewitt became Secretary of the Department of Agriculture, Fisheries and Forestry; Lisa Paul was appointed Secretary of the Department of Education and Training; Patricia Scott took charge of the new Department of Human Services; and Lynelle Briggs was appointed as Public Service Commissioner. Women who were continuing and extended in their roles were Helen Williams at the Department of Communications, Information Technology and the Arts; and Jane Halton at the Department of Health and Ageing.

There were three Opposition leaders between 2004 and 2007. Mark Latham was Leader of the Opposition during the October 2004 federal election. When the Labor Party lost that election and Mark Latham resigned in January 2005, Kim Beazley returned to the Labor leadership before being replaced by Kevin Rudd in December 2006. On the face of it, that could have been seen as an instability within the Labor Party, but it ultimately won the election in 2007 with Kevin Rudd as leader and ended the Howard Government's 11 years and 267 days in power.

Fourth Howard Ministry (as of 26 October 2004 with Cabinet ministers shown in bold type)

John Howard	**Prime Minister**	**LPA**	**NSW**
John Anderson	**Deputy Prime Minister, Minister for Transport and Regional Services**	**NPA**	**NSW**
Mark Vaile	**Minister for Trade**	**NPA**	**NSW**
Peter Costello	**Treasurer**	**LPA**	**Vic**
Alexander Downer	**Minister for Foreign Affairs**	**LPA**	**SA**
Senator Robert Hill	**Minister for Defence and Leader of the Government in the Senate**	**LPA**	**SA**
Dr Brendan Nelson	**Minister for Education, Science and Training**	**LPA**	**NSW**
Senator Nick Minchin	**Minister for Finance and Administration and the Deputy Leader of the Government in the Senate**	**LPA**	**SA**
Tony Abbott	**Minister for Heath and Ageing**	**LPA**	**NSW**
Philip Ruddock	**Attorney-General**	**LPA**	**NSW**
Senator Ian Campbell	**Minister for the Environment and Heritage**	**LPA**	**WA**
Senator Helen Coonan	**Minister for Communications, Information Technology and the Arts**	**LPA**	**NSW**
Warren Truss	**Minister for Agriculture, Fisheries and Forestry**	**LPA**	**QLD**

Senator Amanda Vanstone	**Minister for Immigration and Multicultural and Indigenous Affairs**	**LPA**	**SA**
Kevin Andrews	**Minister for Employment and Workplace Relations**	**LPA**	**Vic**
Senator Kay Patterson	**Minister for Family and Community Services**	**LPA**	**Vic**
Ian Macfarlane	**Minister for Industry, Tourism and Resources**	**LPA**	**QLD**
Joe Hockey	Minister for Human Services	LPA	NSW
Peter McGauran	Minister for Citizenship and Multicultural Affairs	NPA	Vic
Senator Rod Kemp	Minister for the Arts and Sport	LPA	Vic
Senator Chris Ellison	Minister for Justice and Customs	LPA	WA
Senator Ian Macdonald	Minister for Fisheries, Forestry and Conservation	LPA	QLD
Senator Eric Abetz	Special Minister of State	LPA	Tas
Fran Bailey	Minister for Small Business and Tourism	LPA	Vic
Mal Brough	Minister for Revenue and Assistant Treasurer	LPA	QLD
Gary Hardgrave	Minister for Vocational and Technical Education, Minister Assisting the Prime Minister	LPA	QLD
Julie Bishop	Minister for Ageing	LPA	WA
Jim Lloyd	Minister for Local Government, Territories and Roads	LPA	NSW
De-Anne Kelly	Minister for Veterans' Affairs, Minister Assisting the Minister for Defence	NPA	QLD
Peter Dutton	Minister for Workforce Participation	LPA	QLD
Warren Entsch	Parliamentary Secretary to the Minister for Industry, Tourism and Resources	LPA	QLD
Dr Sharman Stone	Parliamentary Secretary to the Minister for Finance and Administration	LPA	Vic
Christopher Pyne	Parliamentary Secretary to the Minister for Health and Ageing	LPA	SA
Bruce Billson	Parliamentary Secretary to the Minister for Trade	LPA	Vic
Teresa Gambaro	Parliamentary Secretary to the Minister for Defence	LPA	QLD
Gary Nairn	Parliamentary Secretary to the Prime Minister	LPA	NSW
John Cobb	Parliamentary Secretary to the Minister for Transport and Regional Services	NPA	NSW

Chris Pearce	Parliamentary Secretary to the Treasurer	LPA	Vic
Greg Hunt	Parliamentary Secretary to the Minister for Environment and Heritage	LPA	Vic
Senator Richard Colbeck	Parliamentary Secretary to the Minister for Agriculture, Fisheries and Forestry	LPA	Tas
Pat Farmer	Parliamentary Secretary to the Minister for Education, Science and Training	LPA	NSW
Sussan Ley	Parliamentary Secretary to the Minister for Family and Community Services	LPA	NSW

During the life of the Fourth Howard Government there were 57 changes to the ministry, which is much higher than in any of the previous Coalition administrations. Notably, Peter McGauran, Julie Bishop, Chris Ellison, Mal Brough and Joe Hockey were all appointed to Cabinet during the Fourth Howard Government while Malcolm Turnbull went from the backbench to Parliamentary Secretary and then to the Cabinet within one term, having been elected with a background as a merchant banker and high-profile lawyer. Turnbull's meteoric rise could be seen as rapid and unusual.[7] Prior to Turnbull, few had risen to Cabinet rank within one term.[8] By the time Liberal Party leadership was being discussed among Cabinet members and the question of whether Howard should stand down was canvassed, Turnbull was a prominent voice and 'strongly agitating for it'.[9] Although Turnbull fended off questions about his ambitions in his first term in parliament, he was 'universally believed to be chasing the top job'.[10]

Also of note was Andrew Robb, who entered the House of Representatives having spent seven years as the Liberal Party Federal Director. He was elected in 2004, made Parliamentary Secretary in 2006 and was in the outer ministry as Minister for Vocational and Further Education by 2007.

Below are the changes that were made to the ministry during the Howard Government's fourth term:

Cabinet

- John Anderson: Deputy Prime Minister, Minister for Transport and Regional Services (to 6 July 2005)
- Mark Vaile: Minister for Trade (to 10 August 2006); Deputy Prime Minister (from 6 July 2005); Minister for Transport and Regional Services (from 10 August 2006)
- Senator Robert Hill: Minister for Defence, Leader of the Government in the Senate (to 27 January 2006)
- Dr Brendan Nelson: Minister for Education, Science and Training (to 27 January 2006); Minister for Defence (from 27 January 2006)
- Senator Nick Minchin: Minister for Finance and Administration, Vice-President of the Executive Council, Deputy Leader of the Government in the Senate (to 27 January 2006); Leader of the Government in the Senate (from 27 January 2006)
- Malcolm Turnbull: Minister for the Environment and Water Resources (from 23 January 2007)
- Senator Helen Coonan: Minister for Communications, Information Technology and the Arts, Deputy Leader of the Government in the Senate (from 27 January 2006)
- Warren Truss: Minister for Agriculture, Fisheries and Forestry (to 6 July 2005); Minister for Transport and Regional Services (from 6 July 2005 to 10 August 2006); Minister for Trade (from 10 August 2006)
- Senator Amanda Vanstone: Minister for Immigration and Multicultural and Indigenous Affairs, Minister Assisting the Prime Minister for Indigenous Affairs (to 27 January 2006); Minister for Immigration and Multicultural Affairs (from 27 January 2006 to 23 January 2007)

- Kevin Andrews: Minister for Employment and Workplace Relations, Minister Assisting the Prime Minister for the Public Service (to 23 January 2007); Minister for Immigration and Citizenship (from 23 January 2007)
- Joe Hockey: Minister for Employment and Workplace Relations, Minister Assisting the Prime Minister for the Public Service (from 23 January 2007)
- Senator Kay Patterson: Minister for Family and Community Services, Minister Assisting the Prime Minister for Women's Issues (to 27 January 2006)
- Julie Bishop: Minister for Education, Science and Training, Minister Assisting the Prime Minister for Women's Issues (from 27 January 2006)
- Mal Brough: Minister for Families and Community Services and Indigenous Affairs (from 27 January 2006)
- Peter McGauran: Minister for Agriculture, Fisheries and Forestry (from 6 July 2005)
- Senator Ian Campbell: Minister for the Environment and Heritage (to 23 January 2007); Minister for Human Services (30 Jan 2007 to 9 March 2007)
- Senator Chris Ellison: Minister for Human Services (from 9 March 2007)

Outer ministry

- Peter McGauran: Minister for Citizenship and Multicultural Affairs (to 6 July 2005)
- Senator Rod Kemp: Minister for the Arts and Sport (to 30 January 2007)
- Senator Chris Ellison: Minister for Justice and Customs (to 9 March 2007)

- Senator David Johnston: Minister for Justice and Customs (from 9 March 2007)
- Senator Ian Macdonald: Minister for Fisheries, Forestry and Conservation (to 27 January 2006)
- Joe Hockey: Minister for Human Services (to 23 January 2007)
- Senator Eric Abetz: Special Minister of State (to 27 January 2006); Minister for Fisheries, Forestry and Conservation (from 27 January 2006)
- Mal Brough: Minister for Revenue and Assistant Treasurer (to 27 January 2006)
- Gary Hardgrave: Minister for Vocational and Technical Education, Minister Assisting the Prime Minister (to 23 January 2007)
- Andrew Robb: Minister for Vocational and Further Education (from 23 January 2007)
- Julie Bishop: Minister for Ageing (to 27 January 2006)
- De-Anne Kelly: Minister for Veterans' Affairs, Minister Assisting the Minister for Defence (to 27 January 2006)
- Peter Dutton: Minister for Workforce Participation (to 27 January 2006); Minister for Revenue and Assistant Treasurer (from 27 January 2006)
- John Cobb: Minister for Citizenship and Multicultural Affairs (6 July 2005 to 27 January 2006); Minister for Community Services (from 27 January 2006 to 30 January 2007)
- Senator Nigel Scullion: Minister for Community Services (from 30 January 2007)
- Bruce Billson: Minister for Veterans' Affairs, Minister Assisting the Minister for Defence (from 27 January 2006)
- Gary Nairn: Special Minister of State (from 27 January 2006)
- Dr Sharman Stone: Minister for Workforce Participation (from 27 January 2006)

- Senator Santo Santoro: Minister for Ageing (from 27 January 2006 to 16 March 2007)
- Christopher Pyne: Minister for Ageing (from 18 March 2007)
- Senator George Brandis SC: Minister for the Arts and Sport (from 30 January 2007)

Parliamentary secretaries

- Warren Entsch: Parliamentary Secretary to the Minister for Industry, Tourism and Resources (to 27 January 2006)
- Dr Sharman Stone: Parliamentary Secretary to the Minister for Finance and Administration (to 27 January 2006)
- Christopher Pyne: Parliamentary Secretary to the Minister for Health and Ageing (to 18 March 2007)
- Senator Brett Mason: Parliamentary Secretary to the Minister for Health and Ageing (from 18 March 2007)
- Bruce Billson: Parliamentary Secretary to the Minister for Trade (to 6 July 2005); Parliamentary Secretary to the Minister for Immigration and Multicultural and Indigenous Affairs (from 6 July to 27 January 2006); Parliamentary Secretary to the Minister for Foreign Affairs (to 27 January 2006)
- Teresa Gambaro: Parliamentary Secretary to the Minister for Defence (to 27 January 2006); Parliamentary Secretary to the Minister for Foreign Affairs (from 27 January 2006 to 30 January 2007); Parliamentary Secretary to the Minister for Immigration and Citizenship (from 23 January 2007); Assistant Minister for Immigration and Citizenship (from 18 March 2007)
- Gary Nairn: Parliamentary Secretary to the Prime Minister (to 27 January 2006)

- John Cobb: Parliamentary Secretary to the Minister for Transport and Regional Services (to 6 July 2005)
- Greg Hunt: Parliamentary Secretary to the Minister for the Environment and Heritage (to 30 January 2007); Parliamentary Secretary to the Minister for Foreign Affairs (from 30 January 2007)
- Senator Richard Colbeck: Parliamentary Secretary to the Minister for Agriculture, Fisheries and Forestry (to 27 January 2006); Parliamentary Secretary to the Minister for Finance and Administration (from 27 January 2006)
- Sussan Ley: Parliamentary Secretary to the Minister for Family and Community Services (Children and Youth Affairs) (to 27 January 2006); Parliamentary Secretary to the Minister for Agriculture, Fisheries and Forestry (from 27 January 2006)
- De-Anne Kelly: Parliamentary Secretary to the Minister for Transport and Regional Services (from 29 September 2006); Parliamentary Secretary to the Minister for Trade (from 27 January 2006 to 29 September 2006)
- Senator Sandy Macdonald: Parliamentary Secretary to the Minister for Trade (from 6 July 2005 to 27 January 2006); Parliamentary Secretary to the Minister for Defence (from 27 January 2006 to 30 January 2007)
- Andrew Robb: Parliamentary Secretary to the Minister for Immigration and Multicultural Affairs (from 27 January 2006 to 23 January 2007)
- Malcolm Turnbull: Parliamentary Secretary to the Prime Minister (from 27 January 2006 to 23 January 2007)
- Tony Smith: Parliamentary Secretary to the Prime Minister (from 23 January 2007)
- Peter Lindsay: Parliamentary Secretary to the Minister of Defence (from 30 January 2007)

- Bob Baldwin: Parliamentary Secretary to the Minister for Industry, Tourism and Resources (from 27 January 2006)

APPENDIX 2
SUCCESSION COMMENTARY

ALAN WILSON

5 December 1994	John Howard, Peter Costello and Ian McLachlan meet to discuss the leadership of the Parliamentary Liberal Party. Howard says, 'I said that I would only serve one or two terms … We reached no understanding.' In his memoirs, Costello writes that Howard said: 'If Downer resigns and you stand aside, I only want one term. Then I would stand aside in the next term to let you have a go.' McLachlan makes a note of the meeting, which is not made public until 10 July 2006.
22 February 1997	In an interview with the *Weekend Australian*, reflecting on his first year in office, Howard says: 'every party should have a 10-year transition strategy'. He adds: 'While my health lasts and I've got my marbles, you stay. But when that changes, you don't.'
21 July 1998	On a radio program, Costello raises the question of leadership, claiming that Liberal colleagues have asked him to replace Howard: 'Look, bear this in mind, I helped John Howard become leader and I did that because I thought he was the right person to lead the party and he has my full support'.

21 July 1998   Asked to comment on Costello's remarks, Howard says, 'in any political party you'll always have, particularly if it's big and a big majority, you'll always have a few people who are a bit unhappy with the boss, that's always the case. Bob Menzies had it, every prime minister's had it. I am not concerned by it at all. I think people are always after the top job in politics – nothing unusual about that. I'd be the last person to decry ambition.'

25 July 1999   On the eve of his 60th birthday Howard says, 'I don't have any intention of retiring'.

23 September 1999   An article in the *Australian Financial Review* suggests that Costello appears to put a timetable on his future by saying: 'I've got another Budget or two in me, I suppose. I've done four.' Asked whether he had discussed his next step, beyond the Treasury, with the prime minister, he paused and said, 'Well, I'm Treasurer and I'm looking forward to next year's Budget. They'll get easier I hope.'

23 September 1999   Asked if he agrees with Costello, who 'appears to have put a timetable on his future and, I suppose, with that yours and he says he's only got another budget or two in him', Howard says: 'I can understand that Peter finds the job very arduous' and 'he actually raised the article with me. He was a little surprised, so he told me, with the tone of it. He said he was just stating the obvious that he didn't want to stay Treasurer forever and I think that's perfectly understandable.'

24 September 1999	Asked to place a timetable on his tenure as prime minister, Howard said these were 'matters for the party but can I just say that as I feel at the moment, I have never felt more in control of the situation. The team is working well. I don't think the government has been in better shape.'
27 September 1999	Asked: 'Mr Howard, do you see Peter Costello as your successor as prime minister?', Howard replies: 'I am not thinking of any successors, I am thinking of winning the next election and remaining prime minister'.
26 July 2000	On his 61st birthday Howard says he will lead the Liberal Party into the next election. 'I have said before that if the party wants me to lead it to another election, which will be at the end of next year, I am happy to do so. After that, obviously one has to recognise, I'll then be in my 63rd or 64th year', he says. 'And nothing is forever.'
29 July 2000	Howard refuses to be drawn on who should succeed him, but insists his comments that fuelled speculation on the Liberal leadership were 'honest and deliberate'. Howard, who has said Costello would 'make a very good prime minister', says he was not anointing anybody. 'What I've said is that I'll lead the party to the next election if it wants me to and obviously some time after that I'd start thinking about the future', he said.

25 May 2001

Howard is asked by Neil Mitchell in a radio interview: 'Will you serve all the next term if you're elected?' He replies: 'Well my position on that I made clear. I want to get a lot of things done in the next term. I said I'd look at the situation around the time of my 64th birthday and I've said that before and I'm not altering that. But I've got to tell you the last thing on my mind at the moment is retirement from politics. I'm loving it.'

31 May 2001

Howard is asked by Jeremy Cordeaux in a radio interview: 'What're your plans?' Howard replies: 'My plans are to stay around for quite a while … I've said that when I reach my 64th birthday which will be in a couple of years' time I'll just think about my future. I haven't taken it any further than that and I thought it was the honest open thing to do to say that. I think I said that almost a year ago. But at the moment the last thing I'm thinking about is retiring.' He adds: 'If at some time in the future I decide to leave politics, well the Party Room will choose a successor and it will also, if that successor happens to be somebody who's now the deputy leader, namely Peter Costello, then obviously they'll have to choose somebody else to take Peter's place. But that is all well into the future and it is not for me to say who should have what position. That is a matter for the Liberal Party Room at the time.'

27 July 2001

In a review of Shaun Carney's biography of Costello, Michelle Grattan quotes: 'Mr Costello saw Mr Howard's 2000 comments flagging likely retirement at 64 as indicating "his leader had deduced that he could make it through one more election but not two", and "Costello felt that Howard was sending a signal to him: take it easy, I know I have to go but there's no point in trying to push me".'

4 October 2001   Asked 'will you commit that if you win the next election you will serve the full term in the parliament?' Howard responds: 'as you know I said that when I got to the age of 64 I'd think about my future, I said that about a year ago. Quite frankly the last thing I want to do at present is leave government.'

13 October 2001   In an interview in the *Australian*, Howard talks openly of succession, saying: 'If I go, Peter Costello will become the leader'. He also says, 'You shouldn't assume I will retire. But I'm being very upfront that it's something two years into my term I'll decide – whether I'm going to run again. We have no witnesses. We don't even have a deal. We have nothing of the kind.'

12 April 2002   Responding to questions about the leadership of the Liberal Party, Howard says: 'The question of my successor will be a matter for the parliamentary party, if and when there's a vacancy and there's no vacancy'.

17 April 2002   Howard is asked, 'what do you think your heir apparent, Peter Costello, will be like as prime minister, eventually?' He says, 'it's a purely hypothetical issue', and adds 'Nobody's immortal but when you are in a job and enjoying it and I hope, without sounding in any way presumptuous, doing it tolerably well, I won't put it any more strongly than that, you don't start talking about who might be doing it in the future'.

28 November 2002   Howard and Costello confirm that they have privately discussed the Liberal leadership. 'We have private discussions about a lot of things', says Howard. Asked whether he wants to succeed Howard, Costello says, 'Let's see what happens next year'.

2 January 2003 — Howard is under pressure from Coalition MPs to stay on as prime minister until after the 2004 election because of concern over marginal seats, the *Australian* reports.

21 February 2003 — Howard is asked by Neil Mitchell in a radio interview: 'have you decided yet whether you will stay past your 64th birthday?' Howard responds: 'I haven't made a decision yet about my long-term future'. Responding to a comment that whereas he had been hinting before at retiring mid-term he was now 'going to go straight through to the next election', Howard says he is 'going to see this issue [the war in Iraq] through'.

26 February 2003 — In his diary, Howard writes about Costello: 'I raised the leadership issue and told him that I had not made up my mind. I said several times that there was no guarantee that I would go.'

2 June 2003 — Howard writes: 'On 2 June 2003, I saw Peter Costello in my Canberra office and told him of my decision [to stay] … He argued during our hour-long discussion last Monday morning [2 June 2003] that the party's best interests would be served by a transition now … There was, however, overwhelming support in the parliamentary party for me to stay. There has been a very positive reaction to the decision.'

3 June 2003 — Howard tells Liberal MPs he will continue as prime minister as long as the party wants him. Costello later confesses: 'It wasn't my happiest day'.

16 November 2003	In a discussion with journalist Peter Wilmoth, Costello says: 'We [Howard and Costello] had a discussion in February. He had indicated for many years he was going to consider his position and announce it in July. We discussed what that decision might be and yet not made a final decision at that point. It was very, very open as to what the decision might be. As a consequence of that I knuckled down and I did the budget … and the next discussion we had was in June.' He adds: 'Frankly I think if I'd have stood up and done the "hail, fellow, well met" bonhomie – [puts on happy voice] "Sure, nothing better's ever happened to me in my life, this is a wonderful event" – first of all it would not have been credible and secondly the public would have been entitled to say "You're not genuine"'. Asked if he felt 'as though it was going to be a huge journey ahead to become prime minister?', Costello replies: 'Oh look, it's more this, that you operate under a set of assumptions for a number of years, the assumptions change … You've got to put this in context. There are far worse things that happen to a lot of people than me. At the end of that day it wasn't my happiest day, right? Still alive, still got my health, I've got my family and I've got my job. So we're going to move on.'
8 March 2004	Howard plays down leadership speculation, saying he will: 'remain Leader of the Liberal Party for so long as the party wanted me to and while it remained in the party's interest that I should'.
7 May 2004	Costello supporters raise the prospect of a leadership handover after the election. 'I think most people expect that if we win the next federal election there will be a peaceful, harmonious transition from Howard to Costello', Senator George Brandis says.

28 May 2004 — Neil Mitchell asks Howard: 'If you win the next election, will you stay the full term?' Howard responds: 'I'll stay as long as the party wants me to and it's in the party's best interests'. He adds: 'I mean it's not tricky. It's a statement of the truth. Somebody who has been in parliament for a few years, as I have, who enjoys very good health, who likes the job, but sensibly that is the attitude I should have and it's the attitude I do have and it's the attitude I will continue to have.'

24 August 2004 — Howard hints at political longevity, telling an audience of retirees: 'I think people should continue in the workforce for as long as they want to and as long as they're making a contribution and age is irrelevant'.

30 August 2004 — Costello says: 'In the next three years, I am seeking to be Treasurer in the government to serve under Mr Howard, and that's what I am doing, and ruling out challenging'.

9 February 2005 — Announcing that the Asia Pacific Economic Co-operation summit will be held in Sydney in 2007, Howard adds, 'the Australian prime minister will host that meeting … I am not going to comment on that except to say that I'll continue to occupy this position for so long as my party wants me to'.

8 March 2005 — In an article in the *Bulletin*, Costello refuses to deny he was led to believe that Howard would pass the leadership to him in the third term.

30 April 2005 — In an interview published in the *Australian*, Howard squashes Costello's immediate leadership hopes by declaring 'I'm not going anywhere'. Speaking in Athens he says: 'I still have got plenty of ideas and there are lots of things I want to do. I am not planning my post-prime-ministerial life.'

30 April 2005   Asked: 'Are you going to stay on for a fifth term?', Howard responds: 'I have not formed any different position than I had at the time of the election, and that is that I'll remain in the job I now have for so long as my party wants me to and I have not changed that position'.

1 May 2005   On *Meet the Press*, Costello refuses to rule out a leadership challenge. 'I don't think the events of the last 24 hours have helped the government or the Liberal Party', he says, referring to the coverage of Howard's so-called 'Athens declaration'.

2 May 2005   In the *Australian* an editorial says that Howard 'challenged [his] own deputy to come and take the leadership or go away'.

4 May 2005   The *Age* says that Costello would not remain as Howard's deputy or Treasurer beyond early 2006, and quotes an unnamed source as saying, 'Howard needs to understand that there will be a transition this term – the only question is whether it will be smooth or messy'.

30 August 2005   Costello adds momentum to his leadership push when he tells the Nine Network: 'I'm the Treasurer, I'm the deputy leader of the Liberal Party, so I feel in a sense that I do lead in this country. I've done 10 budgets, I've been responsible for the economy and people's jobs and mortgage interest rates for, you know, the last nine-and-a-half years, so I feel in many respects I do.'

7 October 2005   Two days before the anniversary of his fourth election victory, Howard denies he is thinking of retiring.

4 December 2005	Leadership tensions are fuelled when Howard tells the Nine Network it was Costello who first raised the idea of appointing Robert Gerard to the RBA board. Gerard later resigned after disclosing his family company had been in dispute with the Australian Tax Office for 14 years.
7 December 2005	Costello publicly rejects challenging Howard and commits himself to delivering the 2006 Budget.
22 April 2006	An article in the *Sydney Morning Herald* reported: 'But now they [Costello supporters] acknowledge the leadership decision is Mr Howard's to make whenever he chooses. Mr Costello has no plans to challenge for the leadership, that Costello would not stay on as Howard's deputy or Treasurer beyond early 2006, and quotes an unnamed source as saying, "Howard needs to understand that there will be a transition this term – the only question is whether it will be smooth or messy".'
15 May 2006	Asked if he owed 'it to the public to actually express or declare your position?', Howard responds: 'the direct communication I had with the Australian people before the last election was that I would remain the Leader of the Liberal Party for so long as my party wanted me to and it was in the party's best interests. Now I was re-elected with an increased majority which indicates that the Australian people are happy with that response and that's the position.'

9 July 2006   In the Sunday *Herald Sun*, Glenn Milne reports that Howard made a promise at a secret meeting in 1994 to step aside for Costello, according to the only witness in the room. The then Opposition spokesman on the environment, Ian McLachlan, was a witness to the vow and made notes of the meeting. The notes specifically refer to 'undertaking' as a description of the conversation.

10 July 2006   Costello describes a conversation of 5 December 1994 at which he says: 'Howard asked me not to nominate for the Liberal Party leadership because he did not want a vote in the Party Room. He told me that he intended to do one and a half terms as prime minister and then would hand over.'

10 July 2006   In the *Australian*, Glenn Milne reports that Costello was asked: 'Can I just ask you a plain, simple question? Is there an understanding between you and Mr Howard as to his departure?' Costello replied: 'Look, these things have worked in the interests of the Australian people and the people concerned and there is no point in speculating on it'.

10 July 2006   Ian McLachlan – the third man at the leadership meeting on 5 December 1994 – releases the note he has kept, supporting Costello's version: 'Meeting Monday Dec 1994. Undertaking given by JH at a meeting late pm in PC's room that if AD [Alexander Downer] resigned and Howard became PM then one and a half terms would be enough and he would hand over to PC. IMcL.'

10 July 2006	Asked: 'how do you answer claims that you have been dishonourable over Mr Costello?', Howard responds: 'The situation is very simple, there was no deal made. There were lots of discussions at that time, including one in which Mr McLachlan was present, that did not involve the conclusion of a deal.' He adds: 'I openly said at the time of the last election that I would remain the leader of the Liberal Party for so long as the party wanted that and it was in the party's best interests. That was the condition on which I was elected and that remains my position.'
11 July 2006	Asked about Howard's response to his comments of 10 July, Costello responds: 'I have told you the truth, there is nothing new about this. I have known this for 12 years. He has known of this. We have worked together knowing the truth of all of this.'
11 July 2006	Costello says: 'There has been a lot in the papers the last couple of days, and I have never spoken about these events before, but since others have, the public is entitled to know the full truth. I did not ask Mr McLachlan to relate these matters but his account is entirely accurate. [The prime minister] told me that he intended to do one and a half terms as prime minister and then would hand over. I did not seek that undertaking, he volunteered it, and I took him at his word. Obviously, that did not happen.'

12 July 2006   Howard says: 'I've indicated that the leadership of the party is something that is determined by the views of the Parliamentary Party and that remains my position. And no, let me make it quite clear, no agreement was entered into between Mr Costello and me about the future. It is not my right, nor is it his right. The question of who leads the Liberal Party is a matter for the Liberal Party Room.' He adds: 'I will remain the Leader of the Liberal Party as long as the party wants me to, and it's in the party's best interests that I do so. Now that was my position three years ago when I told the party room in June of 2003 that I would continue. It was the position I put to the Australian people, I was re-elected prime minister with an increased majority on the basis of that position and therefore it is proper that I maintain that position. In the end the people who will decide this are the men and women of the Parliamentary Liberal Party, and I really am not going to deviate from that.'

13 July 2006   In the *Herald Sun*, an article by Neil Mitchell describes Costello's performance as 'petulant, arrogant and indulgent' and says that he had 'significantly damaged any hope he has of realising what he seems to believe is his God-given right to ascension'. He adds that Costello said: '[John Howard] is yet to announce what his position is for the next election. He intends to consider his future and he'll let you know when he's done that. He indicated obviously he will consider these matters and he should consider these matters.'

30 July 2006   Howard rings Costello to tell him that he had decided to stay and lead the Coalition. Costello says that the decision was the wrong one and that Howard might not end up facing Beazley at the next election.

31 July 2006 Howard sends a letter to his Parliamentary Liberal Party colleagues regarding his intention to lead the party to the next federal election. He says: 'My soundings tell me that the strong view of the party is that the current leadership team, with me as leader and Peter Costello as deputy leader, should remain in place through to the next election'; and 'Just as the party now wants me to continue as leader I accept that it has a perfect right to change its mind if it judges that to be to the party's benefit. If that were to occur, I would not ignore the party's shift in sentiment.'

31 July 2006 Costello issues a statement in which he says: 'I have spoken to many members of the public and colleagues and it is clear that most people do not support a leadership transition at the current time'.

7 August 2007 In an article in the *Bulletin,* Paul Daley says that on 2 June 2005 Costello had said: 'Howard can't win; I can. We can, but he can't.'

15 August 2007 In an article in the *Age,* Tony Wright says that on 2 June 2005 Costello had set a deadline of April 2006 for Howard to hand the leadership to him, and that if that did not happen he would challenge, and if, as anticipated, that did not succeed, he would go to the backbench and 'carp' my leadership and 'destroy it'.

15 August 2007   Howard says: 'What happened in 2006 was that
I canvassed extensively my colleagues about the
leadership issue and as I indicated publicly my
colleagues expressed an overwhelming view that
they wanted to retain the partnership of me as Prime
Minister and Mr Costello as Treasurer. And I discussed
that matter and before I made my statement I indicated
to Mr Costello that I intended to remain as leader of
the party because that's what the party overwhelmingly
wanted, but it also overwhelmingly wanted him to
continue as Treasurer, and I asked him to continue as
Treasurer and that was all that was involved. And I
remember the day very well, I was in Innisfail, in Far
North Queensland, and I spoke to him on the phone
and he indicated that after consideration, because we'd
spoken the day earlier, he would continue.'

4 September   Howard has a conversation with Alexander Downer
2007   about impending defeat in the forthcoming election
asking, 'Do you think it would help if I went? Could
Costello do better than I could? Perhaps a new leader
would upset Rudd and turn things around?' Howard
gives Downer authority to call members of Cabinet
together to ascertain their attitude.

6 September   Downer meets with some Cabinet colleagues to tell
2007   them of Howard's pessimism about the election
outcome. Most of them do not think that the
government could win under Howard's leadership but
were unconvinced that it would be any better under
Costello.

7 September 2007	Howard asks Downer if Cabinet would be willing to 'own' a request for him to stand aside. Downer tells him that there is absolutely no support for this. Howard suggests that a resignation would look like cowardice, and he would rather go down fighting than desert on the eve of the battle.
9 September 2007	Howard discusses resignation with his family, whose attitude is that he should only give up the leadership if publicly requested to do so by his senior colleagues.
12 September 2007	Howard appears on the *7.30 Report* saying: 'I would expect well into my term, and after those things [that I want to do] have been implemented and battered down, I would probably, certainly form the view well into my term, that it makes sense for me to retire, and in those circumstances, I would expect, although it would be a matter for the party to determine if Peter would take over'.
14 October 2007	Asked: 'Can you tell us a little more about your handover to Mr Costello and that as part of the right leadership team?', Howard replies: 'What I have said is that well into my next term, if I am elected, there will be a leadership transition. And that leadership transition will be from me to the next most experienced person in Australian politics, Mr Costello.'
13 November 2007	Howard says: 'I have indicated time without number that if we are re-elected, then sometime well into the next term there will be a transition to Mr Costello'.

22 November 2007	Responding to a question at the National Press Club, Howard says: 'if we are re-elected, that I will, at some point well into the term, have the transition and it will be to Peter Costello and I base that on my knowledge of the party and my personal strong belief that he's far and away the most qualified person. I mean, he is the next most experienced person in public life in Australia and I think he will do a very good job, very, very good job indeed. So I think it is a very clear position, it's very open, we're not concealing anything, we don't have any secret Kirribilli House pacts.'
24 November 2007	Howard loses government and his seat in House of Representatives election.
29 November 2007	Brendan Nelson elected Leader of the Parliamentary Liberal Party by 45 votes to 42 over Malcolm Turnbull.
18 February 2008	On the ABC TV *Four Corners* program *Howard's End*, former ministers discuss the election outcome and John Howard's role in the election defeat.
16 September 2008	Costello's biography, *The Costello Memoirs*, is launched. In his preface, co-author Peter Coleman says: 'These memoirs record the long saga of the Howard–Costello contest … The dismal details, through to the final catastrophe, are all here.' Chapter 12 is entitled 'Leadership: from Memo to Madness' (pages 223–57).
21 October 2010	Howard's autobiography, *Lazarus Rising*, is published. In Chapter 44, 'The leadership' (pages 599–625), Howard writes, 'The focus of this chapter is the leadership issue and why a transition late in 2006 did not take place'.

<table>
<tr><td>21 October 2010</td><td>In an article in the *Australian*, Paul Kelly includes quotes from Howard's autobiography, *Lazarus Rising*, including: 'Mr Costello completely misread both my temperament and my personality'. Kelly writes, 'In an account that casts Mr Costello as weak and vacillating, Howard expresses surprise that the former Treasurer "imagined I would succumb to the sort of rank amateur pressure placed on me through media briefings"'.</td></tr>
<tr><td>27 October 2010</td><td>Of Howard, Costello writes: 'Now for the first time he "reveals" he intended to stand down as Liberal leader in December 2006 but was prevented from doing so – mainly by me, but also by his colleagues and then by Kevin Rudd and lastly by his own family. So if you want to know who caused all this catastrophe it is Peter Costello. John Howard was responsible for everything except his own retirement, which was all the fault of … well, you know the story by now. He couldn't go, he says, in July 2006 because I pushed him too hard; he would look as if he was running from me. He couldn't go in December 2006 because Kevin Rudd was elected Labor leader and he would look as if he was running from Rudd. He couldn't go when his Cabinet advised him to leave in September 2007 because, according to his family, it would look as if he was running from the voters.'</td></tr>
</table>

21 September
2014

Speaking of Costello in an interview with Janet
Albrechtsen, Howard says: 'He was obviously
disappointed that I didn't retire at some point as
I intended to do at the end of 2006, because the
allegation emerged that I'd welshed on some deal years
earlier … So I resolved as a result of overwhelming
requests from my colleagues to stay and lead the party
to the next election, which was in 2007.' Asked if he
made a deal with Costello, he says: 'No, I didn't make
a deal. I mean what happened in 1994 when we were
talking about the leadership, when Alexander Downer's
leadership was in trouble, I said to him, "Peter, I'll only
stay one and a half terms". That was my feeling at the
time, but he didn't turn around and say to me, "Let's
shake on that, I'll support you for the leadership". He
kept dangling on the issue for another five or six weeks,
which he was entitled to do. He mused on one occasion
about running himself, which is fair enough he had
every right to. And then interestingly enough, some
years later – 2003 – when we had a discussion about
whether I was going to retire or not, he never once
raised the so-called deal.'

NOTES

1   Setting the scene
1   'Andrew Denton interviews Mark Latham', the *Age*, 16 September 2005, <www.
    theage.com.au/national/andrew-denton-interviews-mark-latham-20050916-
    ge0vvx.html>.
2   Quoted in 'Latham trips on "them" to reach us', the *Age*, 16 September 2004,
    <www.smh.com.au/opinion/latham-trips-on-them-to-reach-us-20040916-
    gdjqwm.html>.
3   'Latham unveils super plan', *ABC News*, 10 February 2004, <www.abc.net.au/
    news/2004-02-10/latham-unveils-super-plan/133484>.
4   Catherine McGrath, 'Howard announces new MP superannuation rules', *ABC
    News*, 12 February 2004, <www.abc.net.au/pm/content/2004/s1043892.htm>.
5   Parliamentary Superannuation Bill 2004, Parliament of Australia website,
    2004, <www.aph.gov.au/Parliamentary_Business/Bills_Legislation/bd/
    bd0304/04bd131>.
6   'Troops home by Christmas, Latham pledges', *Sydney Morning Herald*, 7 October
    2004, <www.smh.com.au/national/troops-home-by-christmas-latham-pledges-
    20041007-gdjvbn.html>.
7   'Public backs Latham's Bush attack', the *Age*, 10 December 2003, <www.theage.
    com.au/national/public-backs-lathams-bush-attack-20031210-gdwwo6.html>.
8   Sarah Clarke, 'Peter Garrett to stand for Labor seat', *ABC News*, 10 June 2004,
    <www.abc.net.au/pm/content/2004/s1129232.htm>.
9   David Fickling, 'Rock star's trip from green to MP makes Labor members see
    red', the *Guardian*, 8 June 2004, <www.theguardian.com/world/2004/jun/08/arts.
    australia>.
10 For a detailed treatment of this matter see Tom Frame, 'A certain political
    scandal', in Tom Frame (ed.), *Trials and Transformations, 2001–2004: The Howard
    Government, Volume III*, UNSW Press, Sydney, 2019, chapter 8.
11 'Howard: election to be about trust', *Sydney Morning Herald*, 29 August 2004,
    <www.smh.com.au/national/howard-election-to-be-about-trust-20040829-gdjn4a.
    html>.
12 'Mark Latham's 2004 ALP Campaign Launch Speech', AustralianPolitics.com
    website, 29 September 2004, <australianpolitics.com/2004/09/29/mark-latham-
    alp-campaign-launch-speech.html>; see also 'Latham in a flap over Howard
    handshake', *Sydney Morning Herald*, 27 October 2004, <www.smh.com.au/
    national/latham-in-a-flap-over-howard-handshake-20041027-gdjzxd.html>.

13   Sean Kelly, 'Mark Latham: The outsider', *The Monthly*, August 2019, <www.
      themonthly.com.au/issue/2019/august/1564581600/sean-kelly/mark-latham-
      outsider>.

14   'Mark Latham's famous overly physical hand shake with John Howard revisited',
      News.com.au, 19 September 2014, <www.news.com.au/entertainment/tv/mark-
      lathams-famous-overly-physical-hand-shake-with-john-howard-revisited/news-
      story/ae926777c1a669d8a6d145c15f2e8da0> and 'Mark Latham and John Howard
      shake hands', *ABC News*, 23 March 2019, <www.abc.net.au/news/2019-03-23/
      mark-latham-shakes-john-howards-hand-(one-use-only)/10929958>.

15   'Erratic Latham caused Labor loss: Liberals', *ABC News*, 27 October 2004,
      <mobile.abc.net.au/news/2004-10-27/erratic-latham-caused-labor-loss-liberals/
      575058?pfm=sm&pfmredir=sm> and 'Brian Loughnane: Liberal Party's 2004
      Federal Election Analysis', AustralianPolitics.com website, 27 October 2004,
      <australianpolitics.com/2004/10/27/brian-loughnane-npc-election-analysis.html>.

2   Missing the wood for the trees: Explaining Howard's 2004 victory

1   The two-party preferred concept had been conceived by Joan Rydon rather
      than Malcom Mackerras; see Murray Goot, 'The Transformation of Australian
      Electoral Analysis: The two-party preferred vote – origins, impacts, and critics',
      Australian Journal of Politics and History, vol. 62, no. 1, 2016, pp. 70–72. The
      first preference counts are in Colin A Hughes and BD Graham, *A Handbook of
      Australian Government and Politics 1890–1964*, Australian National University
      Press, Canberra, 1968, pp. 286ff, and at <elections.uwa.edu.au/elecdetail.
      lasso?keyvalue=711&summary=false>; the two-party preferred figures, estimated
      as far back as 1949, are in Malcolm Mackerras, 'The pendulum', in Marian Simms
      & John Warhurst (eds), *Mortgage Nation: The 2004 Australian Elections*, API
      Network and Curtin University of Technology Press, Perth, 2005, p. 290.

2   Graham Richardson, 'Relaxed and comfortable: Correspondence', *Quarterly Essay*,
      issue 20, 2005, p. 69.

3   David Clune, 'Howard at the crossroads? The October 2004 federal
      election', *Australasian Parliamentary Review*, vol. 20, no. 1, 2005,
      pp. 3–4; <search-informit-com-au.simsrad.net.ocs.mq.edu.au/
      documentSummary;dn=200507685;res=IELAPA> ISSN: 1447–9125.

4   Nick Dyrenfurth & Frank Bongiorno, *A Little History of the Australian Labor Party*,
      UNSW Press, Sydney, 2011, p. 183.

5   Mungo MacCallum, *Run, Johnny, Run*, Duffy & Snellgrove, Sydney, 2004, pp. 60,
      87, 101.

6   Mark Latham, *The Latham Diaries*, Melbourne University Press, Melbourne, 2005,
      pp. 417–18; Tim Gartrell, 'The Australian Labor Party', in Simms & Warhurst
      (eds), *Mortgage Nation*, p. 143. At Labor's bi-annual conference, in January, *Sydney
      Morning Herald* journalist Mark Riley had said that the ALP, once the Australian
      Losers Party, was now the Australian Latham Party; MacCallum, *Run, Johnny, Run,*
      p. 30.

7   *Agence France Presse* quoted in Peter Browne, 'Introduction', in Peter Browne &
      Julian Thomas (eds), *A Win and a Prayer: Scenes from the 2004 election*, UNSW
      Press, Sydney, 2005, p. 7.

8   Quoted in Jennifer Byrne, 'Mark Textor', *Bulletin*, 7 September 2004.

9   Rodney Tiffen, 'Must Labor lose?', in Browne & Thomas (eds), *A Win and a Prayer*,
     p. 127. See also Frank Bongiorno, 'The Latham factor', in Tom Frame (ed.) *Trials
     and Transformations, 2001–2004: The Howard Government, Volume III*, UNSW
     Press, Sydney, 2019, p. 185.
10   Latham, *The Latham Diaries*, p. 378.
11   Wayne Errington & Peter van Onselen, *John Winston Howard: The biography*,
     Melbourne University Press, Melbourne, 2007, p. 354.
12   MacCallum, *Run, Johnny, Run*, pp. 131, 264. A three-point buffer had not been
     enough in 1990.
13   Ian McAllister & Clive Bean, 'Leaders, the economy or Iraq? Explaining voting in
     the 2004 elections', *Australian Journal of Politics and History*, vol. 52, no. 4, 2006,
     p. 605.
14   Tony Vermeer, 'Coalition holds winning lead in all key marginals', *Sunday
     Telegraph*, 5 September 2004. The seats polled, all requiring swings of less than
     two percentage points to fall to Labor, were: Dobell, Eden-Monaro, Parramatta,
     Paterson, Richmond (NSW); Deakin, McEwen (Vic); Herbert (Qld); Adelaide,
     Hindmarsh (SA); Canning (WA); Solomon (NT). The various iterations of the poll
     are noted in MacCallum, *Run, Johnny, Run*, pp. 205, 212, 242–43, 270, 274, 284.
     For how each of the pollsters constructed the two-party vote, see Peter Brent, 'Poll
     position: Making sense of opinion polls', in Christian Kerr (ed.), *The Crikey Guide
     to the 2007 Federal Election*, Penguin, Melbourne, 2007, pp. 140–41.
15   Labor 'was never in the lead', David Adams argues, basing his argument simply on
     first preferences in Newspoll; 'The leadership contest: Boy Wonder versus "Honest"
     John', in Simms & Warhurst (eds), *Mortgage Nation*, p. 38.
16   From January to October, Latham reminded his critics after the election, 'the
     Government led in just two out of 22 Newspolls (2PP)'; *The Latham Diaries*,
     p. 400.
17   Dennis Shanahan & Sid Maher, 'Coalition ahead in marginals', the *Australian*,
     8 October 2004.
18   Ian McAllister, 'Online poll report for Friday 8 October, 2004', ANU, 9 October
     2004; author's collection. McAllister's claim that '[a]ll the poll predictions were
     within sampling error' – when the ANU poll favoured Labor by 8, and the
     electorate favoured the Coalition by 5.4, a difference of 13.4 percentage points – is
     highly fanciful; Ian McAllister, 'A margin for error … ', *Bulletin*, 19 October 2004.
     McAllister's claim is not repeated in Rachel Gibson & Ian McAllister, 'Designing
     online election surveys: Lessons from the 2004 Australian election', *Journal of
     Elections, Public Opinion and Parties*, vol. 18, no. 4, 2008, pp. 387–400.
19   Mackerras, 'The pendulum', p. 307.
20   John Howard, 'Election speeches: John Howard, 2004', Museum of Australian
     Democracy, <electionspeeches.moadoph.gov.au/speeches/2004-john-howard>;
     Mark Latham, 'Election speeches: Mark Latham, 2004', Museum of Australian
     Democracy, <electionspeeches.moadoph.gov.au/speeches/2004-mark-latham>.
21   For the response of the betting markets, at every turn, see Andrew Leigh & Justin
     Wolfers, 'Competing approaches to forecasting elections: Economic models,
     opinion polling and prediction markets', *The Economic Record*, vol. 82, 2006, p. 331.
22   Stephen J Duckett, 'Social policy at the 2004 election', *Australian Journal of Social
     Issues*, vol. 42, no. 3, 2007, p. 295.

23   MacCallum, *Run, Johnny, Run*, p. 272; Murray Goot, 'Underdogs, bandwagons or incumbency? Party support at the beginning and end of Australian election campaigns, 1983–2007', *Australian Cultural History*, 2010, vol. 28, no. 1, 2010, p. 74.

24   Quoted in Laurie Oakes, 'The reign of King John', *Bulletin*, 15 December 2004; reprinted in *Power Plays: The real stories of Australian politics*, Hachette, Sydney, 2008, p. 308.

25   John Howard, *Lazarus Rising: A personal and political autobiography*, revised edition, HarperCollins, Sydney, 2013, pp. 567–68.

26   Tom Clarke, *Talking Up a Legacy: Australian prime ministers and the speeches we remember them by*, UWA Publishing, Perth, 2019, p. 96.

27   Quoted in John Warhurst, 'The campaign: Trust and leadership', in Simms & Warhurst (eds), *Mortgage Nation*, p. 18; Browne, 'Introduction', p. 9.

28   Howard, 'Election speeches', p. 2.

29   See Adams, 'The leadership contest', p. 38.

30   In the language of political science, Howard framed the election in terms of 'valence issues', the parties' alternative – and contested – policy prescriptions representing 'position issues'; Donald E Stokes, 'Spatial models of party competition' *American Political Science Review*, vol. 57, 1963, pp. 372–74.

31   MacCallum, *Run, Johnny, Run*, pp. 140–41. Tiffen thought 'the economic situation was probably loaded heavily against a Labor victory'; 'Must Labor lose?', p. 127. For a review of the international evidence along these lines, see Michael S Lewis-Beck & Mary Stegmaier, 'Economic determinants of electoral outcomes', *Annual Review of Political Science*, vol. 3, 2000, pp. 183–219; 'Economic models of voting', in Russell Dalton & Hans-Dieter Klingeman (eds), *The Oxford Handbook of Political Behavior*, Oxford University Press, Oxford, 2007. Contrast this position with that of Don Russell, formerly principal adviser to Paul Keating, pointing to the change of government in 1996, who argued that '[t]he better things got, the easier it became to replace a government'; quoted in David Crowe, 'Economy in the driver's seat', *Australian Financial Review*, 19–20 May 2007. Ahead of the 2004 campaign, Margaret Simons doubted that voters would feel sufficiently relaxed about the economy to allow Latham to convince them that 'it is now acceptable to vote on the basis of social issues'; 'Latham's world: the new politics of the outsiders', *Quarterly Essay*, issue 15, 2004, p. 107.

32   Leigh & Wolfers, 'Competing approaches to forecasting elections', pp. 328–29. For a sceptical view of inflation's importance, see Michael D McDonald & Ian Budge, *Elections, Parties, Democracy: Conferring the median mandate*, Oxford University Press, Oxford, 2005, p. 228.

33   Marian Simms & John Warhurst, 'Introduction and overview', in Simms & Warhurst (eds), *Mortgage Nation*, p. 1.

34   Leigh & Wolfers, 'Competing approaches to forecasting elections', p. 326.

35   Latham, *The Latham Diaries*, pp. 343, 377–78.

36   'Australian economy in 2004', Google search results, <www.google.com/search?q=Australian+economy+in+2004&tbm=isch&source=univ&client=firefox-b-d&sa=X&ved=2ahUKEwjqm4XsjejkAhVDf30KHdUPCFQQsAR6BAgFEAE&biw=192>.

37   Simon Crean, 'The challenge of opposition', in Frame (ed.), *Trials and Transformations*, p. 117.

38   Information from advisers with access to the research.

39   Latham, *The Latham Diaries*, p. 418.

40   Crosby | Textor, 'Positioning statements', 7 October 2004.

41   Brian Loughnane, 'The Liberal campaign', in Simms & Warhurst (eds), *Mortgage Nation*, pp. 134, 137. See also Labor's Evan Thornley, quoted in Steve Lewis, 'Losing the plot', in Nick Cater (ed.), *The Howard Factor: A decade that changed the nation*, Melbourne University Press, Melbourne, 2018, p. 185.

42   See George A Quattrone & Amos Tversky, 'Contrasting rational and psychological analyses of political choice', *American Political Science Review*, vol. 82, no. 3, 1988; reprinted in Daniel Kahneman & Amos Tversky (eds), *Choice, Values, and Frames*, Cambridge University Press, Cambridge, 2000, pp. 457–58. See also Lewis-Beck, *Economics and Elections*, p. 156.

43   Murray Goot & Ian Watson, 'Explaining Howard's success: Social structure, issue agendas and party support, 1993–2004', *Australian Journal of Political Science*, vol. 42, no. 2, 2007, p. 265. The proportions in each category reported here, but not the odds ratios, differ from those in the original.

44   McAllister, *The Australian Voter*, p. 191. The analysis of vote-switchers presented by McAllister and Bean suggests that positive evaluation of how households had performed made switching from the LNP to Labor less likely while evaluations of how the economy had performed had no impact; 'Leaders, the economy or Iraq?', p. 617.

45   Goot & Watson, 'Explaining Howard's success', p. 274.

46   Goot & Watson, 'Explaining Howard's success', p. 274.

47   Brian Costar & Peter Browne, 'How Labor lost', in Browne & Thomas (eds), *A Win and a Prayer*, p. 114.

48   Goot & Watson, 'Explaining Howard's success', p. 274.

49   Latham, 'Election speeches', p. 7.

50   Goot & Watson, 'Explaining Howard's success', p. 274.

51   McAllister, *The Australian Voter*, p. 180.

52   For the Liberal Party ads, and the underlying narrative, see Sally Young, 'Political advertising', in Simms & Warhurst (eds), *Mortgage Nation*, pp. 107–109. The ubiquitous L-plate reworked the theme used against Labor in 1994 by the Northern Territory Country Liberal Party; Gartrell, 'The Australian Labor Party', p. 151. Labor research had alerted the party to Latham's vulnerability on his record as mayor; Latham, *The Latham Diaries*, p. 418.

53   Latham, *The Latham Diaries*, pp. 343, 359, 372.

54   Information from consultant at the heart of the campaign.

55   Annabel Crabb, *Losing It: The inside story of the Labor Party in opposition*, Picador, Sydney, 2005, p. 251. To suggest, as Geoff Robinson does, that the lesson for 'the left' was that 'voters had lost faith in the possibility of public policy affecting their standard of living' was to misread the electorate completely; *Being Left-Wing in Australia: Identity, culture and politics after socialism*, Australian Scholarly Publishing, Melbourne, 2019, p. 157.

56   Crabb, *Losing It*, p. 252.

57   Lagan, *Loner*, p. 171.

58   Gartrell, 'The Australian Labor Party', pp. 149–50. See also Rodney Cavalier, 'The defeat of Labor', in Simms & Warhurst (eds), *Mortgage Nation*, pp. 353–54.

59   Megalogenis, *The Longest Decade*, pp. 13, 310. See also Costar & Browne, 'How
     Labor lost', p. 114.
60   Gartrell, 'The Australian Labor Party', p. 149.
61   George Megalogenis, 'Mortgage Nation', the *Australian*, 16–17 October 2004,
     reproduced in Malcolm Mackerras, 'The pendulum', in Simms & Warhurst (eds),
     Mortgage Nation, p. 303; Tim Colebatch, 'New divide opens up', the *Age*,
     23 October 2004, quoted in Costar & Browne, 'How Labor lost', pp. 114–15.
62   Bob Birrell, Ernest Healy & Lyle Allan, 'Labor's shrinking constituency', *People
     and Place*, vol. 13, no. 2, 2005, pp. 50–67.
63   Simon Jackman, 'Incumbency advantage', in Simms & Warhurst (eds), *Mortgage
     Nation*, pp. 346–47. But cf. Steve Easton & Richard Gerlach, 'Interest rates and the
     2004 Australian election', *Australian Journal of Political Science*, vol. 40, no. 4, 2005,
     pp. 559–66.
64   McAllister & Bean, 'Voting behaviour', p. 319, emphasis added; 'Leaders, the
     economy or Iraq?', p. 619.
65   McAllister & Bean, 'Voting behaviour', p. 329.
66   Clive Bean, Ian McAllister, Rachel Gibson & David Gow, *Australian Election Study,
     2004* [computer file], Canberra, Australian Social Science Data Archive, ANU,
     2005, pp. 60–69.
67   'Strategists feel they "own" an issue only on the assumption that, if it becomes
     salient, more electors on balance are likely to vote for them than if it does not';
     Ian Budge & Dennis Fairlie, 'Party competition – Selective emphasis or direct
     confrontation? An alternative view with data', in Hans Daalder & Peter Mair (eds),
     Western European Party Systems: Continuity & change, Sage, Beverly Hills, 1983,
     p. 282.
68   Goot & Watson, 'Explaining Howard's success', p. 268.
69   Margaret Simons, 'Latham's world: Response to correspondence', *Quarterly Essay*,
     issue 16, 2004, p. 99.
70   Latham, 'Election speeches', pp. 1, 2.
71   Simons, 'Latham's world', pp. 93–94.
72   Latham, *The Latham Diaries*, p. 370.
73   McAllister, 'The Australian federal election', p. 548.
74   Quoted in Warhurst, 'The campaign', p. 18. The emphasis on health and education
     was in line with Labor's market research, though rather than 'health' the research
     emphasised 'Medicare'; Latham, *The Latham Diaries*, p. 418.
75   Latham, *The Latham Diaries*, p. 334.
76   Howard, 'Election speeches', pp. 9–10; Latham, 'Election speeches', pp. 3–6.
77   George Megalogenis, *The Longest Decade*, revised edition, Scribe, Melbourne, 2008,
     p. 200.
78   For Latham on 'aspiration', see: 'Election speeches: Mark Latham, 2004', pp. 8, 11;
     Murray Goot & Ian Watson, 'Are "aspirationals" different?', in David Denemark
     et al., (eds), *Australian Social Attitudes 2: Citizenship, work and aspirations*, UNSW
     Press, Sydney, 2007, pp. 218–19.
79   Warhurst, 'The campaign', pp. 19–22.
80   Loughnane, 'The Liberal campaign', pp. 136, 138.
81   See also Sarah M Cameron & Ian McAllister, *Trends in Australian Political Opinion:
     Results from the Australian election study 1987–2016*, School of Politics and

International Relations, Australian National University, Canberra, 2016, pp. 35, 37.

82 Howard, 'Election speeches', pp. 4, 9. Contrast Jane Green & Will Jennings, *The Politics of Competence: Parties, public opinion and voters*, Cambridge University Press, Cambridge, 2017, p. 122, who use Newspoll data to argue that Labor 'lost its traditional strength' on healthcare during the Howard years.

83 Crabb, *Losing It*, p. 256, citing Labor research. For the coverage and critique of the plan, see Latham, *The Latham Diaries*, pp. 347–48; MacCallum, *Run, Johnny, Run*, pp. 267–70, 277.

84 Labor source, 28 November 2019.

85 Liberal source, 29 October 2019.

86 Crosby|Textor, 'Positioning statements', 7 October 2004.

87 Latham, *The Latham Diaries*, p. 370.

88 Goot & Watson, 'Explaining Howard's success', p. 264.

89 Errington & van Onselen, *John Winston Howard*, p. 342; Latham, 'Election speeches', p. 3.

90 Ian McAllister, 'The Australian federal election, October 2004', *Electoral Studies*, vol. 24, 2005, p. 549; McAllister & Bean, 'Leaders, the economy or Iraq?', p. 617. See also Duckett, 'Social policy at the 2004 election', p. 295.

91 Goot & Watson, 'Explaining Howard's success', p. 264.

92 Latham, *The Latham Diaries*, p. 347. For MacCallum, Labor was 'in with a big chance' at the end of week four, and 'the chance was getting bigger'; *Run, Johnny, Run*, p. 249.

93 Crosby|Textor, 'Positioning statements', 7 October 2004. See also Warhurst, 'The campaign', p. 25; Haydon Manning & John Warhurst, 'The old and new politics of religion', in Simms & Warhurst (eds), *Mortgage Nation*, p. 266.

94 McAllister & Bean, 'Leaders, the economy or Iraq?', pp. 616–17; Duckett, 'Social policy at the 2004 election', p. 295.

95 McAllister, 'The Australian federal election, October 2004', p. 549.

96 Goot & Watson, 'Explaining Howard's success', p. 264.

97 McAllister & Bean, 'Leaders, the economy or Iraq?', p. 617; see also Duckett, 'Social policy at the 2004 election', p. 295.

98 Quoted in Greg Buckman, *Tasmania's Wilderness Battles: A history*, Jacana Books, Sydney, 2008, p. 125.

99 Judith Ajani, *The Forest Wars*, Melbourne University Press, Melbourne, 2007, p. 290. See also Katrina Willis, 'The Australian Greens', in Simms & Warhurst (eds), *Mortgage Nation*, p. 165; Lagan, *Loner*, p. 182. One 'media professional' suggests that 'the swing against Liberals in some metropolitan' seats – 'base-bleeding', Howard called it – was attributable to 'social issues' of concern to 'doctors' wives'. See Fiona Wade, '"You knew what he stood for"', in Frame (ed.), *Trials and Transformations*, p. 343; Howard, *Lazarus Rising*, p. 568.

100 Howard's visit to Richmond (NSW) is noted in MacCallum, *Run, Johnny, Run*, pp. 208–12, 214, 236; Lagan, *Loner*, p. 183.

101 Errington & van Onselen, *John Winston Howard*, p. 359. For the history of the phrase, see Aynsley Kellow, 'Economics and the environment', in Frame (ed.), *Trials and Transformations*, pp. 291, 294.

102 Megalogenis, *The Longest Decade*, pp. 186–87. For John Stone, 'real people' was 'a category which … excludes the "doctors' wives"'; 'Our greatest prime minister?',

in Keith Windschuttle, David Martin Jones & Ray Evans (eds), *The Howard Era*, Quadrant Books, Sydney, 2009, p. 23.

103 Crabb, *Losing It*, p. 260.

104 Latham, *The Latham Diaries*, p. 349; see also Lagan, *Loner*, p. 185.

105 McAllister & Bean, 'Voting behaviour', p. 329. More formally, the effective zero in response to questions like this is much higher than zero.

106 Enterprise Marketing & Research Services [EMRS], 'Forest industry issues survey research report September 2004', cited in Ajani, *The Forest Wars*, p. 289.

107 Willis, 'The Australian Greens', p. 166; Latham, 'Election speeches', p. 10.

108 Crabb, *Losing It*, p. 262.

109 Paddy Manning, *Inside the Greens: The origins and future of the party, the people and the politics*, Black Inc., Melbourne, 2019, p. 233.

110 Crabb, *Losing It*, pp. 263–64; on Latham's dealings with Lennon and the forestry union, see *The Latham Diaries*, pp. 349–52.

111 Lagan, *Loner*, p. 174.

112 My thanks to Antony Green for data on the preference flows.

113 Lagan, *Loner*, p. 182.

114 Arthur Sinodinos, quoted in Sam Crosby, *The Trust Deficit*, Melbourne University Press, Melbourne, 2016, p. 99. Contrast Lagan, *Loner*, p. 187, who has Howard winning both the workers and 'the doctors' wives'.

115 Buckman, *Tasmania's Wilderness Battles*, pp. 125–26; Warhurst, 'The campaign', pp. 22–23; Marcus Haward & Tony McCall, 'Tasmania', in Simms & Warhurst (eds), *Mortgage Nation*, pp. 228–29; Ajani, *The Forest Wars*, pp. 131–35, 288–94; Nick Burston (comp), '10 years in 25 pictures', in Cater (ed.), *The Howard Factor*, p. 333.

116 Crosby, *The Trust Deficit*, pp. 98–100.

117 Latham, *The Latham Diaries*, p. 352.

118 Latham, *The Latham Diaries*, pp. 352, 373.

119 Haward & McCall, 'Tasmania', p. 229.

120 Jackman, 'Incumbency advantage', p. 340. The terms 'rural' and 'provincial' come from the Australian Electoral Commission.

121 Mackerras, 'The pendulum', pp. 298–99.

122 Gartrell, 'The Australian Labor Party', pp. 146–47; see also McAllister, 'The Australian federal election', p. 549; Latham, *The Latham Diaries*, p. 379.

123 Errington & van Onselen, *John Winston Howard*, p. 358.

124 Manning, *Inside the Greens*, p. 234. It 'was *the* catastrophe of the Latham campaign'; Lagan, *Loner*, p. 186.

125 John Caples, 'Libs ahead in Bass', and 'Result is a wake-up call to MHRs', *Sunday Examiner*, 12 September 2004, pp. 1, 5, 8. There had been 200 interviews in each of the state's five seats. Perhaps Labor's pre-selection in June of Peter Garrett, the prominent environmentalist, for the safe Sydney seat of Kingsford Smith, had already alarmed voters in Tasmania. See MacCallum, *Run, Johnny, Run*, pp. 122, 128; Lagan, *Loner*, p. 184.

126 Haward & McCall, 'Tasmania', pp. 228–29, 231; Mackerras, 'The pendulum', p. 298. Doubts about the efficacy of the issue are also expressed by Ajani, *The Forest Wars*, pp. 290, 294. On Adams, see Latham, *The Latham Diaries*, p. 351.

127 Mackerras, 'The pendulum', p. 301.

128 MacCallum, *Run, Johnny, Run*, pp. 280–82; Leigh & Wolfers, 'Competing approaches to forecasting elections', p. 331.

129 Latham, *The Latham Diaries*, p. 370.

130 McAllister & Bean, 'Leaders, the economy or Iraq?', p. 616.

131 John Wanna, 'Political chronicles: Commonwealth of Australia', *Australian Journal of Politics and History*, vol. 51, no. 2, 2005, p. 276; Nick Cater, *The Lucky Culture and the Rise of an Australian Ruling Class*, HarperCollins, Sydney, 2013, p. 189; Paul Kelly, *Triumph and Demise: The broken promise of a Labor generation*, updated edition, Melbourne University Press, Melbourne, 2014, p. 40.

132 Dennis Shanahan & David Tanner, 'Nationals gain from Labor's miner complications', *Weekend Australian*, 29 February–1 March 2020.

133 Howard, 'Election speeches', p. 3.

134 John Howard, 'The view from Kirribilli', in Frame (ed.), *Trials and Transformations*, p. 353. In his autobiography, Howard calls his account of the election 'Blue collars and green sleeves – Latham's implosion'; *Lazarus Rising*, ch. 36.

135 Goot & Watson, 'Explaining Howard's success', p. 274.

136 Errington & van Onselen, *John Winston Howard*, p. 357; Murray Goot, 'Neither entirely comfortable nor wholly relaxed: Public opinion, electoral politics and foreign policy', in James Cotton & John Ravenhill (eds), *Trading on Alliance Security: Australia in world affairs 2001–2005*, Oxford University Press, Melbourne, 2007, pp. 275–77.

137 Robert Manne, *Left, Right, Left: Political essays 1977–2005*, Black Inc., Melbourne, p. 363; James Curran, 'The ANZUS cornerstone', in Daniel Baldino, Andrew Carr & Anthony J Langlois (eds), *Australian Foreign Policy: Controversies and debates*, Oxford University Press, South Melbourne, 2014, p. 127.

138 Megalogenis, *The Longest Decade*, p. 289. Bongiorno, who called it 'the most serious error' of Latham's leadership, thought it a turning-point for Labor in the polls; 'The Latham factor', pp. 184–85. Similarly, Nicholas Stuart, *Kevin Rudd: An unauthorised political biography*, Scribe, Melbourne, 2007, p. 253, thought Latham's announcement marked 'the moment from which his collapse in the polls had begun'. See also Paul D Williams, 'The 2004 federal election: Why Labor failed', *Australian Quarterly*, vol. 76, no. 5, 2004, p. 5; <search-informit-com-au.simsrad.net.ocs.mq.edu.au/documentSummary;dn=200501216;res=IELAPA>.

139 I am grateful to William Bowe for the Newspoll data and to John Stirton for the ACNielsen data; for Morgan, see Morgan Poll, <www.roymorgan.com/morganpoll/federal-voting/2pp-voting-intention-trend-1901-2019>.

140 MacCallum, *Run, Johnny, Run*, p. 154.

141 Howard, 'Election speeches', p. 4.

142 Latham, 'Election speeches', p. 10.

143 Geoffrey Barker, 'The dog that didn't bark', in Browne & Thomas (eds), *A Win and a Prayer*, pp. 31, 34. See also Kingston, *Still Not Happy, John!*, p. 6; Warhurst, 'The campaign', p. 25; MacCallum, *Run, Johnny, Run*, p. 163; James Jupp, 'The ethnic dimension', in Simms & Warhurst (eds), *Mortgage Nation*, p. 251.

144 McAllister & Bean, 'Leaders, the economy or Iraq?', pp. 607, 612; emphasis retained.

145 Goot, 'Neither entirely comfortable nor wholly relaxed', pp. 272, 277.

146 Murray Goot, 'Questions of deception: Contested understandings of the polls on WMD, political leaders and governments in Australia, Britain and the United States', *Australian Journal of International Affairs*, vol. 60, no. 1, 2007, pp. 41–64; McAllister & Bean, 'Leaders, the economy or Iraq?', p. 613.

147 Howard quoted in Tom Conley, 'Issues in Australian foreign policy', *Australian Journal of Politics and History*, vol. 51, no. 2, 2005, p. 267; Goot, 'Neither entirely comfortable nor wholly relaxed', pp. 278–79.

148 Greg Sheridan, *The Partnership: The inside story of the US–Australian alliance under Bush and Howard*, UNSW Press, Sydney, 2006, pp. 249, 299; Bean et al. (eds), *Australian Election Study*, 2004, p. 63. For audience reactions to mentions of Iraq during the leaders' debate, see MacCallum, *Run, Johnny, Run*, p. 231.

149 Ian McAllister, 'Australian public opinion toward the Iraq war', in Ramesh Thakur & Jack Cunningham (eds), *Australia, Canada, and Iraq: Perspectives on an invasion*, Dundurn, Toronto, 2015, p. 288.

150 McAllister & Bean, 'Voting behaviour', p. 329. The figures ignore those (4 per cent) who didn't answer the question.

151 Goot & Watson, 'Explaining Howard's success', p. 264.

152 Cited in Lagan, *Loner*, p. 87.

153 McAllister & Bean, 'Voting behaviour', p. 331; McAllister & Bean, 'Leaders, the economy or Iraq?', pp. 619–20.

154 Latham, *The Latham Diaries*, p. 419. See also Lagan, *Loner*, pp. 84–91; Ann Capling, '"Allies but not friends": Anti-Americanism in Australia', in Richard Higgott & Ivona Malbašić (eds), *The Political Consequences of Anti-Americanism*, Routledge, Abingdon, 2008, p. 146; Erik Paul, *Little America: Australia, the 51st state*, Pluto Press, London, 2006, pp. 43, 226.

155 Gartrell, 'The Australian Labor Party', pp. 143–52.

156 Robert Manne, 'Murdoch's war', the *Monthly*, July 2005, <www.themonthly.com.au/monthly-essays-robert-manne-murdochs-war-how-lovestruck-teenager-angry-man-and-ambitious-baron-made->; reprinted in *Making Trouble: Essays against the new Australian complacency*, Black Inc., Melbourne, 2011, p. 181.

157 McAllister, 'The Australian federal election', p. 546.

158 Goot, 'Neither entirely comfortable nor wholly relaxed', p. 283.

159 Gartrell, 'The Australian Labor Party', p. 146; see also Latham, *The Latham Diaries*, p. 342. See Leigh & Wolfers, 'Competing approaches to forecasting elections', p. 328, for the bookies.

160 Lagan, *Loner*, pp. 160–63; Leigh & Wolfers, 'Competing approaches to forecasting elections', p. 328.

161 Gartrell, 'The Australian Labor Party', p. 146. The bookies tell a different story; Leigh & Wolfers, 'Competing approaches to forecasting elections', p. 328.

162 Goot & Watson, 'Explaining Howard's success', p. 264.

163 Goot & Watson, 'Explaining Howard's success', p. 264.

164 Barker, 'The dog that didn't bark', pp. 32, 41.

165 Loughnane, 'The Liberal campaign', p. 134.

166 Conley, 'Issues in Australian foreign policy', p. 257.

167 Goot & Watson, 'Explaining Howard's success', p. 264.

168 McAllister & Bean, 'Voting behaviour', p. 329; Goot & Watson, 'Explaining Howard's success', p. 264.

169 Eric Richards, *Destination Australia: Migration to Australia since 1901*, UNSW Press, Sydney, 2019, p. 335.

170 Scott Burchill, 'The trouble with empathy', *Griffith Review*, no. 8, 2005, p. 117.

171 Murray Goot, 'Turning around the votes – The 2001 election', in Frame (ed.), *Trials and Transformations*, pp. 97–98. For attitudes to asylum seekers, see Anne Pedersen, Farida Fozdar & Mary Anne Kenny, 'Battling boatloads of prejudice: An interdisciplinary approach to activism with asylum seekers and refugees in Australia', in Diane Bretherton & Nikola Balvin (eds), *Peace Psychology in Australia*, Springer, New York, 2012, pp. 123–28. For the 'myths' about them, see Jane McAdam & Fiona Chong, *Refugee Rights and Policy Wrongs*, UNSW Press, Sydney, 2019, ch. 3.

172 Latham, *The Latham Diaries*, pp. 335, 344; Gartrell, 'The Australian Labor Party', p. 143; Wanna, 'Political chronicles', p. 274; Margo Kingston, *Still Not Happy, John!: 2007 election edition*, Penguin, Melbourne, 2007, pp. 8–10; Tom Frame, 'A certain political scandal', in Frame (ed.), *Trials and Transformations,* pp. 134–37.

173 Errington & van Onselen, *John Winston Howard*, p. 354.

174 Adams, 'The leadership contest', p. 35. Frame nominates the *Tampa* controversy, the decision to invade Iraq, and 'children overboard' as the focus of these criticisms; 'A certain political scandal', p. 119. For Textor 'dishonesty' meant 'acting essentially in an inconsistent way, so [others] have no idea about your behaviours'; quoted in Byrne, 'Mark Textor'. The ironic sobriquet 'Honest John' had been bestowed in the 1970s when Howard had been treasurer, and his reputation among his critics for dishonesty had continued from there; see MacCallum, *Run, Johnny, Run*, pp. 1–2, 86, 88, 131, 180, 190, 194, 197, 199ff.

175 MacCallum, *Run, Johnny, Run*, p. 194; Browne, 'Introduction', pp. 8–9; Latham, *The Latham Diaries*, p. 419; Wade, '"You knew what he stood for"', pp. 341–42, on the anti-Howard websites. The reference was to government claims in 2001 about asylum seekers in boats throwing their children overboard, a claim challenged in the run-up to the election, yet again, this time by a former public servant of the staff of Defence Minister Peter Reith; see Manne, *Left, Right, Left*, pp. 359–61.

176 Latham, *The Latham Diaries*, pp. 332–33, 334.

177 Michael Gordon, 'PM lied over children: poll', the *Age*, 8 September 2004. Howard and Latham were both rated 'trustworthy' (6–10 on a scale of 0–10) by 43 per cent; ACNielsen Issues Report, 6 September 2004.

178 Dennis Shanahan, 'Voters warming to vision of Latham', the *Australian*, 22 September 2004. On two measures – 'has a vision for Australia', and 'understands the major issues' – the differences were 179.

179 Dennis Shanahan, 'Latham loses advantage on "caring"', the *Australian*, 21 July 2004.

180 Allan Gyngell, *Fear of Abandonment: Australia in the world since 1942*, La Trobe University Press, Melbourne, 2017, p. 262.

181 Quoted in Latham, *The Latham Diaries*, p. 418.

182 [Newspoll, ACNielsen, Morgan] Galaxy, which did not ask about preferred prime minister, noted that 'Mr Howard tied with the Labor leader at 42 per cent on the question of who had been the election's most impressive performer'; Michael Harvey, 'Close call: Howard, Latham neck and neck', *Herald Sun*, 8 October 2004.

183 For the phrase, see Dyrenfurth & Bongiorno, *A Little History of the Australian*

Labor Party, p. 185. See also Brent's claim that 'there is absolutely no evidence to support the proposition that an opposition leader with a high satisfaction rating has a better chance of being elected than one with a low rating'; 'Poll position', p. 143.

184 Loughnane, 'The Liberal campaign', p. 139.

185 Judith Brett, 'Relaxed and comfortable: Response to correspondence', *Quarterly Essay*, issue 20, 2005, p. 93.

186 'Readiness' is always likely to be a problem for any untried leader up against a veteran. Early concerns about Latham's 'readiness' are noted in MacCallum, *Run, Johnny, Run*, p. 128.

187 Bean et al. (eds), *Australian Election Study, 2004*, pp. 40–44; Bean and McAllister, 'Voting behaviour', pp. 326–31. Given that in other surveys 'likeability' is a variable in its own right, 'liked' was an infelicitous choice for the aggregate variable. [Cf. Browne, p. 8 re Morgan poll on trust.]

188 Clive Bean & Anthony Mughan, 'Leadership effects in parliamentary elections in Australia and Britain', *American Political Science Review*, vol. 83, 1989, p. 1171.

189 Clive Bean, 'The electoral influences of party leader images in Australia and New Zealand', *Comparative Political Studies*, vol. 26, 1993, p. 129; Daniel Kahneman, *Thinking, Fast and Slow*, Allen Lane, London, 2011, pp. 90–91, for Todorov.

190 John Bartle & Ivor Crewe, 'The impact of party leaders in Britain: Strong assumptions, weak evidence', in Anthony King (ed.), *Leaders' Personalities and the Outcomes of Democratic Elections*, Oxford University Press, Oxford, 2002, p. 90.

191 David Runciman, *Where Power Stops: The making and unmaking of presidents and prime ministers*, Profile Books, London, 2019, p. 193.

192 Imre Salusinszky, 'The Howard idiom', in Cater (ed.), *The Howard Factor*, p. 202; emphasis in the original. See also Irving Saulwick, 'Latham's world: Correspondence', *Quarterly Essay*, issue 16, 2004, p. 92; Judith Brett, 'Relaxed and comfortable: The Liberal Party's Australia', *Quarterly Essay*, issue 19, 2005, p. 36. Howard presented his election spending as an act of 'mateship' not 'class or envy'; cited in Lagan, *Loner*, p. 169.

193 Clarke, *Talking Up a Legacy*, p. 73.

194 Judith Brett, 'The new liberalism', in Robert Manne (ed.), *The Howard Years*, Black Inc., Melbourne, 2004, pp. 82ff; also in Robert Manne & Chris Feik (eds), *The Words That Made Australia: How a nation came to know itself*, second edition, Black Inc., Melbourne, 2014, pp. 425ff. For the strange view that Howard suffered from an almost complete 'lack of understanding of political symbolism', see Errington & van Onselen, *John Winston Howard*, p. 358.

195 Howard, *Lazarus Rising*, pp. 486ff. For a picture, see Nick Burston (comp.), '10 years in 25 pictures', in Cater (ed.), *The Howard Factor*, p. 332.

196 Loughnane, 'The Liberal campaign', pp. 139–41.

197 Simons, 'Latham's world: Response to correspondence', p. 95. The allegation that he struck his wife was 'simply untrue'.

198 Gartrell, 'The Australian Labor Party', pp. 145, 151; see also Latham, *The Latham Diaries*, p. 418. ACNielsen reported in similar terms from focus groups in Parramatta; 'Affection for Latham, but no keys to Lodge', *Sydney Morning Herald*, 28 September 2004.

199 Simons, 'Latham's world', pp. 2–3, 19; John Button, 'Latham's world: Correspondence', *Quarterly Essay*, issue 16, 2004, p. 69.

200 Arthur Sinodinos quoted in Errington & van Onselen, *John Winston Howard*, p. 354.

201 Latham, *The Latham Diaries*, p. 333. See Bill Clinton, *My Life*, Hutchinson, London, 2004, p. 435, for Latham's source.

202 Bean et al. (eds), *Australian Election Study, 2004*, pp. 35–36; Philip Senior & Peter van Onselen, 'Re-examining leader effects: Have leader effects grown in Australian federal elections 1990–2004?', *Australian Journal of Political Science*, vol. 43, p. 231.

203 Senior & van Onselen, 'Re-examining leader effects', pp. 233–34.

204 Senior & van Onselen, 'Re-examining leader effects', pp. 236–40.

205 Loughnane, 'The Liberal campaign', pp. 134, 139.

206 Gartrell, 'The Australian Labor Party', p. 148; Latham, *The Latham Diaries*, pp. 333–34, 359.

207 Bean et al. (eds), *Australian Election Study, 2004*, pp. 35–36; McAllister & Bean, 'Leaders, the economy or Iraq?', pp. 616–17.

208 Latham, 'Election speeches', p. 2. Latham's 'readiness' was no doubt a hesitation in research about voting for Labor.

209 MacCallum, *Run, Johnny, Run*, pp. 179–80; Young, 'Political advertising', pp. 110–12. The trope itself was an old one. In 1972, for example, the Liberals presented Gough Whitlam as really Bob Hawke with a mask; 'When Labor speaks, who is really talking?' [illustration], in Laurie Oakes & David Solomon, *The Making of an Australian Prime Minister*, Cheshire, Melbourne, 1973. In 2004, the British Conservatives considered 'vote Blair, get Brown' as their campaign slogan until they discovered George Brown would be an asset to Labour's vote; Michael A Ashcroft, *Smell the Coffee: A wake-up call for the Conservative Party*, Michael A Ashcroft, np, 2005, p. 67.

210 Gartrell, 'The Australian Labor Party', pp. 147–48. Public polling, conducted earlier in the year, suggesting that the prospect of Costello as prime minister would have made voters less likely to vote Liberal, is reported in MacCallum, *Run, Johnny, Run*, p. 112. One explanation: 'like all treasurers, he was deeply unpopular with the electorate'; MacCallum, *Run, Johnny, Run*, p. 53.

211 Latham, *The Latham Diaries*, pp. 360, 372.

212 Loughnane, 'The Liberal campaign', p. 137.

213 Cited in Latham, *The Latham Diaries*, p. 370.

214 Leigh & Wolfers, 'Competing approaches to forecasting elections', p. 331.

215 On the extent to which betting markets follow the polls, contrast Simon Jackman, 'All that glitters: Betting markets and the 2013 Australian federal election', in Carol Johnson & John Wanna (eds), *Abbott's Gambit: The 2013 Australian Federal Election*, ANU Press, Canberra, 2015, with Leigh & Wolfers, 'Competing approaches to forecasting elections'.

216 Rodney Tiffen, 'Australia: Gladiatorial parties and volatile media in a stable polity', in Jesper Strömbäck & Lynda Lee Kaid (eds), *The Handbook of Election News Coverage Around the World*, Routledge, New York, 2008, p. 118.

217 Tiffen, 'Australia', p. 119.

218 Aaron Patrick, *The Surprise Party: How the Coalition went from chaos to comeback*, Black Inc., Melbourne, 2019, p. 192.

219 Author's calculation. The final polls are reported in Dennis Shanahan & Sid Maher, 'Coalition ahead in marginals', the *Australian*, 8 October 2004.

220   Errington & van Onselen, *John Winston Howard*, p. 358.

221   Murray Goot, 'To the second decimal point: How the polls vied to predict the national vote, monitor the marginals and second-guess the Senate', in Marian Simms & John Wanna (eds), *Julia 2010: The caretaker election*, ANU E Press, Canberra, 2012, p. 106.

222   Mackerras, 'The pendulum', p. 299; Charles Richardson & Christian Kerr, 'The best seats in the House', in Kerr (ed.), *The Crikey Guide to the 2007 Federal Election*, p. 26.

223   Tiffen, 'Must Labor lose?', pp. 125–26.

224   Crosby, *The Trust Deficit*, p. 99. See also Tiffen, 'Must Labor lose?', p. 128.

225   Errington & van Onselen, *John Winston Howard*, p. 360.

226   Loughnane, 'The Liberal campaign', p. 139; MacCallum, *Run, Johnny, Run*, p. 262.

227   Loughnane, 'The Liberal campaign', p. 134; John Howard, 'The view from Kirribilli', p. 353.

228   Errington & van Onselen, *John Winston Howard*, p. 358.

229   Crabb, *Losing It*, pp. 264–65.

230   Errington & van Onselen, *John Winston Howard*, pp. 358–59. Similarly, Dyrenfurth & Bongiorno on 'the crucial last week'; *A Little History of the Australian Labor Party*, p. 184.

231   Warhurst, 'The campaign', p. 24; see also p. 19, where it appears as one of the campaign's 'significant dates'. For the handshake, see Burston, '10 years in 25 pictures', p. 333.

232   Errington & van Onselen, *John Winston Howard*, p. 360. See also Adams, 'The leadership contest', p. 41'.

233   Latham, *The Latham Diaries*, p. 369.

234   Crabb, *Losing It*, pp. 264–65; Latham, *The Latham Diaries*, p. 121.

235   Claire Kimball, 'Enough rope for a Windsor knot', *Sun-Herald*, 24 November 2019; Nicola Berkovic, 'From first lady of Labor to the bench', the *Australian*, 12 September 2019.

236   Howard, *Lazarus Rising*, pp. 314, 560, 567, 582.

237   McAllister, *The Australian Voter*, p. 229.

238   Loughnane, 'The Liberal campaign', p. 134. See also Willis, 'The Australian Greens', p. 167; Ian Ward, 'Queensland', in Simms & Warhurst (eds), *Mortgage Nation*, pp. 198–99; Manning, *Inside the Greens*, p. 231.

239   Howard, *Lazarus Rising*, pp. 567–68. On Anzac Day, under Howard, contrast Mark McKenna, 'Anzac Day: How did it become Australia's national day?', in Marilyn Lake & Henry Reynolds with Mark McKenna & Joy Damousi (eds), *What's Wrong with Anzac? The militarisation of Australian history*, UNSW Press, Sydney, 2010, pp. 123–29, with Mervyn F Bendle, *Anzac and Its Enemies: The history war on Australia's national identity*, Quadrant Books, Sydney, 2015, pp. 201ff. For 'the black armband', see Geoffrey Blainey, 'Drawing up a balance sheet of our history', *Quadrant*, vol. 37, no. 7–8, July–August 1993, pp. 10–15, reprinted as 'From three cheers to the black armband', in Robert Manne & Chris Feik (eds), *The Words that Made Australia: How a nation came to know itself*, Black Inc., Melbourne, 2012, pp. 193–203. See also Errington & van Onselen, *John Winston Howard*, p. 350, on Howard's attempt to push 'Australian values'.

240   Graham Wallas, *Human Nature in Politics*, fourth edition, Constable, London,

1908/1948, p. 84. 'Word association: national security = a Liberal strength … economic management = a Liberal strength'; Latham, *The Latham Diaries*, pp. 342, 343.

241 Loughnane, 'The Liberal campaign', pp. 137, 139.

242 Wanna, 'Political chronicles', p. 276.

243 Barry Jones, 'Where are we coming from? Where are we going?', in Jones (ed.), *Coming to the Party*, p. 7.

244 *Lateline*, ABC television, 12 October 2004, quoted in David O'Reilly, *The New Progressive Dilemma: Australia and Tony Blair's legacy*, Palgrave Macmillan, Basingstoke, 2007, p. 191. See also Lewis, 'Losing the plot', p. 184.

245 Loughnane, 'The Liberal campaign', p. 134.

246 Mark Textor & John Scales to Brian Loughnane, 'Strategic Memorandum', Crosby | Textor, 3 May 2004, p. 2.

247 Loughnane, 'The Liberal campaign', p. 134.

248 Crosby | Textor, 'Positioning statements', 7 October 2004.

249 Wallas, *Human Nature in Politics*, pp. 83–85,

250 Bean et al., *Australian Election Study, 2004*, pp. xii–xiii, for the list.

251 *Australian Election Study, 2004*, p. 15.

252 Goot & Watson, 'Explaining Howard's success', p. 255, for McAllister's reckoning, 2006–04. The most persuasive attack on issues as the determinant of the vote, but from a quite different position to that of McAllister, see Christopher H Achens & Larry M Bartels, *Democracy for Realists: Why elections do not produce responsive government*, Princeton University Press, Princeton, 2016.

253 Ian McAllister, 'The personalization of politics', in Dalton & Klingeman (eds), *The Oxford Handbook of Political Behavior*.

254 Ian McAllister & Stephen Quinlan, 'Leader or party? Evaluating the personalization of politics thesis', Canadian Political Studies Association, 27 May 2019, pp. 4, 17. For an example of the 'prevailing narrative', see Sheridan, *The Partnership*, p. 250.

255 Graeme Starr, *Carrick: Principles, politics and policy*, Connor Court, Ballan, 2012, p. 145.

256 Neal Blewett, 'Personal reflections on the art of elections', in Kerr (ed.), *The Crikey Guide to the 2007 Federal Election*, p. 237.

257 Don Watson, *Recollections of a Bleeding Heart: A portrait of Paul Keating PM*, anniversary edition, Vintage, Sydney, 2002/2011, pp. 330, 350, 588, 674, 702.

258 *The IPSOS Mackay Report: Exploring the mind & mood of Australia: Aspirations*, Ipsos Australia, Sydney, 2004, p. 9; Hugh Mackay, 'An election decided long beforehand', *Sydney Morning Herald*, 11 October 2004.

259 'Best poll in our Galaxy', Galaxy Research, press release [c13 October 2004].

260 Leigh & Wolfers, 'Competing approaches to forecasting elections', p. 328.

261 Andrew Gelman & Gary King, 'Why are American presidential elections campaign polls so variable when votes are so predictable?', *British Journal of Political Science*, vol. 23, 1993, pp. 409–51.

3 The 'continuing work' of industrial relations

1 Commonwealth Parliamentary Debates, 26 May 2005 and reported in the *Australian*, 27 May 2005.

2   Greg Combet with Mark Davis, *The Fights of My Life*, Melbourne University Press, Melbourne, 2014, p. 172.

3   John Howard, *Lazarus Rising: A personal and political autobiography*, Harper Collins, Sydney, 2010, p. 561.

4   Howard, *Lazarus Rising*, p. 561.

5   Peter Hartcher, *To the Bitter End*, Allen & Unwin, Sydney, 2009, p. 77.

6   Paul Kelly, *The March of the Patriots*, Melbourne University Press, Melbourne, 2009, p. 303.

7   Howard, *Lazarus Rising*, p. 569.

8   Combet, *The Fights of My Life*, p. 174.

9   Combet, *The Fights of My Life*, p. 186.

10   Hartcher, *To the Bitter End*, p. 86.

11   Hartcher, *To the Bitter End*, p. 84.

12   Combet, *The Fights of My Life*, p. 186.

13   Combet, *The Fights of My Life*, p. 199.

14   Shaun Carney, the *Age*, 19 May 2012.

15   Madonna King, *Hockey*, University of Queensland Press, Brisbane, 2014, p. 184.

16   King, *Hockey*, p. 185.

17   King, *Hockey*, p. 188.

18   Combet, *The Fights of My Life*, p. 203.

19   John Howard, Address to *Howard Government Retrospective II*, Old Parliament House, Canberra, 15 November 2017.

20   Bernard Keane, 'Why Australian workers can't win', *Crikey*, 8 November 2019.

21   Geoff Gilfillan & Chris McGann, 'Trends in union membership in Australia', Australian Parliamentary Library, 15 October 2018.

22   Ewin Hannan, 'Campaign forgot voters', the *Australian*, 9 August 2019.

23   Ewin Hannan, 'Westacott calls for accord to save enterprise bargaining system', the *Australian*, 30 October 2019.

4   Restrained law-making and unrestrained terror

1   Graeme Dobell, 'Great Australian foreign policy speeches: Howard on 9/11 and the US alliance', *Interpreter*, 15 August 2014.

2   John Howard, *Commonwealth Parliamentary Debates* (Reps), 17 September 2001, p. 30 739.

3   *Criminal Code Act 1983* (NT), Sch I, Pt III, Div 2.

4   Bret Walker, Independent National Security Legislation Monitor, *Annual Report* (2011), p. 13 and Appendix 7.

5   Daryl Williams MP, Attorney-General, 'New counter-terrorism measures', media release, 2 October 2001.

6   Security Legislation Amendment (Terrorism) Bill 2002; Suppression of the Financing of Terrorism Bill 2002; Criminal Code Amendment (Suppression of Terrorist Bombings) Bill 2002; Border Security Legislation Amendment Bill 2002; and the Telecommunications Interception Legislation Amendment Bill 2002.

7   Australian Security Intelligence Organisation Legislation Amendment (Terrorism) Bill 2002.

8   Ben Saul, 'Defining terrorism: A conceptual minefield', in Erica Chenoweth et al. (eds), *Oxford Handbook of Terrorism*, 2019, pp. 34–49.

9 Gilbert + Tobin Centre of Public Law, Submission 25, Security Legislation Review Committee, 1 February 2006.

10 *Criminal Code Act 1995* (Cth), s 100.1.

11 Andrew O'Neill, 'Degrading and managing risk: Assessing Australia's counter-terrorist strategy', *Australian Journal of Political Science*, vol. 42, no. 3, 2007, pp. 471–87, 485.

12 See, for example, Malcolm Turnbull, press conference, London, United Kingdom, 11 June 2017.

13 National Commission on Terrorist Attacks upon the United States, *The 9/11 Commission Report*, 2004, p. xvi.

14 Anthony Reilly, 'The processes and consequences of counter-terrorism law reform in Australia: 2001–2005', *Flinders Journal of Law Reform*, vol. 10, no. 1, 2007, pp. 81–103, 100.

15 George Williams, 'A decade of Australian anti-terror laws', *Melbourne University Law Review*, vol. 35, no. 3, 2011, pp. 1136–1176, 1145.

16 A comprehensive list of this legislation can be obtained from the author, Dr Nicola McGarrity.

17 Kent Roach, *The 9/11 Effect: Comparative counter-terrorism*, Cambridge University Press, Cambridge, 2011, p. 309.

18 Andrew Lynch, 'Legislating with urgency – The enactment of the *Anti-Terrorism Act (No 1) 2005*', *Melbourne University Law Review*, vol. 30, no. 3, 2006, pp. 747–81, 779.

19 Ben Golder & George Williams, 'Balancing national security and human rights: Assessing the legal response of common law nations to the threat of terrorism', *Journal of Comparative Policy Analysis*, vol. 8, no. 1, 2006, pp. 43–62, 57.

20 Philip Thomas, 'Legislative responses to terrorism', the *Guardian*, 12 September 2002.

21 Daryl Williams, *Commonwealth Parliamentary Debates* (Reps), December 2002, pp. 1040–43.

22 Jenny Hocking, *Terror Laws: ASIO, counter-terrorism and the threat of democracy*, UNSW Press, Sydney, 2004, p. 196.

23 John Howard, Prime Minister of Australia, 'Anti-Terrorism Bill', media release, 2 November 2005.

24 Senate Legal and Constitutional Legislation Committee, *Provisions of the Anti-Terrorism Bill (No 2) 2005*, p. 4.

25 Eminent Jurists Panel on Terrorism, Counter-terrorism and Human Rights, International Commission of Jurists, *Assessing Damage, Urging Action*, 2009, p. 21.

26 Hocking, *Terror Laws*, p. 218.

27 John Faulkner, *Commonwealth Parliamentary Debates* (Sen), 16 June 2003, p. 11 432.

28 Lynch, 'Legislating with urgency', pp. 747–81, 780.

29 Liora Lazarus & Benjamin Goold, 'Introduction – Security and human rights: The search for a language of reconciliation' in Liora Lazarus & Benjamin Goold (eds), *Security and Human Rights*, Bloomsbury, London, 2007, pp. 1–24.

30 Sophie Mirabella, *Commonwealth Parliamentary Debates* (Reps), 11 September 2006, p. 65.

6 Controlling the Senate

1 Andrew Robb MP, quoted in Sandra O'Malley & Susanna Dunkley, 'We went too far, Libs reformer says of WorkChoices', *Canberra Times*, 14 December 2007; Brian

Loughnane, Federal Director of the Liberal Party, quoted in Dennis Shanahan, 'Selling of WorkChoices tops blame list', the *Age*, 26 November 2007.

2   Paul Kelly, *Triumph and Demise: The broken promise of a Labor generation*, Melbourne University Press, Melbourne, 2014, pp. 70–72.

3   Kelly, *Triumph and Demise*, pp. 111–12.

4   Gwynneth Singleton, 'Industrial relations: Pragmatic change', in Scott Prasser & Graeme Starr (eds), *Policy and Change: The Howard mandate*, Hale & Iremonger, Sydney, 1997, pp. 192–207.

5   Singleton, 'Industrial relations: Pragmatic change', pp. 192–207.

6   Kelly, *Triumph and Demise*, p. 111.

7   John W Howard, *Lazarus Rising: A personal and political autobiography*, HarperCollins, Sydney, 2010, p. 568.

8   Liberal and National Coalition, *Our Plans for Australia: Election 2004*, 'An enterprise culture', pp. 37–38.

9   Senator George Brandis, 'The Australian Senate and responsible government', in Nicholas Aroney, Scott Prasser & JR Nethercote (eds), *Restraining Elective Dictatorship: The upper house solution?*, University of Western Australia Press, Perth, 2008, p. 90.

10 WorkChoices refers to the amendments made to the *Workplace Relation Act 1996* by the *Workplace Relations Amendment (Work Choices) Act 2005*, which began on March 2006.

11 Harry Evans, 'The case for bicameralism', in Aroney, Prasser & Nethercote, *Restraining Elective Dictatorship*, p. 73.

12 Scott Prasser, JR Nethercote & Nicholas Aroney, 'Upper houses and the problem of elective dictatorship', in Aroney, Prasser & Nethercote, *Restraining Elective Dictatorship*, p. 2.

13 Harry Evans, 'The Senate', in Clive Hamilton & Sarah Maddison (eds), *Silencing Dissent: How the Australian Government is controlling public opinion and stifling debate*, Allen & Unwin, Sydney, 2007, p. 201.

14 Harry Evans, 'The Senate', in Hamilton & Maddison, *Silencing Dissent*, p. 201.

15 David Clune, 'Howard at the Crossroads?: The October 2004 federal election', *Australasian Parliamentary Review,* vol. 20, no. 1, 2005, p. 7.

16 Gerard McManus, 'The PM who fell to pride', *Herald Sun*, 29 November 2007.

17 Judith Brett, 'Exit Right: The unravelling of John Howard', *Quarterly Essay*, Black Inc, Melbourne, 2007, p. 62.

18 Marian Sawer, 'Markets good, governments bad: The philosophy of the New Right', *Current Affairs Bulletin*, vol. 64, no. 2, July 1987, pp. 26–32.

19 Richard D French, 'Political capital', *Representation*, vol. 47, no. 2, 2011, pp. 215–30.

20 The Menzies Coalition Government won seven elections in succession, the Hawke–Keating Labor administrations five, and the Fraser Coalition three.

21 These figures and assessments are drawn from Scott Bennett, Gerald Newman & Andrew Kopras, 'Commonwealth Election 2004', *Research Brief*, Commonwealth Parliamentary Library, Canberra, 14 March 2005, p. 17 and Clune, 'Howard at the Crossroads', p. 16.

22 Charlotte R Riley, 'Echoes of Labor's "longest suicide note in history"', *Australian Financial Review*, 18 December 2019.

23   Neil Brown, 'Two years as a minister in the Fraser Government', speech to Liberal
     Speakers' Group Annual General Meeting, Brisbane 12 March 1985; Liberal
     Party of Australia, Report of the Committee of Review (Valder Review), *Facing the
     Facts*, September, Canberra, September, 1983; Paddy P McGuiness, 'Sorry 7 years
     economic policy', *Australian Financial Review*, 24 February 1983; Russell Barton,
     'Seven years of contradictions', the *Age*, 7 March 1983.

24   Gerard Henderson, 'The Liberals: Why another period of lost opportunity
     would be the end', the *Australian*, 24 January 1987; Peter Tiver, 'Liberals in the
     Doldrums', *Current Affairs Bulletin*, vol. 64, no. 7, November 1987, pp. 4–11.

25   Howard, *Lazarus Rising*, p. 136.

26   Paul Kelly, *The End of Certainty: The story of the 1980s*, Allen & Unwin, Sydney,
     1992, pp. 36–37; Paul Kelly, 'Rethinking Australian Governance: The Howard
     legacy', *Australian Journal of Public Administration*, vol. 65, no. 1, March 2006,
     pp. 7–24.

27   Howard, *Lazarus Rising*, p. 649.

28   Brett, *Exit Right*, p. 62.

29   John W Howard, 'The Liberal–National parties' industrial relations policy:
     Deregulation by providing an enterprise focus', *The Economic and Labour Relations
     Review*, vol. 1, no. 2, December 1990, pp. 34–47; John W Howard, 'Industrial
     relations in Australia … A Liberal view', *Current Affairs Bulletin*, vol. 68, no. 1,
     June 1991, pp. 12–16.

30   See Singleton, 'Industrial relations: Pragmatic change', in Prasser & Starr, *Policy
     and Change*, pp. 194–95, for discussions of the differences between the 1992
     Jobsback! policy statement and the Coalition's 1996 industrial relations election
     platform.

31   Gwynneth Singleton, 'On the waterfront: The Howard Government's approach
     to industrial relations', in Gwynneth Singleton (ed.), *The Howard Government:
     Australian Commonwealth administration 1996–1998*, UNSW Press, Sydney, 2000,
     p. 140.

32   Singleton, 'On the waterfront', p. 140.

33   John Howard MP, Transcript of the Victory Speech of the Prime Minister Elect,
     Wentworth Hotel, 2 March 1996.

34   Brett, *Exit Right*, p. 6.

35   John W Howard, 'Reflections on Australian federalism', address to Menzies
     Research Centre, 11 April 2005.

36   Howard, *Lazarus Rising*, p. 566.

37   See Jamie Briggs, Senior Adviser to Prime Minister on Industrial Relations
     2006–07, quoted in Kelly, *Triumph and Demise*, p. 115.

38   Howard, *Lazarus Rising*, p. 566.

39   Brett, *Exit Right*, p. 64.

40   Senator Chris Evans (WA), 'A not so humble anniversary: A year of government
     Senate control', *Online Opinion*, 11 July 2006.

41   Senator John Hogg, 'An opposition view of the Australian Senate', in Aroney,
     Prasser & Nethercote, *Restraining Elective Dictatorship*, p. 100.

42   Scott Bennett, *The Australian Senate*, Research Paper no. 6, Commonwealth
     Parliamentary Library, Canberra, 2003–04, p. 8.

43   John Uhr, 'How democratic is parliament? A case study in auditing the

performance of parliaments', *Democratic Audit of Australia*, June 2005, p. 35.

44   Bennett, *The Australian Senate*, p. 10; Uhr, 'How democratic is parliament?', p. 3.

45   This critique is based on Gwynneth Singleton, 'The Senate a paper tiger', in Chris Aulich & Roger Wettenhall (eds), *Howard's Fourth Government: Australian Commonwealth administration 2004–2007*, UNSW Press, Sydney, 2008, pp. 75–94.

46   Singleton, 'The Senate a paper tiger', pp. 88–89.

47   Harry Evans, 'The Rudd Administration and the Senate: Business as usual', in Chris Aulich & Mark Evans (eds), *The Rudd Government: Australian Commonwealth Administration 2007–2010*, ANU Press, Canberra, pp. 87–95.

48   Singleton, 'The Senate a paper tiger', p. 76.

49   See for discussion: GS Reid, 'Australia's Commonwealth Parliament and the Westminster model', *Journal of Commonwealth Political Studies*, vol. 2, no. 2, 1964, pp. 89–100; John Uhr & John Wanna, 'The future roles of parliament', in Michael Keating, John Wanna & Patrick Weller (eds), *Institutions on the Edge: Capacity for governance*, Allen & Unwin, Sydney, 2000, pp. 10–44.

50   The United Kingdom and Canadian upper houses are appointed, and the United States Senate was not elected till 1913 (previously selected by state legislatures).

51   New Zealand abolished its upper house in 1950. In Canada there have been no upper houses in the provinces since 1968.

52   Kelly, 'Rethinking Australian governance', p. 16.

53   Evans, 'The Howard Government and Parliament', in Singleton (ed.), *The Howard Government*, p. 30.

54   Evans, 'The Rudd administration and the Senate', in Aulich & Evans, p. 94.

55   From 1919 to 1979 the Labor Party's federal platform proposed abolition of the Senate.

56   Labor abolished the upper house in Queensland in 1922 through quite nefarious means – see Justice Bruce H McPherson, 'A constitutional history of the Parliament of Queensland', in Aroney, Prasser & Nethercote, *Restraining Elective Dictatorship*, pp. 229–47. In NSW a Labor government in 1961 failed in its referendum to abolish the Legislative Council. Most other state Labor branches, although supporting abolition of their upper houses, took no steps to implement this policy.

57   Paul Keating MP, *Commonwealth Parliamentary Debates* (Reps), 4 November 1992, p. 2547.

58   Paul Keating MP, *Commonwealth Parliamentary Debates* (Reps), 5 November 1992, p. 2733.

59   Phil Lewis, 'Industrial relations and the labour market', in Aulich & Wettenhall, *Howard's Fourth Government*, p. 176.

60   Brett, *Exit Right*, p. 62.

61   Brett, *Exit Right*, p. 68.

62   Kelly, *Triumph and Demise*, pp. 111–12.

63   Kelly, *Triumph and Demise*, p. 111.

64   Greg Combet, ACTU Secretary, quoted in Kelly, *Triumph and Demise*, p. 110.

65   Kelly, *Triumph and Demise*, p. 110.

66   Lewis, 'Industrial relations and the labour market', p. 185.

67   Lewis, 'Industrial relations and the labour market', pp. 170–73.

68   Lewis, 'Industrial relations and the labour market', p. 177.

69 Daile White, 'Workplace rights and the states', in *Upholding the Australian Constitution*, vol. 29, Proceedings of the 29th Conference of The Samuel Griffith Society, 2018, pp. 89–102.

70 Kelly, *Triumph and Demise*, p. 117.

71 Howard, *Lazarus Rising*, p. 584.

72 Richard F Fenno, *Home Style: House members in their districts*, Scott Foresman, Glenview, 1978, p. 241.

73 Kelly, *Triumph and Demise*, pp. 115–17.

74 Howard, *Lazarus Rising*, pp. 649–50.

75 Brett, *Exit Right*, p. 22.

76 Peter Costello (with Peter Coleman), *The Costello Memoirs*, Melbourne University Press, Melbourne, 2008.

77 Costello, *The Costello Memoirs*, p. 294.

78 Peter Costello, 'Failure in 2007 was all Howard's doing', *Sydney Morning Herald*, 27 October 2010.

79 Peter van Onselen & Wayne Errington, *John Winston Howard*, Melbourne University Press, Melbourne, 2007.

80 Howard, *Lazarus Rising*, pp. 621–22.

81 *Inquiry into Certain Australian Companies in Relation to the UN Oil-for-Food Programme* was a royal commission appointed in October 2005 and reported in November 2006 – both Howard and Foreign Affairs Minister Alexander Downer appeared as witnesses.

82 See Stephen Bartos, 'Sweeping the wheat under the carpet – how much we have learnt from the AWB oil for food kickbacks scandal?' in Scott Prasser & Helen Tracey (eds), *Royal Commissions & Public Inquiries: Practice and potential*, Connor Court, Melbourne, 2014, pp. 233–47.

83 Tom Frame, *Trials and Transformations, 2001–2004: The Howard Government, Volume III*, UNSW, Sydney, 2019, Part I, pp. 15–63, and pp. 119–51.

84 Brett, *Exit Right*, p. 1.

85 David Owen & Jonathan Davidson, 'Hubris syndrome: An acquired personality disorder? A study of US presidents and UK prime ministers over the last 100 years', *Brain*, vol. 132, 2009, pp. 1396–1406.

86 Jim Bulpitt, 'The discipline of the New Democracy: Mrs Thatcher's domestic craft', *Political Studies*, vol. XXXIV, 1986, p. 19. This apparent bias is reflected in a 2013 survey of Australian academics of prime ministerial performance that included six Labor prime ministers among the top eight. This seems odd given that three led their party to massive defeats and Labor has only held office nationally for 30 per cent of the time since Federation – see Patrick Weller, *The Prime Ministers' Craft*, Oxford University Press, Oxford, 2018, p. 22.

87 Howard, *Lazarus Rising*, p. 569–70.

88 Tony Abbott MP, interview, ABC, 19 July 2010.

89 Kelly, *Triumph and Demise*, p. 109.

90 Mark Evans, Michelle Grattan & Brendan McCaffrie (eds), *From Turnbull to Morrison: The trust divide: Australian Commonwealth Administration 2016–2019*, Melbourne University Press, Melbourne, 2019.

91 Anthony J Makin & Sam Strong, 'New measures of factor productivity in Australia: A Sato approach', *Applied Economics*, vol. 45, 2013, pp. 2413–22.

92   Paul Keating MP, speech to the Institute of Directors, Melbourne, 21 April 1993.
93   Lewis, 'Industrial relations and the labour market,' p. 184.
94   Austin S Holmes, 'The good fight', *The Economic Record*, vol. 57, no. 1, March, 1981, pp. 1–11.

7   Indigenous affairs
1   John Howard, *Lazarus Rising: A personal and political autobiography*, HarperCollins, Sydney, 2010, p. 283.
2   Howard, *Lazarus Rising*, pp. 280, 588.
3   Patrick Mullins, *Tiberius with a Telephone: The life and stories of William McMahon*, Scribe, Melbourne, 2018, p. 479.
4   Mullins, *Tiberius with a Telephone*, p. 482.
5   Mullins, *Tiberius with a Telephone*, pp. 482–83.
6   Howard, *Lazarus Rising*, p. 204.
7   Paul Strangio, Paul 't Hart & James Walter, *The Pivot of Power: Australian prime ministers and political leadership 1949–2016*, Miegunyah Press, Melbourne, 2017, p. 224.
8   John Howard, *Commonwealth Parliamentary Debates* (hereafter CPD) (Reps), 3 July 1998, p. 6050.
9   Strangio, 't Hart & Walter, *Pivot*, p. 224.
10   Howard, CPD, 3 July 1998, p. 6050.
11   Howard, *Lazarus Rising*, p. 259.
12   Howard, *Lazarus Rising*, p. 225.
13   Howard, CPD, 11 April 1989, p. 1330.
14   Howard, CPD, 2 March 1995, p. 1412.
15   Howard, CPD, 30 October 1996, p. 6158.
16   Howard, CPD, 3 July 1998, p. 6050.
17   Howard, *Lazarus Rising*, p. 276.
18   Howard, *Lazarus Rising*, p. 283.
19   Howard, CPD, 27 May 1997, p. 4113.
20   Howard, *Lazarus Rising*, p. 256.
21   Howard, CPD, 2 March 1995, pp. 1411, 1412.
22   Howard, CPD, 30 October 1996, p. 6158.
23   Howard, CPD, 27 May 1997, p. 4111.
24   John Howard in David Furse-Roberts (ed.), *Howard: The art of persuasion, selected speeches 1995–2016*, Jeparit Press, Brisbane, 2018, p. 252.
25   CPD, 30 October 1996, p. 6155.
26   Howard, CPD, 27 May 1997, p. 4111.
27   Howard, CPD, 27 May 1997, p. 4112.
28   John Howard, 'The Liberal tradition: The beliefs and values which guide the federal government', the 1996 Sir Robert Menzies Lecture, <pmtranscripts.dpmc. gov.au/sites/default/files/original/00010171.pdf>.
29   John Howard, 'Opening address to the Australian Reconciliation Convention – Melbourne 1997', <www.austlii.edu.au/au/other/IndigLRes/car/1997/4/pmspoken. html>. In commenting on an earlier version of this chapter, Howard was emphatic that he will never agree to refer to the colonisation of Australia as an 'invasion'.
30   Howard, *Lazarus Rising*, p. 277.

31   Howard, CPD, 3 June 1999, p. 6017.
32   Howard, CPD, 26 August 1999, p. 9205.
33   Heidi Norman, *What do We Want? A political history of Aboriginal Land Rights in New South Wales*, Aboriginal Studies Press, Canberra, 2015, pp. 180–85.
34   McMullan, CPD, 1 June 2004, pp. 29 679.
35   The members of the NIC were: Sue Gordon, Wesley Aird, Archie Barton, MaryAnn Bin-Sallik, Miriam Rose Baumann, Joseph Elu, Robert Lee, Adam Goodes, Sally Goold, John Moriarty, Warren Mundine, Joe Procter, Michael White and Tammy Williams.
36   John Howard, 'To stabilise and protect – Little Children Are Sacred [Address to The Sydney Institute on 25 June 2007]', *Sydney Papers*, vol. 19, no. 3, 2007, pp. 68–76, p. 70.
37   Macklin, CPD, 7 August 2007, p. 68.
38   Luke Buckmaster, Diane Spooner & Kevin Magarey, 'Income management and the *Racial Discrimination Act*', <www.aph.gov.au/About_Parliament/ Parliamentary_Departments/Parliamentary_Library/pubs/BN/2011-2012/ IncomeManagementRDA)>.
39   Melissa Lovell, 'The normalisation of income management in Australia: Analysis of the parliamentary debates of 2007 and 2009–10', *Australian Journal of Social Issues*, vol. 51, no. 4, 2016, pp. 433–48, p. 436.
40   Lovell, 'The normalisation', p. 441.
41   Quoted in Calla Wahlquist, 'Indigenous voice proposal "not desirable", says Turnbull', the *Guardian*, 26 October 2017, <www.theguardian.com/australia-news/2017/oct/26/indigenous-voice-proposal-not-desirable-says-turnbull>.
42   Cressida Fforde, Lawrence Bamblett, Ray Lovett, Scott Gorringe & Bill Fogarty, 'Discourse, deficit and identity: Aboriginality, the race paradigm, and the language of representation in contemporary Australia', *Media International Australia*, vol. 149, no. 1, 2013, pp. 162–73.
43   Howard's approach to Indigenous rights can be seen as consistent with the philosophical commitment described by journalist Paul Kelly as a 'common law view of rights' which opposes the tendency of 'bills of rights' to empower the unelected judiciary at the expense of the elected legislature. See Paul Kelly, 'Re-thinking Australian governance: the Howard legacy', Occasional Paper Series 4/2005, Academy of the Social Sciences in Australia, Canberra, 2005, p. 17. Insofar as Indigenous rights are part of 'international law', Howard's approach to them also asserts the right of Australians to maintain their own customary notions of fairness, thus celebrating the nation against the world.
44   Kerry McCallum & Lisa Waller, 'The intervention of media power in Indigenous policy-making', *Media Information Australia*, vol. 149, no. 1, 2013, pp. 139–49, 145.
45   Jackie Huggins & Rod Little, 'A rightful place at the table', in Shireen Morris (ed.), *A Rightful Place*, Black Inc, Melbourne, 2017, pp. 147–72, 163.
46   As confirmed by the High Court of Australia in *Kartinyeri v Commonwealth* (1998) 195 CLR 337; 152 ALR 450, and in *Kruger v Commonwealth* (1997) 2 AILR 371; 190 CLR 1; 146 ALR 126.

8   **Energy and the environment**

1   And, as well, climate alarmists who link every weather event to climate change and demand action that would be hugely disruptive across the globe.

2   The COVID-19 recession might provide an unplanned reduction in emissions.

3   *Climate Change 2001: The scientific basis*, Intergovernmental Panel on Climate Change (IPCC) website, <www.ipcc.ch/site/assets/uploads/2018/03/WGI_TAR_full_report.pdf>.

4   President Bush had announced that the United States would commence steps to withdraw from the Protocol in March 2001.

5   Although I believe that there might have been a doorstop media interview on 10 September that noted climate had been discussed.

6   'Gas boom as China signs $25bn deal', *Sydney Morning Herald*, 9 August 2002, <www.smh.com.au/national/gas-boom-as-china-signs-25bn-deal-20020809-gdfiz2.html>.

7   David Kemp and I were told by a vice-president of Exxon at a meeting in the Australian Embassy in Washington DC in 2001 that after the victory was confirmed they had 'picked up the phone and told George that the (Clean Skies) caps were dead'.

8   'Global Greenhouse Challenge: The way ahead for Australia', joint media release, Minister for the Environment and Heritage Dr David Kemp and Minister for Foreign Affairs Alexander Downer, 15 August 2002.

9   'Global Greenhouse Challenge', 2002.

10   I had a considerable role in the drafting and negotiation with other department secretaries of this statement for consideration by ministers.

11   These papers have not yet been released. Ken Henry and I were the principal architects of the scheme that ministers proposed to Cabinet.

12   Guy Pearse, *High and Dry: John Howard, climate change and the selling of Australia's future*, Penguin, Sydney, 2007, p. 86. I cannot comment on the accuracy of this statement as I was not present at the Cabinet meeting.

13   Again, I am unable to comment on the accuracy and veracity of this statement.

14   With the minor distraction of the Manildra ethanol scandal. The Department of the Environment, *inter alia*, had to spend $4.2 million definitively proving the accuracy of automative and fuel industry experts' advice that long-term use of ethanol blends in excess of 20 per cent would seriously damage most existing vehicles' engines.

15   *Securing Australia's Energy Future*, Commonwealth of Australia, 2004.

16   Prime minister's foreword, *Securing Australia's Energy Future*, p. iii.

17   There was much else in the White Paper to commend it, but here the focus is on the link to climate policy.

18   Pearse, *High and Dry*, p. 87.

19   As was proposed by the sensible but stillborn National Energy Guarantee (NEG).

20   Ironically, I had led the team of officials which had negotiated the first stage of the RFA under the Keating Government, bringing to an end a long period of dispute including the logging truck blockade of Parliament House.

21   Bureau of Meteorology press release, 5 January 1999, 'Record warm year for Australia in 1998'.

22   Tim Flannery, *The Weather Makers: The history and future impact of climate change*, Text Publishing, Melbourne, 2005.

23   Anthony Downs, *Up and Down with Ecology – The issues attention cycle*, Public Interest, 1972, p. 28.

24   Lowy Institute Poll 2019, <www.lowyinstitute.org/publications/lowy-institute-poll-2019>.

25   I had retired from the Australian Public Service in early 2004, having stood aside from running the department in 2003 after declining a further term as secretary. I was approached by the state governments to develop a scheme which I undertook with Jon Stanford, a colleague at Allen Consulting.

26   House of Representatives Standing Committee on Industry and Resources, *Australia's Uranium – Greenhouse-friendly fuel for an energy-hungry world: A case study into the strategic importance of Australia's non-fossil fuel energy industry*, Commonwealth of Australia, Canberra, November 2006.

27   National Archives of Australia *PM Transcripts*, release date: 15/05/2006; release type: Interview Transcript ID: 22287.

28   Working to Marius Kloppers, chief executive, I drafted the BHP-Billiton submission to the review with the assistance of colleagues from consulting firm Allen Consulting.

29   Sharon Masher, 'Too hot to handle? Uranium and nuclear power in Australia's energy mix', *Australian Resources and Energy Law Journal*, vol. 26, no. 3, p. 335.

30   I was called by Peter Conran, Cabinet Secretary and Adviser to the Prime Minister, for advice.

31   Quoted by Marc Hudson in 'Ten years of backflips over emissions trading leave climate policy in the lurch', the *Conversation*, ABC website, 8 December 2016.

32   Prime minister press release: Prime Ministerial Task Group on Emissions Trading, 10 December 2006, Canberra, <parlinfo.aph.gov.au/parlInfo/download/media/pressrel/68QL6/upload_binary/68ql61.pdf;fileType=application%2Fpdf#search=%22media/pressrel/68QL6%22>.

33   *Report of the Prime Ministerial Task Group on Emissions Trading*, ISBN 978-0-9803115-4-9 (paperback); ISBN 978-0-9803115-5-6 (PDF), 31 May 2007, p. 84.

34   Emissions from the power sector, transport and stationary energy continued to grow strongly until the Global Financial Crisis (GFC) and the introduction of a carbon tax.

35   Lowy Institute Poll 2019, <www.lowyinstitute.org/publications/lowy-institute-poll-2019>.

10   Hearts and heads: The challenge of welfare reform

1   Report produced by the Reference Group on Welfare Reform, 'A new system for better employment and social outcomes', February 2015, <www.dss.gov.au/sites/default/files/documents/02_2015/dss001_14_final_report_access_2.pdf>.

2   Report of the Reference Group on Welfare Reform, *Participation Support for a More Equitable Society*, July 2000.

3   The members of the Reference Group included: Patrick McClure, CEO, Mission Australia (Chair); Wayne Jackson, Deputy Secretary, Department of Family and Community Services (Deputy Chair); Professor Peter Dawkins, Director, Melbourne Institute of Applied Economic and Social Research, University of

Melbourne; Elizabeth Morgan, Social Policy Specialist with Morgan, Disney and Associates; Jim Longley, Senior Finance Executive, Commonwealth Bank of Australia; Professor Mark Lyons, Director, School of Management, UTS; Jane Schwager, CEO, Benevolent Society, New South Wales. A Welfare Review Team under the leadership of Serena Wilson, a senior executive of the Department of Family and Community Services, and seven departmental staff acted as Secretariat. Dr Marie Leech, National Manager, Mission Australia Research and Social Policy Unit, and Peter Sandeman, General Manager, Mission Australia Community Services, also provided the Reference Group with specialist advice. They independently researched social policy initiatives throughout the OECD, especially in the United Kingdom and New Zealand. They brought a more balanced approach to the concept of mutual obligation, stressing the importance of government and business obligations as well as individual obligations. They also introduced the concepts of social inclusion, community capacity building, social enterprise and social innovation.

4 *Participation Support for a More Equitable Society*, p. 2.

5 *Participation Support for a More Equitable Society*, p. 3.

6 *Participation Support for a More Equitable Society*, p. 4.

7 *Participation Support for a More Equitable Society*, p. 3.

8 *Participation Support for a More Equitable Society*, p. 4.

9 *Participation Support for a More Equitable Society*, p. 6.

10 *Participation Support for a More Equitable Society*, p. 32.

11 *Participation Support for a More Equitable Society*, p. 35.

12 *Participation Support for a More Equitable Society*, pp. 45ff.

13 Patrick McClure, *Seize the Day: From priest to CEO*, Longueville Books, Sydney, 2011, p. 88.

14 'Budget 2001–02 "What's new what's different"', Department of Social Services website, <www.dss.gov.au/about-the-department/publications-articles/corporate-publications/budget-and-additional-estimates-statements/2001-02-budget-and-additional-estimates/budget-2001-02-whats-new-whats-different/australians-working-together-helping-people-to-move-forward>.

15 McClure, *Seize the Day*, p. 90.

16 *Participation Support for a More Equitable Society*, pp. 37ff.

17 *A New System for Better Employment and Social Outcomes*, February 2015, pp. 127ff.

18 'Welfare reform to save billions', the *Australian*, 14 October 2019, pp. 1ff.

11 The Howard Government and the rise of the Australian Greens

1 Bureau of Meteorology 'Recent rainfall, drought and southern Australia's long-term rainfall decline', April 2015, <www.bom.gov.au/climate/updates/articles/a010-southern-rainfall-decline.shtml>.

2 Australian Politics and Elections Archive 1856–2018, Election of 24 November 2007, <www.elections.uwa.edu.au/elecdetail.lasso?keyvalue=1337>.

3 See Gillian Fisher, *Half Life: The NDP, peace, protest and party politics*, State Library of NSW Press, Sydney, 1995.

4 See Randall Doyle, 'Turning point in Van Diemen's Land: Bob Brown, Bob Hawke and the Franklin River dam crisis of 1983', *Grand Valley Review*, vol. 29, no. 1, 2005, pp. 47–63.

5   See *Sydney Morning Herald*, 'Brown kicked out of parliament', 23 October 2003.

6   See David Charnock, 'Can the Australian Greens replace the Australian Democrats as a "third party" in the Senate?', *Australian Journal of Political Science*, vol. 44, no. 2, 2009, pp. 245–58.

7   Kevin Rudd, 2007 Australian Federal Election Speech, 14 November, <electionspeeches.moadoph.gov.au/speeches/2007-kevin-rudd>.

8   Keith Suter, 'The politics of climate change and the dismissal of Kevin Rudd', *Journal of the Indian Ocean Region*, vol. 6, no. 2, 2010, pp. 267–73.

9   See Jon Hovi, Detlef F Sprinz & Guri Bang, 'Why the United States did not become a party to the Kyoto Protocol: German, Norwegian, and US perspectives', *European Journal of International Relations*, vol. 18, no. 1, 2010, pp. 129–50.

10   See *Sydney Morning Herald*, 'I won't sign Kyoto agreement: PM', 27 May 2004.

11   See Julian Glover, 'The lucky country?', the *Guardian*, 23 November 2007.

12   John Howard, Transcript of the Prime Minister, The Hon John Howard MP, Address to the National Press Club, Great Hall, Parliament House, 25 January 2007, <parlinfo.aph.gov.au/parlInfo/download/media/pressrel/K81M6/upload_binary/k81m68.pdf;fileType=application%2Fpdf#search=%22media/pressrel/K81M6%22>.

13   Bill McCormick, 'Murray-Darling Basin water issues', Parliamentary Library, Canberra, 2010, <www.aph.gov.au/About_Parliament/Parliamentary_Departments/Parliamentary_Library/pubs/BriefingBook43p/murraydarlingissues>.

14   'Half-hearted climate change response', the *Age*, 30 July 2005.

15   Emma Young, 'Australia announces "cap and trade" CO_2 scheme', *New Scientist*, 17 July 2007.

12   **A view from Eden-Monaro**

1   'Questions without notice', Hansard, Parliament of Australia website, 19 September 2007, <parlinfo.aph.gov.au/parlInfo/search/display/display.w3p;db=CHAMBER;id=chamber%2Fhansardr%2F2007-09-19%2F0049;query=Id%3A%22chamber%2Fhansardr%2F2007-09-19%2F0000%22>.

2   'Questions without notice', 19 September 2007.

3   'Questions without notice', 19 September 2007.

16   **The succession that wasn't**

1   David Adams, 'Staying on', in Chris Aulich & Roger Wettenhall (eds), *Howard's Fourth Government, Australian Commonwealth Administration 2004–2007*, UNSW Press, Sydney, 2008, p. 264.

2   Wayne Errington & Peter van Onselen, *John Winston Howard: The definitive biography*, Melbourne University Press, Melbourne, 2007, p. 402.

3   Quoted in Cameron Hazlehurst, *Menzies Observed*, Allen & Unwin, Sydney, 1979, pp. 371–74.

4   Malcolm Fraser with Margaret Simons, *Malcolm Fraser: The political memoirs*, Miegunyah Press, Melbourne, 2010, pp. 616–17.

5   Fraser with Simons, *Malcolm Fraser*, p. 617.

6   Quoted in Troy Bramston, *Paul Keating: The big-picture leader*, Scribe, Melbourne, 2016, p. 371.

7   Peter Costello with Peter Coleman, *The Costello Memoirs*, Melbourne University Press, Melbourne, 2008, pp. 343–46.
8   Quoted in Peter Hartcher, *To the Bitter End*, Allen & Unwin, Sydney, 2009, p. 130.
9   Paul Daley, 'Not happy John', *Bulletin*, 29 May 2007.
10   Hartcher, *To the Bitter End*, p. 131.
11   Quoted in Hartcher, *To the Bitter End*, p. 135.
12   Costello, *The Costello Memoirs*, p. 257.

17   The dead bounce budget
1   Sir Arthur Fadden, Treasurer from 1949 to 1958, delivered 11 budgets. Harold Holt, the first member for Higgins, delivered seven budgets as Treasurer from 1958–66. No budget surpluses were recorded.
2   In reference to John Howard's 'five minutes of economic sunlight', a politically devastating putdown of the Keating Government's economic program in Peter van Onselen & Wayne Errington, *John Winston Howard: The definitive biography*, Melbourne University Press, Melbourne, p. 211.
3   'Costello crafts a clever Budget', the *Australian*, 9 May 2007.
4   'Shrewd package lacks big data', *Australian Financial Review*, 9 May 2007.
5   'Costello provides vision beyond the pork-barrelling', the *Age,* 9 May 2007.
6   'Happy marriage of clever politics and sound economics', *Sydney Morning Herald*, 9 May 2007.
7   'Politically correct', *Herald Sun*, 9 May 2007.
8   'Something for almost everybody', *Advertiser*, 9 May 2007.
9   Peter Hartcher, 'The budget ends the easy ride', *Sydney Morning Herald*, 11 May 2007, <www.smh.com.au/national/the-budget-ends-the-easy-ride-20070511-gdq3zr.html>.
10   *Commonwealth Parliamentary Debates* (CPD), House of Representatives, Thursday 10 May 2007, p. 129.
11   CPD, 10 May 2007, p. 134.
12   Dennis Shanahan, 'Most popular budget on record, but no bounce', the *Australian*, 15 May 2007, p. 1.
13   Peter Costello, doorstop interview, Gold Coast International Hotel, 15 May 2007, <www.petercostello.com.au/transcripts/2007/3320-telstra-newspoll-budget-doorstop-interview-gold-coast>.
14   'Dead bounce brings danger of spendfest', the *Australian*, 15 May 2007.
15   Marian Simms, 'The campaigns', *Australian Cultural History*, vol. 27, no. 2, 2009, pp. 87–96; Dennis Shanahan also alludes to the five previous budgets not giving the Howard Government a sudden lift in the first poll after the budget and had gotten a 'delayed' bounce in only two: 'Costello hoping to boost end-of-term results', the *Australian*, 15 May 2007.
16   Peter Costello, doorstop interview, Spring Road Gardens, Malvern, 14 October 2007, <www.petercostello.com.au/transcripts/2007/3231-election-doorstop-interview-malvern>.
17   Peter Costello, interview with Neil Mitchell, 3AW, 16 October 2007, <www.petercostello.com.au/transcripts/2007/3224-tax-cuts-economic-management-election-07-visy-amcor-decision-interview-with-neil-mitchell-3aw>.
18   Newspaper editorial comments summarised in the *Age*, 23 November 2007, p. 13.

19   Peter Costello, press conference, Treasury Place, Melbourne, 25 November 2007,
      <www.petercostello.com.au/transcripts/2007/3176-post-election-press-conference-
      treasury-place-melbourne>.
20   Costello, *Costello Memoirs*, p. 294.
21   Costello, *Costello Memoirs*, p. 294.
22   Costello, *Costello Memoirs*, p. 294.
23   John Howard discussing the election at a UNSW Canberra-hosted dinner at the
      National Press Club, 4 March 2020.

18   John Howard: Conservative, liberal, or what?

1   Donald Horne, *Looking for Leadership: Australia in the Howard years*, Penguin,
      Melbourne, 2001; Robert Manne, *The Barren Years: John Howard and Australian
      political culture*, Text Publishing, Melbourne, 2001; Guy Rundle, 'The
      Opportunist: John Howard and the triumph of reaction', *Quarterly Essay*, Black
      Inc., Melbourne, 2001.
2   John Howard, address at the launch of the publication 'The Conservative',
      Parliament House Canberra, 2005, <pmtranscripts.pmc.gov.au/release/
      transcript-21912>. See also Gregory Melleuish, 'Is the Broad Church broad
      enough or has Menzies Liberal Party run its course?', *Meanjin*, March 2019.
3   Zachary Gorman, 'George Reid's anti-socialist campaign in the evolution of
      Australian liberalism', in G Melleuish (ed.), *Liberalism and Conservatism*, Connor
      Court, Ballarat, 2015, pp. 17–38.
4   George Reid, election speech, 23 October 1906, <electionspeeches.moadoph.gov.
      au/speeches/1906-george-reid>; Billy Hughes, election speech, 27 March 1917,
      <electionspeeches.moadoph.gov.au/speeches/1917-billy-hughes>.
5   Malcolm Fraser, The Daniel Mannix Memorial Lecture: 'Sir Robert Menzies: In
      search of a balance', <archives.unimelb.edu.au/explore/collections/malcolmfraser/
      resources/postparliamentspeeches/the-daniel-mannix-memorial-lecture-sir-robert-
      menzies-in-search-of-balance>.
6   Robert Menzies, *The Forgotten People*, Angus & Robertson, Sydney, 1943, pp. 11–17.
7   Gregory Melleuish, 'EG Whitlam: Reclaiming the initiative in Australian History',
      in J Hocking (ed.), *Making Modern Australia: The Whitlam Government's 21st
      century agenda*, Monash University Press, Melbourne, 2017, pp. 308–35.
8   Melleuish, 'Is the Broad Church broad enough?'.
9   Zachary Gorman & Gregory Melleuish, 'Menzies and Howard on themselves:
      Liberal memoir, memory and myth making', *History Australia*, vol. 15, no. 1, 2018,
      pp. 7–22.
10   William Morris Hughes, *The Case for Labor*, Sydney, Sydney University Press,
      1970, pp. 59–65.
11   Bruce Smith, *Liberty and Liberalism*, Longman Green, New York, 1889.
12   Frederic W Eggleston, *Reflections of an Australian Liberal*, FW Cheshire,
      Melbourne, 1953, p. 203.
13   Stephen Chavura & Gregory Melleuish, 'Conservative instinct in Australian
      political thought: The Federation debates, 1890–1898', *Australian Journal of
      Political Science,* vol. 50, no. 3, 2015, pp. 512–28.
14   Robert Menzies, 'Politics as an art', in *Speech Is of Time*, Cassell, London, 1958,
      pp. 183–92.

15	John Howard, election speech, 26 September 2004, <electionspeeches.moadoph. gov.au/speeches/2004-john-howard>; John Howard, election speech, 12 November 2007, <electionspeeches.moadoph.gov.au/speeches/2007-john-howard>.

16	Robert Menzies, election speech, 2 September 1940, <electionspeeches.moadoph. gov.au/speeches/1940-robert-menzies>.

17	Menzies, *The Forgotten People*, pp. 1–10.

18	Malcolm Fraser, election speech, 30 September 1980, <electionspeeches.moadoph. gov.au/speeches/1980-malcolm-fraser>.

19	John Howard, *The Australia I Believe In*, Liberal Party of Australia, Canberra, 1996, pp. 21, 24, 36.

20	National and Liberal Parties, *Future Directions: Summary*, December 1988, p. 2.

21	John Howard, *Lazarus Rising: A personal and political autobiography*, HarperCollins, Sydney, 2010, pp. 486–97.

22	Howard, *Lazarus Rising*, p. 567.

23	Gregory Melleuish, 'The Machiavellian takeover of Australian universities', *Quadrant*, vol. 62, nos 1–2, 2018, pp. 66–74.

24	Gregory Melleuish, 'David Syme, Charles H Pearson and the democratic ideal in Australia', *Australian Journal of Political Science*, vol. 44, no. 2, 2009, pp. 213–28.

25	Gregory Melleuish, *Cultural Liberalism in Australia*, Cambridge University Press, Cambridge, 1995, p. 154.

26	Gregory Melleuish, 'Sir Robert Menzies and Australian education', in John R Nethercote (ed.), *Menzies: the shaping of modern Australia,* Connor Court, Brisbane, 2016, pp. 257–77.

27	Bartholomew A Santamaria, *The Earth Our Mother*, Challenge Press, Melbourne, 1945.

**19	The Howard Government and ministerial staff**

1	Maria Maley, 'Understanding the divergent development of the ministerial office in Australia and the UK', *Australian Journal of Political Science*, vol. 53, issue 3, 2018, pp. 320–35.

2	John Valder, *Facing the Facts: Report of the Committee of Review*, Liberal Party of Australia, Canberra, 1983.

3	Maley, 'Understanding the divergent development of the ministerial office in Australia and the UK', pp. 9–11.

4	Senate, *Personal Employee Positions as at 1 October 2019*. Total numbers depend on which staff are counted. These figures count all staff working for ministers and assistant ministers but do not count staff who assist backbenchers, such as the Members and Senators Support Unit.

5	Senate, *Personal Employee Positions as at 1 February 2020*. This number includes the staff in the Cabinet Office.

6	Anne Tiernan, 'Advising Howard: Interpreting changes in advisory and support structures for the Prime Minister of Australia', *Australian Journal of Political Science,* vol. 41, no. 3, 2006, pp. 309–24.

7	RAW Rhodes & Anne Tiernan, *Lessons in Governing*, Melbourne University Press, Melbourne, 2014, p. 59.

8	Don Watson, *Recollections of a Bleeding Heart: A portrait of Paul Keating PM*, Knopf, Sydney, 2002.

9   Paul Strangio, Paul 't Hart & James Walter, *The Pivot of Power: Australian prime ministers and political leadership, 1949–2016*, Miegunyah Press, Melbourne, 2017, pp. 198–234.

10   Anne Tiernan, *Power Without Responsibility*, UNSW Press, Sydney, 2007, pp. 151–70.

11   Tiernan 'Advising Howard: Interpreting changes in advisory and support structures for the Prime Minister of Australia', p. 317.

12   Allan Behm, *No, Minister: So you want to be a chief of staff?*, Melbourne University Press, Melbourne, 2015, p 17; Laura Tingle, 'Malcolm Turnbull walks to power in the company of Howard-era memories', *Australian Financial Review*, 15 September 2015.

13   Tiernan, 'Advising Howard', p. 312.

14   Anne Tiernan, 'Staffing the PM's Office: A key to national leadership' in Tom Frame (ed.), *Back From the Brink, 1997–2001: The Howard Government, Volume II*, UNSW Press, Sydney, 2018, p. 92.

15   Tiernan, 'Staffing the PM's Office', pp. 92–93; Rhodes & Tiernan, *Lessons in Governing*, pp. 61–62.

16   Tiernan, 'Advising Howard', p. 310.

17   Tiernan, 'Staffing the PM's Office', pp. 92–93.

18   John Wanna, 'From afterthought to afterburner: Australia's Cabinet Implementation Unit', *Journal of Comparative Policy Analysis: Research and Practice*, vol. 8, no. 4, 2006, pp. 347–69.

19   One of the key issues revealed by the Cabinet Implementation Unit was 'over promising' on the speed with which initiatives could be implemented in Cabinet submissions.

20   Paul Strangio, Paul 't Hart & James Walter, *The Pivot of Power: Australian prime ministers and political leadership, 1949–2016*, pp. 198–234.

21   The exception was the short period when Arthur Sinodinos performed the role as a minister.

22   Department of the Prime Minister and Cabinet, *Cabinet Handbook: 13th edition*, Commonwealth of Australia, Canberra, 2019.

23   Matt Stafford, Arthur Sinodinos, Peter Conran and Andrew Shearer worked as political advisers in the Howard period. Simon Atkinson is the exception.

24   Martin Parkinson, *Secretary's Address 2018*, 18 December 2018, IPAA/APSC.

25   Peter Shergold, *Learning from Failure*, Commonwealth of Australia, Canberra, 2015, pp. 30–35.

26   Senate Select Committee on a Certain Maritime Incident, *Report*, Commonwealth of Australia, Canberra, 2002.

27   Patrick Weller, *Don't Tell the Prime Minister*, Scribe, Melbourne, 2002, p. 72.

28   For example Anne Tiernan, *Power Without Responsibility*, UNSW Press, Sydney, 2007.

29   Shergold, *Learning from Failure*, p. 33.

30   Commonwealth of Australia, *Our Public Service, Our Future: Independent review of the Australian Public Service*, 2019.

31   Maley, 'Understanding the divergent development of the ministerial office in Australia and the UK', p. 11.

32   Paul Tilley, *Changing Fortunes: A history of the Australian Treasury*, Melbourne University Press, Melbourne, 2019, p. 424.

33   Tilley, *Changing Fortunes*, p. 416.
34   Auditor-General, *Award of Funding under the Community Sport Infrastructure Program*, Auditor-General Report, no. 23, 2019–2010, pp. 36, 38, 47.
35   Peter Shergold, *Australia's Public Sector: Fit for purpose?*, address to the IPAA National Conference, 17 October 2018.
36   Andrew Podger, *Protecting and Nurturing the Role and Capability of the Australian Public Service, Parliamentary Library Lecture*, 10 September 2019.

20   Prepared for opposition?
1   Peter van Onselen & Philip Senior, *Howard's End: The unravelling of a government*, Melbourne University Press, Melbourne, 2008.
2   Richard Katz & Peter Mair, 'Changing models of party organisation and party democracy: The emergence of the cartel party', *Party Politics*, no. 1, 1995, pp. 5–28; Richard Katz & Peter Mair, 'The cartel party thesis: A restatement', *Perspectives on Politics* 7, no. 4, 2009, pp. 753–66.
3   Dean Jaensch, *The Liberals*, Allen & Unwin, Sydney, 1994.
4   David Kemp, 'A leader and a philosophy', in Henry Mayer (ed.), *Labor to Power: Australia's 1972 election*, Angus & Robertson, Australasian Political Studies Association, 1973.
5   Paul Webb & Thomas Poguntke, *The Presidentialization of Politics: A comparative study of modern democracies*, Oxford University Press, London and New York, 2005.
6   'Costello won't stand for Libs leadership', *Sydney Morning Herald*, 25 November 2007, <www.smh.com.au/national/costello-wont-stand-for-libs-leadership-20071125-1co6.html>.
7   Annabel Crabb, *Stop at Nothing*, Black Books, Melbourne, 2016.
8   Mark Colvin, 'Liberals look to conservative heartland', *PM*, Australian Broadcasting Corporation, 1 December 2009, <www.abc.net.au/radio/programs/pm/liberals-look-to-conservative-heartland/1164994>.
9   Paul Kelly, *Triumph and Demise: The broken promise of a Labor generation*, Melbourne University Press, Melbourne, 2014.
10   André Kaiser, 'Parliamentary opposition in Westminster democracies: Britain, Canada, Australia and New Zealand', *The Journal of Legislative Studies*, vol. 14, no. 1, 2008, pp. 20–45.
11   Marija Taflaga, 'Politics, policy development and political communication during opposition: The Federal Liberal Party of Australia 1983–1996 and 2007–2013', 2016, <openresearch-repository.anu.edu.au/handle/1885/112342>.
12   Kevin Theakston, 'Winston Churchill, 1945–51', in Timothy Heppell (ed.), *Leaders of the Opposition: From Churchill to Cameron*, Palgrave Macmillan, Basingstoke, 2012; Robert Menzies, *The Measure of the Years*, London, Coronet Books, 1972, chapter 2.
13   Graham Maddox, *Australian Democracy in Theory and Practice*, 5th edn, Pearson Education Australia, Sydney, 2005.
14   See Jennings for the strongest articulation of this mode of opposition.
15   For example, see George Brandis, 'We Believe: The Liberal Party and the liberal cause', University of Melbourne, Melbourne, 22 October 2009, <australianpolitics.com/2009/10/22/brandis-liberal-cause.html>.

16   Maria Hawthorne, Melissa Jenkins, & Kate Corbett, 'Nelson's sorry speech sparks anger', *Sydney Morning Herald*, 13 February 2008, <www.smh.com.au/national/nelsons-sorry-speech-sparks-anger-20080213-1rx7.html>.

17   Taflaga, 'Politics, policy development and political communication during opposition'.

18   For a collection of essays both supportive and critical of the Howard Government's legacy see Peter van Onselen (ed.), *Liberals and Power: The road ahead*, Melbourne University Press, Melbourne, 2008.

19   Margaret Fitzherbert, 'Credible candidates win marginal seats', in Peter van Onselen (ed.), *Liberals and Power: The road ahead*, Melbourne University Press, Melbourne, 2008; Taflaga, 'Politics, policy development and political communication during opposition'.

20   Marija Taflaga, 'A more aggressive parliament? An examination of Australian parliamentary behaviour 1996 to 2012', Australian Political Studies Association Conference, University of Tasmania, 2012.

21   Sarah Cameron & Ian McAllister, *Trends in Australian Political Opinion: Results from the Australian Election Study 1987–2019*, Australian National University, Canberra, 2019, p. 99.

22   Laura Tingle, 'Tony Abbott is creating a Whitlam government of our time', *Sydney Morning Herald*, 14 August 2015.

23   Heath Aston & Mark Kenny, 'Labor giving green light to budget's deficit levy', *Sydney Morning Herald*, 16 May 2014.

24   Jode Kelly, 'Swan unleashes on Hockey's view of election costings', the *Australian*, 12 September 2011, <www.theaustralian.com.au/national-affairs/swan-unleashes-on-hockeys-view-of-election-costings/news-story/a398cbf0ec157f69fe67d382882727ab>.

25   Wayne Errington, 'The Liberal Party: Electoral success despite organisational drift', in Narelle Miragliotta, Anika Gauja & Rodney Smith (eds), *Contemporary Australian Political Party Organisations*, Monash University, Melbourne, 2015, pp. 15–23.

26   For trends around the world see Susan Scarrow, *Beyond Party Members: Changing approaches to partisan mobilization*, Oxford University Press, Oxford, 2014; and Anika Gauja, *Party Reform: The causes, challenges, and consequences of organisational change*, Oxford University Press, Oxford, 2016; for the LPA specifically see John Ruddick (ed.), *Make the Liberal Party Great Again*, Wilkinson Publishing, Melbourne, 2018.

27   Anne Davies, 'NSW Liberals reject Tony Abbott-backed plan for preselections', the *Guardian*, 10 February 2018, <www.theguardian.com/australia-news/2018/feb/10/nsw-liberals-reject-tony-abbott-backed-plan-for-preselections>; Brian Costar, 'The National Party: The resilient party', in Miragliotta et al. (eds), *Contemporary Australian Political Party Organisations*.

28   Shane Stone quoted in Maria Hawthorne, 'Fed: Stone bids farewell to federal Liberal presidency', Australian Associated Press, 24 June 2005.

29   Liberal Party of Australia, Committee of Review & John Valder, *Facing the Facts: Report of the Committee of Review*, Liberal Party of Australia, 1983.

30   Tony Staley & Liberal Party of Australia, 'Review of the 2007 Federal Election Campaign & Review of the Liberal Party Federal Constitution', September 2008.

31   For plebiscites, see Narelle Miragliotta, 'Explaining the (lack of) use of radical candidate selection methods by Australia's major parties', *Australian Journal of Politics & History*, vol. 59, no. 1, 1 March 2013, pp. 113–26, <doi.org/10.1111/ajph.12007>; for factionalism, see Ian Hancock, *The Liberals: A history of the NSW division of the Liberal Party of Australia, 1945–2000*, Federation Press, Sydney, 2007.

32   Hancock, *The Liberals*.

33   Imre Salusinszky & John Wiseman, 'State of the Nation: The view from the *Weekend Australian*'s political writers', the *Australian*, 29 March 2008; Imre Salusinszky, 'Lib trio quit as reform stalls', the *Australian*, 29 May 2008.

34   Peter Reith, 'Review of the 2010 federal election', Liberal Party Australia, Canberra, 25 May 2011.

35   Marija Taflaga & Katrine Beauregard, 'The merit of party institutions: Women's descriptive representation and conservative parties in Australia and the United Kingdom', *Journal of Women, Politics & Policy*, vol. 41, no. 1, 23 February 2020, pp. 66–90, <doi.org/10.1080/1554477X.2020.1701934>.

36   Fitzherbert, 'Credible candidates win marginal seats'.

37   Ainslie van Onselen, 'It's Time: Women & affirmative action in the Liberal Party', *AQ: Australian Quarterly*, vol. 80, no. 4, 1 July 2008, pp. 4–40, <doi.org/10.2307/20638564>; Judith Troeth, 'Modernising the parliamentary Liberal Party by adopting the organisational wing's quota system for preselections', Canberra, 23 June 2010, <apo.org.au/system/files/57011/apo-nid57011-98866.pdf>.

38   Marija Taflaga & Jennifer Curtin, 'Australia: Political development and data for 2018', *European Journal of Political Research Political Data Yearbook*, no. 58, 2019, <doi.org/10.1111/2047-8852.12234>.

39   Shane Stone, 'Chapter 15: Federal president Liberal Party of Australia', The Stone Family in Australia website, <www.stonefamilyinaustralia.com.au/shane_stone/story/chapter-15-federal-president-liberal-party-of-australia>.

40   Troels Bøggild, 'Politicians as Party Hacks: Party loyalty and public distrust in politicians', *The Journal of Politics*, 25 February 2020, <doi.org/10.1086/708681>.

21   The Howard Government: A pictorial review

1   Formerly the Ceremonial and Hospitality Branch.

23   Postscript

1   Tom Frame (ed.), 'Setting the scene', *Trials and Transformations, 2001–2004: The Howard Government, Volume III*, UNSW Press, Sydney, 2019, pp. 1–12.

2   Nick Cater (ed.), *The Howard Factor: A decade that transformed a nation*, Melbourne University Press, Melbourne, 2006.

3   Cater, *The Howard Factor*, p. 348.

4   Cater, *The Howard Factor*, p. 348.

5   David Barnett & Pru Goward, *John Howard: Prime Minister*, Viking, Melbourne, 1997.

6   Cater, *The Howard Factor*, p. xi.

7   Leak in Cater (ed.), *The Howard Factor*, p. 200.

8   Megalogenis in Cater (ed.), *The Howard Factor*, p. 317.

9   Russ Radcliffe, *Man of Steel: A cartoon history of the Howard years*, Scribe, Melbourne, 2007.
10   Radcliffe, *Man of Steel*, p. 1.
11   Radcliffe, *Man of Steel*, p. 2.
12   Radcliffe, *Man of Steel*, p. 3.
13   Radcliffe, *Man of Steel*, p. 4.
14   Judith Brett, *Exit Right: The unravelling of John Howard*, *Quarterly Essay*, issue 28, Scribe, Melbourne, December 2007.
15   Peter van Onselen & Philip Senior, *Howard's End: The unravelling of a government*, Melbourne University Press, Melbourne, 2008; Peter Hartcher, *To the Bitter End: The dramatic story behind the fall of John Howard and the rise of Kevin Rudd*, Allen & Unwin, Sydney, 2009.
16   Peter van Onselen (ed.), *Liberals and Power: The road ahead*, Melbourne University Press, Melbourne, 2008.
17   George Brandis, 'John Howard and the Australian liberal tradition', in van Onselen (ed.), *Liberals and Power*, p. 79.
18   Brandis, 'John Howard and the Liberal tradition', p. 79.
19   Norman Abjorensen, 'First termers', 28 November 2008, *Inside Story*, 26 November 2008, <www.insidestory.org.au/first-termers>; see also Abjorensen, *John Howard and the Conservative Tradition*, Australian Scholarly Publishing, Melbourne, 2008.
20   Norman Abjorensen, 'First termers'.
21   George Megalogenis, *The Longest Decade*, Scribe, Melbourne, 2006 (updated 2008). The other major survey of the 1990s and 2000s – Paul Kelly's *The March of the Patriots: The struggle for modern Australia*, Melbourne University Press, Melbourne, 2009 – concludes with the November 2001 election.
22   George Megalogenis, *The Longest Decade*, 2008, p. 2.
23   Peter Costello with Peter Coleman, *The Costello Memoirs*, Melbourne University Press, Melbourne, 2008.
24   Tony Abbott, *Battlelines*, Melbourne University Press, Melbourne, 2009.
25   Abbott, *Battlelines*, p. xi.
26   Keith Windschuttle, David Martin Jones & Ray Evans (eds), *The Howard Era*, Quadrant Books, Sydney, 2009.
27   Margo Kingston, *Not Happy, John! Defending our democracy*, Penguin, Melbourne, 2004; Margo Kingston, *Still Not Happy, John!*, Penguin, Melbourne, 2007.
28   David Martin Jones in Windshuttle et al., *The Howard Era*, p. 3.
29   Peter Reith, *The Reith Papers*, Melbourne University Press, Melbourne, 2015.
30   Reith, *The Reith Papers*, p. 3.

Appendix 1
1   'Fourth Howard ministry', Prime Minister of Australia media release issued 22 October 2004, <pmtranscripts.pmc.gov.au/release/transcript-21536>.
2   'Howard reshuffles cabinet', ABC interview with Catherine McGrath on 14 July 2004, <www.abc.net.au/pm/content/2004/s1154030.htm>.
3   'Howard unveils new ministry', ABC News, 22 October 2004, <www.abc.net.au/news/2004-10-22/howard-unveils-new-cabinet/571978>.
4   John Howard, press conference at the Blue Room, Parliament House on 22 October 2004, <pmtranscripts.pmc.gov.au/release/transcript-21538>.

5   John Howard, doorstop interview, 28 October 2004, <pmtranscripts.pmc.gov.au/release/transcript-21539>.

6   Press conference, Parliament House, 22 October 2004.

7   Maria Maley, 'Parliamentary Experience in Australian Ministerial Careers 1996–2007', *Australian Journal of Politics & History*, vol. 64, no. 2, 2018, p. 242.

8   In more recent times, Simon Crean went into the ministry as the Minister for Science and Technology after the 1990 election. He was appointed to the Cabinet as Minister for Primary Industries and Energy in the following year. Bob Hawke was appointed shadow minister for Industrial Relations once elected in 1980. In February 1983, he was Leader of the Opposition and then became Prime Minister after a landslide victory, achieving a 24-seat swing, in March 1983.

9   Peter Costello, *The Costello Memoirs*, Melbourne University Press, Melbourne, 2008, p. 252.

10   Paddy Manning, *Born to Rule?*, Melbourne University Press, Melbourne, 2018, p. 286.

ACKNOWLEDGMENTS

UNSW Canberra is grateful to AT Kearney, particularly its executives Robert Holt and Craig Pandey, for the company's generous support of the Fourth Howard Government Retrospective Conference held in November 2019; to Sky News Extra for broadcasting the conference presentations; the staff of the National Press Club in Canberra for their assistance in staging the conference, and the Museum of Australian Democracy (Director, Daryl Karp AM), the National Archives of Australia (Director General, David Fricker) and the National Museum of Australia (Director, Dr Mat Trinca AM) for their continuing goodwill towards the Howard Library at Old Parliament House.

The editor is most grateful to his UNSW colleagues Professors Michael Frater FTSE, David Lovell and Harvi Sidhu, and Howard Library teammates Andrew Blyth, Annette Carter, Trish Burgess, Alan Wilson and Dr Fiona Wade, and to Adjunct Professor JR Nethercote for his generous assistance with copy-editing and proof-reading the manuscript. Any errors or flaws remain the sole responsibility of the editor.

INDEX